COMPUTING

A Problem-Solving Approach with FORTRAN 77

T. RAY NANNEY

**Professor of Computer Science
Furman University**

D0164643

Prentice-Hall, Inc.
Englewood Cliffs, New Jersey 07632

Library of Congress Cataloging in Publication Data

Nanney, T. Ray
    Computing: a problem-solving approach with
FORTRAN 77.

    Includes index.
        1. FORTRAN (Computer program language)
2. Electronic digital computers—Programming.
I. Title.
QA76. 73. F25N36   001.64'24   80-28220
ISBN 0-13-165209-5

To

Elizabeth Nanney

who inspired this work and helped
with every phase of its development.

*Editorial/production supervision and
    interior design: Service to Publishers*
Cover design: Lee Cohen
*Manufacturing buyer: Joyce Levatino and
    Gordon Osbourne*

Printed in the United States of America

10 9 8 7 6 5 4 3 2

PRENTICE-HALL INTERNATIONAL, INC., London
PRENTICE-HALL OF AUSTRALIA PTY. LIMITED, Sydney
PRENTICE-HALL OF CANADA, LTD., Toronto
PRENTICE-HALL OF INDIA PRIVATE LIMITED, New Delhi
PRENTICE-HALL OF JAPAN, INC., Tokyo
PRENTICE-HALL OF SOUTHEAST ASIA PTE. LTD., Singapore
WHITEHALL BOOKS LIMITED, Wellington, New Zealand

CONTENTS

Chapter

Chapter

PREFACE

This book is a text for a beginning course in computer science in a liberal arts environment. The organization of topics in the book is the result of the continual evolution of a course that has been taught at Furman University since 1968. For the majority of students at Furman, this course would be the only one that they would take in computer science. Yet, many of them would later be required to write computer programs both in courses and in independent study in their own disciplines. It was essential, therefore, that the students have the opportunity to become good programmers. I had observed in previous introductory courses that many intelligent, motivated, nonscience students had great difficulty mastering the material in the traditional programming-oriented introductory course. I believed this problem to be a result of the teaching method used to present the material, not the inadequacies in the abilities of the students.

The format of the present course crystallized in the summer of 1975 during a six-week visit to the laboratory of Professor Seymour Papert of the Artificial Intelligence Laboratory at the Massachusetts Institute of Technology. In his laboratory, I observed average 10- and 11-year-old children writing relatively complex programs in the computer language LOGO. This reinforced my belief that any motivated college student should be able to learn programming. Many of the techniques used in this book have their origin in ideas found in the work of Professor Papert.

The material in this book has been used in approximately 24 sections of the introductory computer science course during the period from 1975 to 1980. Although the evidence is rather qualitative, there appears to have been a significant improvement in the performance of students, especially nonscience majors, using the approach. Grades have improved, more programs have been completed, and students report having more fun than in previous years.

I am grateful to my colleagues James H. Keller and E. James Runde, who were willing to use this book while it was still evolving and who gave me valuable feedback. Three of my former students, C. Joseph Bridwell, James M. Coggins, and Cary A. Coutant, helped me in many ways. I am especially grateful to Seymour Papert, who gave me a stimulating place to work during the most crucial part of the writing.

T. RAY NANNEY

TO THE STUDENT

There are many approaches to the study of computing. This book emphasizes the writing of computer programs, but it also presents many other important aspects of computing. The course is essentially nonmathematical and is designed to be useful to both science and nonscience majors. No previous knowledge of computers, programming, or other specialized skills is required.

Regardless of your future interests and activities, it will be difficult (probably impossible) to avoid contact with computers. Consequently, in this book you will be introduced to programming, terminology, computer languages, applications, and social implications of computers. If you work conscientiously to master the material, at the end of the course you should be able to use the computer to solve problems that interest you. You should also have gained insight into many other important topics in computing.

The writing of computer programs is intimately associated with problem solving, so considerable attention will be given to a systematic approach to problem solving. At the end of the course many of you will find it easier to analyze and solve problems. A thorough understanding of the contents of the course will also improve your ability to think logically and critically.

An important side benefit of our study will be an enhanced understanding of the nature of language and the difficulties associated with using language in a precise, unambiguous manner. In fact, to solve a problem using a computer *requires* that language be used with precision. There is considerable truth to the statement that "computer science is more closely associated with linguistics and communication than with mathematics."

Studying computing can and should be exciting and fun. It is, however, quite different from anything you have studied previously; if you get behind, it can be almost impossible to catch up. It can also be a disastrous mistake to wait until the last minute to undertake a programming assignment. A problem that is quite easy for 95% of the class can be time consuming and difficult for you. The only safe assumption is that the problem will take longer than you had planned.

In writing computer programs, the following somewhat contradictory attitude is suggested: strive for perfection, but do not be upset or embarrassed by a mistake. When you write a program, you should try to write it so perfectly that correct answers are obtained when the program is first run on the computer. Yet it is not the nature of human beings to be perfectly accurate. So if you make a mistake, it is not a catastrophe—correct the mistake and rerun the program.

A major goal of this course is to learn to write computer programs using the FORTRAN language. Traditionally, in such a course you would learn a small part of the language and immediately begin programming. In contrast, we will not begin writing FORTRAN programs until an overview of computing has been presented and some principles have been discussed. This approach appears to have the following advantages:

1. The introductory material will aid you in organizing your thinking about how to solve the problem for which you want to write a program. This is helpful for everyone and is especially valuable for students with nonscientific or nonmathematical backgrounds.
2. The initial study of programming principles helps you to develop and use good programming techniques from the beginning of the course. This is invaluable when the programs become longer and more difficult.
3. The knowledge of programming principles gained in the first part of the course makes a language like FORTRAN easier to learn and reduces frustration. The experimental evidence suggests strongly that students become better programmers because of the introductory material.

LIST OF FIGURES

Figure

LIST OF TABLES

TABLE 1.1 *Number of computers used in the United States*

Year	Number of computers
1950	~12
1955	1,000
1960	6,000
1965	30,000
1976	220,000

TABLE 1.2 *Ownership of general-purpose conventional computers within the United States, 1976*

Ownership by industrial classification		Percent of computers
Manufacturing industry		31.0
Electric machinery	3.5%	
Nonelectric machinery	4.5%	
Other process manufacturing	9.7%	
Other manufacturing	11.0%	
Transportation equipment	2.3%	
Miscellaneous business		13.3
Advertising, employment, equipment, rental, engineering services, other professional services		
Banking, credit, insurance, real estate, and other financial institutions		13.4
Trade (wholesale and retail)		13.1
Educational institutions (schools, universities, libraries)		5.7
State and local government		5.7
Federal government		3.4
Transportation carriers		2.9
Medical and health services		2.7
Printing and publishing		2.4
Communications		1.9
Utilities (electric, gas, and sanitary services)		1.6
Other professional services		1.9
Petrochemical industry		1.0

Source: Ruth M. Davis, "Evolution of Computers and Computing," *Science, 195* (March 18, 1977), 1100; by permission.

computer explosion had begun. The approximate number of computers in use in the United States at the end of various years is given in Table 1.1. In a 1967 report to the president of the United States,* it was estimated that 80,000 computers would be in use by the end of 1975. This estimate was far too low; improved computer tech-

Computers in Higher Education, Report of the President's Science Advisory Committee, The White House, Washington, D.C., February 1967, p. 58.

nology and the resulting reduced costs made the acquisition of a computer attractive to many organizations. In 1976, the number of computers in use was 220,000.

The federal government owned all computers in the early 1950s; its share has now dropped to only 3.4 percent. At present, the manufacturing industry, miscellaneous businesses, and banking institutions own most of the computers. Ownership information (1977) is summarized in Table 1.2. The diversity of the industries represented supports the view that the computer revolution is here.

1.2 THE SPEED OF THE COMPUTER

The ability of computers to perform tasks at amazing speeds is well known. The fastest computers can perform more than 10 million elementary operations in a second and simultaneously operate many attached devices. For example, a large computer could, in 1 second, calculate the payroll for more than 1000 employees, print more than 100 checks, update records for 2000 students, and make various statistical or scientific calculations. This speed gives us tremendous power to manipulate information.

There is however, another aspect of computing power to be considered: the power of computers to expand the human intellect. Computers make it possible for us to think thoughts that were never before possible. The source of this power is the ability of the computer to manipulate symbols at fantastic speeds. It can be argued that a mere increase in speed could not significantly change what we can do and think, but this argument is invalid. Consider the following analogy:

> The ability to do work can be expressed in terms of horsepower. For example, to fly a small jet plane may require engines having 50,000 horsepower. There is no way to use 50,000 horses to supply the power to fly the plane. Something new has become possible because of the concentration of power in a small package.

Another very descriptive view of the way the speed of the computer changes what we can do has been given by Rice and Rice:

> It is difficult to comprehend the speed of current computers. The fact is that this speed is more than quantitative. It is qualitative in the sense that it has changed the basic nature of computation. A usual way to illustrate how a quantitative change can be qualitative is to consider a gift of money to a student. A gift of $.05 is meaningless. A gift of $50 (1000 times as much) is nice, but does not change the student's basic outlook about money. A gift of $50,000 (a million times as much) is very nice, but one soon finds that it buys a very limited number of sports cars, fancy clothes, round-the-world cruises and summer cottages. Thus this gift soon evaporates and the student is still faced with where the next dollar is coming from. A gift of $50,000,000 (a billion times as much) completely changes things. It is no longer possible to spend this much money on personal living. Thus the cost of a car, a house or a suit becomes meaningless. There is no longer any point to earning money if it has to be spent on personal

items. The ratio between 5 cents and $50,000,000 is the ratio of current to old computing speeds.*

Several comments must be made about this statement. First, it was written in 1969; since that time, computing speeds have increased by a factor of 10. Second, the word *computation* must not be used in too narrow a sense. The computer is not merely a superfast calculator; it can also manipulate symbolic information such as the alphabet.

1.3 THE DECREASING COST OF COMPUTERS

In 1968, the college at which I teach purchased some additional computer memory for $22,000. In 1979, we could have purchased 32 times as much memory for approximately $5600. If the prices of automobiles had been changing at the same rate, a car selling in 1968 for $6000 would have sold in 1979 for $47 instead of approximately $12,000.

The computer industry trade paper, *Computerworld*,[†] April 1979, in a two-page advertisement describing the value of their paper as an advertising medium, emphasized the statement: "If the auto industry had done what the computer industry has done in the last 30 years, a Rolls-Royce would cost $2.50 and get 2,000,000 miles per gallon." This astounding decrease in cost is due primarily to the increase in the volume of production and to improvements in technology which allow many more circuit elements to be placed in a given area. Between 1959 and 1977, the number of circuit components increased from 1 to more than 260,000 elements per unit area. Some projections predict at least a doubling in the number of elements per unit area each year until approximately 1990.

1.4 THE COMPUTER AS PROBLEM SOLVER

Suppose that you have a problem to solve. You would begin by collecting information relevant to the problem. If the amount of information is large, you might record it in some way; otherwise, you will simply memorize it. If you know a technique for solving the problem, you will then apply an appropriate sequence of steps to the information to produce an answer. Finally, you present the answer. You solve the problem by transforming the raw data into the form required as a solution to the problem.

When a computer is used for this task, a similar set of steps is required. This leads to the functional description shown in Figure 1.1.

A computer can thus be defined as an information-processing machine.

*J. K. Rice and J. R. Rice, *Instructor's Guide for Introduction to Computer Science* (New York: Holt, Rinehart and Winston, Inc., 1969), p. 45.

[†]Copyright 1979 by CW Communications/Inc., Newton, Mass. 02160; reprinted from *Computerworld*.

CHAPTER 1 COMPUTERS AND COMPUTER SCIENCE

There is hardly an area of human endeavor that has not been affected by computers. Banks use computers to print your bank statements; utility companies compute your usage of their services and a computer prints your bill; computers are used as inventory control in department stores; airline personnel check your reservations using a computer. They are everywhere—in business, industry, government, education, sciences, and all present-day technology. This widespread use of computers in our society is due primarily to the generality of tasks that computers can perform, the tremendous speed of computer operations, and the decrease in the cost of computers.

1.1 COMPUTERS IN SOCIETY

In 1974, I heard an IBM executive refer to the rapid spread of computer usage as "the insidious revolution." He explained that the general population rarely sees a computer, almost never works with a computer (computer billing being an exception), and is unaware of the diversity of computer applications and their pervasiveness in society. His claim was that without the public's realization, we have become so dependent upon computers that society could not be maintained in its present form without them.

Let us expand our perspective regarding computer applications by briefly considering the history* of modern computing. The first large-scale electronic computer, ENIAC, was completed in 1946 and was used by the United States Army Ordnance Corps primarily to compute ballistic tables. In the early 1950s all computers were owned by the federal government and were used for census studies, weapons calculations, weapons delivery and control, cryptographic applications, nuclear design, nuclear engineering, inventory, and logistic applications. In 1954, the UNIVAC I computer was delivered to General Electric Company for commercial use, and the

*Much of this information has been abstracted from Ruth M. Davis, "Evolution of Computers and Computing," *Science*, *195* (March 18, 1977), 1096–1102, copyright 1977 by the American Association for the Advancement of Science; and Saul Rosen, "Electronic Computers: A Historical Survey," *Computing Surveys*, *1* (March 1969), 7–36. Copyright 1969, Association for Computing Machinery, Inc., reprinted by permission.

> **Computer System**
>
> accept information
> store information
> transform information
> retrieve information
> display information

FIGURE 1.1   *Functional description of a computer*

When you solve a problem, you follow some set of rules to ensure that the steps are done in the proper sequence. In many cases, you would find it quite difficult to state precisely what these rules are. (We solve problems without knowing how we do it!) To use a computer, we first store in it a set of instructions, called a *program*, which, when executed, will solve the problem without human assistance. The program must be written in a language that the computer can understand.

Computers store the instructions which they are to execute in the *memory* of the computer. This allows the instructions to be manipulated at a rate dependent upon the internal speed of the computer. Storing the instructions in computer memory makes the computer a universal problem-solving machine; to change the problem being solved, it is necessary only to change the set of instructions stored in memory. One machine can be used to solve a variety of problems. This *stored program concept*, which vastly expands the power of computers, was first suggested by John von Neumann, an eminent mathematician who also made fundamental contributions to game theory and quantum mechanics.

The stored-program concept is used to distinguish a computer from a calculator —a calculator does not have the ability to store a program in memory and subsequently replace that program with another. Although a calculator may be powerful for solving engineering or scientific problems, its inability to enter a new program and execute it, automatically limits the range of the calculator's application.

The physical units that constitute the computer are known as the *hardware*. The computer manufacturer may also design and implement a set of programs, known as the *software*, to make the computer easier to use. The software for a large computer is very complex, and many worker-years of programming effort may be required to produce it. A user of a computer normally interacts only with the software, so that to a large degree the software appears to the user to be the computer. We will call the combination of hardware and software for a computer the *computer system*.

1.5   HIGH-LEVEL VIEW OF COMPUTER STRUCTURE

Understanding computers (or anything for that matter) involves levels of knowledge. Some levels for hardware and software are shown in Figure 1.2. To use a computer, it is not necessary to understand its operation at all levels, and the same is true of its hardware and software. Most of this book is concerned with communicating with

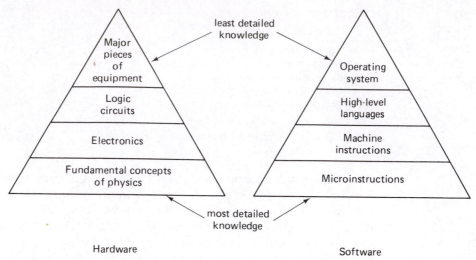

FIGURE 1.2 *Some levels of knowledge for hardware and software*

the computer using a high-level language, but before proceeding we must consider the high-level structure of the hardware to develop a vocabulary.

The least detailed view of the computer treats it as a structure with three major components: a component to receive instructions and data from the outside world, a component to perform the instructions to produce an "answer," and a component to communicate the "answer" to the outside world (see Figure 1.3).

The box marked *input* represents all the devices that can be used to enter

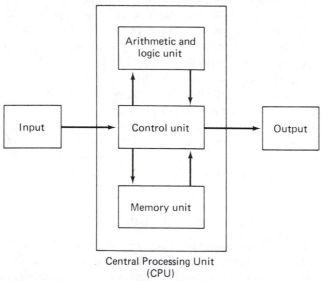

FIGURE 1.3 *Major components of a computer*

TABLE 1.3 *Input/output devices*

Input only	Output only	Both input and output
Card reader	Line printer	Terminals
Console keyboard	Card punch	Magnetic tape drive
Paper tape reader	Paper tape punch	Magnetic disk drive
Mark sense reader	Console printer	
	Plotter	

instructions or data for manipulation by the computer. The box marked *output* represents all the devices that can be used to make the results known to the outside world. The *central processing unit* (CPU) is the heart of the computer and controls the operation of all components of the system. The memory unit stores the instructions and the data, the control unit manages the activities of all the components of the system, and the arithmetic and logic unit performs arithmetic and makes logical decisions related to the user's program.

As the diagram implies, a computer does not ordinarily consist of a single box. Normally, there is a separate unit for each input or output device and some devices serve as both input and output units (see Table 1.3).

Suppose that a simple computer consisted of a card reader (input), a CPU, a disk drive (input and output) for auxiliary storage of information, and a line printer (output). To use the computer, you would write in an appropriate language a set of instructions (or program) which you want the computer to execute and then punch the instructions into cards using a keypunch. The data that the instructions are to manipulate are also punched into cards. The computer program, followed by the data, is placed in the card reader, which transmits the contents of the cards to the CPU. Using previously written programs stored on the disk, the CPU decides what your instructions are to do and then executes them. The answers are printed by the line printer.

1.5.1 Some Components of the Central Processing Unit

Memory Unit

Computer memory consists of *cells* in which information can be stored. The physical realization of a memory cell in a particular computer depends upon the state of technology at the time a computer is designed and upon its projected selling price—more expensive computers will tend to incorporate more expensive components. Since the invention of computers, the physical form of memory cells has changed from arrays of relays, to arrays of vacuum tubes, to arrays of magnetic cores, to arrays of solid-state devices. Fortunately, you do not have to be concerned about the physical form of a memory cell while you are learning to use a computer, but you do need to understand some fundamental aspects of operation that are independent of the construction of the cell.

Each computer memory cell has an address and contents: the *address* is the identifying number of a cell, and the *contents* (or *value*) are what is stored in a cell. The difference in these concepts can be visualized by using the classic "post-office-box" analogy.

A post office has boxes for the use of its customers. Each box has an address and, perhaps, contents. The address of your box is quite different from its contents (a letter) and you would never confuse the two. But experience has shown that you are likely to forget the distinction between address and contents during the writing of computer programs.

The post-office-box analogy extends even further. The size of a letter or package that can be placed in a box is limited by the size of the box. The number of alphabetic characters that can be placed in a computer memory cell is limited by the design of the cell. Typically, a memory cell of the smallest, least expensive computer can hold one character, a cell of a more expensive computer can hold two characters, and a cell of the most expensive computers can hold four to six characters. A memory cell can also be used to store numbers; the size of the cell limits the size of the number that can be placed in it. For the integers, many computers have the range – 32,768 to +32,767.

There are several important ways in which the post-office-box analogy fails. In contrast with a post office box, which may be empty, a computer memory cell always contains a value. The reading of the contents of a memory cell does not change the contents of the cell—this is called *nondestructive readout*. It is as if a new copy of a letter, identical in every way with the original, were created within the post office box whenever a letter is removed. Another difference is that a post office box may have several different letters at a given time; a computer memory cell contains exactly one value. When a new value is stored in a memory cell—a process known as *destructive readin*—the previous value is completely erased.

A common mistake in writing programs is to forget that a memory cell contains a value. The value may be left over from the previous use of the computer, but it will be there. It is essential to avoid using these "accidental" values in your programs; initializing the contents of memory cells—that is, setting the contents of memory cells to required initial values—can be vital.

Another way in which the post-office-box analogy fails is that the time interval to access any given memory cell is independent of the cell to be accessed. In the case of post office boxes, the time required to access a particular box depends upon one's physical distance from the box. The term *random-access memory* (RAM) is used to indicate that computer memory cells can be accessed in any sequence and that the access time is the same for each cell. This is analogous to being able to take books from a bookshelf in any order. Computers sometimes have a second type of memory, known as *read-only memory* (ROM), which has the property that the contents of a cell can be read in a normal manner but special apparatus is required to store a new value in a cell. Read-only memory is used to store important components of the software.

Control Unit

The control unit of the computer manages the execution of the program stored in memory and, in some computers, performs functions related to the operation of the input/output devices. Programs in computer memory consist of sequences of statements which the circuitry of the computer has been designed to interpret and execute. This language—the *machine language*—is the only language the computer can understand directly; a statement in any other language must be translated into machine language before the computer can use it. A single statement in machine language is called a *machine instruction*.

In the control unit, the *instruction register*, a special hardware device, is used to interpret and execute machine-language instructions. The contents of a memory cell are first copied into the instruction register. Then in a series of steps the circuits associated with the register determine whether the contents of the register constitute a legitimate machine instruction, and then the circuits determine what actions to perform for the instruction. Finally, the actions are performed, after which the next instruction is placed in the register and the sequence is repeated. Another register, the *program counter*, contains the address of the next instruction to be executed.

Arithmetic and Logic Unit

The arithmetic and logic unit is the component of the CPU in which numerical calculations, comparison of values, and logical operations are performed. A common technique for making calculations is to use a register, the *accumulator*, to hold values involved in a computation. Adding two numbers using the accumulator requires the execution of a sequence of machine instructions equivalent to:

1. Loading the first value into the accumulator.
2. Adding a copy of the second value to the contents of the accumulator and leaving the resulting answer in the accumulator.
3. Storing the answer in a memory cell.

These steps are similar to those you take to add two numbers using a hand calculator. You key in the first number, causing it to be displayed by the calculator (the display is analogous to the accumulator). Then you key in the second number, push the add key, and the answer appears in the display. Finally, you save the answer, perhaps by jotting it on a note pad.

The actual technique used by a computer for making calculations may be very similar to that just considered, but it may also be quite different. Large, expensive computers designed basically for solving scientific problems requiring many hours per given problem will probably use complex hardware to speed the computational process. In most cases the user of a computer does not have to be concerned with how the calculations are actually made.

1.5.2 The Input/Output Processor

As more input/output units are attached to a computer, the CPU must devote a larger fraction of time to manipulating these devices. Eventually, as even more are added, the CPU has inadequate available time to perform useful calculations. One solution used by some modern computers is to incorporate a specialized CPU, the *input/*

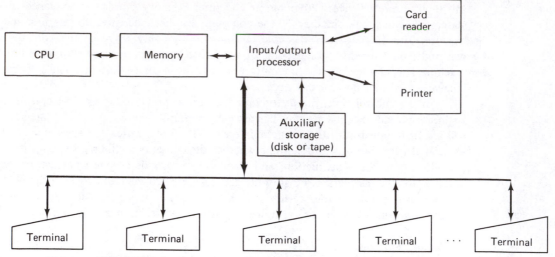

FIGURE 1.4 *Functional description of a small time-sharing computer*

output processor, to control the devices. Figure 1.4 shows the structure of a small time-sharing computer which has an input/output processor. Notice that the processor has direct access to computer memory.

The adding of an input/output processor to a computer can be viewed as the addition of a "special-purpose computer" to the system. Generally, we will not be interested in the operation of the new CPU because it operates other hardware and is not involved directly in using the computer to solve problems. The trend is to use microcomputers as components of terminals, card readers, printers, and other input/output devices, so that the workload of controlling the devices is distributed even more widely.

1.6   MICROCOMPUTERS AND MINICOMPUTERS

The terms "microcomputer" and "minicomputer" are used to categorize computers by cost and capability. *Microcomputers* can cost as little as $5 each in large quantities, and they typically have memory cells that can hold only a single alphabetic character. The CPU of a microcomputer is formed chemically on a small chip (usually made of silicon), producing what is called an *integrated circuit*. Microcomputers are particularly suitable for incorporation into household appliances, electronic equipment, complex tools, and electronic games to automate the operation of the device. Despite their small size and cost, microcomputers have capabilities that compare favorably with those of the early computers. (See Table 1.4, which compares the 1946 ENIAC with the Fairchild F8, a microcomputer.) The number of microcomputers in use in 1980 was estimated to be more than 10 million.

At the upper end of the cost scale are computers priced from half a million to millions of dollars. These computers have many input/output devices, storage for large amounts of information, and the ability to execute several programs concurrently.

TABLE 1.4 *Comparison of the ENIAC and Fairchild F8 computers*

Parameter	ENIAC	Fairchild F8	Comments
Size	3000 cubic feet	0.011 cubic foot	300,000 times smaller
Power consumption	140 kilowatts	2.5 watts	56,000 times less power consumption
Read-only memory	16K bits (relays and switches)	16K bits	Equal amount
Random-access memory	1K bits (flip-flop accumulators)	8K bits	8 times more RAM in F8
Clock rate	100 kilohertz	2 megahertz	20 times faster clock rate with F8
Transistors or tubes	18,000 tubes	20,000 transistors	About the same
Resistors	70,000	None	F8 uses active devices as resistors
Capacitors	10,000	2	5000 times less in F8
Relays and switches	7500	None	
Add time	200 μseconds (12 digits)	150 μseconds (8 digits)	About the same
Mean time to failure	Hours	Years	More than 10,000 times as reliable
Weight	30 tons	<1 pound	

Source: J. G. Linvill and C. L. Hogan, "Intellectual and Economic Fuel for the Electronics Revolution," *Science, 195* (March 18, 1977), 1107–1113, Table 1; copyright 1977 by the American Association for the Advancement of Science.

Intermediate in capability between microcomputers and computers are *minicomputers.* The term is ambiguous and should be used with care because some minicomputers have capabilities that exceed those of large computers of a few years ago. Further, a large minicomputer may have capabilities that exceed those of some computers. There is a tendency to use the term "minicomputer" to refer to computers having memory cells that hold two alphabetic characters.

1.7 THE RELIABILITY OF COMPUTERS

Do computers make errors? This question is highly ambiguous. If the question means, do computers ever produce invalid results, then the answer is yes. Almost without exception, however, the invalid result arises because a human being made an error in preparing data or in writing the computer program. If the question refers to the mechanical components (which have many moving parts), the answer is also yes. In fact, in a typical computer center a significant amount of money is spent maintaining the printer, card reader, and other mechanical parts. If the question refers to the central processing unit of the computer, which contains the memory and electronic circuitry for making computations, then the theoretical answer is yes, but the practical answer is no.

What can that last statement mean? First, let us concede that any electronic equipment will eventually experience a malfunction. Computer designers and manufacturers recognize this potential for error and have designed computers that test themselves automatically for faulty performance. The testing is usually done using parity bits. (The word *bit* is an acronym taken from the words *bi*nary digi*t*.) The parity technique works as follows:

1. All information stored in the computer is stored in coded form; for example, the alphabetic character "A" is encoded by some computers as

    1100 0001

    The actual set of codes used by any particular computer need not concern us now because the encoding and decoding is done automatically by the system. However, the study of coding principles is important for anyone who has a serious interest in computing, and this subject is considered in more advanced courses.

2. Suppose that the system has just read and encoded the character "A"; the circuitry automatically attaches another bit called the parity bit which is set to either 0 or 1 as required to give an odd number of 1 bit (odd parity). Thus, "A" becomes

    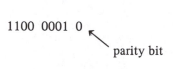

    1100 0001 0

    parity bit

3. Whenever information is manipulated, it is tested to determine whether or not the datum still has odd parity. If any bit has been changed (an error), the datum will no longer have odd parity. The computer detects this error, signals the operator that a parity error has occurred, and stops. The computer will not operate until the problem has been found and fixed.

Notice that although an error occurred, the machine stopped itself instead of producing an invalid answer. It will be necessary to rerun the work that was being done when the problem arose. The final answer, however, usually can be trusted.

If you have been alert, you probably have detected a flaw in the previous discussion. Suppose that two errors occur simultaneously in the same datum. Then the parity would be unchanged; the errors would not be detected and the results would be invalid answers or other catastrophes. It is estimated that such a double error should occur no more than one time in 30,000 years.

Computers now can detect a change in parity and automatically correct the error without stopping the computer. For example, one widely used, moderately priced computer has 5 checking bits for every 16 bits of data. This allows the automatic correcting of errors mentioned above, and also allows the detection of two simultaneous errors in a datum.

1.8   COMPUTER SCIENCE

It is extremely difficult to give a meaningful definition of any broad area of human knowledge. Circular definitions such as, "Mathematics is the subject studied by mathematicians, and mathematicians are people who study mathematics," can be difficult to avoid. Often a definition has meaning only after a person has studied a subject and knows what kinds of activities are associated with the subject. Moreover, the specialists in a subject view the subject differently and would define the discipline in ways that correspond to their own tastes.

To obtain a better grasp of the nature of computer science, let us examine the structure of the subject (see Figure 1.5). Please note that this is my personal viewpoint; other people would probably describe a different structure. Also keep in mind that knowledge cannot be neatly parceled into blocks as indicated in the diagram—everything is related to everything else.

The indicated branches of computer science are briefly described below:

Hardware: The design and construction of digital computers. Emphasis is given to making computers more reliable, faster, and capable of storing larger quantities of information. Advances may require the invention of new devices.

Programming methodology: The study of methods and approaches for writing more reliable programs with less effort. Includes the development of computer languages for particular problem domains.

Systems programming: The development of programs to improve the operating efficiency of the computer (the system), including programs to make the computer operate itself and to translate computer languages.

Information structures: The study of methods for representing information within the computer, with emphasis on the relationship between the pieces of information.

Artificial intelligence: The study of methods for making computers behave intelligently. Includes the study of robots.

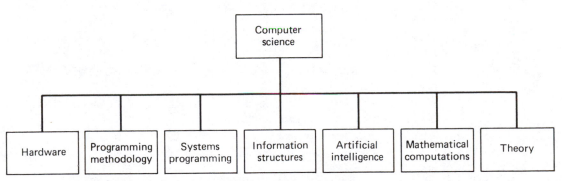

FIGURE 1.5   *A structure of computer science*

Mathematical computations: The development of methods for performing complex mathematical computations with computers. Includes the study of errors in computations. The resulting methods are especially useful in the sciences.

Theory: The study of the foundations of computer science. This branch is highly mathematical and includes formal languages (some linguistics), automata theory (the theory of machines), computability (the theory of what can be computed), complexity theory (the study of complexity of processes), and algorithm development (the study of problem-solving methods).

In our foregoing description of computer science, no mention was made of applications of computers to solve problems of practical and economic value. For example, a very important subject is data processing, which uses computers in business applications and which employs a large number of people. It is not, however, usually considered to be a part of computer science.

The breadth of computer science should now be evident. When you have completed this book, you will have a reasonable understanding of programming methodology and to a lesser degree an understanding of the hardware and the systems programming.

REVIEW QUESTIONS

1. What does the term "insidious revolution" mean when it is applied to the rapid spread of computers?

2. What were the first uses of computers? When did computers start to be used for commercial purposes? What is the approximate distribution of computers by type of industry?

3. What factors are responsible for the increasing widespread use of computers?

4. How can computers be used to allow human beings to expand their intellectual power?

5. Give a description of a computer system as an information-processing machine.

6. Define the terms program, memory, stored-program concept, hardware, software, and computer system.

7. What are the major components of a computer, and what is the purpose of each term?

8. What is a memory cell? What is meant by the terms "address" and "contents" of a memory cell?

9. Describe the post-office-box analogy for computer memory. How does the analogy fail?

10. What is the meaning of each term: nondestructive readout, destructive readin, random-access memory, and read-only memory?

11. What is machine language, and why is it important?

12. What is a register? Give the name and purpose of three registers normally found in computers.

13. What is an input/output processor? How does it improve the efficiency of operation of a computer?

14. What is meant by the terms "microcomputer" and "minicomputer"? Compare the capabilities of modern microcomputers and early computers.

15. What parts of a computer are most likely to malfunction?

16. What are parity bits, and how are they used?

17. Why is it difficult to define the term "computer science"?

REVIEW QUIZ

1. Computer science is a branch of (A) mathematics, (B) engineering, (C) linguistics, (D) programming, (E) none of the previous answers.

2. The power of computers results primarily from (A) the speed of computers, (B) the ability of computers to perform arithmetic, (C) the ability of computers to store huge amounts of information, (D) the low cost of computers, (E) the small size of computers.

3. A device that is more reliable than a computer is (A) an automobile, (B) a desk calculator, (C) a television receiver, (D) a telephone, (E) none of the previous answers.

4. According to the description in terms of major components of a simple (non-time-sharing) computer, (A) all information stored in the memory unit must first pass through the control unit, (B) all information stored in the memory unit has its origin in the input unit, (C) the control processing unit has two major components, (D) the actions of the output unit are under the control of the memory unit, (E) the memory unit communicates directly with the arithmetic and logic unit.

5. A device used for both input and output is (A) a plotter, (B) a magnetic disk, (C) a console keyboard, (D) a card punch, (E) a card reader.

6. A topic that is *not* considered to be a branch of computer science is (A) information structures, (B) hardware, (C) artificial intelligence, (D) data processing, (E) systems programming.

7. Malfunctions in the electronics of a computer (A) never occur, (B) occur but are not detected, (C) are detected using parity bits, (D) are corrected automatically using parity bits, (E) two of the previous answers.

8. A fundamental difference between a computer and a calculator is: (A) a calculator contains integrated circuits, (B) a computer uses the stored-program concept, (C) a computer has memory cells, (D) a calculator has an accumulator, (E) a calculator uses machine language.

9. An important difference between the post-office-box analogy of computer memory and actual computer memory is that computer memory (A) uses destructive readout, (B) uses nondestructive readin, (C) does not use addresses, (D) stores more than one value in a cell, (E) always contains values.

10. The type of industry that owns the largest number of computers is (A) banking, (B) educational institutions, (C) government, (D) printing, (E) manufacturing.

11. In a computer system, the software component that involves the least detailed knowledge for its use is (A) the major pieces of equipment, (B) the high-level languages, (C) the operating system, (D) the fundamental concepts of physics, (E) microinstructions.

12. The component of the central processing unit that contains the address of the next instruction to be executed is (A) an accumulator, (B) a program counter, (C) an instruction register, (D) a read-only memory, (E) a random-access memory.

EXERCISES

1. Various researchers in computer technology have predicted that in the early 1980s nearly every family in this country will have its own computer. Discuss the possibility that the prediction is valid.

2. The answers you give for the following depend, in part, on your previous experience with computers. At the end of the course your answers will probably be different.
   a. If you had a "home computer," what would you do with it? Make a list of possible applications.
   b. How is the computer used in the field that you have chosen for a career?
   c. Assume that you are a professional writer. How could you use a computer to help with your work?

3. Consult a computer hobby magazine such as *Byte* or *Creative Computing* and determine:
   a. The current cost of a small computer.
   b. The location of several nearby computer stores.

4. By consulting the literature supplied by the manufacturer of the computer used by your school, obtain a functional description of that computer.

5. It has been proposed that a microcomputer would be a valuable component in many home appliances. Find some examples of products for the home that have had microcomputers incorporated.

6. Obtain descriptions for the more expensive hand "calculators" manufactured by Texas Instruments and Hewlett-Packard. Should these devices be considered computers? How do you decide?

CHAPTER 2 COMMUNICATION, INFORMATION, AND LANGUAGE

2.1   A MODEL OF COMMUNICATION

From the previous discussion of the functional description of computers, we conclude that one of our fundamental problems will be communicating to the computer what is to be done. Thus it is appropriate for us to consider a general model of communication before undertaking a study of computing. Such a model is shown in Figure 2.1.

To gain insight into the model, let us consider a radio broadcast. The announcer is the information source and has a message to convey to you. The spoken message (transmitted message) is detected by the microphone (first stage of the transmitter); the resulting signal is converted into an electromagnetic wave which is broadcast by the station antenna (the last stage of the transmitter). The radio wave (the transmitted signal) travels through space (the channel) and reaches the radio receiver antenna (the first stage of the receiver). The radio loudspeaker (the last stage of the receiver) produces sound that allows you to receive the message.

Noise is introduced into the broadcast by improperly functioning equipment and by distortion of the wave as it travels through the atmosphere. This results in the popping, hissing, and variation in sound intensity with which we are familiar. In the case of computers, the noise and distortion are kept at extremely low levels.

The broadcasting of a television program fits the communication model in a manner that is similar to the radio broadcast. An important difference between radio and television, however, is the amount of information that must be transmitted in unit time, a quantity known as the *bandwidth* of the channel. To transmit music of high quality over radio requires a bandwidth equivalent to the frequency of vibration of the highest pitched sound, or approximately 15,000 cycles per second. AM radio settles for 5000 cycles per second. To create a television picture requires a total of approximately 4,000,000 pieces of information per second, or 800 times as much information as required for an AM radio broadcast. The concept of bandwidth is also important in computing. For example, if two computers use the same amount of time for adding two numbers, but the number of digits added by the first computer is twice as many as added by the second computer, then the first computer does more work in unit time (because of its greater bandwidth).

A conversation between two people is an especially interesting application of the

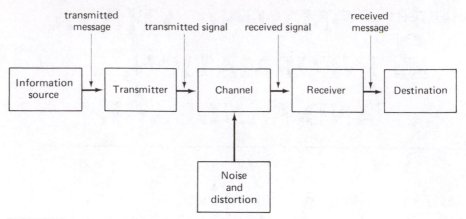

FIGURE 2.1 *General model of communication*

communication model. The lips of one person constitute the transmitter, and the ears of the second person are the receiver. As the conversation proceeds, the individuals are alternately transmitters and receivers. The ambiguity of natural language causes a considerable portion of the conversation to be devoted to clarifying what the individuals are trying to communicate. When we communicate with a computer, this process of determining what is meant is not possible—and perhaps it will never be possible. Since the computer is incapable of understanding any more than what we tell it, we must be very careful to tell the computer *exactly* what we mean. It is not unusual to hear a student complain: "The computer did what I asked it to do, not what I meant for it to do."

When we use a computer, the communication process can be visualized:

1. Human beings, as the information source, prepare data or instructions in a suitable language which is sent using appropriate equipment (e.g., a terminal or card reader) through wires (the channel) to the destination (the computer memory). Recall that noise and distortion play no role in this process. The precise use of language is, however, essential.

2. The computer, acting upon the instructions stored in its memory, performs operations to obtain an answer. The computer will eventually send the answers to the human beings.

3. The communication process is reversed. The computer is the information source. It sends the "computed" results through wires and prints them on a sheet or perhaps displays them on a television screen so that the human beings can read them. (Other techniques are also possible.)

If the process proceeds as described, the computer is said to be operating in the *batch-processing* mode. If a terminal is being used, the computer can transmit results at intermediate stages of the processing. We can examine these results and either direct the computer to continue or can modify the processing by sending new instructions—this is an example of *interactive computing*.

2.2   INFORMATION

This section briefly considers the concept of information—a concept that plays a fundamental role in constructing, using, and understanding computers. Information theory was invented by Norbert Wiener and Claude Shannon. In 1948, Wiener published a famous book, *Cybernetics, or Control and Communication in the Animal and in the Machine*, which recognized that the manipulation of information is essential to the functioning of organisms. In the same year, Claude Shannon published his great work, *A Mathematical Theory of Communication*. You should realize that the word *information* will be used in this section in a technical sense and that the meaning is not the same as in ordinary conversation. It has been noted that this is a prime example of scientists' ruining an otherwise good word. Shannon himself did not like using the word, but he could not find another that was as close to being right.

The goal of the communication process is to transfer information from a source to a destination. In ordinary discourse, information refers to knowledge, and the communication process involves the transfer of knowledge. Such a statement, however, does not tell us very much. In science we wish to have a definition of information that tells how to measure the amount of information in a message. It is generally conceded, for example, that the amount of information in a message depends upon the extent to which it is "news." For the definition to be intuitively and aesthetically pleasing, it should satisfy the condition that

> the minimum time to transmit the information (or the minimum cost to transmit it) should increase as the amount of information increases.

As a first guess, let us assume that the amount of information in a message can be determined by counting the number of words in it. For example, consider the following telegram, which is sent from one businessman to another:

> Dear Sam, it was a real pleasure to talk with you by phone this morning. As you requested, I have reserved the meeting rooms and made arrangements for lunch to be served during the business meeting. All the people we discussed have agreed to attend. I will pick you up at the airport on Friday morning at eight thirty. I am looking forward to seeing you again and to having a successful business meeting. Sincerely, John.

This message contains 76 words, and it is apparent that this number could be reduced by eliminating *redundancy* and editing the message using telegraphic style. Then the message might read:

> Sam, rooms reserved, lunch served. All will attend. Will pick you up at eight thirty Friday at airport. John.

This message of 19 words contains all the essential information of the original message. The technique of counting words is obviously not going to be adequate in determining the amount of information in the message. The message size can be reduced even further. (1) If John is Sam's only business contact in the city from which the message is sent, John's name could be omitted. (2) If it had been agreed that the meeting would be on Friday, that fact could be omitted. (3) If Sam normally travels by plane, the airport need not be mentioned. (4) Sam's name need not be mentioned, since the fact that he receives it meant it was addressed to him. The message now becomes:

> Rooms reserved, lunch served. All attend. Pickup at eight thirty.

The message has now been reduced to 10 words. An even greater reduction can be obtained using a procedure commonly employed by college students when making long-distance calls. Sam and John agree that if everything can be arranged—rooms, lunch, all attend, and airport pickup—a simple coded message will be sent. The telegram is then reduced to the following word:

> OK

Our analysis has led us to an extremely significant conclusion:

> The amount of information contained in a message depends upon what the receiver already knows.

We shall see that this conclusion has important implications for communications between human beings and computers. Finally, notice that if the receiver knows the content of the message before receiving it, no information is received.

This simple but important conclusion is just the beginning of Shannon's work on information. He derived equations for computing the amount of information in a message and developed a precise theory of information. Since we do not need more detail for our study, the subject will not be considered further here. The mathematically inclined reader will find the book by Gordon Raisbeck* to be an interesting introduction to the subject.

2.3 FEATURES OF NATURAL LANGUAGES

An essential feature of the communication process is the existence of a language in which information can be encoded for transmission to the receiver. This section summarizes some important features of natural language and compares them with computer languages. Peter Naur, a noted Danish computer scientist who played a key role in the development of the computer language ALGOL, discussed this subject in an elegant paper, "Programming Languages, Natural Languages, and Mathematics," which you should read.†

2.3.1 Complexity of Language

All natural languages are complex in the sense that there are no primitive natural languages. Natural languages are so complex that we are, despite numerous theories

---

*Gordon Raisbeck, *Information Theory* (Cambridge, Mass.: The MIT Press, 1963).
†Peter Naur, "Programming Languages, Natural Languages, and Mathematics," *Communications of the ACM* (December 1975), 678.

and a volume of literature on the subject, very far from understanding how any natural language really works. We do not know enough, for example, to develop computer programs that make good translations from one natural language to another. We do not understand how children are able to learn any natural language without any restrictions as to the form of the language. In contrast, all computer languages are completely understood; moreover, relative to natural languages, all computer languages are quite simple and primitive.

Natural language is used primarily in verbal communication. This is important, as it allows individuals to use their knowledge in verbal interchanges to eliminate ambiguities and finally to communicate ideas and concepts. With computers the situation is quite different—the computer "knows" only what we have been able to tell it, and our ability to convey knowledge to the computer is quite limited. The implication for computer languages, that is, languages which allow communication between human beings and computers, is very important. Recall that in the communication process the information content of a message depends upon what the receiver already knows. What does the computer know? Very little. Consequently, computer languages (and communication with the computer) require a precision of expression that exists in very few areas of human communication—perhaps in some scientific writing, mathematics, and musical composition.

Two eminent linguists, Benjamin L. Whorf and Edward Sapir, hypothesize that what we can think depends upon the language we know. To the degree that this hypothesis is true, you can expect your thinking to be changed by learning a computer language. The habits of precision in thinking that you will develop should help you in many subjects and activities outside computer science.

2.3.2 Redundancy

All natural languages have considerable redundancy associated with them. This is a valuable characteristic for verbal communication, since it allows us to understand each other in the presence of appreciable noise and distortion. Even when several words have been missed in a conversation, we can frequently infer the meaning of the speaker.

Redundancy in natural languages arises in several ways. In the English language some redundancy is introduced by the difference in the frequency of occurrence of the alphabetic characters (see Table 2.1). In cryptography the frequency table is sufficient to allow breaking of simple codes.

The tendency of characters to occur in definite sequences (q is followed by u, t is usually followed by h, etc.) introduces additional redundancy. Words are followed by predictable patterns of other words. It has been estimated that one-third of the words used in conversations consist of the set "the-of-and-to-a-that-is-I-for-be-was-as-you-with-he-on-by-not." The word order required by English syntax introduces even more redundancy. All this produces high redundancy, approximately 75 percent, in normal conversation; but very low redundancy is the rule for most computer languages. A single incorrect character will usually make a computer program completely unintelligible to the computer.

TABLE 2.1 *Frequency of occurrence of characters of the English alphabet*

Character	Frequency of occurrence
Space	0.2
E	0.105
T	0.072
O	0.0654
A	0.063
N	0.059
I	0.055
R	0.054
S	0.052
H	0.047
D	0.035
L	0.029
C	0.023
F, U	0.0225
M	0.021
P	0.0175
Y, W	0.012
G	0.011
B	0.0105
V	0.008
K	0.003
X	0.002
J, Q, Z	0.001

2.3.3 Ambiguity

Many statements in natural languages are ambiguous and imprecise. This is the primary factor that prevents satisfactory computer translation of natural languages. Usually, the ambiguity in a sentence is not noticed until someone asks the meaning, and in the larger context of a conversation an inherently ambiguous sentence may have a clear interpretation. Consider the meaning of the following*:

The boss fired the salesman with enthusiasm.

Possible meanings:
1. The boss fired the salesman who was enthusiastic.
2. The boss enjoyed firing the salesman.
3. The boss instilled enthusiasm in the salesman.

*D. Terence Langendoen, *The Study of Syntax* (New York: Holt, Rinehart and Winston, Inc., 1969), pp. 12–14. Copyright © 1969 by Holt, Rinehart and Winston, Inc. Reprinted by permission of Holt, Rinehart and Winston.

The scriptwriter was promoted for his entertaining new ideas.

Possible meanings:
1. The scriptwriter was promoted because he considered new ideas.
2. The scriptwriter was promoted because he had entertaining new ideas.

Ralph took my picture.

Possible meanings:
1. Ralph photographed me.
2. Ralph photographed the picture belonging to me.
3. Ralph made off with the pictorial representation of me.
4. Ralph made off with the picture belonging to me.

My favorite ambiguous sentence is, "Time flies like an arrow." Bryan Higman* has noted that the assumed meaning of the words affects our analysis of the sentence. Most people assume:

Time	*flies*	*like*	*an*	*arrow.*
noun subject	verb	adverbial preposition	article	noun

but apply a different interpretation to:

Fruit	*flies*	*like*	*a*	*banana.*
noun used adjectively	noun	verb	article	noun

In the early 1960s the sentence was submitted to an elaborate computer program at Harvard, which tried to deduce the structure of sentences on the basis of thousands of rules. The program deduced that "Time flies like an arrow" has four different meanings:

1. The concept, time, moves forward in the same way an arrow does.
2. Time the movement of insects (i.e., flies) in the same manner the movement of an arrow is timed.
3. A species of insects, time-flies, enjoy an arrow.
4. Measure the speed of the insects that resemble an arrow.

For natural languages, ambiguity is not necessarily a disadvantage, and it could even be an advantage. Naur has speculated that this impreciseness makes it easier for a language to evolve and allows speakers to express new ideas. In poetry, ambiguity can give an author the opportunity to express several ideas with a single phrase. For computer language, however, ambiguity is a disaster.

*Bryan Higman, *A Comparative Study of Programming Languages* (New York: American Elsevier Publishing Company, Inc., 1969), p. 9.

2.3.4 Syntax, Semantics, and Logical Validity

In using either a natural language or a computer language, we must be concerned with the syntax, semantics, and logical validity of what we are communicating. In this discussion, *syntax* will refer to the set of grammar rules for a language, *semantics* will refer to the meaning of a statement, and *logical validity* will refer to the truth or falsity of a statement. Consider, as examples, the following sentences:

Green ideas sleep furiously.*

1. This sentence is syntactically valid, that is, it follows English grammar rules.
2. I don't know what the sentence means; the semantics are not clear to me.
3. Because I don't know what the sentence means, I cannot say anything about its logical validity.

In computer science an average grade of 105 is required to make a final grade of C.

1. The sentence obeys the syntax rules.
2. I understand the meaning (semantics) of the sentence.
3. The sentence is not logically valid since a much lower average grade is required for making a final grade of C.

When you are learning to use a computer language, you will probably make errors involving syntax, semantics, and logic. Errors in syntax will be discovered immediately by the computer, which will print an appropriate message at the end of the program. Errors in semantics will arise because of a failure to understand how a computer language statement operates; for example, many students who are learning FORTRAN have difficulty with the "DO" statement because they do not realize in detail what the computer will do when the DO statement is encountered. The computer cannot detect errors of this type, so the program runs but produces the wrong answer. Errors of the logical validity type arise when the program is not a true representation of the problem you are trying to solve utilizing the computer. The problems cannot be detected by the computer, and they are frequently very difficult for us to find and correct.

2.4 COMPUTER LANGUAGES

Computer languages are all much simpler than natural languages in the sense that computer languages are completely understood and are much easier to learn. The quality of computer languages differs. This is also true for natural languages. It has been suggested that a language is better as it is able to express greater amounts of meaning with simpler mechanisms. The difference in the "power" of computer languages will be quite obvious during the discussion of low-level and high-level languages.

*Noam Chomsky, *Syntactic Structures* (The Hague: Mouton Publishers, 1957), p. 15. Reproduced by permission of Mouton Publishers.

Communicating with a computer using a computer language can be, however, more difficult than communicating with another person. The reason for this has been mentioned already:

The amount of information contained in a message depends upon what the receiver already knows.

The difficulty in using computer languages arises because, contrary to our interpersonal experience, the receiver of the message (the computer) "knows" practically nothing. Generally, the computer's "understanding" of languages will be quite small, because this understanding is limited by what the designers of the computer language have assumed will be the nature of the communication process. If you use any computer language extensively, you will occasionally be irritated by some unnatural limitation in the language; but if you wish to use the language, you must submit to the method assumed by the language designer.

2.4.1 Machine and Assembly Language

Every computer has an associated *machine language*, the nature of which depends upon the design of the particular machine. For each type of instruction, there will be electronic circuitry to interpret and execute the instruction, each of which will take the form of a long sequence of bits. For example, a typical instruction to add two numbers is

$$1000\ 0000\ 0110\ 1001$$

The circuitry must decode this binary number to discover that addition is requested, and then the circuitry must perform the addition using the appropriate numbers.

Machine language is a computer's "native language" and the only language that the computer can use directly. If a set of computer instructions is written in any language other than machine language, the instructions must be translated into machine language before the computer can execute them. Usually, a computer will have an *assembly language* that is directly related to its machine language. In assembly language a mnemonic code is used to represent the operation to be executed, and symbols are used for *operands*, that is, the quantities upon which the operations act. For example, consider the following machine instruction:

$$1000\ 0000\ 0110\ 1001$$

If the leftmost 8 bits are used to represent the operation to be done (addition) and the rightmost 8 bits are used to represent the operand (the value of X), the machine language instruction could be conveniently expressed as

$$\text{ADD X}$$

In assembly language programming, instructions are written using mnemonic operation codes and symbolic operands. An assembly-language instruction must be

TABLE 2.2 *Corresponding assembly- and machine-language instructions:*
$$C = A + B$$

Assembly language	Machine language
LOAD A	1100 0000 1011 0101
ADD B	1000 0000 0001 1110
STORE C	1101 0000 0110 1001

translated into a machine-language instruction before it can be executed. Each assembly-language instruction will be translated into one machine-language instruction by a special program called an *assembler*. The term one-to-one translation is used to describe this process. Table 2.2 shows a portion of a program to calculate $C = A + B$.

Writing a computer program directly in machine language is extremely difficult because it is almost impossible for us to remember and use so many bits without making an error. Assembly language is much easier to use than machine language, but it is also relatively difficult because problems still must be solved at the level of the elementary operations performed by the computer—human beings do not ordinarily think at such a detailed level in solving problems. Assembly language is an example of a *low-level* language.

2.4.2 High-Level Languages

Many high-level computer languages have been developed to make the use of computers easier. Such languages make it possible to solve problems using notation that is convenient and normal for us. For example, the high-level computer language FORTRAN was designed for solving mathematical problems. In FORTRAN, the algebraic equation

$$Z = Y^2 + (2A + C)X - 50$$

is written as

$$Z = Y**2 + (2*A+C)*X-50 \quad \text{where} \quad * \quad \text{means multiply}$$
$$** \quad \text{means raise to a power}$$

A root of the quadratic equation is computed using the FORTRAN statement

$$X = (-B+SQRT(B**2-4*A*C))/(2*A) \quad \text{where} \quad / \quad \text{means divide}$$
$$SQRT \quad \text{means take the square root}$$

Typically, a single high-level statement will be translated into many machine-language instructions. For example, the FORTRAN statement given above for computing the value of Z is translated into approximately 10 machine-language statements by a special program known as a *compiler*. The term *one-to-many translation* is used to describe this process.

2.4.3   The Need for Higher-Level Languages

Some problems such as the writing of a program to control the internal operation of a terminal usually require using assembly language, and the writing of such programs can be fun. Normally, however, computer programming should be done using a higher-level language. This is true for a variety of reasons:

1. It is difficult to think at the very detailed level required by assembly languages. It can be very aggravating to break down your thoughts about a problem to the assembly-language level—the required attention to details interferes with solving the problem. Alfred North Whitehead noted:

   > It is a profoundly erroneous truism, repeated by all copy-books and by eminent people when they are making speeches, that we should cultivate the habit of thinking of what we are doing. The precise opposite is the case. Civilisation advances by extending the number of important operations which we can perform without thinking about them. Operations of thought are like cavalry charges in a battle—they are strictly limited in number, they require fresh horses, and must only be made at decisive moments.

2. It is usually more time-consuming to write an assembly-language program to solve a problem than to use a higher-level language to solve the same problem. For most problems the extra time required for assembly-language programming is not justified.

3. High-level-language programs for a problem normally require fewer steps than a corresponding solution in an assembly language. The individual program statements more nearly resemble English and hence are easier to understand. The programs are easier to modify. Since computer programs for business organizations seem to undergo continual change, a process called "program maintenance," these programs should be written in a higher-level language whenever possible.

2.4.4   Problem-Solving Domains—Various Higher-Level Languages

There is an astounding variety of natural languages—more than 2700 have been discovered. Most of these are spoken by only a few hundred or a few thousand people, approximately 100 of the languages are used by a million or more people, and only 13 of the languages are used by more than 50 million people. An analogous situation exists in computing: thousands of high-level computer languages have been invented, but only a small number have obtained widespread acceptance and usage. Some of the best-known high-level computer languages are given in Table 2.3. (Jean Sammet describes 120 of the best-known languages in her book, *Programming Languages*.)

TABLE 2.3 *High-level computer languages*

Name (acronym)	Description
ALGOL	Algorithmic Language
APL	A Programming Language
BASIC	Beginners All-Purpose Symbolic Instruction Code
COBOL	Common Business-Oriented Language
FORTRAN	Formula Translation
LISP	List Processor
PASCAL	(is not an acronym)
PL/I	Programming Language I
RPG	Report Program Generator
SNOBOL	String-Oriented Symbolic Language

The analogy between natural languages and computer languages extends even further. First, computer languages evolve in much the same way as natural languages. For example, work on the FORTRAN language began in 1954. Since then three different versions of the language have been widely used, with each subsequent version containing a substantial number of new features. A similar evolution has occurred with other computer languages.

A second area of similarity between natural languages and computer languages is the existence of dialects. Computer manufacturers who also supply the compilers often add special, nonstandard features to a language. If a program uses the nonstandard features, it is probable that the program will have to be modified before it can be run on a different manufacturer's computer.

Why are there so many programming languages? Basically, they make the solving of a particular class of problems easier. Thus each programming language has a particular problem-solving domain for which it was designed. Each language has the capability of being useful in areas outside its normal problem-solving domain, but such usage is unnatural and unsatisfying. Again, an analogous situation exists regarding natural languages. A given natural language is not well suited for solving all possible types of problems, with the result that specialized languages have been invented for areas such as mathematics, music, and the sciences. English could have been used for any of these subjects, but such usage would have been awkward, inconvenient, and might even have impeded progress in a subject. Imagine describing a musical score in English.

To make the previous discussion concrete, let us consider the languages COBOL, FORTRAN, and LISP. COBOL was developed for solving accounting, report writing, and data-file maintenance problems for business. FORTRAN was developed for solving scientific and mathematical problems, and LISP was developed to manipulate lists of information for studies in the area of artificial intelligence. Each language produces programs that look very different from programs written in the other languages. Consider the case of arithmetic. Suppose that we want to add the values of A and B and assign the sum as the value of C. Appropriate statements for these languages are

FORTRAN   C = A + B

COBOL	ADD A TO B GIVING C
LISP	(SET (QUOTE C) (PLUS A B))

For computations in science and mathematics, FORTRAN is superior to COBOL, but for writing business reports, COBOL is superior to FORTRAN. When a person uses the computer to solve a problem, considerable time can be saved by selecting a language designed for that class of problems. For example, writing a COBOL program to make a statistical computation might take many hours. Writing a FORTRAN program to solve the same problem would probably take 20 to 30 minutes. Equivalent amounts of time could be saved by using COBOL instead of FORTRAN to generate a complex report. The message should be clear—if you are planning to be a computer professional, you will need to learn many computer languages so that you can select the one most appropriate for a particular task. If you are planning to use the computer as a tool in the subject area that interests you, you should learn the computer language that applies most directly to your field.

Learning your first computer language involves learning a new way to think. Learning a second, third, or fourth computer language is made easier by the knowledge absorbed from the previous language: each involves a new way to think. It can be an exciting intellectual experience.

REVIEW QUESTIONS

1. What are the components of the general model of communication?
2. How is the concept of bandwidth related to communication?
3. Compare the batch-processing and interactive-processing modes of computing.
4. How does the knowledge of a receiver affect the information content of a message?
5. What is the implication for information theory for communication between a human being and a computer?
6. Compare natural languages and computer languages with respect to their complexity, use in communication, redundancy, and ambiguity.
7. Give the meaning of each term: syntax, semantics, logical validity.
8. In using a computer language, what will be the effect of an error in:
   a. Syntax?
   b. Semantics?
   c. Logical validity?
9. Why is communication with a computer often more difficult than communication with another human being?
10. What are the relationships between and differences in machine language, assembly language, and high-level language?
11. What are the differences between a low-level computer language and a high-level computer language?
12. What is an assembler?
13. What is a compiler?
14. Why should a higher-level language normally be used instead of an assembly language in solving problems with a computer?
15. Why are there so many high-level computer languages?

16. Give the primary purpose for which the languages FORTRAN, COBOL, and LISP are used.

1. A concept that is *not* essential in a general model of communication is (A) redundancy, (B) a receiver, (C) a transmitted signal, (D) noise, (E) a channel.

2. Information in going from a source to a destination (A) passes through the bandwidth, (B) has the amount of noise reduced, (C) is transmitted through a channel, (D) is interpreted by the transmitter, (E) none of the previous answers.

3. The amount of information that can be communicated in unit time is limited primarily by (A) the size of the transmitter, (B) the bandwidth of the channel, (C) the physical dimensions of the receiver, (D) the presence of noise in the source, (E) the physical size of the channel.

4. Ordinarily, during the processing of computer programs the only errors that can be discovered by the computer involve (A) noise, (B) semantics, (C) logical validity, (D) syntax, (E) redundancy.

5. The "native language" of a computer (A) depends upon its design, (B) is the machine language, (C) is a low-level language, (D) is produced by an assembler, (E) all the previous answers.

6. A one-to-one translation is a characteristic of (A) FORTRAN, (B) an assembler, (C) a high-level language, (D) a compiler, (E) a binary number system.

7. An example of a low-level language is (A) English, (B) a compiler, (C) an assembly language, (D) BASIC, (E) two of the previous answers.

8. The most complex language listed is (A) English, (B) machine, (C) FORTRAN, (D) assembly, (E) COBOL.

9. The most suitable language for solving a business-oriented problem is (A) ASSEMBLY, (B) FORTRAN, (C) COBOL, (D) LISP, (E) ALGOL.

10. Assembly language should be used to solve a problem (A) to save programming time, (B) to make debugging easier, (C) to reduce the number of program statements, (D) only when there is no convenient, available high-level language for solving the problem, (E) two of the previous answers.

11. A knowledge of several computer languages (A) allows selection of a language that is suitable for solving the problem of interest, (B) may involve learning different ways to think, (C) is easier to achieve after one language has been learned well, (D) will require learning several sets of syntax rules, (E) all the previous answers.

1. Discuss the nature of noise and distortion in the communication process between human beings.

2. Devise a communication technique that will allow you, with minimum words, to notify your parents that you will be home for the weekend. Suppose that the telephone is to be used in the communication process and that you wish to minimize the phone costs. What can you do?

3. Speculate on the following. Consult the linguistics literature and compare your speculations with that of experts.
   a. Are some natural languages more complex than others? (Is this sentence ambiguous? If it is, what are some possible interpretations?)
   b. Is the Whorf-Sapir hypothesis valid?

4. In 1922, the eminent linguist Otto Jaspersen suggested

   that language ranks highest which goes farthest in the art of accomplishing much with little means, or, in other words, which is able to express the greatest amount of meaning with the simplest mechanism.

   a. Assume that the statement is true, and develop a set of criteria for deciding which modern natural language is best.
   b. Criticize Jaspersen's statement.
   c. What would Jaspersen probably conclude about high- and low-level computer languages?

5. Give reasons why English is not well-suited to serve as a computer programming language.

6. In the following phrase, some characters have been replaced by asterisks. What was the original phrase?

   T* BE *R NOT TO **

   Why can such phrases be interpreted?

7. Each of the following sentences is ambiguous. Give two interpretations for each sentence.
   a. Mary is a beautiful swimmer.
   b. The bill is large.
   c. Jeff received a blow on the head.
   d. John ate a half baked chicken.
   e. David bought a guaranteed used car.
   f. Visiting relatives can be a nuisance.
   g. The shooting of the hunters was awful.

8. Find a poem in which ambiguity is important.

9. Discuss the syntax, semantics, and logical validity of the statement: Computer science is less difficult than mathematics or philosophy.

ALGORITHMS

3.1 PROCESSES

A *process* is a series of activities that take place in a definite sequence; notice that there is a direct relation between the passage of time and the completion of individual steps leading to the completion of the overall process. Many of our normal activities can be considered to be processes, although we do not ordinarily think of them in such a formal way. For example, studying for a quiz, driving a car, cooking a meal, and buying groceries are all processes.

Our interest in processes arises because the computer performs its activities in definite, discrete steps over some time interval—that is, the computer performs processes. To describe what the computer is to do, it would be convenient to have a method for describing processes. Many such methods exist, but some are more suitable for describing computer processes than others. As an example of a description of a process, consider the following recipe for making French-style bread:

> Combine $1\frac{1}{2}$ packages of active dry yeast and 2 cups of warm water (100 to 115°F approximately) with 1 tablespoon of granulated sugar in a large bowl and allow to proof. Mix 1 tablespoon of salt with 5 to 6 cups of all-purpose flour and add to the yeast mixture, a cup at a time, until you have a stiff dough. Remove to a lightly floured board and knead until no longer sticky, about 10 minutes, adding flour as necessary. Place in a buttered bowl and turn to coat the surface with butter. Cover and let rise in a warm place until doubled in bulk, $1\frac{1}{2}$ to 2 hours. Punch down the dough. Turn out on a floured board and shape into two long, French-style bread loaves. Place on a baking sheet that has been sprinkled with 3 tablespoons of yellow cornmeal but not buttered. Slash the tops of the loaves diagonally in two or three places and brush with an egg wash made of 1 tablespoon of egg white mixed with 1 tablespoon of cold water. Place in a cold oven, set the temperature at 400°F, and bake 35 minutes, or until well browned and hollow-sounding when the tops are rapped.

Using the recipe, we can identify a definite sequence of steps to be executed in a specific order. Instead of this narrative style, however, a computer scientist would probably display the individual steps on different-numbered lines as follows:

1. Combine $1\frac{1}{2}$ packages of active dry yeast and 2 cups of warm water (100 to 115°F approximately) with 1 tablespoon of granulated sugar in a large bowl.

2. If the mixture does not proof, start over.
3. Mix 1 tablespoon of salt with 5 to 6 cups of all-purpose flour.
4. While the dough is not stiff, add the flour, a cup at a time, to the yeast mixture.
5. Remove to a lightly floured board.
6. While the dough is sticky, knead the dough, adding flour as necessary.
7. Place in a buttered bowl.
8. While the surface is not coated with butter, turn the dough.
9. Cover the dough and let rise in a warm place until doubled in bulk, $1\frac{1}{2}$ to 2 hours.
10. Punch down the dough.
11. Turn out on a floured board and shape into two long, French-style loaves.
12. Prepare a baking sheet by sprinkling with 3 tablespoons of cornmeal. Do not butter the baking sheet.
13. Place the loaves on the baking sheet.
14. Slash the loaves diagonally in two or three places.
15. Prepare an egg wash made of 1 tablespoon of egg white mixed with 1 tablespoon of cold water.
16. Place in a cold oven.
17. Set the temperature at 400°F.
18. Bake 35 minutes or until well browned and hollow-sounding when the tops are rapped.

A *flowchart* is another technique used to describe processes. In a flowchart the activities are written within blocks whose shapes indicate the nature of the step. For example, Figure 3.1 shows the standard symbols. The flowchart symbols are con-

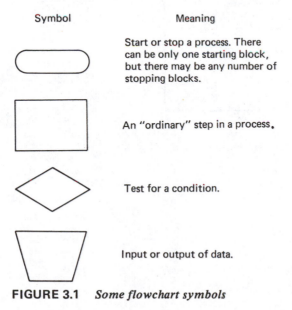

Symbol	Meaning
	Start or stop a process. There can be only one starting block, but there may be any number of stopping blocks.
	An "ordinary" step in a process.
	Test for a condition.
	Input or output of data.

FIGURE 3.1 *Some flowchart symbols*

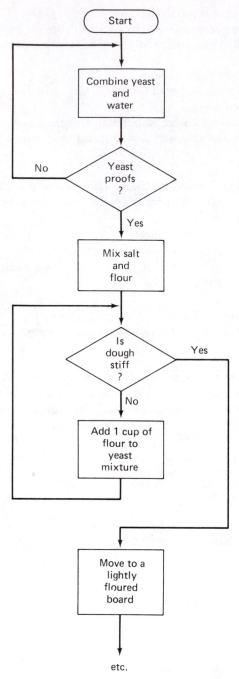

FIGURE 3.2 *Part of a flowchart for making French bread*

nected by arrows that indicate the sequence of execution of steps. In some cases, the overall logic is obvious and the arrowheads are omitted from the lines connecting the blocks. A portion of a flowchart for the making of French-style bread is given in Figure 3.2.

Flowcharts provide a graphic way of displaying processes, but it is time-consuming to draw the blocks. In addition, as the process grows more complex, the flowchart will extend over many pages, and there will be some difficulty in deciding where to place the blocks. For these reasons, flowcharts will be used rarely in the remainder of the course. Instead, an outline-like format will be used for the instructions, with indentations giving the level of logic of the steps in the process. This technique will be discussed later when we are ready to use it.

3.2 EFFECTIVE PROCEDURES

The baking of French-style bread is certainly a process, but it is not a process that all people could follow without difficulty. In my case, there are several undefined terms in the process. What are the meanings of "proof," "stiff" (how stiff?), "lightly floured," "sticky," "punch the dough," and "until brown" (how brown?). Because of these uncertainties, it is unlikely that I could bake the bread without first having some instruction—and maybe not even then in my case. What would it take to describe the process so that anyone could do it? One requirement is that there must be no uncertainty in how to interpret the language, but this requirement poses another problem, since all natural languages are inherently ambiguous. A solution is to use an unambiguous computer language to describe a process. For this course, therefore, a process will be considered to be completely described when it is expressed in an appropriate computer language. It is an interesting result that our quest for precision in describing processes has led us to use a machine (the computer) and an artificial language.

Some processes are more interesting than others. One such concept, the effective procedure, is defined as follows:

A *procedure* is a process performed by a computer.

An *effective procedure* is a procedure that terminates if a solution can be found, but otherwise it may not terminate.

For example, a *perfect number* is an integer that is equal to the sum of all its divisors except itself. Therefore, 6 is a perfect number ($1 + 2 + 3 = 6$), but 8 is not a perfect number ($1 + 2 + 4 = 7$). It is not known whether there is an infinity of perfect numbers. Consequently, an effective procedure for finding perfect numbers would find a given perfect number, print it, and then halt. The procedure could be executed again and again to find subsequent perfect numbers. If an attempt were made to find another after the largest perfect number were found (assuming that a finite number of perfect numbers exists), the procedure would never stop executing.

As another example, consider the following well-known puzzle.

Ten holes are bored in a block to form a triangle:

Each hole except one is filled with a movable peg, usually a golf tee. The object is to move the tees by jumping another tee to land in an empty hole. Any tee that is jumped is removed. The object is to finish with a single tee on the board.

A computer program to solve the puzzle has found hundreds of solutions, but for one particular starting position, no solution has ever been found, despite the use of considerable computer time. Is the computer program an effective procedure, meaning that no solution is possible for the starting position in question? Has the program not run long enough? Does the program contain a bug? As far as I have been able to determine by experimentation and by literature search, the answers are not known.

3.3 ALGORITHMS

An algorithm is a restriction of effective procedures to cases that always terminate. Thus,

An *algorithm* is a procedure written in a clear, unambiguous manner which is guaranteed to terminate in a finite time and either give an answer or indicate that no answer is possible.

There are, for example, many algorithms for determining whether or not an integer is a prime. One of the simplest (but not efficient) is indicated in Figure 3.3. In this description of the algorithm, the statements, from line 4 through line 9 are to be repeated as long as the condition "the integer is less than the number" is true. When the integer and number are equal, the condition is false, and the number must be a prime. Thus, when the condition becomes false, statement 11 is executed next. You should test your understanding of the algorithm by trying it with several numbers, such as 7 and 9.

The discovery and development of algorithms and effective procedures is an intellectually challenging activity. In some cases the task is so difficult that the discovery of an algorithm is sufficient to make its inventor famous. As you learn computer science, make a mental distinction between finding an algorithm and implementing it using FORTRAN or some other computer language. Most of your difficulties will have to do with finding an algorithm.

```
 1. Select a number.
 2. Assign the value 2 to a test value.
 3. WHILE (the test value is less than the number)
 4.        Divide the number by the test value.
 5.        IF   (there is no remainder)
 6.               THEN   Print "The number is not prime."
 7.                      STOP
 8.               ELSE   Increase the value of the test value by 1.
 9.        ENDIF
10. ENDWHILE
11. Print   "The number is a prime."
12. STOP
```

FIGURE 3.3   *Algorithm for determining whether or not an integer is a prime*

3.4   COMPUTABILITY THEORY

Unsuccessful attempts to find effective procedures to solve important problems in mathematics have led to the development of a new branch of mathematics, *computability theory*, which investigates whether or not an answer can be obtained for a problem. A particularly famous problem, which for centuries resisted all attempts to solve it, is the trisection of an angle using only a straightedge and a compass. Computability theory has shown that there is no solution to the problem of trisecting the angle as it is classically stated.

Whenever a problem resists all efforts by many people to find a solution, computability theory is used to determine if a general solution is possible. The theory is difficult and highly mathematical, with the result that attempts to use it are not always successful. This subject is very important to computer scientists and is presented in advanced courses.

REVIEW QUESTIONS

1. What is a process?
2. What is the relation between a process and a computer?
3. What methods are used to describe processes?
4. Define an effective procedure.
5. What is the relationship between an effective procedure and an algorithm?

REVIEW QUIZ

1. A process (A) involves the passage of time, (B) may involve discrete steps, (C) can be described in narrative form, (D) may be described with a flowchart, (E) all of the previous answers.
2. An algorithm (A) describes an effective procedure, (B) describes a process, (C) is ambiguous, (D) does not terminate, (E) all the previous answers.
3. The listed activity that will probably be most difficult is (A) describing a process, (B) finding an algorithm to solve a problem, (C) writing a computer program to solve a problem, (D) finding an effective procedure to solve a problem, (E) eliminating errors from computer programs.

4. Investigation of whether or not a problem has a solution is the primary concern of (A) algorithm development, (B) drawing a flowchart, (C) process description, (D) computability theory, (E) two of the previous answers.

EXERCISES

1. Convert into a flowchart the algorithm for determining whether an integer is a prime (Figure 3.3).

2. List five processes that you perform on a regular basis.

3. Describe in detail any one of the processes that you listed as an answer to Exercise 2.

4. Can the computation of your average quiz grade for this course be considered algorithmic in nature? Explain your answer.

5. Does the process of computing a person's pay form an algorithm? Explain your answer.

6. Give an example of a process that cannot be described as an algorithm.

7. Some researchers believe that an important portion of a person's knowledge is a set of procedures. Comment on this idea.

CHAPTER 4 SOME PROGRAMMING CONCEPTS

Before we actually start using a computer, we need to learn some fundamental programming concepts. To illustrate the ideas, we use a simple computer language whose operation is particularly easy to visualize. Programs written in the language should be "hand-simulated." This approach allows us to separate the ideas from the extraneous details that must be learned to operate the computer, and simultaneously gives practice in thinking about the execution of computer programs.

Some important concepts that will be discussed are:

1. Computer program
2. Bugs
3. Debugging
4. Planning
5. Procedure
6. Formal parameter
7. Argument
8. Subprocedure
9. Naming
10. State
11. Local
12. Global
13. Extensibility

Be sure that you understand these concepts as they are presented. Because they occur in real computer languages, a knowledge of them can make it easier to learn a computer language.

The approach taken in this chapter is based upon the work of Seymour Papert and his associates (at the Massachusetts Institute of Technology), who have developed a high-level computer language, LOGO, for manipulating learning environments. Using LOGO, they have successfully taught grammar-school children many important concepts about computing and thinking. In honor of their work, we shall call the pseudo-language used here MLOGO (Modified LOGO).

4.1 CONCEPT OF A COMPUTER PROGRAM

By definition, a *computer program* is a set of instructions designed to cause the computer to perform a set of actions of interest to us. Thus a computer program always has a clearly defined goal to accomplish. This sounds very simple and straightforward, but developing a computer program can be very challenging. Developing a computer program for complex problems may take us to the very limit of what we know how to do. Even when we know what we want to do and approximately how to accomplish it, most of us do not have appropriate experience in using language with the precision required for writing a computer program. In contrast with natural languages, computer languages are unambiguous, have low redundancy, and use a rigid syntax. The computer "knows" only what the language designer has been able to build into the language translator. This means that you must supply all—100 percent—of the information the computer requires to solve the problem. In learning to develop computer programs, you will be learning to think in a new way—a precise way that can be useful in any area of human endeavor whether the computer is being used or not.

The goal-oriented nature of a computer program leads to an important property: the program either works perfectly or it fails. In the event a program executes but produces the wrong answer, the program is said to contain a *bug*. The process of eliminating bugs, *debugging*, is quite important, and we will later consider it in detail.

4.2   DISPLAY TURTLES

The language that we shall use involves instructions for manipulating a "turtle." These instructions are actually for a computer that controls the turtle. (Although we are not going to use a computer for the work in this chapter, we will talk about using it.) Turtles come in two forms: a robot turtle, which moves around on the floor in response to instructions, and a display turtle, which draws pictures on a television screen (cathode ray tube or CRT). The robot turtle actually uses a pen, but the display turtle merely leaves a trail on the CRT as the turtle moves. Our goal will be to write programs that will draw interesting figures by making the turtle move. For convenience, we consider only the display turtle in the remaining part of the discussion.

The CRT screen will be the surface on which the turtle moves. When the computer begins its operation, the turtle will be displayed as a small arrowhead in the center of the CRT screen. The point of the arrowhead indicates the direction in which the turtle's nose is pointing. The location at which the shaft attaches to the arrowhead is the position of the pen. At any time the location of the turtle can be determined by finding the arrowhead on the screen. The turtle can step forward or backward or rotate to the left or to the right. The CRT screen is divided into 400 units of one step per unit in both the horizontal and vertical directions. The screen can also be treated as an x, y grid of steps, with the origin of the axes being the center of the screen. Figure 4.1 illustrates this.

The primitive instructions for manipulating the turtle are very simple and are summarized in Table 4.1.

Now let us consider a computer terminal session using the turtle. We sit down, turn on the terminal, and the screen lights up, showing the turtle at the center. Now we make the turtle draw a square for us. Type the instructions at the terminal keyboard:

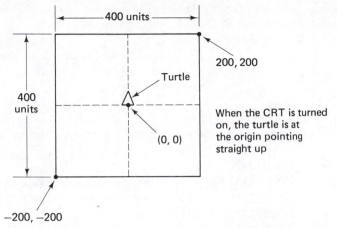

FIGURE 4.1 *CRT screen for display turtles*

TABLE 4.1 *Primitive instructions for turtle*

Instruction	Meaning
PENUP	Raise the pen so the turtle can be moved without leaving a trace
PENDOWN	Lower the pen so a trail will be drawn when the turtle moves
FORWARD ⟨value⟩	Move the turtle forward ⟨value⟩ number of steps (do not change the direction it is pointing)
BACKWARD ⟨value⟩	Move the turtle backward ⟨value⟩ number of steps (do not change the direction it is pointing)
RIGHT ⟨value⟩	Rotate the turtle to the right (clockwise) by ⟨value⟩ degrees
LEFT ⟨value⟩	Rotate the turtle to the left (counterclockwise) by ⟨value⟩ degrees

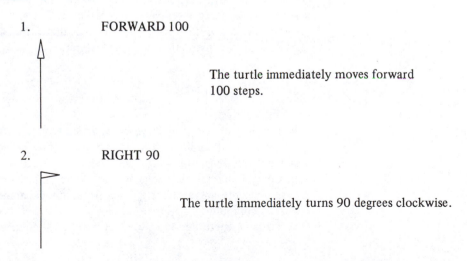

1. FORWARD 100

The turtle immediately moves forward 100 steps.

2. RIGHT 90

The turtle immediately turns 90 degrees clockwise.

3.   FORWARD 100

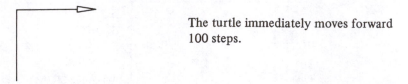

The turtle immediately moves forward 100 steps.

The steps are repeated as

RIGHT 90
FORWARD 100   Each step is executed immediately after it is
RIGHT 90   typed in. Notice that the turtle has been returned
FORWARD 100   to its original state.
RIGHT 90

to give

There are several important features associated with this simple program:

1. The turtle (more accurately, the language) is being used in the *execution mode*. In this mode, an action is performed as soon as a signal is sent from the terminal, indicating that a complete instruction has been entered. Execution mode allows one's logic to be checked as the problem is being solved, but for some purposes it is not convenient.

2. When the turtle is stationary, it can be described completely by giving its state, that is, its x-coordinate, y-coordinate, heading in degrees, and pen position. Before an instruction is executed, the turtle is in a state, and then, as a result of the instruction, it changes states.

$$\text{state 1} \xrightarrow[\text{(change of state)}]{\text{instruction execution}} \text{state 2}$$

The concepts of *state* and *change of state* are very powerful and have applications in many disciplines. If you start to looking consciously for states in common situations, you will be amazed how often the concept applies. Incidentally, all digital computers use the state and change-of-state concepts. These concepts are extremely valuable in understanding the dynamic behavior of computers.

3. The turtle was returned to its original state. This required that the turtle turn

through 360 degrees. An important theorem, the Total-Turtle-Trip (T^3) theorem, can be deduced:

When a turtle makes a round trip (returns to its original state), it turns a whole number of 360 degrees.

4.3 DEFINITION MODE

When we know exactly how to draw a figure (or think we know), the *definition mode* is more convenient than the execution mode. In the definition mode, all other actions are suspended to allow a sequence of instructions to be defined and given a name. The word "TO" indicates that the definition mode is to be entered, and the word "END" designates there is nothing more to be done in definition mode. The set of instructions that is defined is called a *procedure*, and every procedure must have a name. The word that immediately follows "TO" is the name of the procedure. To define the procedure SQUARE, we type the following:

```
TO    SQUARE
10    FORWARD    100
20    RIGHT      90
30    FORWARD    100
40    RIGHT      90
50    FORWARD    100
60    RIGHT      90
70    FORWARD    100
80    RIGHT      90
90    RETURN
END
```

The word "RETURN" when encountered during execution mode means to return to doing whatever was in progress when the procedure was entered. The numbers that appear before the instructions (10, 20, 30, etc.) are called *statement numbers*, and they are used merely to identify the instructions. Statement numbers are optional, but we will always include them to make it easy to discuss particular statements.

After the system returns to the execution mode, we can cause a square having sides of length 100 steps to be drawn whenever we wish by typing SQUARE. The procedure SQUARE has become part of the language and is now an instruction in the same manner that FORWARD is an instruction. For this reason the language is said to be *extensible* with respect to its operations. The importance of this concept, *naming*, as an aid to thinking cannot be overemphasized. Whenever we can identify an idea with sufficient precision to enumerate the individual steps and give the process a name, we can stop being concerned with the details. In my opinion, this is a technique that plays a central role in the advancement of many intellectual disciplines.

4.4 ARGUMENTS

Our procedure for drawing a square contains a deficiency: all squares drawn by it have sides of 100 steps. The procedure can be generalized by using formal parameters and arguments. The new definition becomes

```
TO    SQUARE    SIDE
10    FORWARD   SIDE
20    RIGHT     90
30    FORWARD   SIDE
40    RIGHT     90
50    FORWARD   SIDE
60    RIGHT     90
70    FORWARD   SIDE
80    RIGHT     90
90    RETURN
END
```

Any symbol that follows the name of a procedure (e.g., SIDE in our definition of SQUARE) is called a *formal parameter*. When a procedure is used in the execution mode, an actual value, known as an *argument*, is substituted for a formal parameter. The following illustrate the substitution of arguments (25, 50, and 100) for the formal parameter SIDE:

SQUARE 25   draws a square of side length 25
SQUARE 50   draws a square of side length 50
SQUARE 100   draws a square of side length 100

Using an argument provides a technique for allowing a value to be input into a procedure and substituted wherever the argument appears in the definition. There is no limit to the number of arguments that a procedure may have.

4.5 NAMES AND VALUES

When a variable is used in a programming language, it is necessary to make a distinction between the name of the variable and its value. In the definition of SQUARE, the argument SIDE refers to the value of the variable SIDE. As a further example, consider the statement

$$\underbrace{SIDE}_{\text{name of result}} = \underbrace{SIDE + 10}_{\substack{\text{values to be used} \\ \text{in the computation}}}$$

This is interpreted as "make the name SIDE refer to the value of SIDE plus 10." If the value of SIDE is initially 50, then after the statement is executed, the name SIDE will refer to the value of 60. Operations of this type are of great importance in computing.

A name such as SIDE will be assumed to be the name of a computer memory cell. The cell will contain some value. This can be visualized as

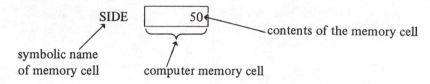

In terms of this model, the statement

$$SIDE = SIDE + 10$$

is interpreted as

take the contents of the cell whose name is SIDE, add 10 to this value, and finally store the resulting value as the new value of the cell whose name is SIDE.

Thus the value 60 is stored as the new value of SIDE.

Notice that the statement SIDE = SIDE + 10 is not an algebraic equation, since the equals sign means "store the value computed for the right-hand side as the value of the left-hand side." This process is called *assignment*; that is, a new value is assigned to the cell which is named on the left of the *assignment operation* (i.e., the equals sign).

The statement

$$COUNT = COUNT + 1$$

means: take the current value of COUNT, add 1 to this value, and store the results as the new value of COUNT. A statement such as COUNT = 0, in which no calculation is necessary on the right-hand side, means to assign 0 as the value of COUNT.

4.6   BUGS AND DEBUGGING

We shall now define a procedure to draw equilateral triangles of any size. Consider the following:

TO	TRIANGLE	SIDE
5	FORWARD	SIDE
10	RIGHT	60

15	FORWARD	SIDE
20	RIGHT	60
25	FORWARD	SIDE
30	RIGHT	60
35	RETURN	
END		

Does the procedure TRIANGLE actually draw a triangle? To find the answer, we "play computer"; that is, we perform the instructions in the same way the computer would. This is what we get:

If we had been using a display turtle, it would have been immediately obvious that a problem exists. "Playing computer" is more work, but it is a standard technique for testing programs.

Our procedure contains a bug, and we must find the problem and correct it. We discover that we should have turned 120 degrees instead of 60. The correct procedure is

TO	TRIANGLE	SIDE
10	FORWARD	SIDE
20	RIGHT	120
30	FORWARD	SIDE
40	RIGHT	120
50	FORWARD	SIDE
60	RIGHT	120
70	RETURN	
END		

Notice that the new procedure satisfies the Total-Turtle-Trip theorem.

The process of discovering and correcting errors is known as *debugging*. In the real world, debugging is an extremely important and commonly occurring activity. Furthermore, finding a bug is not a catastrophe; one merely corrects it. (Contrast this with many academic environments in which the emphasis is on being "right.") Recognition of a bug may be opportunity in disguise. It is not unusual for a bug to result from an inadequately developed concept. In this case the bug alerts us to the problem, and we have the opportunity to refine and clarify our concept. Important intellectual advances can result from the recognition of a bug and the attempts to correct it.

4.7   SUBPROCEDURES

A *subprocedure* is a procedure that is used in the construction of another procedure. Any procedure can be used as a subprocedure. When a subprocedure is used, the following conventions must be followed:

1. The subprocedure must have the same number of arguments as it had when it was originally defined as a procedure.
2. The arguments in the subprocedure must have the same meaning and appear in the same relative position as they did in the original definition as a procedure.
3. Any variable that appears in the argument list of a subprocedure must have been defined previously.

As an example, consider the writing of a procedure to draw a "bowtie."

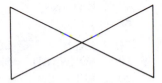

The bowtie consists of two triangles, although they have different orientations. Having made this observation, it is easy to define a procedure for the bowtie using TRIANGLE as a subprocedure. (Assume that the two triangles connect at the origin on the CRT.)

```
TO    BOWTIE      SIDE
10    RIGHT       60
20    TRIANGLE    SIDE
30    RIGHT       180
40    TRIANGLE    SIDE
50    RETURN
END
```

In this example the procedure TRIANGLE is used as if it were an instruction such as FORWARD and RIGHT, which were defined originally as part of the language. Thus the language can be extended to meet our needs by defining procedures. Several additional examples are given below.

```
TO    HOURGLASS    SIDE
10    LEFT         30
20    TRIANGLE     SIDE
30    RIGHT        180
40    TRIANGLE     SIDE
50    RETURN
END
```

```
TO    HOURGLASS   SIDE
10    RIGHT       90
20    BOWTIE      SIDE
30    RETURN
END
```

```
TO    DIAMOND     SIDE
10    TRIANGLE    SIDE
20    LEFT        60
30    TRIANGLE    SIDE
40    RETURN
END
```

```
TO    TREE        SIDE
10    FORWARD     SIDE
20    LEFT        90
30    FORWARD     SIDE/2
40    RIGHT       120
50    TRIANGLE    SIDE
60    RETURN
END
```

4.8   PROGRAMMING EXAMPLES

There are many different and often equally satisfactory ways to solve a particular problem using a computer. To illustrate this point and also to expand our knowledge of programming, we consider next four different procedures for drawing a square. To execute any of the four procedures, we would type, for example, SQUARE 100. A person watching the CRT screen would not be able to tell which method was being used, but internally the procedures have different behaviors (see Figure 4.2).

Method 1: Statements 10, 20, 30, . . . , 80 are executed sequentially, causing the square to be drawn. When the RETURN statement is executed, the computer enters a state for determining what the next instruction is outside the procedure. Once the figure is drawn, the computer hardware continues to display it.

Method 2: A subprocedure DRAWSIDE is defined which draws one side and turns the turtle in preparation for drawing the next side. The command REPEAT has the syntax

REPEAT count, command

```
            Method 1                                    Method 2

TO    SQUARE    SIDE                  TO    SQUARE    SIDE
10    FORWARD   SIDE                  10    REPEAT 4, DRAWSIDE    SIDE
20    RIGHT     90                    20    RETURN
30    FORWARD   SIDE                  END
40    RIGHT     90
50    FORWARD   SIDE                  TO    DRAWSIDE    SIDE
60    RIGHT     90                    10    FORWARD    SIDE
70    FORWARD   SIDE                  20    RIGHT      90
80    RIGHT     90                    30    RETURN
90    RETURN                          END
END


            Method 3                                    Method 4

TO    SQUARE   SIDE                   TO    SQUARE    SIDE
10    COUNT = 4                       10    COUNT = 0
20    REPEAT COUNT, DRAWSIDE SIDE     20    WHILE COUNT < 4, DRAWSIDE2 SIDE COUNT
30    RETURN                          30    RETURN
END                                  END

TO    DRAWSIDE    SIDE                TO    DRAWSIDE2 SIDE COUNT
10    FORWARD    SIDE                 10    FORWARD    SIDE
20    RIGHT      90                   20    RIGHT      90
30    RETURN                          30    COUNT = COUNT + 1
END                                  40    RETURN
                                     END
```

FIGURE 4.2   *Different procedures for drawing a square*

where "command" is any command or procedure
"count" is the number of times the command is
to be repeated

Thus REPEAT 4, DRAWSIDE SIDE means to repeat the command DRAW-
SIDE four times.

Method 3: This method is a variation of the previous one, but the variable
COUNT is used to hold the number of times the command in REPEAT
is to be repeated.

The variables SIDE and COUNT have different properties which
should be recognized. SIDE is defined outside the procedure SQUARE,
and because its value is known both within and without the procedure,
it is called a *global variable*. The variable COUNT is defined and used
entirely within the procedure SQUARE, so it is called a *local variable*.
Other procedures outside SQUARE will have no knowledge of this use
of COUNT.

Method 4: This method uses the WHILE command, which has the syntax

WHILE condition, command

where "command" is any command or procedure
"condition" is a term that evaluates as either true

or false. It involves comparing two values using the relational operators:

=	equal
<	less than
>	greater than
<=	less than or equal
>=	greater than or equal
<>	not equal

The command part of the WHILE statement is executed as long as the condition is true. Thus in

WHILE COUNT < 4, DRAWSIDE2 SIDE COUNT

DRAWSIDE2 will be executed as long as COUNT is less than 4. Notice that DRAWSIDE2 must change the value of COUNT, or an infinite loop would result.

Consider the following procedure for drawing a triangle:

```
TO    TRIANGLE    SIDE
10    REPEAT 3, DRAWSIDE3    SIDE
20    RETURN
END

TO    DRAWSIDE3    SIDE
10    FORWARD    SIDE
20    RIGHT    120
30    RETURN
END
```

This technique is almost identical to the second method used to draw a square. This suggests that a single procedure should be able to draw either a triangle or a square. In fact, we can write a procedure to draw any simple polygon.

```
TO    POLY    SIDE    ANGLE    NUMBEROFSIDES
10    REPEAT NUMBEROFSIDES, DRAWONESIDE    SIDE    ANGLE
20    RETURN
END

TO    DRAWONESIDE    SIDE    ANGLE
10    FORWARD    SIDE
20    RIGHT    ANGLE
30    RETURN
END
```

In the execution mode:

POLY	100	120	3	draws a triangle
POLY	100	90	4	draws a square
POLY	100	60	6	draws a hexagon
POLY	100	45	8	draws an octagon

of a side length of 100 units.

4.9 PLANNING AND TOP-DOWN PROGRAMMING

As problems become more complex, it becomes progressively more difficult to recall simultaneously all the details necessary to solve the problem. In an invaluable planning technique known as *top-down programming*, we assume that subprocedures are available for solving the problem. After the problem is solved using these procedures, the procedures themselves are written. The technique will be illustrated with three examples:

1. Draw a simplified house having the following form:

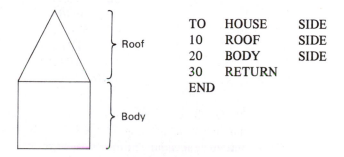

TO	HOUSE	SIDE
10	ROOF	SIDE
20	BODY	SIDE
30	RETURN	
END		

Now define subprocedures for ROOF and BODY.

TO	ROOF	SIDE
10	RIGHT	30
20	TRIANGLE	SIDE
30	RETURN	
END		

TO	BODY	SIDE
10	RIGHT	60
20	SQUARE	SIDE
30	RETURN	
END		

2. Draw a simplified wishing well of the following form:

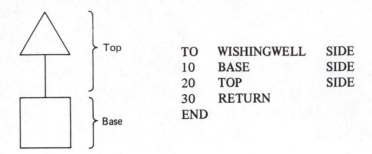

```
TO    WISHINGWELL    SIDE
10    BASE           SIDE
20    TOP            SIDE
30    RETURN
END
```

Now define the subprocedures **TOP** and **BASE**.

```
TO    BASE       SIDE
10    SQUARE     SIDE
20    RETURN
END

TO    TOP        SIDE
10    FORWARD    SIDE
20    RIGHT      90
30    FORWARD    SIDE/2
40    LEFT       90
50    TREE       SIDE
60    RETURN
END
```

Notice the use of an arithmetic expression in line 30. Any arithmetic expression constructed using +, −, ∗ (for multiplication), and / (for division) is permitted as an argument to a procedure.

3. Draw a simplified rocket of the following form:

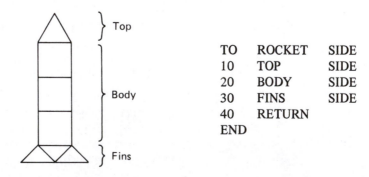

```
TO    ROCKET     SIDE
10    TOP        SIDE
20    BODY       SIDE
30    FINS       SIDE
40    RETURN
END
```

Now define the subprocedures.

TO	TOP	SIDE
10	RIGHT	30
20	TRIANGLE	SIDE
30	RIGHT	60
40	RETURN	
END		

TO	BODY	SIDE
10	SQUARE	SIDE
20	RIGHT	90
30	FORWARD	2* SIDE
40	RIGHT	180
50	SQUARE	SIDE
60	RIGHT	90
70	SQUARE	SIDE
80	RIGHT	90
90	FORWARD	SIDE
100	LEFT	30
110	RETURN	
END		

TO	FINS	SIDE
10	TRIANGLE	SIDE
20	FORWARD	SIDE
30	LEFT	120
40	TRIANGLE	SIDE
50	RETURN	
END		

The more complex the problem to be solved, the more useful the top-down programming approach will be. You are encouraged to use the approach whenever possible.

REVIEW QUESTIONS

1. Define "computer program." Why are natural languages not suitable for writing computer programs?
2. What is a program bug? Why is the concept important?
3. List the primitive instructions for manipulating a display turtle.
4. What is the difference in execution mode and definition mode? How is the mode determined?
5. What factors determine the state of the turtle?
6. Give the steps required to define a procedure. Why do procedures make the language extensible?
7. How are procedures and arguments related? What restrictions exist in using arguments? How do arguments make procedures more powerful?

8. Define "global variable" and "local variable."

9. What is a subprocedure?

10. Explain the top-down approach to writing programs.

1. A concept that is directly related to the concept of a process is (A) extensibility, (B) global, (C) procedure, (D) state, (E) naming.

2. Arguments are used (A) in procedures, (B) in planning, (C) only in the definition mode, (D) as operations, (E) to find bugs.

3. A student had the goal of drawing a house, ⌂, so he used

```
TO      HOUSE
10      SQUARE      100
20      FORWARD     100
30      RIGHT       120
40      TRIANGLE    100
50      RETURN
END
```

(A) His approach worked.
(B) The base of the triangle touched the square at only one point.
(C) The house was lying on its side.
(D) Statement 30 should be changed to 30 RIGHT 60.
(E) None of the previous answers.

4. Given:

```
TO      ROCKET
10      TOP
20      BODY
30      BASE
40      RETURN
END
```

(A) ROCKET is an example of a subprocedure.
(B) Different-size rockets cannot be drawn using ROCKET.
(C) The definition of BODY cannot involve procedures or subprocedures.
(D) The statement TO ROCKET includes inputs.
(E) It is an example of bottom-to-top planning.

5. The statement STEP = STEP + 1 (A) causes the value of STEP to increase by 1, (B) can appear in a procedure, (C) can appear in a subprocedure, (D) all the previous answers, (E) none of the previous answers.

Use the following in answering questions 6 to 9:

Given:

```
TO      POLY STEP ANGLE NUM
10      REPEAT NUM, DRAW STEP ANGLE
20      RETURN
END
```

```
TO      DRAW STEP ANGLE
10      FORWARD STEP
20      RIGHT ANGLE
30      RETURN
END
```

6. A command that would cause an octagon to be drawn is (A) POLY 100 135 8, (B) POLY 100 45 8, (C) POLY 50 60 6, (D) POLY 50 135 8, (E) two of the previous answers.

7. The command POLY 75 180 2 (A) draws a circle, (B) causes POLY to be executed 180 times, (C) draws a rectangle, (D) draws a straight line, (E) is invalid.

8. A concept that POLY does *not* directly illustrate is (A) state, (B) procedure, (C) formal parameter, (D) local variable, (E) global variable.

9. A valid statement is:
   (A) STEP is a local variable.
   (B) ANGLE refers to the name of the variable STEP.
   (C) POLY contains an infinite loop.
   (D) POLY is an example of a global variable.
   (E) NUM is a global variable.

EXERCISES

1. Each of the following is a student-written procedure to draw a figure, but each contains one or more "bugs." Rewrite the procedures eliminating the bugs.

a.
```
TO      HOUSE
10      RIGHT
20      TRIANGLE    SIDE
30      RIGHT       180
40      SQUARE      SIDE
50      RETURN
END
```

b.
```
TO      HOUSE       SIDE
10      TRIANGLE    SIDE
20      RIGHT       90
30      SQUARE      SIDE
40      RETURN
END
```

c.
```
TO      WISHINGWELL   SIDE
10      TRIANGLE      SIDE
20      RIGHT         90
30      FORWARD       SIDE/2
40      RIGHT         90
50      FORWARD       SIDE
60      LEFT          90
70      FORWARD       SIDE/2
80      SQUARE        SIDE
90      RETURN
END
```

d.
```
TO      WISHINGWELL   SIDE
10      RIGHT         30
20      TRIANGLE      SIDE
30      RIGHT         60
40      FORWARD       SIDE/2
50      RIGHT         90
60      FORWARD       SIDE
70      LEFT          90
80      FORWARD       SIDE
90      SQUARE        SIDE
100     RETURN
END
```

2. What figure is drawn by the following, and what is the final state?

```
TO      WHAT        SIDE
10      SQUARE      SIDE
20      FORWARD     SIDE
```

30	LEFT	90
40	SQUARE	SIDE
50	FORWARD	SIDE/2
60	RIGHT	90
70	FORWARD	SIDE/2
80	RIGHT	90
90	SQUARE	SIDE
100	RETURN	
END		

3. Using a top-down approach and subprocedures, write a program to draw the following rocket. You can assume that procedures for a square and a triangle, as listed below, are already available.

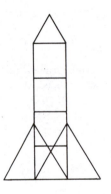

TO	SQUARE	SIDE
10	REPEAT 4, DRAW1	SIDE
20	RETURN	
END		

TO	TRIANGLE	SIDE
10	REPEAT 3, DRAW2	SIDE
20	RETURN	
END		

TO	DRAW1	SIDE
10	FORWARD	SIDE
20	RIGHT	90
30	RETURN	
END		

TO	DRAW2	SIDE
10	FORWARD	SIDE
20	RIGHT	120
30	RETURN	
END		

4. Using a top-down approach and subprocedures, write a program for the following figure. The origin of the figure is marked by a dot.

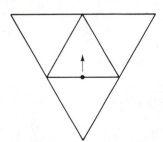

5. Write a program to draw the following figure.

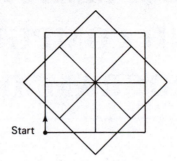

CHAPTER 5

COMPLEXITY AND COMPUTER PROGRAMMING

Complexity is a relative thing. What is complex and difficult for one person may be easy for another. Yet it can be said with certainty that for each of us there is some level of difficulty in computer programming at which the complexities of the task threaten to overwhelm us. Some persons reach this level before others, but all of us eventually reach the barrier. An internationally known computer scientist, Andrei P. Ershov, has stated the situation elegantly:

> In my opinion programming is . . . the most humanly difficult of all professions involving numbers of men. . . . Programmers constitute the first large group of men whose work brings them to those limits of human knowledge which are marked by algorithmically unsolvable problems and which touch upon deeply secret aspects of the human brain.*

Since Ershov's statement in 1972, significant progress has been made in discovering and elucidating methods for reducing the problems posed by complexity. This chapter will present two of these methods, structured programming and stepwise refinement. For many of the programming examples presented in this book, these techniques are, perhaps, not required. But it is important to develop good programming habits at the very beginning.

Before we undertake the study of the major topics of the chapter, there is one important aside to be made. Computer programs can be aesthetically beautiful—some programs are more beautiful than others even though they solve the same problem. Computer programming can result in "logic poems," and I hope you will have the pleasure and satisfaction of creating some. The material of this chapter is designed to help in this quest.

5.1 HUMAN LIMITATIONS

Limitations in the amount of information that the human mind can process cause significant difficulty in computer programming. Psychologists have demonstrated experimentally that the concept of channel capacity applies to the processing

*Andrei P. Ershov, "Aesthetics and the Human Factor in Programming," *Communications of the ACM*, *15* (July 1972), 501–505. Reproduced by permission of the Association for Computing Machinery, Inc.

of information by human beings. In this case, the channel capacity is the upper limit on the extent to which an observer can match responses to the stimuli presented. For many types of sensory data the channel capacity is surprisingly small, approximately 7 bits per second. (This topic was first treated by George A. Miller in a famous scientific paper.*) By recoding the information into more meaningful organizations, called chunks, more than 7 bits (approximately 7 chunks) of information can be processed. For example, if a string of alphabetic characters arranged in some meaningless sequence is presented to a subject, he or she can recall only about seven of the characters. If the characters are arranged into words (chunks), then about 7 words can be recalled. If the words are formed into meaningful sentences (chunks), then approximately 7 sentences can be remembered. The recoding process is therefore very helpful in assisting us to extend our ability to recall facts; but the important fact for computer programming is that despite the recoding process, we can still process only a surprisingly small amount of information.

A similar limit exists for our ability to store information in short-term memory—approximately 7 items are the maximum for most of us. Furthermore, if a person is required to perform some intellectual activity, such as counting backward rapidly by threes, as information is presented, most subjects are unable to remember any of the information that was presented.

The implications of these limitations for computer programming is obvious, in retrospect. (Before 1970 almost no professional programmers used the techniques presented here.)

1. Computer programs should be organized in short, logically independent blocks. The words "short" and "independent" are important. Various names have been given to such blocks, including *module*, *procedure*, *subprogram*, *subroutine,* and *macro.*
2. A given logical block must be sufficiently simple that we have only to manipulate and recall a few facts at a time in writing it.

5.2 STRUCTURED PROGRAMMING

At this point in our study we are in a dilemma. To show the technique for developing programs that is most favored today, we need to know and use concurrently two concepts—structured programming and stepwise refinement. Learning both topics at once can be confusing. Consequently, we will study structured programming first. Then as we learn and use stepwise refinement, we will use structured programming in conjunction with it.

5.2.1 The Size of Complex Programs

As part of your study in this course, most of you will write computer programs having between 75 and 200 statements in them. A few may write programs as long as

*George A. Miller, "The Magical Number Seven, Plus or Minus Two: Some Limits on Our Capacity for Processing Information," *The Psychological Review* (March 1956), 81–97.

500 statements. You can be sure that you will encounter difficulties in getting your logic correct; and if you do not use the methods presented here, as much as 50 percent of your time working on the programs may be used in trying to find and eliminate bugs. Yet, the programs on which you will be working are not considered to be large. One of the leading exponents of structured programming, Edward Yourdon, has classified programs according to size in the following way:

1. *Simple programs:* Programs consisting of 1000 or fewer lines of instructions. Usually written by a single programmer.
2. *Medium-complexity programs:* Programs consisting of more than 1000 but less than 10,000 lines of instructions. Usually written by 2 or 3 programmers.
3. *Complex programs:* Programs consisting of more than 10,000 but less than 100,000 lines of instructions. Usually written by a team of 5 to 20 programmers over a period of 2 to 3 years.
4. *Nearly impossible programs:* Programs consisting of more than 100,000 but less than 1 million lines of instructions. Usually written by a team of 100 to 1000 programmers over a period of several years. Such programs can presently be undertaken only by the very largest companies.
5. *Utterly absurd programs:* Programs consisting of more than 1 million but less than 100 million instructions. These programs require more than 1000 programmers working for up to 10 years, and are limited at present to governments and military organizations.*

Programs costing more than $1,000,000 to write are commonplace. The program OS/360 (an acronym for Operating System 360) which was designed to operate the larger models of the IBM 360 computer series, and hence was used in many computer centers, is estimated to have required more than 2000 worker-years to write. (This puts the lower limit of its cost at about $20,000,000.) The project manager for OS/360, Frederick Brooks, has estimated that at the height of the activity, more than 5000 people, managers, programmers, secretaries, and so on, were working on the development of OS/360. It is a reasonable conclusion that some computer programs are the most complex chains of logical reasoning ever constructed by the human mind.

5.2.2 Testing Complex Programs

Until recent years, the prevailing opinion was that errors were unavoidable in computer programs. This attitude was certainly confirmed by observation. Consider as an example the case of OS/360, which was reissued more than 20 times. Each new release was intended to correct the existing errors in the program, and for each release the number of errors corrected was in the thousands.

For OS/360 and other large programs, no strategy exists for testing the programs for correctness—there is simply not enough time available for the testing. Assume that

*Edward Yourdon, *Techniques of Program Structure and Design* (Englewood Cliffs, N.J.: Prentice-Hall, Inc., 1975), pp. 249–254. Reproduced by permission of Prentice-Hall, Inc.

to be certain a program works, it is necessary to test every logical path through the program. If a program has 45 branch points with each point giving two paths, in theory there could be as many as 2^{45} paths through the program. If it were possible to test a path in one millionth of a second (10^{-6} seconds), slightly more than 1 year would be required to test the program. With 55 branch points, more than 1000 years would be required, and more than 1 million years would be necessary for 65 branch points. Programs containing more than 1000 branch points are common. (For curiosity, I scanned a program of approximately 5000 lines of instructions and found 341 branch points.)

Approximately 50 percent of the program development time has traditionally been used for program testing and corrections. This is obviously a significant amount of time. Edsger W. Dijkstra, an international authority on programming methodology, has pointed out that program testing can show only the absence of errors, but it can never demonstrate program correctness. Dijkstra recommends that we design our programs correctly, so that the time required for program testing can be reduced. The techniques presented in this chapter will be invaluable in avoiding errors in logic while writing programs.

The foregoing remarks should not be interpreted as inferring that program testing is unnecessary. Program testing is always necessary. The remarks were intended to demonstrate that your time is better used in designing a program properly than in trying to test your program exhaustively.

5.2.3 Does Structured Programming Work?

Extravagant claims have been made about the virtues of structured programming, but no evidence has been presented to you to validate these claims. Writing structured programs is, at first, more difficult for some students than writing unstructured programs. Thus it is appropriate for us to justify the initial extra effort that will be required.

In Table 5.1,* results are given for the programming of an information bank that was delivered in 1970 to the *New York Times*. The methods of structured programming and stepwise refinement were used in developing the programs. In addition to the errors listed in Table 5.1, another 25 errors were discovered in the system during approximately a year of operation. Only 13 of the 25 errors were made by the programmers. The evidence strongly indicates that structured programming works.

5.2.4 Rules for Structured Programming

The rules for structured programming had their origin in a classic paper by C. Böhm and G. Jacopini,[†] who showed that any computer program could be written

---

*F. T. Baker, "System Quality Through Structured Programming," *AFIPS-Conference Proceedings*, vol. 41 (Montvale, N.J.: AFIPS Press, 1972), p. 342. Reproduced by permission of AFIPS Press.

[†]C. Böhm and G. Jacopini, "Flow Diagrams, Turing Machines and Language with Only Two Formulation Rules," *Communications of the ACM* (May 1966), 366–371.

TABLE 5.1 *Bugs observed in information bank programs for the New York Times*

		Bugs			
Program	Source lines	Incorrect function	Omitted function	Misinterpreted function	Total
A	12,029	0	0	0	0
B	38,990	9	8	3	20
C	13,421	0	0	1	1
D	18,884	0	0	0	0
	83,324	9	8	4	21

Programming time: 132.0 worker-months = 11 worker-years

Error rate: less than 2 bugs per worker-year

using only three types of structures. Their ideas have been expanded by many others. The first type of structure is called *sequence* and is illustrated below.

Suppose that we wish to calculate a value for X using the following sequence of equations: C = 2 ∗ A− B, D = C/A, and X = B− D, where ∗ means multiplication and / means division. A flowchart for the computation is given in Figure 5.1. Notice

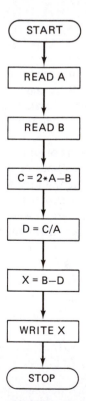

FIGURE 5.1 *Illustration of the sequence structure*

that there is never any question as to what is to be done next; when execution of the program is begun, one step follows the next without debate. There is one way into the program and one way out: this is a requirement for structured programs. The entire program can be represented as a single block:

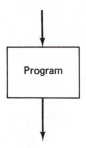

Any number of sequence-type blocks can be combined logically into a single block. For example, consider the computation part of our simple program. These can be combined to give

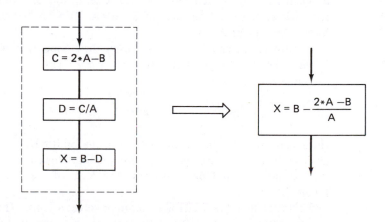

The second type of structure, the *IF structure*, has the form

IF p THEN f ELSE g

which can be represented by the flowchart of Figure 5.2. For the IF structure, the first step is to perform a test on p to determine whether it is true or false. The symbol p is called a *logical condition*, and it may be simple or complex as necessary. A logical condition must always be true or false. Depending upon the outcome of the test, either block f or block g is executed next (not both). Blocks f and g must lead to exactly the same exit point. There is, consequently, one entry point and one exit point for an IF structure, and it may be represented by a single logical block.

As an example of the use of the IF structure, consider a slightly more complicated case of the calculation of X, which was diagrammed in Figure 5.1. Suppose that

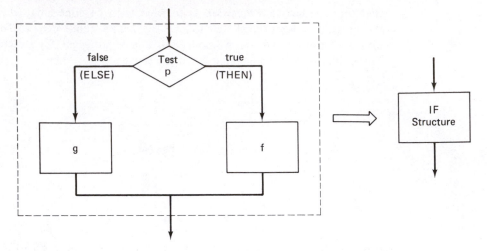

FIGURE 5.2   *The IF structure*

if B is negative (less than zero), X is to be set to the value of minus B, and if B is positive, X is to be set to the value of B − (2∗A−B)/A. A flowchart is given in Figure 5.3
for the resulting program.

Most problems that are solved using the computer involve the repetition of a set
of steps. The third type of structure, the *WHILE structure*, is designed to handle such
cases and has the form

WHILE   p   DO   f

(In actual programs the word "DO" may be omitted as part of WHILE.) The condition p is tested before every execution of the block f to determine whether or not
the execution should be continued. The form of the WHILE structure is given in
Figure 5.4.

Notice that the WHILE structure involves a loop. The block f, which may be
any structure or combination of structures, is to be repeated as long as the condition p
has the value *true*. This implies that something must occur within block f which will
cause p to change its value. (Try to remember this fact, as it is a common source of
error in writing programs.) In writing programs, whenever repetition is required, you
should think immediately of the WHILE structure.

As an example of the use of the WHILE structure, let us examine an extension
of the problem involving the calculation of X. Assume that the calculation of X must
be made for thousands of values of A and B. (The problem is now becoming something for which we would actually use the computer.) The solution given in Figure 5.3
is what we need for a single calculation—it just needs to be repeated for each pair of
A's and B's. Furthermore, let us assume that all the values of A will be positive. In
that case a negative value of A could be used as a signal that the computations have
been completed. A solution to our new problem is to enclose our previous solution

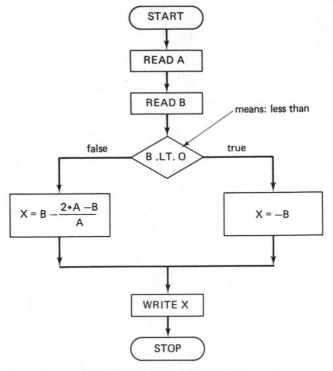

FIGURE 5.3   *Use of the IF structure*

(Figure 5.3) in an appropriate WHILE structure using the value of A as the condition. As long as A is zero or positive, the loop is to be repeated. The new solution is given in Figure 5.5. Notice that an additional READ A statement has been included at the end of the loop to allow the condition to change value; the first READ A immediately

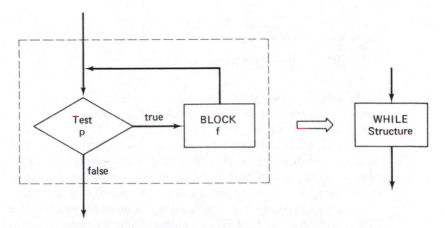

FIGURE 5.4   *The WHILE structure*

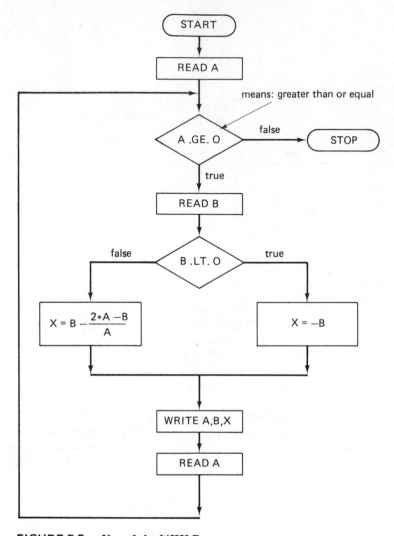

FIGURE 5.5 *Use of the WHILE structure*

after START is outside the loop and is executed only one time. The values of A, B, and the corresponding X are also written. It is usually good style to write the input as well as the output.

In summary, all computer programs can be written using three types of structures: sequence, IF, and WHILE. Programs written using only these structures can be understood by reading from the first statement straight through to the last, in the same way that you would read an essay. The number of errors in a program can be drastically reduced or even eliminated by using structured programming. Structured programs do not use the GO TO statement, which is popular in some computer languages. For that reason, structured programs are sometimes called "GOTOless" programs.

5.3 STEPWISE REFINEMENT OF PROGRAMS

Stepwise refinement is a general problem-solving technique which is especially helpful in coping with the many difficulties that arise in computer programming. That is, it is a method for dealing systematically with program complexity. (Stepwise refinement is very similar to the top-down method introduced in the MLOGO chapter.) Stepwise refinement is, however, not limited to computer problems, and a mastery of the method will be useful in many subject areas. In addition, stepwise refinement does not have to be used in conjunction with structured programming, but we will always do so to obtain the benefits of both methods.

A fundamental concept of stepwise refinement is delaying consideration of details until attention to them becomes absolutely necessary. We first propose a high-level solution, with no attention being given yet to details. For example, suppose that I want to become a millionaire: a high-level solution to my problem is

> Find a product to sell.
> Until I become at least a millionaire:
> > Manufacture the product,
> > Sell it at a profit,
> > Save the profit.

Each of these steps should next be expanded to obtain a better understanding of the problem. These expansions continue with more and more attention being given to detail until a workable solution is found. To prevent the complexity of the problem from overwhelming us, only one step is considered at a time.

5.3.1 Program Development Language (PDL)

It is both convenient and advantageous to have a simple standardized language for the stepwise refinement process. Program Development Language (PDL) was proposed by IBM for this purpose, and it is used as follows:

1. At the highest levels (least detail), use ordinary English to express the steps in the problem.
2. At lower levels (more detail), show the logic of the problem by:
   a. Indenting to signify a more detailed level of logic.
   b. Using structured programming concepts of sequence, IF, and WHILE.

When the most detailed level is reached using PDL, this final result is then translated by the programmer into the computer language he or she wishes to use. For those languages that allow the IF and WHILE structures, the PDL program and the final program may be almost identical. Notice that PDL as we will use it is a combination of stepwise refinement and structured programming.

5.3.2 Examples of the Use of PDL

Example 1

As an example of the method, the calculation of X that resulted in Figure 5.5 will be repeated. The problem would normally be stated as:

The value of X is to be calculated from the values of A and B. When B is negative, $X = -B$; otherwise, $X = B - (2*A-B)/A$. The calculation is to be repeated an unknown number of times. A negative value for A indicates no more calculations are to be made.

Application of PDL (both stepwise refinement and structured programming)

A. Level 1 Solution

```
read input
while (there are calculations to be made)
    make calculations
    write answers
```

B. Level 2 Solution

Any of the steps of the level 1 solution could now be expanded, but it frequently is advantageous to determine first the nature of the condition of WHILE structures. Often clues will be obtained about other parts of the program. The problem statement gives: a negative value for A indicates that no more calculations are to be made. This is equivalent to performing the loop as long as A is zero or positive. This observation allows writing:

```
read input
WHILE (A .GE. 0)
    make calculations
    write answers
```

C. Level 3 Solution

What is the input? We are told that values of A and B are to be input. The value of A must be known before the beginning of the WHILE structure, and the value of A must change within the loop. A possible level 3 solution is therefore

```
READ A
WHILE (A .GE. 0)
```

```
      READ B
      make calculations
      write answers
      READ A
ENDWHILE
STOP
END
```

In this solution, the convention has been adopted of indicating explicitly the end of the WHILE structure by using the ENDWHILE statement. (The ENDIF statement will be used to designate the end of the IF structure.) The command STOP means stop the execution of the program, and END means there is no more program.

D. Level 4 Solution

The final tasks in obtaining a solution to the problem are to make the calculation and to write the answers. The IF statement is needed for the calculation to allow a decision to be made. This leads to our final statement of the program.

```
READ A
WHILE (A .GE. 0)
    READ B
    IF (B .LT. 0)
        THEN X = -B
        ELSE X = B - (2*A-B)/A
    ENDIF
    WRITE A, B, X
    READ A
ENDWHILE
STOP
END
```

The level 4 solution now requires only trivial changes to make it conform to the syntax rules of a computer language. After these changes, the program can be executed on a computer.

There is more than one way to solve a problem as simple as this one and still use stepwise refinement and structured programming. For a more complicated problem, there may be many equally satisfactory computer programs, especially if we are merely trying to obtain the correct answer. Do not be alarmed, therefore, if your program is different from others for the same problem. Programs are also written not only to obtain the correct answer, but to optimize the execution time, the amount of memory needed, or some other factor. Consideration of these factors can complicate the programming task, and more will be said about this subject later.

Example 2

Write a PDL program to calculate, for each student in a class, the student's quiz average. For each student, print the individual grades and the average. The number of grades may be different for different students. To avoid counting the number of grades for each student, a negative grade will be entered to signal that all grades for a student have been read. (There are no negative grades in introductory computer science, so the negative value can be used as a signal.) If the first grade read for a student is negative, all calculations have been completed and the program should stop. Skip a line between the data for different students.

This problem statement is more detailed than you would ordinarily be given. For the normal, less detailed statement you would either have to ask questions or make assumptions about the problem. In dealing with the computer, absolute precision in the use of language is required. Detailed as this problem statement is, it is still ambiguous because there are unknown aspects of the problem. For example, in printing the average for a student, should digits be printed to the right of the decimal?

Fortunately, the problem statement tells us the conditions for changing the flow of logic within the program; that is, when to exit from the WHILE loops. For many problems, you will have to decide upon the signals to be used in the conditions.

In thinking about the solution to the problem, try to visualize how you would solve it using pencil and paper and perhaps a calculator. In a very real sense, the writing of a computer program is equivalent to writing a very precise description of how to solve a problem with pencil and paper without being concerned about how long the calculations would take. Recall that in solving such problems, it is not unusual to make several false starts before finding a solution method; the same situation exists in writing computer programs. Using stepwise refinement and PDL will reduce the number of false starts you need to make. Finally, do not attempt to do too much at any level of the development process—remember our human limitations.

A solution to the example is given below. Try to solve it yourself before you examine the answers given. Remember that there is more than one correct way to write the PDL program. If you have doubts about your solution, show it to the instructor.

A. Level 1 Solution

```
            initialize for the WHILE structure
            WHILE (there are more student averages to be calculated)
                initialize for the calculation of this student's average
                sum and count grades for this student
                calculate and print the student's average
            ENDWHILE
            STOP
            END
```

The term *initialize* means to do all those activities which are necessary before beginning a loop. For example, if the calculation of a student's average is done with a hand calculator, it should be cleared before the grades are added.

B. Level 2 Solution

The condition for entering and repeating the WHILE structure is GRADE .GE. 0. This implies that a grade should be read in the initialization. Another WHILE structure is implied for adding the student's grades. Before we get lost with too many details, we write the next level of solution.

```
READ GRADE
WHILE (GRADE .GE. 0)
      initialize for the calculation of this student's average
      WHILE (GRADE .GE. 0)
          sum and count grades
      ENDWHILE
      calculate and print the student's average
ENDWHILE
STOP
END
```

C. Level 3 Solution

The summing and counting of a student's grades implies that there are variables which should initially be set to zero. The summing of the grades can be accomplished with the statement SUM = SUM + GRADE, which means add the current value of SUM and GRADE to obtain a new value of SUM. Within the inner WHILE structure, it will be necessary to read a new grade to avoid an infinite loop. A grade has already been read, so the reading of a new grade should be postponed until all processing is completed for the original grade. Incorporating these ideas gives

```
READ GRADE
WHILE (GRADE .GE. 0)
    SUM = 0
    COUNT = 0
    WHILE (GRADE .GE. 0)
        WRITE GRADE
        SUM = SUM + GRADE
        COUNT = COUNT + 1
        READ GRADE
    ENDWHILE
    calculate and print the student's average
ENDWHILE
STOP
END
```

D. Level 4 Solution

The calculation section for the average is the only remaining uncompleted part of the program. The original statement of the problem tells us to calculate the average, print it, and skip a line. A new value for GRADE also needs to be read. This grade will either be the first grade for the next student or the signal that all calculations have been completed. The final program is

```
READ GRADE
WHILE (GRADE .GE. 0)
    SUM = 0
    COUNT = 0
    WHILE (GRADE .GE. 0)
        WRITE GRADE
        SUM = SUM + GRADE
        COUNT = COUNT + 1
        READ GRADE
    ENDWHILE
    AVERAGE = SUM/COUNT
    WRITE AVERAGE
    SKIP LINE
    READ GRADE
ENDWHILE
STOP
END
```

We will digress to mention the *relational operators*, such as .GE., which can be used in writing the condition part of WHILE and IF statements. There are six relational operators, and their meanings are summarized in Table 5.2. To be consistent with the conventions of several computer languages, we choose to begin and end each operator with a period.

TABLE 5.2 *Relational operators*

Operator	Meaning
.EQ.	Equal
.NE.	Not equal
.GE.	Greater than or equal
.GT.	Greater than
.LE.	Less than or equal
.LT.	Less than

Now we will work on a program for the famous Fibonacci series, which has a number of surprising applications. For example, it describes in an approximate way the growth of a population of rabbits and the arrangement of leaves in plants. Although we will find it easy to generate the elements of the series, careful thinking is necessary to avoid errors in the computer program. The problem is described below.

Example 3

The Fibonacci series is a sequence of integers that begin as 0, 1, 1, 2, 3, 5, 8, 13, 21, 34, 55, 89, 144, 233, ... The third and subsequent members of the series are computed by adding the previous two members of the series. For example,

$$3rd\ element = 0 + 1 = 1$$
$$4th\ element = 1 + 1 = 2$$
$$5th\ element = 1 + 2 = 3$$
$$6th\ element = 2 + 3 = 5\quad etc.$$

Write a PDL program to generate the series until a term exceeding 20,000 is obtained.

Some planning leads to the following PDL program:

A. Level 1 Solution

```
initialize
write initial values
WHILE (latest term .LE. 20000)
    write the element
    calculate the next element
ENDWHILE
write last element
STOP
END
```

B. Level 2 Solution

What values must be initialized in the program? Reflection leads us to conclude that we must provide the first two terms of the series to the program. We choose to use the assignment operation for initialization rather than reading cards.

```
PREVIOUS-TERM = 0
LATEST-TERM = 1
WRITE PREVIOUS-TERM
WHILE (LATEST-TERM .LE. 20000)
    write LATEST-TERM
    make calculations
ENDWHILE
write LATEST-TERM
STOP
END
```

C. Level 3 Solution

Now we can concentrate on making the calculation. The obvious approach is to add the previous term and the latest term to get a new latest term, that is,

$$\text{LATEST-TERM} = \text{LATEST-TERM} + \text{PREVIOUS-TERM}$$

This is almost correct. Remember that the calculation will be made repeatedly within the WHILE loop. The next time the calculation is made, we will need the value of the LATEST-TERM as it appears on the left of this assignment statement and the LATEST-TERM as it appears on the right (so it can be treated as the PREVIOUS-TERM). But because of the assignment operation, the new value for LATEST-TERM has replaced the old value for LATEST-TERM. We must save the old value of LATEST-TERM before calculating the new value. (This is a common problem in programs, so be conscious of this possible bug.) Our final PDL program is

```
PREVIOUS-TERM = 0
LATEST-TERM = 1
WRITE PREVIOUS-TERM
WHILE (LATEST-TERM .LE. 20000)
    WRITE LATEST-TERM
    SAVE-TERM = LATEST-TERM
    LATEST-TERM = LATEST-TERM + PREVIOUS-TERM
    PREVIOUS-TERM = SAVE-TERM
ENDWHILE
WRITE LATEST-TERM
STOP
END
```

Notice that for this example, only three levels were used in the stepwise refinement process, but for the preceding examples, four levels were used. There is no magic number of levels into which you should divide the development process. The number of levels needed will depend upon the complexity of the problem and upon your experience. For problems that differ in only some minor way from a program you already know, you may be able to write the solution immediately, but for a complex problem with which you have no experience, many levels may be needed. Use PDL and stepwise refinement to help design your programs—it is the design process that is important, not the number of levels used.

5.3.3 Flowchart Technique

Flowcharts may be used instead of PDL in developing problem solutions using stepwise refinement. Flowcharts have the advantage of displaying the logic of the

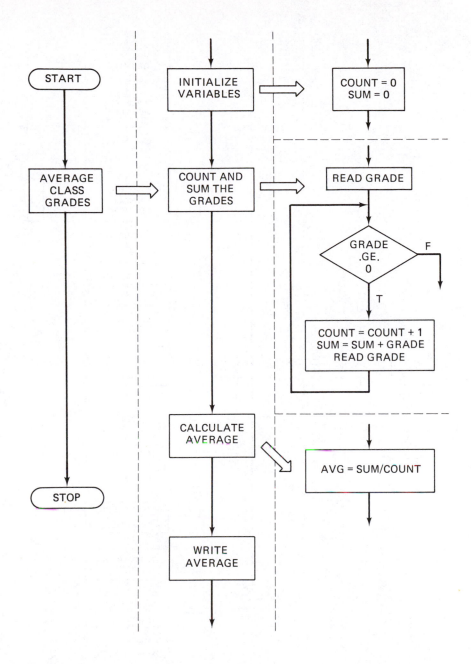

FIGURE 5.6 *Program in flowchart form: class average for a quiz*

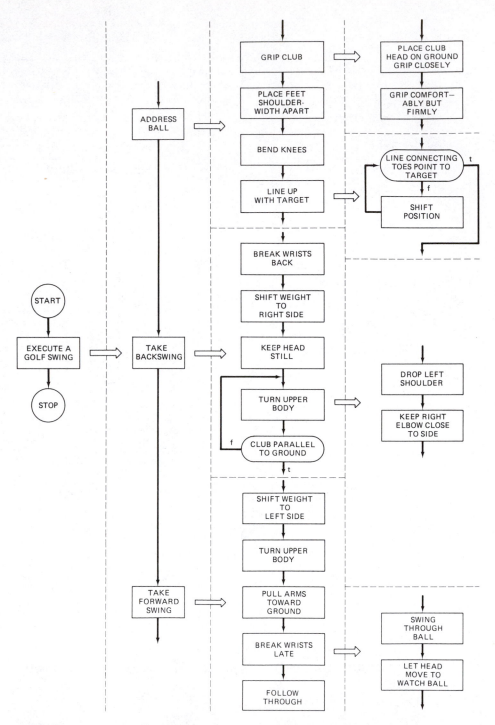

FIGURE 5.7 *Flowchart of a golf swing*

solution in a very graphic manner, but they take longer to prepare. The representation that we use is due to Dinerstein* and is illustrated in Figure 5.6.

In this method, the highest-level flowchart is drawn at the left edge of a page. A vertical dashed line is drawn, and the next level of the flowchart is drawn to the right of the line. An arrow is drawn from the appropriate block of the higher-level flowchart to the corresponding set of blocks at the next level. Portions of the flowchart at a given level may be separated by horizontal dashed lines to assist in associating blocks on different levels. The process is repeated for more detailed levels until a solution is found.

It is easy to write the corresponding PDL program from the flowchart. For each block that has no right-pointing double arrow, write the corresponding PDL statement to obtain

```
COUNT = 0
SUM = 0
READ GRADE
WHILE (GRADE .GE. 0)
    COUNT = COUNT + 1
    SUM = SUM + GRADE
    READ GRADE
ENDWHILE
AVG = SUM/COUNT
WRITE AVG
STOP
END
```

Another flowchart, which describes the process of executing a golf swing, is illustrated in Figure 5.7. This flowchart was devised by a student in an introductory computer science course.

REVIEW QUESTIONS

1. What limitations exist for the processing of information by human beings?
2. In writing computer programs, what should be the nature of the logical blocks that make up a program?
3. Why is the exhaustive testing of computer programs impossible?
4. What are the three types of structures allowed in structured programming?
5. How many entry points and exit points are there for a given block in a structured program?
6. What structures use a condition clause? What are the only allowed values of a condition clause?
7. What is the fundamental idea of the stepwise refinement approach to developing programs?
8. How are top-down programming and stepwise refinement different?

*N. T. Dinerstein, "Does Computer Science Belong in a Liberal Arts College?" *SIGCSE Bulletin, Association for Computing Machinery* (June 1975), 55–64.

9. What are the rules for using PDL?

10. What programming statement is normally not found in structured programs?

1. The psychological concept "chunk" (A) is related to our ability to process information, (B) involves the combining of elementary items of information into more meaningful groups, (C) is related to channel capacity, (D) has important implications for designing computer programs, (E) all of the previous answers.

2. A major goal of structured programming is (A) reducing the number of statements in a program, (B) reducing the number of programming errors, (C) eliminating program testing, (D) reducing the number of variables in a program, (E) eliminating flowcharts.

3. The stepwise refinement of problems (A) is a general problem-solving method, (B) can be used in conjunction with structured programming, (C) is based on bottom-up techniques, (D) requires the use of flowcharts, (E) answers (A) and (B) are correct.

4. In PDL (A) high-level solutions are in computer language, (B) indentation displays levels of logic, (C) low-level solutions are in English, (D) flowcharts are required, (E) all the previous answers are valid.

5. A structure that does not use a condition is (A) sequence, (B) IF, (C) program, (D) ELSE, (E) WHILE.

6. An example of an invalid relational operator is (A) .NE., (B) .LT., (C) .GE., (D) .GT., (E) .EU.

7. A valid statement is:
   (A) All conditions use the .NE. operator.
   (B) Computer programs are restricted to using a single condition.
   (C) Any number of ELSE clauses may appear in an IF structure.
   (D) Relational operators are used to compare arithmetic values.
   (E) All of the previous answers are correct.

8. The test for completion of the loop is the WHILE structure (A) may occur at the bottom of the structure, (B) always occurs at the beginning of the structure, (C) may occur at the beginning of the structure, (D) always occurs at the bottom of the structure, (E) may occur at either the top or bottom of the structure, depending upon the problem to be solved.

9. An important feature of each structure in a structured program is (A) there is exactly one way in and one way out of the structure, (B) the structures must be deduced using stepwise refinement, (C) the structures must be deduced using top-down development, (D) each structure contains a condition, (E) none of the previous answers is valid.

10. The *New York Times* information system project (A) used stepwise refinement techniques, (B) used structured programming techniques, (C) is supporting evidence for the value of structured programming techniques, (D) involved relatively few bugs for programs of such size, (E) all the previous answers are valid.

11. An individual who played an important role in testing the value of structured programming is (A) C. Böhm, (B) G. Jacopini, (C) F. T. Baker, (D) G. A. Miller, (E) F. Brooks.

EXERCISES

1. Assuming that each branch point gives two paths through a program and that a computer can test a path in one millionth of a second, calculate the time required to test all paths in programs containing the following number of branch points. (*Note:* Approximate answers are adequate.)
   a. 5 branch points
   b. 10 branch points
   c. 20 branch points
   d. 40 branch points

2. Using the stepwise refinement technique, draw flowcharts for several of the following:
   a. Driving a car
   b. Making an outline for an essay
   c. Balancing a chemical equation
   d. Asking for a date
   e. Deciding whether to accept a date
   f. Phoning a friend
   g. Deciding what to wear
   h. Putting on lipstick
   i. Drawing a flowchart
   j. Hitting a tennis ball

3. Using stepwise refinement, write structured PDL programs to solve several of the following:
   a. Find the maximum value in a set of 100 positive integers.
   b. Find the minimum value in a set of 100 positive integers.
   c. In a single program, find both the maximum and minimum of a set of values.
   d. Balance a checkbook.
   e. Compute the total cost of several items, the sales tax, and the grand total.
   f. Compute the average height of a group of individuals.
   g. Change a set of distances from miles to kilometers. (1 mile = 1.6 kilometers.)

CHAPTER 6
OVERVIEW OF FORTRAN

You already have a considerable knowledge of FORTRAN as a result of our previous use of PDL to design solutions to problems. There is still, however, much detail that you must master to use FORTRAN effectively. In this chapter, we briefly consider the historical development of FORTRAN and learn the basic facts required to translate PDL programs to FORTRAN. Some aspects of the overall structure of FORTRAN are considered to provide a framework for assimilating the details that will be given in future chapters.

6.1   THE HISTORICAL DEVELOPMENT OF FORTRAN

The version of FORTRAN that we shall use, FORTRAN 77, is the culmination of an extensive development period. A description of the FORTRAN language was first published by the International Business Machine Corporation (IBM) in a preliminary report in November 1954. Development of the language was motivated by the observation that approximately two-thirds of the cost of solving a scientific problem using a computer was associated with the writing of the program. The new language was to provide a convenient way to express any problem of numerical computation and thus to reduce programming costs. Apparently, the original designers of the language gave no thought to the possibility that FORTRAN might be used for business or other nonscientific programming. This was a reasonable assumption at the time, since almost all work being done with computers in 1954 was scientific in nature. (*Note:* The first computer intended for business use, a UNIVAC machine sold to GE, was not delivered until 1954.)

Actual work on the language was begun in the summer of 1954 by a group of IBM employees headed by John W. Backus. Their goal was to implement FORTRAN for the IBM 704 computer, the next large computer to be marketed by the company. Two-and-one-half years later, after an expenditure of 18 worker-years of labor, the implementation was complete. In early 1957, the version was issued for use on the IBM 704. In June 1958, a second version of FORTRAN was issued. IBM did not give special names to these two versions, but users have designated them as FORTRAN I and FORTRAN II. A third version, FORTRAN IV, was described in June 1962 for the IBM 7030 computer. FORTRAN III was never issued by IBM, although it was used within the company. The latest version, FORTRAN 77, was proposed in 1977 by members of the Technical Committee X3J3, American National Standards Institute (a non-IBM organization), which had the goals of improving the language by expanding it and of establishing a standard version of the improved language. We shall be learning FORTRAN 77.

The FORTRAN issued by IBM in 1957 was not intended to be independent of the machine on which it was run; consequently, no attempt was made to produce a formal description of the language. The need to run FORTRAN programs on an ever-increasing number of different types of computers soon resulted in the development of standards for the language. If you are careful in the selection of language features that you use to write a program, you can expect it to run with little or no modification on most computers, regardless of the manufacturer of the computer.

The adoption of FORTRAN by the computer industry at large has obvious advantages for computer users, but there is also a problem: to gain a competitive edge, computer companies often include additional nonstandard features in their FOR-TRAN compilers. Several nonstandard features will be discussed in this book, and each will be identified as being nonstandard so that you can decide whether to use it or not in writing programs. When should you use a nonstandard feature? No simple answer is possible, but I suggest the following guidelines:

1. If it is known that a program will be run on more than one type of computer, use only standard features in writing a program.
2. If guideline 1 does not apply, use any language feature, even a nonstandard one, if it simplifies the problem-solving process.

FORTRAN is quite old relative to other computer languages—all the other major computer languages were invented more recently. There are both advantages and disadvantages related to the age of FORTRAN. One advantage not previously mentioned is the very rapid speed of execution of the machine language programs produced by FORTRAN compilers. At the time of the constructing of the first FORTRAN compiler, there was considerable resistance among programmers to the idea of using a compiler. The programmers believed that they could write machine-language programs which would take fewer memory cells and execute in less time than the corresponding machine program produced by a FORTRAN compiler. To overcome this attitude, the designers of the FORTRAN compiler gave special attention to generating efficient code (machine-language statements) with the compiler. This concern with efficiency eventually led to the development of special *optimizing compilers* that take relatively long times for the compiling process but produce extremely efficient programs.

Large IBM computers normally have two FORTRAN compilers: (1) an ordinary compiler that performs the compilation process rapidly but does not attempt to produce the most efficient code, and (2) an optimizing compiler. During the development and debugging of a program the ordinary compiler is used to save compilation time. When all testing is complete, the optimizing compiler is used to obtain a very efficient machine-language program for subsequent executions.

The compilers for the dialects of FORTRAN known as WATFOR and WATFIV emphasize fast compilation instead of the production of efficient machine-language programs. These compilers were designed and implemented at the University of Water-loo (hence, the WAT portion of the names) for use by students. Normally, students tend to compile a program several times during the debugging process, with the result that compiling consumes more computer time than executing the program. Therefore, in a student-oriented environment, these compilers can save a considerable amount of computer time. In addition, various features were added to make the language more convenient for student use. WATFOR and WATFIV are used by many college and university computer centers.

6.2   CLASSIFICATION OF FORTRAN STATEMENTS

FORTRAN statements are divided into four basic categories, based upon the primary function of the statements. Within a given category, there may be various types or even subtypes of statements. For example, the IF statement is a member of the category of control statements, and there is more than one type of IF statement. The four basic categories are:

1. *Declaration statements:* Declaration statements give the compiler information that is needed about the nature or value of the variables used by a program. All declaration statements are called nonexecutable statements, since they are used by the compiler and not by the resulting machine-language program. For example, the statement REAL I,J notifies the compiler that the variables I and J are to have values containing decimals.

2. *Assignment statements:* Assignment statements cause computations to be performed and save the resulting answer by assigning it as the value of a variable. Many examples of assignment statements, such as X = B − (2∗A−B)/A, have been given in previous PDL programs.

3. *Control statements:* Control statements change the execution of statements from their normal sequential pattern to some other pattern. In the writing of structured programs using PDL, the control statements IF . . . THEN . . . ELSE and WHILE were essential.

4. *Input/output statements:* Input/output statements cause the input or the output of data. In their simplest form, these statements in FORTRAN resemble those used in PDL, but much more complicated forms are possible. There are more rules for input/output statements than for any other type.

Notice that our approach to learning FORTRAN is proceeding from areas of little detail to areas of greater detail, and thus has some features of a top-down approach. This chapter will be followed by chapters on assignment statements, several types of control statements, and input/output statements. All the details will not be presented. Other chapters will go deeper into the details of the language. With each deeper level of detail studied you will gain a greater mastery of the language and will discover new ways of writing programs.

6.3   FORMAT OF FORTRAN STATEMENTS

When FORTRAN was first introduced, the most convenient way to enter data into the computer was to keypunch the data into cards. Terminals had not been invented. The designers assumed, therefore, that the set of **FORTRAN** statements that constitute a program would be keypunched into cards and the deck of cards would be submitted to the compiler. The card format for a statement is still used even if the program is entered at a terminal.

The card format to be used for a **FORTRAN** statement is shown in Figure 6.1. The card is divided into four fields (a group of columns make up a field):

1. Statement number field.
2. Continuation indicator field.
3. FORTRAN statement field.
4. Card identification field.

Only the first 72 columns of a card are used for a **FORTRAN** statement. This number of columns is entirely arbitrary and was chosen because it was convenient for use with the **IBM 704** for which **FORTRAN** was originally implemented. Today, 72 columns are still used, although the number no longer has significance.

Columns 1 to 5 are reserved for an optional, identifying *statement number*. If a given statement is to be referenced by some other statement, then it must be given a statement number; it must be a positive, nonzero integer; it must also be different from other statement numbers used in the program. The statement number can be entered anywhere in columns 1 to 5. For example, it is equally satisfactory to enter the number 15 in columns 1 and 2 or in columns 4 and 5. This flexibility is possible because the compiler deletes all blanks from the statement before other processing is done. (An exception involving FORMAT statements will be discussed later.)

The *FORTRAN statement* proper (i.e., the statement excluding the statement number) can be entered anywhere in columns 7 to 72. Extra blank spaces may be included whenever you wish to make the statement more readable. For example, the

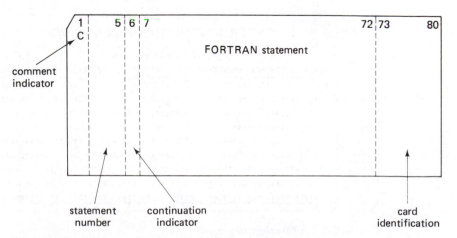

FIGURE 6.1 *Card layout for FORTRAN statements*

compiler will treat the statements

$$X=B-(2*A-B)/A$$

and

$$X = B - (2*A - B)/A$$

as identical statements, since the compiler will automatically delete the blank spaces before proceeding with the compilation. [*Note:* You will save yourself considerable confusion if you realize now that a blank space is an alphabetic character. In writing English sentences (or in writing computer programs), the blank (or space) is the most frequently occurring "alphabetic character." Youcouldhavetroublereadingthisifthere werenospaces.] When a FORTRAN statement card is read by the computer, the contents of all the first 72 columns are stored. If a column is empty (i.e., has no holes), the computer code for a blank is stored. Although statements can be punched anywhere in columns 7 to 72, a program is easier to read and to understand when successive statements begin in the same column and when indenting is used to indicate logic. This approach is recommended.

FORTRAN statements can become quite long—too long to fit on a single card. When this problem arises, punch any nonzero character into column 6 of the next (second) card, and continue punching the statement. A punch in column 6 will be interpreted by the compiler to mean that the card containing the punch is merely a continuation of the previous card. This technique can be applied to several consecutive cards as necessary (see Figure 6.2). One method of punching a statement that requires three continuation cards is to punch 1 in column 6 of the first continuation card, 2 in

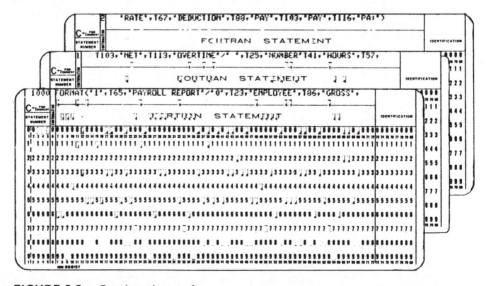

FIGURE 6.2 *Continuation cards*

column 6 of the second continuation card, and 3 in column 6 of the third continuation card. (There will be a total of four cards for this statement; the first card has a blank in column 6.) A, B, and C would have been just as satisfactory.

Column 1 has a special use. If a "C" or an "*" is punched in column 1, the card becomes a *comment card*, which is used to explain some portion of a program to its readers. Such cards are ignored by the compiler. Any number of comment cards may appear in a program interspersed with FORTRAN in any manner the programmer wishes.

The last eight columns of the card (columns 73 to 80) are ignored by the compiler, so you can enter anything you wish (including nothing) to identify the cards. For large or important programs the convention is to enter the name of the program, abbreviated as necessary, and the number of the card.

Special FORTRAN coding forms are available which correspond to the card layout just described. These forms can be very helpful in an environment in which programs are punched by keypunch operators who have no knowledge of FORTRAN. Usually, students do not bother to use the forms when punching their own programs.

6.4 MODE OF VARIABLES

FORTRAN can use integers or real numbers. An *integer* is a number that does not contain a decimal:

$$12 \qquad 0$$
$$-97 \qquad 3001$$

The maximum and minimum values that an integer variable may have is determined by the size of the memory cell that holds it, and this depends upon the computer being used. For a 16-bit memory cell, the allowed range for an integer is $-32,768$ to $32,767$.

A *real number* is any number that contains a decimal:

$$1.00 \qquad 0.004627$$
$$-2.010 \qquad 5732.073$$
$$0.97321 \qquad -45.95$$

The allowed range of values for a real variable also depends upon the computer used. A typical range is -1.0×10^{-77} to $+1.0 \times 10^{77}$.

Within a FORTRAN program, a variable, for example X, can have integer values or real values but not both. The type of value, integer or real, is called the *mode* of the variable. It is the responsibility of the programmer to tell the compiler the mode of each variable used in a program.

The most direct way of designating the mode of variables is to use the declaration statements INTEGER and REAL. As an example, assume that A, B, and C should refer to integer values and that X and Y should refer to real values. Appropriate declaration statements would be

INTEGER A, B, C

REAL X, Y

The goal of declaration statements such as REAL and INTEGER is to give to the compiler the information needed for the compilation process. The following rules regarding declaration statements are true for most compilers:

1. Declaration statements must be placed at the beginning of a program before the executable statements.
2. There is no required sequence for declaration statements. For example, REAL statements can appear either before or after INTEGER statements, and the two types can be intermixed within the declaration statements.
3. A given type of declaration statement can appear in a program as many times as a programmer wishes. Consider the statement

INTEGER A, B, C

This could be replaced by

INTEGER A, B
INTEGER C

or by

INTEGER A
INTEGER B
INTEGER C

or by a sequence in which the variables appear in a different order such as

INTEGER C
INTEGER A
INTEGER B

Each set of these statements will be interpreted by the compiler to mean the same thing.

Defining variables to be of integer or real mode will have a significant effect on the results of arithmetic operations. In FORTRAN when integer division is done, the remainder is dropped. The process of dropping the remainder is called *truncation*. For example, for $A = 3$ and $B = 4$, the computation

$$X = A/B$$

gives X = .75 if A and B are real mode and X = 0.0 if they are integer mode. Similar considerations apply to constants. In the conversion of Fahrenheit temperatures to Celsius temperatures the computations

$$(1) \quad F = 9/5*C + 32$$

and

$$(2) \quad F = 9./5.*C + 32.$$

give quite different answers. The quotient of 9/5 is 1, since both constants are integers, and truncation occurs when integers are divided. Thus computation (1) is equivalent to F = C + 32; but computation (2) gives the expected answer, because the constants are of real mode.

6.5 RULES FOR NAMING VARIABLES

The following rules apply to the names of variables in FORTRAN:

1. Names of variables may consist of from 1 to 6 characters selected from the set of alphabetic characters A to Z, and the set of digits 0 to 9.
2. The first character of the name of a variable must be alphabetic (PAY, AMOUNT, A1234, TEMPTR).
3. In the absence of a REAL or INTEGER statement involving the variable, the *first* character of the variable *implies* the mode of the variable:
   a. First character I through N implies the integer mode. (Notice that I and N are the first two characters of the word *integer*.)
   b. First character A to H or O to Z implies the real mode.

The following are examples of valid variables and their implied modes:

Variable	Mode	Variable	Mode
I	Integer	HELP	Real
IJ	Integer	ORBIT	Real
J	Integer	WEIGHT	Real
J12X	Integer	C	Real
KXYZ	Integer	X	Real
MASS	Integer	X1	Real
NEXT	Integer	ANSWER	Real
INTGER	Integer	GRADE	Real
KAP	Integer	SUM	Real
M5431X	Integer	ZIP	Real
IF	Integer	X1Y34	Real

Now we shall consider examples of names that are almost correct, but contain an error. A study of such errors, which will be called "near-misses," can be invaluable in clarifying a concept and will be considered whenever a new idea is considered. (Incidentally, the most successful programs for teaching concepts to computers require the submission of near-miss examples to the computer.)

Invalid variable	Reason
TEMPERATURE	Too many characters
1ST	Begins with a number
X1,000	A comma is not allowed
NX(15	A left parenthesis is not allowed
N=M	An equals mark is not allowed—in some cases the compiler would interpret this as an arithmetic statement
X+Y	A plus sign is not allowed
VELOCITY	Too many characters
$PAY	A dollar sign is not allowed
X1.67	A decimal is not allowed
FINAL.	A decimal is not allowed

It is improbable that you will make any error in naming variables when the variable is isolated as it is in this discussion. In the context of a problem you are trying to solve, however, it is relatively easy to make an error. For example, in the statement

$$VELOCITY = DISTANCE/TIME$$

notice that both velocity and distance contain too many characters. (Correct: VELOC = DISTNC/TIME.) Check your understanding and power of observation by finding the errors, if any, in the following statements before you read the answers:

1. PRESS = CONST*MOLES*TEMP/VOLUME
2. PAY = GROSS−FEDTAX−STTAX−DEDUCTIONS
3. FICA = RATE*(16,500 − TOTALPAY)
4. GROSS = $2.30*HOURS − TAX
5. AVERAGE = (GRADE1 + GRADE2 + GRADE3)/3.
6. AREA = 2.*π*RADIUS**2

Answers:

1. Correct.
2. DEDUCTIONS contains too many characters.
3. 16,500 contains a comma, and TOTALPAY contains too many characters.
4. $2.30 contains a dollar sign.
5. AVERAGE contains too many characters.
6. π is not an allowable character.

Note that a long, well-designed statement can be made totally invalid by one small error, such as the omission or addition of a comma, parenthesis, or a period. Therefore, a long, well-designed program containing only one such statement will also be made totally invalid. This required precision in using a computer language does not correspond to our use of a natural language. If you misspell one word in an English composition, the professor will still understand your essay; but a single syntax error in a computer program causes the whole program to be rejected by the compiler.

6.6 ASSIGNMENT STATEMENTS

Assignment statements in FORTRAN are very similar to algebraic equations: with the operators +, -, *, /, and ** meaning, respectively, addition, subtraction, multiplication, division, and exponentiation. If you construct a statement using the rules of algebra subject to the restriction given below, the statement will probably be correct. Examples of valid FORTRAN assignment statements that we have used in previous PDL programs are

$$C = 2*A$$

$$D = C/A$$

$$X = B - D$$

$$X = -B$$

$$X = B - (2*A - B)/A$$

$$COUNT = COUNT + 1$$

Statements of much greater complexity can be written, of course, but further discussion of details will be delayed until Chapter 8.

Before proceeding, it is essential for you to recognize a fundamental difference in FORTRAN assignment statements and algebraic equations. In FORTRAN the equals sign (=) means *assignment*; it does not mean "is equal to." *Assignment* means the storing of a value in a memory cell, replacing whatever was in the cell by the new value. (A similar situation was considered in the discussion of MLOGO.) For example, suppose that cells X and Y contain 1.02 and 999.63, respectively. The situation is

$$X \quad \boxed{1.02} \qquad Y \quad \boxed{999.63}$$

Then the FORTRAN arithmetic statement

$$X = Y$$

means to assign the value of Y as the new value of X, giving

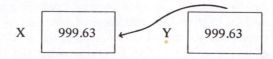

This interpretation of the meaning of "=" is responsible for the FORTRAN rule:

> In an assignment statement, the only quantity that can appear to the left of an equals sign is the name of a variable. The name must refer to a single value.

The statements

$$SUM = SUM + GRADE \qquad (1)$$

and

$$COUNT = COUNT + 1 \qquad (2)$$

are legitimate FORTRAN statements, although they are invalid in algebra. FORTRAN interprets the statement as

(1) Add the values of SUM and GRADE and assign the result as the new value of SUM.
(2) Add 1 to the current value of COUNT and let the result be the new value of COUNT.

What we have been doing in the discussion of assignment statements is making a distinction between the *name* of a memory cell (i.e., X, Y, SUM, GRADE, or COUNT) and the *value* stored in a memory cell. The compiler will associate the name of a variable with the *address* (i.e., the identifying number) of a memory cell. The *contents* of a memory cell during the execution of a program will be the value of the variable associated with the memory cell. These concepts were described in Chapter 1 using the classic "post-office-box" analogy.

6.7 CONTROL STATEMENTS

Control statements are used in FORTRAN for making decisions, performing loops, and stopping the computer. FORTRAN contains a GOTO statement, a computed GOTO statement, three types of IF statements, a DO statement for controlling loops, and other control statements. Yet FORTRAN is not convenient for writing structured programs. Some of its control statements give the programmer too much opportunity to write programs in an undisciplined manner, which can make the programs very difficult to understand, debug, and modify. We therefore restrict our present use of control statements to IF . . . THEN . . . ELSE, WHILE, STOP, and END. The form of the IF . . . THEN . . . ELSE statement is the same as that used in PDL:

IF (condition) THEN
        .
        .
        .
        block of statements to be executed if the condition is true
        .
        .
        .
ELSE
        .
        .
        .
        block of statements to be executed if the condition is false
        .
        .
        .
ENDIF

The relational operators (.EQ., .NE., .LT., etc.) are the same for PDL and FORTRAN.
    The WHILE statement is identical to the statement as it was used in PDL; consequently, it has the form

WHILE (condition)
        .
        .
        .
        block of statements executed repeatedly as long as the
                        condition remains true
        .
        .
        .
ENDWHILE

(*Note:* The WHILE statement is a nonstandard feature of FORTRAN.)

The statement STOP is the last statement executed in a FORTRAN program. In modern computers, the STOP statement does not actually halt the computer, but instead, causes an exit from the program, so that no other statements in the program can be executed.
    The END statement marks the end of the program and acts as a signal to the compiler that all the FORTRAN statements have been read. This use of END is analogous with our use of END in MLOGO and PDL.

6.8   INPUT/OUTPUT STATEMENTS

Input and output of values are accomplished in FORTRAN by using the READ and WRITE statements. Another statement, the FORMAT statement, is used in conjunction with READ and WRITE to describe the manner in which the data are placed on a card, a line of print, or another document. Many options exist for using these statements, giving the programmer maximum flexibility for input of data and for writing complex reports. In this section only the simplest features of input/output will be considered. Discussion of FORMAT statements will be delayed until Chapter 7.

List-directed input/output statements allow the programmer to ignore the details of how the data are to be read or printed, and they are easier to use than other input/output statements. Consequently, they can be very helpful to an individual who is learning FORTRAN.

The syntax of the list-directed input statement is:

READ (5,*) list of variables

where 5 is the identifying code for the standard input device, usually a card reader; by using a different number, a different input device could be selected

   * is the signal to the compiler that free format input is to be used

   "list of variables" is a series of names of variables in the left-to-right sequence in which the corresponding values are to be read; the names in the list must be separated by commas

Suppose that you need to read the values X, Y, and Z from a card. Then an appropriate READ statement is

READ (5,*) X,Y,Z

The data associated with these variables can be punched into the card beginning with any column. The leftmost value on the card will be associated with X, the middle value with Y, and the rightmost value with Z. Successive values on a card should be separated by one (or more) blank columns or by a comma. For example, the card could appear as

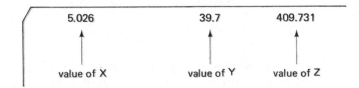

When list-directed input is used, the compiler will generate instructions to search through a card to locate the values associated with the list of variables, regardless of where the values are punched.

Additional examples of list-directed READ statements are:

READ (5,*) GRADE

READ (5,*) RATE, HOURS, DEDUCT

READ (5,*) FREQ, MASS

READ (5,*) N, X, Y, A, Z

READ (5,*) A,B,C,D,E,J,K,L,Q,R,S,M,X,N

Some points to remember when using list-directed input are*:

1. Values for variables must be punched into cards in the same sequence as they are found in the READ statement.
2. Real and integer variables may occur in any desired order in a READ statement.
   a. Punched values must agree in mode with the corresponding variables.

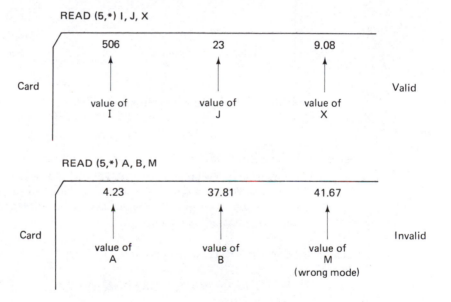

   b. Real values may contain a decimal; the decimal can also be implied to be immediately after the rightmost digit by omitting the decimal.
   c. Integer values can never contain a decimal.
3. Additional cards will be read as necessary to obtain as many values as there are variables.

*These rules may vary slightly from one compiler to another.

READ (5,*) A, B, C, D

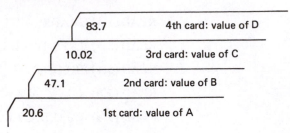

4. If a card contains more values than are needed for correspondence with the variables in a READ statement, then, upon execution of the READ statement, the extra values are ignored and are not available for subsequent use in the program.

READ (5,*) X, Y

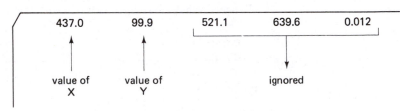

The syntax of the list-directed output statement is:

WRITE (6,*) list of variables

where 6 is the identifying code for the standard output device, usually a line printer
 * is the signal to the compiler that free-format output is to be used
 "list of variables" is a series of names of variables in the left-to-right sequence in which the corresponding values are to be printed; the names in the list must be separated by commas

Sample list-directed WRITE statements are:

WRITE (6,*) GRADE1, GRADE2, AVERAG

WRITE (6,*) SUM, LAST

WRITE (6,*) MEAN, MEDIAN, MAX, MIN, COUNT, STDDEV

WRITE (6,*) X, Y, Q, M, L, R, S, T, WXYZ

WRITE (6,*) A, B, C, ROOT1, ROOT2

The list-directed WRITE statement is even easier to use than the READ statement. Merely list the variables in the left-to-right order in which you wish to have the values printed. When the statement is executed, the values will be printed across a line using whatever spacing the compiler writers chose when they wrote the compiler. You will have no control over the spacing between values or the number of digits printed to the right of the decimal in real numbers; but by giving up this control, you avoid having to write an additional FORTRAN statement. If you try to print more values than can be accommodated on a line, additional lines will automatically be used.

There is a possibility that the compiler you are using will print some (or all) real values in exponential format when you use list-directed output. In exponential notation, a real number is expressed as a combination of a fractional part and an exponential part. For example, 537.01 is expressed as 0.53701E 03, where 0.53701 is the fractional part and E 03 is the exponential part. The E 03 represents the power to which 10 must be raised so that the product of the fraction and the power of 10 will give the original number. Let us convert from exponential form to real form:

given: 0.75362E 02

$$0.75362 \qquad \text{fractional part}$$

$$E\ \underline{02} = 10^2 = 100 \qquad \text{exponential part}$$

$$0.75362E\ 02 = 0.75362 \times 100$$
$$= 75.362$$

By convention the fractional part is always written with the most significant digit (7 in the last example) placed just to the right of the decimal. Exponential notation is especially useful for representing very large or very small real numbers. Table 6.1 gives several more examples.

TABLE 6.1 *Examples of exponential notation for real numbers*

Real number	Exponential notation
40372.1	0.403721E 05
0.403721	0.403721E 00
−0.000403721	−0.403721E−03
0.000000000403721	0.403721E−09
−403721000000.	−0.403721E 12

6.9 SUBPROGRAMS

In our study of MLOGO, procedures and subprocedures played an important role in the development of programs using top-down programming techniques. The FORTRAN equivalent of a procedure is called a *subprogram*. The importance of subprograms as intellectual tools in programming can hardly be overemphasized, and we will be using them throughout our study of FORTRAN.

There are four types of FORTRAN subprograms:

1. Intrinsic functions.
2. Functions.
3. Subroutines.
4. Statement function.

The details for each type will be discussed when we are ready to use a particular type of subprogram. In this chapter, intrinsic function will be used, so a brief introduction is appropriate. More detail will be given later.

An *intrinsic function* is a prewritten subprogram that is considered to be a standard part of the FORTRAN language. Many of these functions have been written to perform additional mathematical operations. For example, the intrinsic function SQRT, which can be used to compute the square root of real numbers, has the form

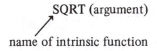

where the argument must be of real mode. To compute the square root of X and assign the result as the value of A, one can write

$$A = SQRT(X)$$

For SQRT the argument can be any legitimate real-mode arithmetic expression, and SQRT can be used in an arithmetic expression wherever a regular arithmetic operator is allowed. The statement

$$Z = (X + SQRT(2.5*X**2+Y**2))/(A+B)$$

is legitimate. Unfortunately, we do not get a correct answer if we use

$$R = SQRT(NUM)$$

since the argument of SQRT must be in the real mode. Another intrinsic function, FLOAT, can be used to produce the real-mode equivalent of NUM:

$$X = FLOAT(NUM)$$

Finally, the SQRT of NUM can be obtained:

$$R = SQRT(FLOAT(NUM))$$

6.10 SAMPLE PROGRAMS

Now that some features of each type of FORTRAN statement have been considered, several programs will be developed to illustrate them. Stepwise refinement and

PDL will be used in the development process. The last step—the translation from PDL to FORTRAN—will be almost trivial.

As our study of FORTRAN proceeds, notice that the difficult part of using the computer is finding a solution method and expressing it unambiguously in some language. Translating the solution into an available computer language is relatively easy. The sample programs discussed in the text are selected to illustrate various approaches to problem solving, some classical algorithms, and various language features of FORTRAN.

Example 1: Payroll Report

Write a FORTRAN program to print a payroll report. For each employee a data card will be read containing the employee's identification number, hours worked, hourly rate, and tax to be deducted. All this information is to be printed together with the gross pay before deductions, the net pay after all deductions, and the gross pay from overtime work in excess of 40 hours per week. The overtime rate is 1.5 times the regular rate.

This example is highly simplified relative to what should be done for a real payroll report. If the program were being written to be used in actual business activities, there would be many additional features included, such as the computation of the tax by the computer. In future chapters, the problem will be expanded to make it more realistic.

A. Level 1 Solution

We know directly from the statement of the problem that

> For each employee
>> read input
>> make computations, taking into account overtime hours
>> write input and pay

B. Level 2 Solution

Expand the previous solution by giving explicit names to variables and by stating a partial solution for the overtime computation. Overtime depends upon hours worked in excess of 40 hours, and this can be tested in an IF statement.

For each employee

```
READ EMPNUM, HOURS, RATE, DEDUCT
IF (HOURS .LE. 40.) THEN
    compute pay
    WRITE EMPNUM, HOURS, RATE, DEDUCT, GROSS, NET
ELSE
    compute pay
    WRITE EMPNUM, HOURS, RATE, DEDUCT, GROSS, NET, OVPAY
ENDIF
```

Notice the construction of the condition in the IF statement:

IF (HOURS .LE. 40.) THEN

The variable HOURS is of real mode, and its value is compared with 40., a real mode constant. Comparisons give unpredictable results unless the values compared have the same mode. Be careful in future work.

The two output statements differ only in the appearance of OVPAY (for overtime pay) at the end of the second statement. Why not remove the WRITE statements from the IF statement and have WRITE EMPNUM, HOURS, RATE, DEDUCT, GROSS, NET, OVPAY after ENDIF? Such a technique will work, but it has the feature of always printing a value for OVPAY even if the value is zero because the employee did not work more than 40 hours. Then to determine whether a person earned overtime pay, it will be necessary to examine the value printed in the OVPAY column to see if it is nonzero. For the method suggested, a value will be printed in the OVPAY column only when overtime pay has been earned.

C. Level 3 Solution

Insert statements for computing the pay.

For each employee

```
READ EMPNUM, HOURS, RATE, DEDUCT
IF (HOURS .LE. 40.) THEN
    GROSS = HOURS*RATE
    NET = GROSS-DEDUCT
    WRITE EMPNUM, HOURS, RATE, DEDUCT, GROSS, NET
ELSE
    OVPAY = 1.5*(HOURS-40.)*RATE
    GROSS = 40.*RATE + OVPAY
    NET = GROSS-DEDUCT
    WRITE EMPNUM, HOURS, RATE, DEDUCT, GROSS, NET, OVPAY
ENDIF
```

D. Level 4 Solution

The final step in the design of the program is to generalize it to work for an arbitrary number of employees. This is accomplished by embedding solution 3 in a WHILE loop, which will be repeated until a negative EMPNUM is encountered. Remember that a new EMPNUM should be read before the WHILE condition is tested.

In this solution stage, the translation from PDL to FORTRAN will be completed by modifying the READ and WRITE statements. In the future, we will use FORTRAN input/output statements in the PDL solutions.

To illustrate the use of the INTEGER and REAL statements, we assume that EMPNUM should be an integer variable and NET should be a real variable.

```
REAL NET
INTEGER EMPNUM
READ (5,*) EMPNUM, HOURS, RATE, DEDUCT
WHILE (EMPNUM .GE. 0)
    IF (HOURS .LE. 40.) THEN
        GROSS = HOURS*RATE
        NET = GROSS-DEDUCT
        WRITE (6,*) EMPNUM, HOURS, RATE, DEDUCT,
                                            GROSS, NET
    ELSE
        OVPAY = 1.5*(HOURS-40.)*RATE
        GROSS = 40.*RATE + OVPAY
        NET = GROSS-DEDUCT
        WRITE (6,*) EMPNUM, HOURS, RATE, DEDUCT,
                                            GROSS, NET, OVPAY
    ENDIF
    READ (5,*) EMPNUM, HOURS, RATE, DEDUCT
ENDWHILE
STOP
END
```

Output from the program is shown in Figure 6.3.

Caution: The card containing a negative EMPNUM to signal the end of processing must also contain values for HOURS, RATE, and DEDUCT, even though they will never be used; otherwise, the list-directed READ statement will continue to read cards trying to find these values. Eventually, this will cause an abnormal termination of the program.

Example 2: *Manhattan Island Problem*

In 1626, Manhattan Island was purchased from the Indians for $24. This money could have been invested in a bank at 5 percent interest compounded annually instead of buying the island. The principal and accumulated interest would be astoundingly large today. Write a program that reads a card with the date of this year on it, and calculate the value of the investment at the end of this year. To show the rate of growth of the investment, print the value of the investment at 10-year intervals beginning with 1630.

```
1  C
2  C              SIMPLE PAYROLL REPORT
3  C
4        REAL NET
5        INTEGER EMPNUM
6        READ(5,*)EMPNUM,HOURS,RATE,DEDUCT
7        WHILE( EMPNUM .GE. 0)
8           IF( HOURS .LE. 40. )THEN
9              GROSS=HOURS*RATE
10             NET=GROSS-DEDUCT
11             WRITE(6,*)EMPNUM,HOURS,RATE,DEDUCT,GROSS,NET
12          ELSE
13             OVPAY = 1.5*(HOURS-40.)*RATE
14             GROSS=40.*RATE+OVPAY
15             NET=GROSS-DEDUCT
16             WRITE(6,*)EMPNUM,HOURS,RATE,DEDUCT,GROSS,NET,OVPAY
17          ENDIF
18          READ(5,*)EMPNUM,HOURS,RATE,DEDUCT
19       ENDWHILE
20       STOP
21       END
```

1001	38.0000	2.75000	26.1000	104.500	78.4000	
1002	42.0000	2.75000	27.4500	118.250	90.8000	8.25000
1003	36.0000	3.25000	25.3700	117.000	91.6300	
1004	39.5000	3.10000	28.4000	122.450	94.0500	
1005	46.5000	3.35000	31.7000	166.663	134.962	32.6625
1006	43.0000	3.20000	29.6000	142.400	112.800	14.4000
1007	40.0000	3.00000	30.0000	120.000	90.0000	
1008	51.5000	2.75000	29.5000	157.438	127.938	47.4375

FIGURE 6.3 *Payroll report*

A. *Level 1 Solution*

> initialize
> read value of this year
> WHILE (year being considered .LE. this year)
>   make calculation
>   IF (year is exactly divisible by 10) THEN
>   write year, value
>   ENDIF
>   increase year being considered
> ENDWHILE
> IF (year is not exactly divisible by 10) THEN
>   write year, final value
> ENDIF
> STOP
> END

B. *Level 2 Solution*

```
INTEGER YEAR, THISYR
YEAR = 1626
VALUE = 24.00
READ (5,*) THISYR
WHILE (YEAR .LE. THISYR)
    VALUE = VALUE + 0.05 *VALUE
    IF (YEAR is exactly divisible by 10) THEN
        WRITE (6,*) YEAR, VALUE
    ENDIF
    YEAR = YEAR +1
ENDWHILE
IF (year is not exactly divisible by 10) THEN
    WRITE (6,*) YEAR, VALUE
ENDIF
STOP
END
```

Does this proposed solution work for the first and last years? (It was noted previously that initial and final states are often special cases that require special attention.) The initial year is handled satisfactorily, but there is an error for the final year. In the final WRITE statement, does the year printed correspond to the year for which the value was calculated? No. VALUE was computed for the previous year. In the next solution, YEAR = YEAR - 1 must be inserted before the last IF statement.

Also notice that the IF statements have no ELSE section. This is a legitimate option.

C. *Level 3 Solution*

The remaining difficulty is to determine whether or not the year is exactly divisible by 10. Most people invest considerable time and effort before they discover a method. You might want to try to solve the problem on your own before examining the technique suggested in the next paragraph.

One way of determining whether an integer is exactly divisible by another is to make use of the truncation property of integer division. If an integer is exactly divisible by a second integer, the remainder is zero; the quotient times the second integer will produce the first integer as its value. For example,

$$(50/10)*10 = 50$$

same

but

$$(53/10)*10 = 50$$

different

In general, the following is valid for exactly divisible integers:

$$INT1 - (INT1/INT2)*INT2 = 0$$

For example,

$$50 - (50/10)*10 = 50 - (5)*10$$
$$= 50 - 50$$
$$= 0 \quad \therefore 50 \text{ is exactly divisible by } 10$$

$$53 - (53/10)*10 = 53 - (5)*10$$
$$= 53 - 50$$
$$\neq 0 \quad \therefore 53 \text{ is not exactly divisible by } 10$$

$$1970 - (1970/10)*10 = 1970 - (197)*10$$
$$= 1970 - 1970$$
$$= 0 \quad \therefore 1970 \text{ is exactly divisible by } 10$$

$$143 - (143/13)*13 = 143 - (11)*13$$
$$= 143 - 143$$
$$= 0 \quad \therefore 143 \text{ is exactly divisible by } 13$$

You should remember this technique for use in other programs. Our final solution is:

```
INTEGER YEAR, THISYR
YEAR = 1626
VALUE = 24.00
READ (5,*) THISYR
WHILE (YEAR .LE. THISYR)
    VALUE = VALUE + 0.05*VALUE
    IF ((YEAR - (YEAR/10)*10) .EQ. 0) THEN
        WRITE (6,*) YEAR, VALUE
    ENDIF
    YEAR = YEAR + 1
ENDWHILE
YEAR = YEAR - 1
IF((YEAR - (YEAR/10)*10) .NE. 0) THEN
    WRITE(6,*)YEAR, VALUE
ENDIF
STOP
END
```

The output for the program is given in Figure 6.4. The final answer is, as anticipated, a very large number. A characteristic of real-mode computations is that only the leftmost seven significant digits (approximately, depending upon the computer and other factors) of an answer are retained in computer memory. In the computation performed by this program, VALUE needs to retain more digits to be completely accurate—the answer is, therefore, an approximate value. It is a much more difficult problem to compute the final answer, correct to the nearest penny.

Example 3: Prime Numbers

A prime number is a number that is exactly divisible only by 1 and itself. The numbers 1, 2, 3, 5, 7, 11, 13, and 17 are examples of prime numbers. Write a program to find and print all the prime numbers less than 1000.

A. Level 1 Solution

From the statement of the problem, it is apparent that a loop is needed in which each of the numbers less than 1000 will be tested for being a prime number. This leads to the PDL solution:

```
initialize
WHILE (NUMBER .LT. 1000)
    determine whether or not NUMBER is prime
    IF (NUMBER is prime) THEN
        write NUMBER
    ENDIF
    increase NUMBER
ENDWHILE
STOP
END
```

B. Level 2 Solution

The major difficulty in expanding the level 1 solution is finding a reasonable way of determining whether or not NUMBER is a prime. The most obvious way of proceeding is to divide NUMBER by each of the integers starting with 2, checking each time to determine if the value of NUMBER is exactly divisible by the integer. If no exact divisor is found before the integers become as large as NUMBER, a prime has been discovered.

In general, a "brute-force" approach to problem solving such as the method just described is not acceptable. For example, if we had to find all the primes less than 1 billion, the method would be far too time-consuming even using a computer. Often, however, examination of a brute-force solution will lead to refinements that give an acceptable or even elegant solution. We start with the brute-force solution and try to improve it.

```
1 C
2 C                 MANHATTAN ISLAND PROBLEM
3 C
4         INTEGER YEAR,THISYR
5         YEAR=1626
6         VALUE=24.00
7         READ(5,*)THISYR
8         WHILE( YEAR .LE. THISYR)
9            VALUE=VALUE+0.05*VALUE
10           IF( (YEAR-(YEAR/10)*10) .EQ. 0 ) THEN
11              WRITE(6,*)YEAR,VALUE
12           ENDIF
13           YEAR=YEAR+1
14        ENDWHILE
15        YEAR=YEAR-1
16        IF( (YEAR-(YEAR/10)*10) .NE. 0) THEN
17           WRITE(6,*)YEAR,VALUE
18        ENDIF
19        STOP
20        END
```

```
1630   30.6308
1640   49.8943
1650   81.2725
1660   132.384
1670   215.640
1680   351.255
1690   572.158
1700   931.985
1710   1518.10
1720   2472.83
1730   4027.98
1740   6561.16
1750   10687.4
1760   17408.7
1770   28357.0
1780   46190.5
1790   75239.5
1800   122557.
1810   199633.
1820   325181.
1830   529686.
1840   862802.
1850   .140541E+07
1860   .228927E+07
1870   .372898E+07
1880   .607412E+07
1890   .989410E+07
1900   .161164E+08
1910   .262520E+08
1920   .427617E+08
1930   .696543E+08
1940   .113460E+09
1950   .184814E+09
1960   .301042E+09
1970   .490366E+09
1980   .798754E+09
1981   .838692E+09
```

FIGURE 6.4 *Manhattan Island Problem*

To implement the method, the statement "determine whether or not NUMBER is prime" in the level 1 solution will be replaced by a WHILE loop, which tests NUMBER for exact divisibility by the integers less than the value of NUMBER, that is:

```
"determine          initialize
whether or =====> WHILE (INTEGR .LT. NUMBER)
not NUMBER              test NUMBER for exact divisibility by INTEGR
is a prime"             IF (INTEGR is an exact divisor) THEN
                            make INTEGR large enough to get out of the loop
                            set indicator for not a prime number
                        ENDIF
                        increase INTEGR
                    ENDWHILE
```

Thus, the level 2 solution is

```
initialize
WHILE (NUMBER .LT. 1000)
    initialize
    WHILE (INTEGR .LT. NUMBER)
        test to determine if INTEGR is an exact divisor of NUMBER
        IF (INTEGR is an exact divisor) THEN
            make INTEGR large enough to get out of the loop
            set indicator for not a prime number
        ENDIF
        increase INTEGR
    ENDWHILE
    IF (indicator designates a prime number) THEN
        WRITE (6,*) NUMBER
    ENDIF
    increase NUMBER
ENDWHILE
STOP
END
```

C. Level 3 Solution

Let PRIME be an integer variable having the interpretation

PRIME = 1   NUMBER is a prime number

PRIME = 0   NUMBER is not a prime number

The technique of the last example can be used to check NUMBER for exact division by INTEGR. We make REMAIN an integer variable and use

```
REMAIN = NUMBER - (NUMBER/INTEGR)*INTEGR
```

Then the third-level solution becomes

```
INTEGER PRIME, REMAIN
NUMBER = 1
WRITE (6,*) NUMBER
NUMBER = 2
WRITE (6,*) NUMBER
WHILE (NUMBER .LT. 1000)
   PRIME = 1
   INTEGR = 2
   WHILE (INTEGR .LT. NUMBER)
      REMAIN = NUMBER - (NUMBER/INTEGR)*INTEGR
      IF (REMAIN .EQ. 0) THEN
         INTEGR = NUMBER
         PRIME = 0
      ENDIF
      INTEGR = INTEGR + 1
   ENDWHILE
   IF (PRIME .EQ. 1) THEN
      WRITE (6,*) NUMBER
   ENDIF
   NUMBER = NUMBER + 1
ENDWHILE
STOP
END
```

D. Level 4 Solution

How can the previous solution be improved? As a first guess, we try to reduce the number of values of INTEGR that are used in the testing procedure. Reflection (how long depends upon the person reflecting!) leads to the conclusion that if NUMBER is an odd number, there will be no point in testing for division by any even number. A method of incorporating this into the program is to test outside the WHILE loop for "even-ness" and to use only odd values of INTEGR within the loop. This gives

```
INTEGER PRIME, REMAIN
NUMBER = 1
WRITE (6,*) NUMBER
NUMBER = 2
WRITE (6,*) NUMBER
NUMBER = 3
```

```
        WHILE (NUMBER .LT. 1000)
            PRIME = 1
            INTEGR = 3
            REMAIN = NUMBER - (NUMBER/2)*2
            IF (REMAIN .EQ. 0) THEN
                INTEGR = NUMBER
                PRIME = 0
            ENDIF
            WHILE (INTEGR .LT. NUMBER)
                REMAIN = NUMBER - (NUMBER/INTEGR)*INTEGR
                IF (REMAIN .EQ. 0) THEN
                    INTEGR = NUMBER
                    PRIME = 0
                ENDIF
                INTEGR = INTEGR + 2
            ENDWHILE
            IF (PRIME .EQ. 1) THEN
                WRITE (6,*) NUMBER
            ENDIF
            NUMBER = NUMBER +1
        ENDWHILE
        STOP
        END
```

The computer output for this program is given in Figure 6.5.

E. Level 5 Solution

The level 4 solution just considered is about as satisfactory as can be conveniently written with the FORTRAN you know now; there are, however, additional improvements that can be made. In this section other ideas from FORTRAN will be introduced in just sufficient detail to make two changes to the program. The new ideas will be presented systematically and in detail later.

The first modification rests on the observation that the quotient obtained using a particular divisor will subsequently become a divisor. For example, assume that 17 is being tested as a possible prime.

Divisor	Quotient	Product
2	8	16
3	5	15
4	4	16
5	3	15
6	2	12
etc.	etc.	etc.

```
 1 C
 2 C          PRIME NUMBERS LESS THAN 1000
 3 C
 4         INTEGER PRIME,REMAIN
 5         NUMBER=1
 6         WRITE(6,*)NUMBER
 7         NUMBER=2
 8         WRITE(6,*)NUMBER
 9         NUMBER=3
10         WHILE( NUMBER .LT. 1000)
11            PRIME=1
12            INTEGR=3
13            REMAIN=NUMBER-(NUMBER/2)*2
14            IF(REMAIN .EQ. 0) THEN
15               INTEGR=NUMBER
16               PRIME=0
17            ENDIF
18            WHILE( INTEGR .LT. NUMBER )
19               REMAIN=NUMBER-(NUMBER/INTEGR)*INTEGR
20               IF( REMAIN .EQ. 0 ) THEN
21                  INTEGR=NUMBER
22                  PRIME=0
23               ENDIF
24               INTEGR=INTEGR+2
25            ENDWHILE
26            IF( PRIME .EQ. 1 ) THEN
27               WRITE(6,*)NUMBER
28            ENDIF
29            NUMBER=NUMBER+1
30         ENDWHILE
31         STOP
32         END


                  1
                  2
                  3
                  5
                  7
                 11
                 13
                 17
                 19
                 23
                 29
                 31
                 37
                 41

                  .
                  .
                  .

                953
                967
                971
                977
                983
                991
                997
```

FIGURE 6.5 *Prime numbers less than 1000−method 1*

As the divisor increases, the quotient decreases; for this particular case, there would be no point in testing divisors greater than 4, as all the potential exact divisors will have already appeared either as the divisor or the quotient. Another way of seeing this point is to note that

$$NUMBER \leqslant QUOTIENT * DIVISOR$$

Since for the example being considered:

2 is not an exact divisor,	8 cannot be an exact divisor
3 is not an exact divisor,	5 cannot be an exact divisor
etc.	

The largest integer we will ever need to consider as a possible exact divisor is the square root of NUMBER. Thus, in the level 4 solution, we should have

$$LIMIT = \text{square root of } NUMBER$$

and WHILE (INTEGR .LT. NUMBER) should be replaced by

$$WHILE \ (INTEGR \ .LE. \ LIMIT)$$

Would these changes really make the solution better? Consider the testing of 997 for being a prime. The square root of 997 (after truncation) is 31. Thus only the divisors through 31 need be tested, and those from 32 through 996 can be ignored. A very significant reduction in the computer time required for testing is obtained, and the proposed method is an improvement. The value of LIMIT can be computed using the intrinsic function SQRT:

$$LIMIT = SQRT(FLOAT(NUMBER))$$

The other change we want to make is intended to improve the clarity of the program. The inner WHILE loop should be repeated as long as both the following conditions are satisfied: (1) no exact divisor has been found, and (2) the divisor is less than or equal to the limit. FORTRAN allows the combining of conditions in using the logical operator .AND. (operators .OR. and .NOT. can also be used). The status of the division process is given by PRIME, the divisor is INTEGR, and LIMIT is the name of the upper limit; thus the condition can be expressed as

$$WHILE \ ((PRIME \ .EQ. \ 1) \ .AND. \ (INTEGR \ .LE. \ LIMIT))$$

This change allows the elimination of the two appearances of the statement

$$INTEGR = NUMBER$$

```
1  C
2  C          PRIMES LESS THAN 1000
3  C
4          INTEGER PRIME,REMAIN
5          NUMBER=1
6          WRITE(6,*)NUMBER
7          NUMBER=2
8          WRITE(6,*)NUMBER
9          NUMBER=3
10         WHILE( NUMBER .LT. 1000)
11            PRIME=1
12            INTEGR=3
13            REMAIN=NUMBER-(NUMBER/2)*2
14            IF(REMAIN .EQ. 0) THEN
15               PRIME=0
16            ENDIF
17            LIMIT=SQRT(FLOAT(NUMBER))
18            WHILE( (PRIME .EQ. 1) .AND. (INTEGR .LE. LIMIT))
19               REMAIN=NUMBER-(NUMBER/INTEGR)*INTEGR
20               IF( REMAIN .EQ. 0 ) THEN
21                  PRIME=0
22               ENDIF
23               INTEGR=INTEGR+2
24            ENDWHILE
25            IF( PRIME .EQ. 1 ) THEN
26               WRITE(6,*)NUMBER
27            ENDIF
28            NUMBER=NUMBER+1
29         ENDWHILE
30         STOP
31         END

                 1
                 2
                 3
                 5
                 7
                11
                13
                17
                19
                23
                29
                31
                37
                41

                 .
                 .
                 .

               953
               967
               971
               977
               983
               991
               997
```

FIGURE 6.6 *Prime numbers less than 1000—method 2*

The final solution is shown below, and the computer printout is shown in Figure 6.6.

```
INTEGER PRIME, REMAIN
NUMBER = 1
WRITE (6,*) NUMBER
NUMBER = 2
WRITE (6,*) NUMBER
NUMBER = 3
WHILE (NUMBER .LT. 1000)
    PRIME = 1
    INTEGR = 3
    REMAIN = NUMBER - (NUMBER/2)*2
    IF (REMAIN .EQ. 0) THEN
        PRIME = 0
    ENDIF
    LIMIT = SQRT (FLOAT(NUMBER))
    WHILE ((PRIME .EQ. 1) .AND. (INTEGR .LE. LIMIT))
        REMAIN = NUMBER - (NUMBER/INTEGR)*INTEGR
        IF (REMAIN .EQ. 0) THEN
            PRIME = 0
        ENDIF
        INTEGR = INTEGR + 2
    ENDWHILE
    IF (PRIME .EQ. 1) THEN
        WRITE (6,*) NUMBER
    ENDIF
    NUMBER = NUMBER +1
ENDWHILE
STOP
END
```

6.11   PROGRAMMING ERRORS AND DEBUGGING

If you use stepwise refinement and give careful attention to the design of a program, your programs will tend to be free of errors. It is inevitable, however, especially as you are learning to write programs, that a program will fail to behave as you expected. Then you must find the bug and correct it.

The process of executing a FORTRAN program is displayed in Figure 6.7. The FORTRAN program that you write and keypunch is called the *source program*. The *object program* is the machine-language program that is produced by the compiler from your source program. Finally, the object program is executed to produce answers. Errors may occur at any stage of this process.

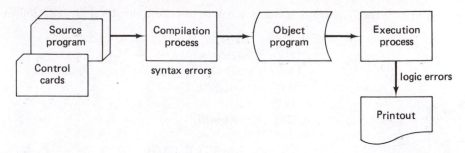

FIGURE 6.7 *Steps in executing a program*

6.11.1 Errors in Control Cards

The computer system is given directions to perform work by means of *control cards*. Normally, a separate card is required for each major activity you want performed such as compiling a FORTRAN source program or executing a previously prepared machine-language program. These commands form the control language, a high-level language that you must learn for the computer that you are using.

Suppose that sufficient time has passed for the computer to have completed work on your program but that no printout has been produced. (The term "sufficient time" is ambiguous and depends upon your computer installation. It may be only a few minutes or several hours, depending upon local circumstances. Ask some knowledgeable person how much time is required for a program.) You should suspect an error in the control cards. Ask the instructor, laboratory assistant, or other appropriate person to determine whether or not the computer is processing your program. If it is found that your program is not being processed, a control-card error occurred. Some possibilities are:

1. *Syntax error in control card:* You may not have followed the syntax rules for the control cards. For example, embedded blanks may not be allowed, but you may have inadvertently inserted a space.
2. *Control cards in wrong sequence:* If the control cards are out of proper sequence, your deck may be entirely rejected, or only a portion of the correct work may be completed. For example, a correct compilation but no execution of the object program suggests that the control cards are in the wrong sequence, or that a required control card is missing.
3. *Incorrect account identification or password:* An incorrect name for your account or an incorrect password will cause your entire deck to be rejected. You will not get a printout or any other clue as to what is wrong.
4. *Missing last control card:* If your system requires a control card such as EOJ to identify the end of your job deck, omitting this card may cause your deck to be ignored.

6.11.2 Syntax Errors

Syntax errors are errors in the FORTRAN statements that are discovered during the compilation stage. For each error a message will be printed. The messages may be inserted after the statements containing the errors, or the messages may all be printed in sequence at the bottom of the printout.

Generally, syntax errors are easy to correct. Examine each statement that contains an error to determine how you violated the syntax rules. Usually, the error message will be quite helpful in discovering the error in a statement. Some common errors are:

1. *Misspelling a keyword:* Keypunch errors involving the interchanging of a pair of characters, such as FI instead of IF, or INTERGER instead of INTEGER, are a common cause of these. The error message may give no clue to the problem, since the compiler may not be able to identify the error correctly. Normally, a message of the type

$$**\text{UNRECOGNIZABLE STATEMENT}$$

is printed.

2. *Missing parenthesis:* In complex arithmetic expressions the number of left-hand and right-hand parentheses may not agree. The compiler will catch this.
3. *Invalid name for a variable:* You may accidentally begin the name of a variable with an invalid character or use a name that contains too many characters.
4. *Keypunching beyond column 72:* If in keypunching a statement you go beyond column 72, it is likely that the compiler will detect an error in the statement. The printed error message will give no hint of what is actually wrong. Furthermore, careless reading of the card or corresponding line on the printout makes the statement appear to be valid. Whenever you have a long statement that contains a syntax error, check the possibility that you typed too much on the card.

In some circumstances the compiler may print error messages when, in fact, no genuine error exists in statements. For example, an important requirement for using variables in FORTRAN is that the variables must have been defined previously. A variable is said to be defined if a value has been read for it or if a value has been given to it by an assignment statement. Consider the following portion of a program:

.
.
.

REED (5,*) A,B,C,D
X = A + B

$$Y = 2.5 * A + B - C$$
$$Z = D ** 2 - B * C$$
.
.
.

The input statement contains a syntax error—REED was keypunched instead of READ. The compiler properly prints an error message for that statement. Since the REED statement is invalid, the variables A, B, C, and D have undefined values. This causes the computations for X, Y, and Z to be invalid, and an error message will be printed for each of these statements. To correct this portion of the program, only the REED statement has to be changed.

6.11.3   Logic Errors

When your program compiles correctly but then produces invalid output as a result of the execution stage of processing, the program contains one or more logic errors. The cause of a logic error can be extremely difficult to find. Some common errors are:

1. *No printout:* If no printout is produced by your program, then:
   a. The wrong logical unit number (device number) was used in the **WRITE** statement; or
   b. The **WRITE** statements could not be reached because of some other logic error in the program.

   The first thing you should do is to check the device number used in the **WRITE** statement. If it is correct, check the logic that leads to the **WRITE** statement. Give special attention to the "conditions" tested in IF statements and WHILE loops.

2. *Invalid printout:* Suppose that your program produces a printout but the answers are wrong. The "algorithm" you selected and implemented may contain a flaw, or you may have made an error in implementing the algorithm. Some possible logic errors that you should check are:
   a. Failure to initialize variables.
   b. Incorrect conditions in IF or WHILE statements.
   c. Input is not what is expected.
   d. Incorrect use of the language.

   Suppose that you intended to test for I = 1 in an IF statement; then the statement

   $$IF \ I = 1$$

   is an invalid IF statement but it is a valid assignment statement

   $$IFI = 1$$

   Thus the compiler would not find a syntax violation.

3. *Infinite loop:* As a precaution whenever you execute a program, use the time parameter that is part of the control cards. The form and location of the parameter will depend upon the computer system you are using, but its purpose is always to let you set an upper limit for how long your program can execute. Using TIME = 20 will prevent the program from looping more than 20 seconds. (This is a reasonable time limit for most programs in this book.) When execution stops, a message will be printed such as

**TIME LIMIT EXCEEDED

Infinite loops can arise in a variety of ways, including the following:
a. A variable used to control a loop is not initialized.
b. An "end-of-data" flag is accidentally omitted from the data deck—this may result in the loop terminating and printing an error message, such as

**OUT OF DATA ON UNIT #5

c. An incorrect condition may be used in a WHILE statement.
d. In a WHILE loop, the loop-controlling variable may not be changed within the loop.

The possible errors discussed thus far should convince you that an almost endless number of errors can occur in programs. The best protection against logic errors is a carefully designed program, but bugs still occur. The ability to debug programs is a skill that improves with practice. Once you have experienced a particular error, you will be less likely to repeat it.

If your program contains a bug, you should take a systematic approach to finding it. One method that is often suggested is hand simulation of the program. In this approach you pretend you are the computer, executing each statement in sequence and recording the values of all variables. Actually, this method does not work very well. The mind-set that caused you to write the program in a particular way will likely cause you to interpret the program in the way you think it is working rather than the way it is actually working. Also, for large or complex programs, this approach is too time-consuming and prone to errors.

A second strategy for discovering a bug is to try to find the area of the program in which it occurs. If a partial printout is obtained, check the statements immediately after the last WRITE statement that was executed. If this fails, additional WRITE statements should be added at strategic locations within the program. A WRITE statement can be placed after each READ statement to assure that the input values are correct. A WRITE statement can be placed after each statement in which the value of some critical variable is changed. The appearance of a strange value for a variable is a clue that something has gone wrong. If the program is aborting (i.e., stopping in an abnormal way) with no hint of where this is occurring in the program, insert WRITE statements to indicate that a particular location in the program has been reached. Then you can determine the area of the program in which the error occurs.

If you have an infinite loop and examination does not reveal any problem with the condition or the loop-controlling variables, insert a WRITE statement within the loop to print the values of the loop-controlling variables. If one or more of these variables produce strange values, try to find the reason. If the values of these variables are reasonable, check the condition. It may be necessary to print values for the condition.

Alas, all the techniques discussed above may fail and you may want to cry or at least put the program away for a while. A good idea is to discuss the program with someone else. It is amazing how often you will discover the problem while describing to someone else what you have done. Also, the other person may immediately find the problem, since he or she will be examining your work from a fresh point of view. Programming should not be a solitary activity.

As an example of a simple program that must be debugged, consider the following. Hopefully, if you had written the program, it would not contain errors, because you would have given adequate attention to the design. Also, for such a simple program you would be likely to discover more than one error at a time. Our goal in this discussion, however, is to illustrate the ideas just presented.

```
1       COUNT = 0.0
2       READ (5,*)GRADE
3       WHILE (GRADE .LT. 0.0)
4           COUNT = COUNT + 1
5           TOTAL = TOTAL + GRADE
6       ENDWHILE
7       AVERAGE = TOTAL/COUNT
8       WRITE (6,*)AVERAGE
9       STOP
10      END
```

When the program is submitted for execution, the compiler writes the message

**INVALID VARIABLE

after lines 7 and 8. We note that AVERAGE contains too many characters, so we rekeypunch the appropriate cards using the name AVER.

Now when the program is submitted, it compiles and begins execution. Then the program aborts and prints

**ATTEMPTED DIVISION BY ZERO

In this case, it is easy to determine where the error occurred—it must be in line 7, since that is the only place division occurs. This implies that COUNT has the value zero. How can this be? Each passage through the loop causes COUNT to increase by 1. We must conclude that the statements in the loop were never executed. This implies that the condition in the WHILE statement is wrong. We realize the relational operator should have been .GE., so we repunch the card and submit the program again. The program compiles and begins execution. Eventually, the following message is printed:

**TIME LIMIT EXCEEDED

The submitted program has the form

```
1       COUNT = 0.0
2       READ (5,*)GRADE
3       WHILE (GRADE .GE. 0.0)
4           COUNT = COUNT + 1
5           TOTAL = TOTAL + GRADE
6       ENDWHILE
7       AVER = TOTAL/COUNT
8       WRITE (6,*)AVER
9       STOP
10      END
```

For this simple program, there is only one loop, so it is obvious that once the loop is entered, the program never exits from the loop. How can this occur? The WHILE condition must always be true, which implies that GRADE is not being treated properly. After examination of the loop, we notice that a statement

READ (5,*)GRADE

should be inserted between lines 5 and 6.

After the correction is made and the cards resubmitted, the value 2107.850 is printed. This is an unreasonable answer, since the average must be no greater than 100. The problem is that TOTAL was not initialized. The statement

TOTAL = 0.0

should be added between lines 1 and 2. If it were not apparent what the problem is, a reasonable next step would be to print the current values of COUNT, TOTAL, and GRADE just prior to reading the next value of GRADE. The first line printed would probably have a peculiar value for TOTAL, and the nature of the difficulty would become apparent.

REVIEW QUESTIONS

1. Who was the leader of the group that first implemented FORTRAN? When was the work done?
2. What is the name of the most recent version of FORTRAN?
3. Explain the term "optimizing" compiler.
4. What versions of FORTRAN have been designed primarily for student use?
5. Why are declaration statements said to be nonexecutable? Give two examples of declaration statements.

6. Describe the card layout for FORTRAN statements. What will happen if a statement extends to column 75 of a card?

7. How many card columns can be used for data for a FORTRAN program?

8. What happens to "blanks" that appear in a FORTRAN statement? What does this imply about the statements you prepare?

9. Describe the technique for continuing long statements over several cards.

10. How are comment cards identified? Where may they be placed in programs?

11. What is the meaning of the term "mode"? Describe two methods for indicating the mode of variables. Which method takes precedence?

12. List the rules for naming variables.

13. Describe the difference of interpretation of the "equals sign" in algebra and FORTRAN?

14. What is the purpose of control statements in FORTRAN?

15. What is the signal that an input/output statement is to use list-directed techniques? Why is this type of statement so easy to use?

REVIEW QUIZ

1. Which of the following is *not* a category of FORTRAN statements?
   (A) arithmetic, (b) declaration, (C) control, (D) assignment, (E) input/output.

2. An *invalid* statement is:
   (A) Statement numbers can be placed anywhere in columns 1 to 5 of a card.
   (B) Ordinarily, "blanks" do not affect the meaning of a FORTRAN statement.
   (C) Comments can appear only at the beginning of a FORTRAN program.
   (D) Columns 73 to 80 are ordinarily used for identification purposes.
   (E) Placing a "C" in column 1 of a card is one way to indicate that a card is a comment.

3. If column 6 of a card contains a nonzero character, (A) the compiler will ignore the card, (B) the compiler will treat the card as a continuation of the previous card, (C) the compiler will treat the card as a comment, (D) the action taken by the compiler depends upon the character punched in the column, (E) two of the previous answers.

4. An example of a valid declaration statement is: (A) REAL DIVISOR; (B) INTEGER X = -12; (C) INTEGER I, N, MASS, TEMP; (D) INTEGER REAL, FREQUENCY; (E) two of the previous answers.

5. A valid name for a variable is (A) INTEGER, (B) 2 X, (C) PAYRATE, (D) QUIP, (E) two of the previous answers.

6. A valid name for a variable that is implied to be in the integer mode is (A) HIGH, (B) KINDNESS, (C) ROOT, (D) MINUS, (E) PLUS.

7. An example of a valid integer-mode constant is (A) 2976, (B) 2.07, (C) -2374, (D) -2961.93, (E) two of the previous answers.

8. An example of a valid assignment statement is (A) I+J = K+L; (B) ANSWERS = X + 2421; (C) 2*X+Y = Z; (D) 19 = I; (E) I = I+1.

9. An example of a valid control statement that is a nonstandard feature of FORTRAN is (A) GOTO, (B) STOP, (C) IF, (D) WHILE, (E) END.

10. The statement

$$\text{READ } (5,*) \text{ X,I,J}$$

(A) always reads three cards, (B) reads three real values, (C) will assign the first value read as the value of J, (D) illustrates list-directed input, (E) two of the previous answers.

11. Given a card having the following values punched:

    5026   39.7   409.731

    A read statement that could not be used for reading the card is (A) READ (5,*) C,B,A; (B) READ (5,*) A,B,C; (C) READ (5,*) K,X,Y; (D) READ (5,*) K,L,Y; (E) two or more of the previous answers.

12. For list-directed output statements, (A) the order in which values are printed is the same as the order that variables appear in the output statement, (B) attempting to print more than one line causes an error, (C) the programmer controls the spacing across a line, (D) the programmer controls the number of digits printed to the right of the decimal point in real-mode values, (E) all variables used in a statement must have the same mode.

13. An example of a valid nonexecutable statement is (A) X = Y + 1.5; (B) STOP; (C) WRITE (6,*) I, X, J, Y; (D) INTGER XYZ; (E) REAL MASS1.

14. The process of truncation is important in (A) integer-mode subtraction, (B) integer-mode division, (C) integer-mode multiplication, (D) real-mode subtraction, (E) real-mode division.

15. Additional arithmetic operations in FORTRAN (A) are made possible by functions, (B) are restricted to integer mode, (C) are restricted to real mode, (D) have special names such as SQRT, (E) two of the previous answers.

PROGRAMMING EXERCISES

1. The transcendental number e (value = 2.7182818) can be calculated using the series

$$e = 1 + \frac{1}{1!} + \frac{1}{2!} + \frac{1}{3!} + \frac{1}{4!} + \cdots$$

Compute the value of e to an accuracy of five significant figures, stopping the computation as soon as this accuracy is obtained. Print the number of terms (include the initial 1) that were required. Do not use the value of e in your program.

2. A factor is an exact divisor of a number, excluding 1 and the number itself. Write a program that reads a series of integers, computes all factors of each integer, and prints each integer and its corresponding factors.

3. Print a table that shows the cost of driving a car 1 mile as a function of the miles per gallon obtained by the car and the cost of a gallon of gasoline. Rows of the table should correspond to the cost of gasoline, starting with 60¢ per gallon, stepping 10¢ per row to a final cost of $2.00 per gallon. Columns in the table correspond to 10, 15, 20, 25, and 30 miles per gallon. For simplicity, assume that the cost of purchasing and maintaining the car is 25¢ per mile over the life of the car and that all remaining cost is due to the cost of the gasoline.

4. Write a program to compute the monthly service charge on a bank checking account. The charge is 10¢ each for the first 10 checks, 5¢ each for the next 10

checks, and 3¢ for each check after the 20th check. A surcharge of $1 is added if the minimum balance falls below $200. If the minimum balance is $1000 or greater, all checks are charged at the rate of 2¢ each. Make up your own data to test the program.

5. A rubber ball initially at rest 72 inches above the ground is allowed to fall. The ball bounces several times, eventually coming to rest on the ground. On each bounce the ball rebounds one-third of the distance through which it fell. Compute and print the height of the ball on each bounce until the ball stops bouncing. (Use the integer mode for the calculation.)

6. IQ University charges $90 for each semester hour of credit, $200 per term for a regular room, $250 per term for an air-conditioned room, and $400 per term for food. All students are charged a $30 matriculation fee. Graduating students must also pay a $35 diploma fee. Write a program that computes the fees which must be paid by a set of students.

7. The surface area and volume of a sphere is needed for a large number of spheres. The area is given by $4\pi r^2$, and the volume is given by $4/3\pi r^3$, where r is the radius of the sphere and π is 3.141593. Write a program that computes and prints surface area and volume for each sphere.

8. At $0°C$ the pressure of 1 mole of O_2 gas as a function of the volume in which the gas is confined can be computed using the equation

$$P = \frac{22.414}{V - 0.0318} - \frac{1.36}{V^2}$$

where the volume is in liters and the pressure is in atmospheres. Compute the pressure exerted by O_2 when it is confined to volumes from 1 to 50 liters. Make the calculations at intervals of 1 liter.

9. The grade-point average for a student is computed by dividing the total quality credits earned by the number of semester hours attempted. Quality credits per semester hour depend upon the grade according to the scheme

Grade	Quality points per semester hour
A	4
B	3
C	2
D	1
All other	0

Compute and print the grade-point average for each student in a group of students. Each student will have several adjacent data cards, and the number of cards may not be the same for each student. Encode the grade as 1, 2, 3, 4, and 5 for A, B, C, D, and other, respectively. A data card should contain a student ID code, a code for the grade, and the number of semester hours of credit for the course. Print all input data.

CHAPTER 7 MORE INPUT/OUTPUT

In computing, many situations arise in which it is essential to have more control over the input and output of values than is possible with list-directed techniques. As more input data are required in a problem, it becomes important to organize the data in a systematic manner. This can save computer time, facilitate the keypunching of data by more than one person, and reduce the number of errors in the data. Explicit control of the printing position of output values is often a requirement for computer-printed reports. For example, in the printing of a payroll check, the amount of the check must be placed in a particular location determined by the preprinted form of the check; the employee's identification number, social security tax, state tax, federal tax, and so on, must also be printed in specific predetermined positions. Almost all computer-printed reports for business have this property of requiring that values be printed in predetermined positions. Also, scientific and statistical reports are easier to read and interpret when the data are printed with appropriate titles, column headings, and other explanatory information. In general, computer-printed reports should contain enough information to be self-explanatory.

7.1 SIMPLE FORMAT STATEMENTS AND READING OF DATA

7.1.1 Integer-Mode Specification

Control of the location of values in input and output is obtained by using a FORMAT statement in conjunction with a READ or WRITE statement. For information punched into a card or printed on a line, the FORMAT statement gives the position and other descriptive information for the values that are to be read or printed. Let us examine a few examples before we list the rules. For the pair of statements

READ (5,1000) NEXT, MAX, MIN
1000 FORMAT (I10,I5,I12)

1. The asterisk within the parentheses of the READ statement has been replaced by the number of the FORMAT statement, 1000, which the READ statement will use.
2. Enclosed within the parentheses of the FORMAT statement is a shorthand description of the card from which the values of NEXT, MAX, and MIN will be read.

a. The notation I10 specifies that an integer value is to be read from a field 10 columns wide; that is,

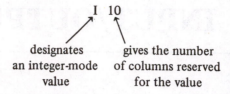

I 5 specifies an integer field 5 columns wide, and I12 specifies an integer field 12 columns wide.

b. Considering the specifications in the FORMAT statement in order of their left-to-right occurrence, the following description of the input card can be constructed:

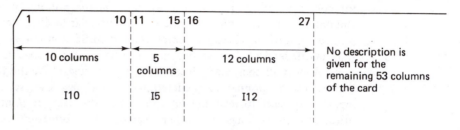

3. The variables in the READ statement are to be associated (in order of their appearance in the list of variables) with the fields specified in the FORMAT statement. Thus the associations are

READ (5,1000) NEXT, MAX, MIN

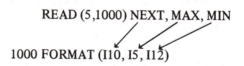

1000 FORMAT (I10, I5, I12)

or in pictorial form the data card will be

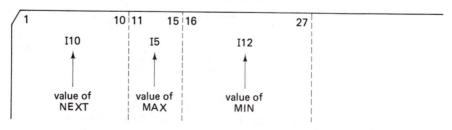

This READ statement can be paraphrased in English as:

Using the standard input device and the FORMAT statement 1000 as a guide to the location of values, read the value of NEXT, followed by the value of MAX, followed by the value of MIN.

Consider the pair of statements

READ (5,1005) I,K
1005 FORMAT (I7,I8)

These statements specify that the value of I is to be read from the first 7 columns of a card, and the value of K is to be read from the next 8 columns, that is, columns 8 to 15.

Here is a tricky example:

READ (5,1010) K,L,M,N
1010 FORMAT (I10)

The FORMAT statement describes a card containing only one field, which appears in columns 1 to 10; so how can the computer read the values of the four variables K, L, M, and N? The computer must read values from four consecutive cards. Thus, the specifications in the FORMAT statement will be repeated for subsequent cards, as needed, to complete the reading of the values. (*Note:* This rule applies regardless of the mode of the variables.)

Integer values should be punched into fields in data cards right-justified; that is, the rightmost digit of the number should always be placed in the rightmost column of the field. Blank columns, if any, should always appear to the left of the number. Failure to remember and use this rule will cause a value different from what you intended to be associated with the number. Suppose that you intend for the value 37 to be read and associated with the variable NUM using the statements

READ (5,1020) NUM
1020 FORMAT (I5)

Then the possible ways of punching 37 into the field of the data card are ("b" is used to designate a "blank" column) as follows:

bbb37	Correct
bb37b	Incorrect: gives 370 as the value
b37bb	Incorrect: gives 3700 as the value
37bbb	Incorrect: gives 37000 or, depending upon the computer, a different negative number as the value (because of integer overflow), or "VALUE OUT OF RANGE"

7.1.2 Real-Mode Specifications

Real values are specified in FORMAT statements by abbreviations of the type F10.2, where the F means *floating-point number* (a synonym for real number), the 10 gives the field width on the data card, and the .2 gives the number of digits to the right of the decimal. Some typical real-mode specifications are

Specification	Field width	Digits to right of decimal
F10.2	10	2
F8.4	8	4
F12.6	12	6
F5.0	5	0
F10.5	10	5

READ and FORMAT statements are used for reading real values in a way that is almost identical with the procedure described for integer values. The major modification is to use real specifications in the FORMAT statement instead of integer specifications. The statement

1030 FORMAT (F10.2, F5.0, F12.4)

describes a data card containing three consecutive fields for real values in columns 1 to 10, 11 to 15, and 16 to 27:

The statements

READ (5,1030) X,Y,Z

1030 FORMAT (F10.2, F5.0, F12.4)

would result in the reading of the values of X, Y, and Z from a data card having the fields just described. When the values are keypunched into the data card, ordinarily the decimal should also be punched.

Actually, keypunching the decimal is optional, but you must be careful if you omit it. For reading a real value, the compiler generates a sequence of machine instructions that performs the following actions:

1. Scan the field in the data card as specified in the FORMAT statement searching for a decimal.
2. If a decimal is found, store the numerical value actually found in the field and ignore the d part of the specification F$w.d$, where w represents the width of the field on the data card and d represents the number of digits to the right of the decimal (for that case when no decimal is punched in the data card).
3. If no decimal is found, use the d part of the specification F$w.d$ to determine the numerical value.
   a. Find the right-hand boundary of the field.
   b. Count digits, right to left, from the boundary.
   c. Assume the decimal to be just to the left of the dth digit.

For example, suppose that the pair of statements

$$\text{READ } (5,1200) \text{ XY}$$
$$1200 \text{ FORMAT } (F7.1)$$

are used to read the data card

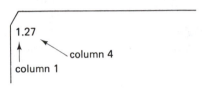

Then the value read and stored in computer memory will be 1.27 (actually, it is stored in exponential form). If the same pair of statements is used to read the card

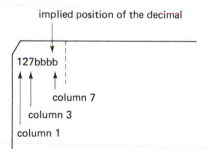

the value stored in memory will be 127000.0, because the specification F7.1 infers that the decimal is immediately to the left of the rightmost position in the field. This leads to the following rule:

If a decimal is punched as part of a real number, the number can be placed anywhere in its field. If the decimal is omitted from a real number, the value should be right-justified and decimal-aligned in its field.

7.1.3 Both Integer- and Real-Mode Specifications in a FORMAT Statement

Both integer and real values can be read from the same card provided that the mode of the variables match in both the READ and FORMAT statements. Examples of valid pairs of statements are

READ (5,1040) X, I, Y

real / integer/ real

1040 FORMAT (F8.2, I10, F12.4)

READ (5,1045) X, N, M

1045 FORMAT (F10.2, I6, I10)

READ (5,1050) L, K, A

1050 FORMAT (I10, I10, F10.4)

Two examples of pairs of statements that are invalid because of invalid matching of modes of variables and specifications are

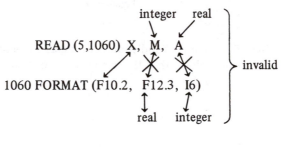

integer   real

READ (5,1060) X, M, A

1060 FORMAT (F10.2, F12.3, I6)   } invalid

real   integer

integer

READ (5,1065) K, L

1065 FORMAT (I10, F12.4)   } invalid

real

7.1.4 Nonexecutability of FORMAT Statements

Throughout this discussion, FORMAT statements have been used to describe the fields in a data card. In the next section, you will see that FORMAT statements are also used to describe fields in a print line. In both cases, FORMAT statements provide purely descriptive information, and they do not cause any action to occur. Like declaration statements, FORMAT statements are nonexecutable. In addition, they can be referenced by more than one statement. For example,

$$\text{READ (5,1070) A, B, N}$$
$$\text{1070 FORMAT (F10.0, F10.2, I5)}$$
$$\text{READ (5,1070) X, Y}$$

is a valid sequence of statements with the first READ statement using all three specifications and the second READ statement using only the first two specifications.

FORMAT statements can be placed anywhere in a program. We will use the convention of placing them after the declaration statements (if any) and before the first executable statement.

7.1.5   Summary of READ and FORMAT Statements

Simple Standard READ Statement

   A. *Form*

$$\text{READ } (a,b) \text{ } list$$

   where *a*   is an unsigned (without + or −) integer constant or an integer variable that is the code for the input device to be used (e.g., card reader)
   b   is an unsigned integer constant that identifies the corresponding FORMAT statement (e.g., 15, 100, 1070)
   list   is a series of names of variables (e.g., A, B, X, NUM) separated by commas

   B. *Rules*
   1. The *list* may contain any number of variables.
   2. Both integer and real variables may appear in any sequence in the *list*.
   3. Each time a READ statement is executed, at least one card will be read.

FORMAT Statement

   A. *Form*

$$b \text{ FORMAT (list of specifications)}$$

   where *b* is an unsigned integer constant used as a statement number to identify the FORMAT statement (e.g., 15, 1070)

Possible specifications (so far) that can appear in the list of specifications are:

Specification type	Form
Integer	I*w*
Real	F*w.d*

where *w* is the width of a field (i.e., number of columns in a field)

d is the number of digits to the right of the decimal

B. *Rules*
   1. FORMAT statements are not executable.
   2. Each must have a unique statement number.
   3. The list of specifications must agree in mode with corresponding variables in any READ statement that references the FORMAT statement.
   4. FORMAT statements may be referenced by more than one READ statement.
   5. FORMAT statements may be placed anywhere in a program.
   6. The set of specifications in a FORMAT statement will be repeated as needed in reading values for variables appearing in a READ statement. (Every new repetition of FORMAT specification implies that a new card is to be read.)

7.2 SIMPLE FORMAT STATEMENTS AND OUTPUT OF DATA

Using a FORMAT statement and a WRITE statement to control the output of data is similar, in many respects, to the input technique just described. The pair of statements

$$\text{WRITE (6,1000) NEXT, MAX, MIN}$$
$$\text{1000 FORMAT (I10, I5, I12)}$$

causes the values of NEXT, MAX, and MIN to be printed on a line. The variables in left-to-right order are associated with the specifications in the FORMAT statement in their left-to-right order, just as was the case for READ and FORMAT pairs:

$$\text{WRITE (6,1000) NEXT, MAX, MIN}$$

$$\text{1000 FORMAT (I10, I5, I12)}$$

Thus this WRITE statement can be paraphrased in English as

Using the standard output device and the FORMAT statement 1000 as a guide to where to print values on a line, print the value of NEXT, followed by the value of MAX, followed by the value of MIN.

For values of 207, 7536, and 193 for NEXT, MAX, and MIN, respectively, the printed line would be

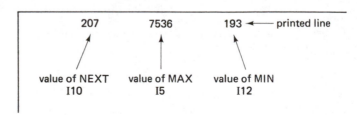

Values of variables are output as the result of the execution of the WRITE statement, which has the form

$$\text{WRITE } (a,b) \text{ } list$$

where *a* is an unsigned integer constant or an integer variable that is the code for the output device to be used (e.g., printer)

  b is an unsigned integer constant that identifies the corresponding FORMAT statement (e.g., 15, 100, 1070)

  list is a series of names of variables (e.g., A, B, X, NUM) separated by commas

7.2.1 Carriage Control

The printing of values differs from the reading of values in a very significant way. When values are printed, both their left-to-right and their up-down positions on the page need to be specified in the program; but when values are read, only information about their left-to-right location is required. Output from a computer needs to be designed in the same way a letter or other document is designed. Questions such as:

1. Should this line be printed at the top of a new page?
2. Should this value be printed on the same line as the last value?
3. Should the report be single-, double-, or triple-spaced?

must be considered. Vertical spacing on a page is indicated by including *carriage control* information (recall that a typewriter has a carriage control lever or a return button) as the first item of information in a FORMAT statement used to describe output. The general form is

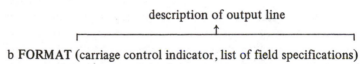

The carriage control indicators are given in Table 7.1.

TABLE 7.1 *Carriage control indicators*[a]

Indicator	Interpretation
1	Skip to a new page before printing
+	Print on the same line as before
b (blank)	Skip to a new line before printing (single spacing)
0	Skip twice before printing (double spacing)

[a] Any character not listed above that appears in the carriage control position will cause single spacing.

Several techniques are available for placing the carriage control character in the FORMAT statement. The simplest involves enclosing the indicator in apostrophes. To print the values of NEXT, MAX, and MIN on a line at the top of a new page, one writes

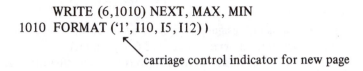

```
      WRITE (6,1010) NEXT, MAX, MIN
1010  FORMAT ('1', I10, I5, I12) )
```

carriage control indicator for new page

Other possibilities are

```
      WRITE (6,1015) NEXT, MAX, MIN
1015  FORMAT (' ', I10, I5, I12)
```

single spacing [keypunch by hitting the apostrophe (') key, followed by the space bar, followed by the apostrophe key]

```
      WRITE (6,1020) NEXT, MAX, MIN
1020  FORMAT ('0', I10, I5, I12)
```

double spacing

```
      WRITE (6,1025) NEXT, MAX, MIN
1025  FORMAT ('+', I10, I5, I12)
```

same line as last printed line

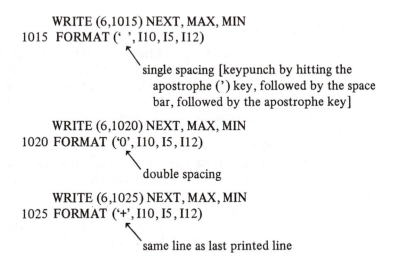

Care must be exercised when printing on the same line as the preceding line to avoid printing on top of previous results, a process known as overprinting.

Another method for indicating the carriage control is to omit the apostrophes and place 1H before the carriage control character. Using this technique gives the following for the previous examples:

```
        WRITE (6,1030) NEXT, MAX, MIN
1030 FORMAT (1H1, I10, I5, I12)
```

↖ new page

```
        WRITE (6,1035) NEXT, MAX, MIN
1035 FORMAT (1H , I10, I5, I12)
```

↖ single spacing (blank space)

```
        WRITE (6,1040) NEXT, MAX, MIN
1040 FORMAT (1H0, I10, I5, I12)
```

↖ double spacing

```
        WRITE (6,1045) NEXT, MAX, MIN
1045 FORMAT (1H+, I10, I5, I12)
```

↖ same line

Discussion of why this works will be given in the section on Hollerith specification (Section 7.3.4).

If you omit the carriage control character from the FORMAT statement, the printout may have an unexpected appearance. The problem is that whenever an output line is printed, a carriage control character is always used—whether you planned it or not. The rule is:

The first character in an output line is *always* used as the carriage control indicator.

This rule is the reason why the carriage control indicator was placed to the left of the other specifications in the FORMAT statement.

In constructing printed reports, it is helpful to visualize the printing of each line using the following model:

1. All information to be printed must first be placed in an *output buffer*. The buffer is a set of memory cells having room to contain the carriage control character plus as many more characters as can be printed on a line (usually 132 characters).
2. A program is executing, and an instruction is encountered to write values. This causes the execution of instructions to:
   a. Fill the output buffer—all 133 positions (carriage control plus 132 character positions)—with the code for a "blank."
   b. Move the data values into the buffer in order of their left-to-right appearance, always filling in the carriage control position first.
   c. Print the contents of the buffer on a line after the values have been placed in the buffer.

Let us observe the operation of this model for a case in which the carriage control character is explicitly placed in the FORMAT statement and for a case in which the carriage control character is merely implied. For both cases, the following values are assumed:

$$NEXT \quad 207$$
$$MAX \quad 7536$$
$$MIN \quad 193$$

For the pair of statements

WRITE (6,1010) NEXT, MAX, MIN
1010 FORMAT ('1', I10, I5, I12)

the buffer is filled with blanks, and then values are moved into the buffer to give

PRINT BUFFER

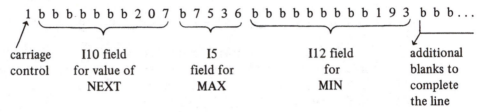

Next, an instruction is executed to print the contents of the buffer. Since the first character in the buffer is 1, a skip is made to the beginning of a new page, and the rest of the buffer contents are printed:

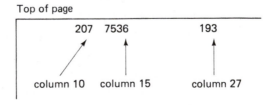

In contrast, consider the pair of statements

WRITE (6,1050) NEXT, MAX, MIN
1050 FORMAT (I10, I5, I12)

in which the FORMAT statement does not explicitly contain a carriage control character. Since there is no explicit carriage control character, the leftmost blank in the field for NEXT goes into the carriage control position of the print buffer, giving:

PRINT BUFFER

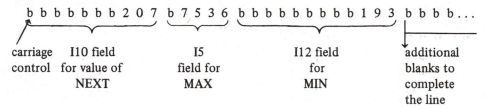

When the instruction is executed to print the contents of the buffer, a blank is used as the carriage control indicator, causing a skip to the next line. The result is:

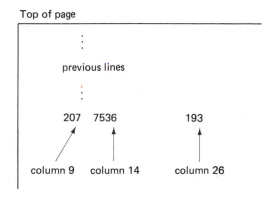

An important side effect of implying the carriage control character has been the shifting of the fields one column to the left on the printed line—the effective width of the field for NEXT is 9 columns (instead of 10), since the leftmost character in the field is used for carriage control and is not printed.

Consider as another example the printing of the values for KX and LX:

$$KX \quad 189$$

$$LX \quad 407$$

using the pair of statements

WRITE (6,1055) KX, LX
1055 FORMAT (I3, I5)

Test your understanding by deciding what the output will be before you examine the following explanation:

There is no explicit carriage control character, so the leftmost of the I3 field for KX will be used for carriage control. This gives for the print buffer:

PRINT BUFFER

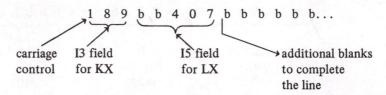

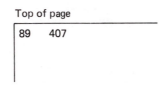

This time the most significant digit of 189 goes into the carriage control position. The result is the skipping to the top of a new page, and the printing of the remaining part of the line.

Top of page

89   407

Consider the following portion of a program:

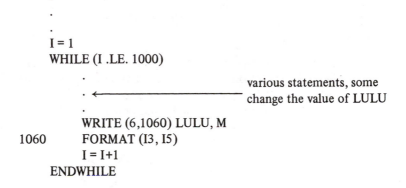

```
        .
        .
        .
        I = 1
        WHILE (I .LE. 1000)
            .
            .                     various statements, some
            .                     change the value of LULU
            WRITE (6,1060) LULU, M
1060        FORMAT (I3, I5)
            I = I+1
        ENDWHILE
```

Suppose that the value of LULU always falls between 100 and 199. Every time the WRITE statement is executed, the leftmost digit of the value of LULU, 1, will be used for carriage control. One thousand pages will be printed, one line per page, with the value of LULU being printed incorrectly. (I have seen fast printers literally spray paper across a room because of this error. Computer-center directors frown on such use of the computer.) The same ideas apply to real numbers.

One of our design goals for writing programs is to make the purpose of each step in the program as clear and obvious as possible. Consequently, we will adopt the convention of always stating explicitly the carriage control character and always enclosing it in apostrophes. Therefore, FORMAT statements used for output on a line printer will begin with the carriage control character enclosed in apostrophes.

7.2.2 Output of Values

The rules for using FORMAT statements for input of values also apply to the output of values if the following two additional rules are included:

1. Carriage control must be considered for output.
2. More digits, usually 132, can be printed on a line than can be read from a card.

The following are valid examples of WRITE and FORMAT statements:

```
      WRITE (6,1000) NEXT, MAX, MIN
1000 FORMAT ('1', I10, I5, I12)

      WRITE (6, 1005) I, K
1005 FORMAT ('b', I7, I8)
```

```
      WRITE (6,1010) K,L,M,N
1010 FORMAT ('1', I10)
```
uses four pages for printing, placing one value at the top of each page

```
      WRITE (6,1011) K,L,M,N
1011 FORMAT ('b', I10)
```
uses one page for printing, placing a value at the left of four different lines

```
      WRITE (6,1020) NUM
1020 FORMAT ('0', I5)

      WRITE (6,1030) X,Y,Z
1030 FORMAT (' ', F10.2, F5.0, F12.4)

      WRITE (6,1040) X,I,Y
1040 FORMAT (' ', F8.2, I10, F12.4)

      WRITE (6,1045) X,N,M
1045 FORMAT (' ', F10.2, I6, I10)

      WRITE (6,1050) L,K,A
1050 FORMAT ('1', I10, I10, F10.4)
```

These examples are simple modifications of the READ and FORMAT pairs that were discussed earlier. The READ has been changed to WRITE, the device code has been changed from 5 to 6, and a carriage control character has been inserted in the FORMAT statements.

When a report is being designed, it is necessary to consider the rules for actual printing of values in their fields. These rules are:

1. Values are *always* printed right-justified in their fields. This is true of both integers and real values. For example, for the values INT = 517 and RELX =

236.457 the statements

WRITE (6,1105) INT, RELX
1105 FORMAT (' ', I5, F10.3)

will print values as

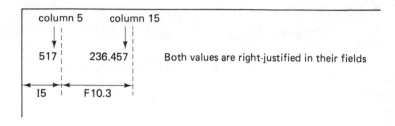

2. The decimal is *always* printed when real values are printed. Thus, the decimal occupies one of the columns of the field and reduces by one the number of columns actually available for printing the digits of the real value.
3. In printing values, the *d* portion of the specification F*w.d* indicates the number of digits that will be printed to the right of the decimal. Additional digits to the right of the decimal are dropped in the printing process, but no change is made in the value of the number in computer memory. For example, consider the printing of different values of X using the statements

WRITE (6,1110) X
1110 FORMAT (' ', F7.2)

Actual value of X in computer memory	Value of X as printed
.0602753	.06
.0075327	.00
.0000989	.00
1.009999	1.00
436.8507	436.85
7056.098	7056.09
− 0.07999999	− 0.07
− 23.18754	− 23.18

4. Attempts to print a value that is too large to fit into a specified field results in an error during the execution of the program, causing the field to be filled with some special character such as an asterisk. (The actual character used depends upon the compiler.) Consider the following examples:

Given:

WRITE (6,1120) INT
1120 FORMAT (' ', I4)

then:

Actual value of INT in computer memory	Value of INT as printed	Comments
397	397	O.K.
20563	*****	Five digits cannot fit in the space reserved for four digits
- 302	- 302	O.K.
- 5981	*****	A column is needed for the negative sign
-31705	*****	Six columns are needed

Given:

WRITE (6,1130) ROOT
1130 FORMAT (' ', F5.2)

then:

Actual value of ROOT in computer memory	Value of ROOT as printed	Comments
27.90367	27.90	O.K.
- 27.90367	*****	Six columns are needed
693.4213	*****	Six columns are needed
4.365842	4.36	O.K.
- 6.403276	- 6.40	O.K.
463905.2	*****	Nine columns are needed
- 463905.2	*****	Ten columns are needed

7.3 LITERAL DATA

Literal data are groups of characters that appear in FORMAT statements in the actual (hence, the term literal) form in which they are to be printed. Techniques involving literal data can be used for printing titles, column headings, or other information that would make a computer printed report more understandable.

7.3.1 The Apostrophe Technique

A particularly convenient and easy technique for manipulating literal data involves enclosing the group of characters in apostrophes and placing them within a FORMAT statement. For example, the statements

WRITE (6,1200)
1200 FORMAT ('1', 'SAMPLE REPORT')

will cause the phrase SAMPLE REPORT to be printed at the top of a page as

SAMPLE REPORT

Notice that:

1. The WRITE statement did not include the names of any variables. The inclusion of such names is optional; but if the name of one or more variables is included, each must have a proper specification and obey the rules cited earlier for WRITE and FORMAT statements.
2. The literal data SAMPLE REPORT is enclosed in apostrophes and follows, in this example, the carriage control character.
3. The carriage control character, 1, is also an example of literal data.

If the carriage control character had been omitted from the FORMAT statement to give

WRITE (6,1210)
1210 FORMAT ('SAMPLE REPORT')

the execution of the WRITE statement would have caused the S in SAMPLE to be used as the carriage control character. The result would be the printing of the phrase

AMPLE REPORT

at the left edge of the next line.

Literal data may be interspersed in any sequence with other specifications in a FORMAT statement. Some examples are:

WRITE (6,1220) X
1220 FORMAT ('1', 'Xb=b', F10.2)   (*b* indicates blank)

WRITE (6,1230) X
1230 FORMAT ('0', F10.2, 'bIS THE VALUE OF X')

WRITE (6,1240) X,Y
1240 FORMAT ('0', 'Xb=b', F10.2, 'bbYb=b', F10.2)

For values of X and Y of 313.2763 and 40726.12, respectively, these statements would print

```
X =     313.27

      313.27 IS THE VALUE OF X

X =        313.27   Y =    40726.12
```

Blank characters (spaces obtained by depressing the space bar of the keypunch) within literal data are treated as legitimate alphabetic characters that are to be encoded and stored within the computer's memory as part of the literal string of characters. A programmer must give attention to what blank spaces are needed. In FORMAT statement 1230, omission of the leading blank in "bIS THE VALUE OF X," that is,

1230 FORMAT ('0', F10.2, 'IS THE VALUE OF X')

would cause the rightmost digit of X and the I of IS to print adjacent to each other.

```
bbbb313.27IS THE VALUE OF X
```

Suppose that it is necessary to print the values of X and Y on a line in a similar manner to that described by FORMAT statement 1240, but with the information for X and Y separated by 10 additional blanks. Two methods of accomplishing this are

WRITE (6,1250) X,Y
1250 FORMAT ('0', 'Xb=b', F10.2, 'bbbbbbbbbb', 'bbYb=b', F10.2)

                                    10 blanks

WRITE (6,1260) X,Y
1260 FORMAT ('0', 'Xb=b', F10.2, 'bbbbbbbbbbbbYb=b', F10.2)

                                    10 blanks

In both cases the spacing across the line is accomplished by inserting 10 additional blank spaces. This technique of inserting blanks will always work, but it is not always convenient—inserting exactly 85 blanks would be an aggravation.

7.3.2   Skip Specification

It can be awkward to use the technique of introducing blank characters that was illustrated at the end of the preceding section. The spacing of literal data and values of variables across a line is simplified by using the skip specification, which has the form

$$nX$$

where X is interpreted as "skip a column" (or "insert a blank character").
n is an unsigned-integer constant, which gives the number of times the skip is to be repeated

Thus

2X   means   skip 2 columns (or insert 2 blanks)

5X   means   skip 5 columns (or insert 5 blanks)

85X   means   skip 85 columns (or insert 85 blanks)

With the skip specification, the FORMAT statement 1250 of the preceding section can be rewritten in a variety of equivalent ways. The statement was

1250 FORMAT ('0', 'Xb=b', F10.2, 'bbbbbbbbbb', 'bbYb=b', F10.2)

Equivalent forms are

1251 FORMAT ('0', 'Xb=b', F10.2, 10X, 'bbYb=b', F10.2)

replaces 'bbbbbbbbbb'

1252 FORMAT ('0', 'Xb=b', F10.2, 12X, 'Yb=b', F10.2)

replaces 'bbbbbbbbbb' and 2 blanks of 'bbYb=b'

1253 FORMAT ('0', 'Xb=', 1X, F10.2, 12X, 'Yb=', 1X, F10.2)

replaces last blank in 'Xb=b'

replaces last blank in 'Yb=b'

7.3.3 Tabulation Specification

The tabulation specification allows the programmer to space items across a line and to avoid the counting of blanks to achieve the spacing. The form of the tabulation specification is

$$Tn$$

where T means tabulate

n is an unsigned integer constant that is the character number (counting carriage control as 1 space) at which the printing will begin for the item immediately following the T specification

The statements

WRITE (6,1250) X, Y
1250 FORMAT ('0', 'Xb=b', F10.2, 'bbbbbbbbbb', 'bbYb=b', F10.2)

with values of 313.2763 and 40726.12 for X and Y, respectively, produce the following line:

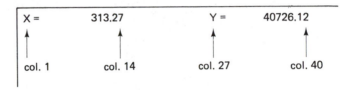

X =	313.27	Y =	40726.12
col. 1	col. 14	col. 27	col. 40

in which the literal 'Yb=b' starts in column 27. This literal could have been located directly at column 27 by preceding it with the specification T28.

WRITE (6,1254) X, Y
1254 FORMAT ('0', 'Xb=b', F10.2, T28, 'Yb=b', F10.2)

causes tabulation to column 27

Suppose that a programmer wishes to print the title SAMPLE REPORT centered at the top of a page. Then the programmer must decide to what column he or she must tabulate before beginning the printing. (This is exactly the same problem a typist would have in preparing a report.) The title contains 13 characters (do not forget the blank that separates the two words in the title) and a printline contains 132 positions; thus starting the word SAMPLE in column 61 will center the title. WRITE and FORMAT statements to accomplish this are

WRITE (6,1270)
1270 FORMAT ('1', T62, 'SAMPLE REPORT')

7.3.4 Hollerith Specification

The "standard" technique for manipulating literal data uses Hollerith specification, which was named in honor of Herman Hollerith, who invented the card code used by keypunches. In this section, the word "standard" means that Hollerith specification is included in nearly every FORTRAN compiler and is thus a standard feature. It does not mean that Hollerith specification is the most frequently used method for manipulating literal data. In fact, programmers tend to use the apostrophe technique if it is a feature of the available compiler.

The form of Hollerith specification is

nH

where H identifies the specification as being Hollerith type, which applies to the
     literal data that follow the H

    n is an unsigned integer constant, which gives the number of literal data char-
     acters that follow the H

To use this specification, place an H immediately before the sequence of literal data characters and place the count of the characters before the H. The count followed by H, in effect, replaces the opening and closing apostrophes used previously to indicate literal data. For example,

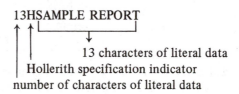

13HSAMPLE REPORT

                  13 characters of literal data
     Hollerith specification indicator
number of characters of literal data

Hollerith-specified data in a FORMAT statement will be printed exactly as it appears (unless it is in the carriage control character position). Thus FORMAT statement 1270 could be rewritten as

WRITE (6,1271)
1271 FORMAT (1H1, T62, 13HSAMPLE REPORT)

where Hollerith specification has been used for both the carriage control character and the title.

Other examples of the use of Hollerith specification are

WRITE (6,1300) X
1300 FORMAT (1H1, 3HX=b, F10.2)

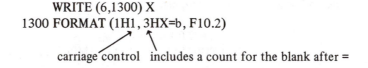

       carriage control   includes a count for the blank after =

```
      WRITE (6,1310) X
1310 FORMAT (1H0, F10.2, 18H IS THE VALUE OF X)
```

carriage control   includes in the count 5 blanks
(note that a blank precedes I in IS)

```
      WRITE (6,1320) X, Y
1320 FORMAT (1H0, 4HXb=b, F10.2, 6HbbYb=b, F10.2)
```

```
      WRITE (6,1330) X, Y
1330 FORMAT (1H0, 4HXb=b, F10.2, T29, 4HYb=b, F10.2)
```

Failure to count literal data characters properly can prevent the program from compiling when Hollerith specification is being used. In the statement

```
1371 FORMAT (1H1, T62, 14HSAMPLE REPORT)
```

too large; counts concluding parenthesis

the last Hollerith count (14) is too large, so it includes the last parenthesis. The compiler therefore considers the last parenthesis to be part of the literal data, which causes the FORMAT statement not to have a concluding parenthesis. This is a syntax error. If the statement is accidentally written as

not counted

```
1372 FORMAT (1H1, T62, 12HSAMPLE REPORT)
```

the literal data string is considered to end with the second R in REPORT. The T that follows the R has no legitimate interpretation by the compiler and a syntax error results. Be very careful when using this Hollerith technique, especially when the literal data string contains blanks! In other words, I hope you have a compiler that allows the apostrophe technique to be used.

7.4   PRINTING REPORTS

The designing of the report(s) to be printed by a program is a major part of the planning process, especially for business-oriented programs. It is not unusual for the details of a computer application to be poorly defined, and the process of completely specifying the output by explicitly describing the reports can be quite helpful in clarifying the problem. Systems analysts, computer specialists who design large-scale computer applications for business and government, produce hand-generated dummy reports as a standard procedure early in the design process. By reviewing the reports with those who requested them, revising the reports, and repeating the review and revision stages as needed, systems analysts clarify the problem they have been asked to solve. Unless you know exactly what your program is to print and, in some cases, where the information is to be printed on a page, you are not ready to write the program.

Suppose that you have been asked to print a conversion chart for Celsius to Fahrenheit temperatures. The first step should be to design the output, which should have:

1. A title

TEMPERATURE CONVERSION TABLE

2. Three headings

        LINE   for line number

        CELSIUS   for the Celsius temperature

        FAHRENHEIT   for the Fahrenheit temperature

3. Values printed under the three headings.

The title contains 28 characters, so 14 characters should appear to each side of the middle of the top line of the report. Consequently, the title should begin in column 53. The heading LINE will be started in column 11 to give a 10-space left-hand margin. (This decision and the subsequent ones described here are arbitrary.) Since a 10-space margin is on the left, a similar margin will be used on the right-hand edge of the page. Thus the heading FAHRENHEIT must end in column 122, which requires that it begin in column 113. The heading CELSIUS will be centered on a line, so it must start in column 65. This gives

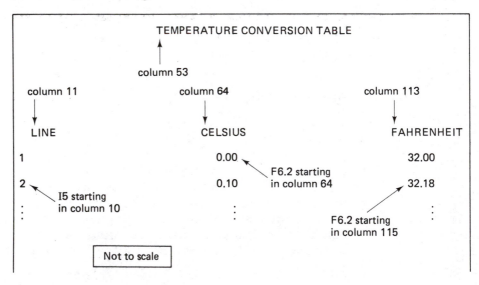

Additional information about the type and location of the data fields has been included in the diagram. Single spacing of data lines is assumed. A blank line is to be inserted between the title and the headings. With the information provided by the report design, it is easy to write the corresponding WRITE and FORMAT statements.

1. *Title*

```
WRITE (6,1000)
1000 FORMAT ('1', T54, 'TEMPERATURE CONVERSION TABLE')
```

2. *Headings*

```
WRITE (6,1010)
1010 FORMAT ('0', T12, 'LINE', T65, 'CELSIUS', T114, 'FAHRENHEIT')
```

3. *Output data*

```
WRITE (6,1020) LINENO, C, F
1020 FORMAT ('b', T11, I5, T65, F6.2, T116, F6.2)
```

A program that produces this report starting with C = 0.0 and proceeding in steps of 0.10°C through 100°C is

```
1000 FORMAT ('1', T54, 'TEMPERATURE CONVERSION TABLE')
1010 FORMAT ('0', T12, 'LINE', T65, 'CELSIUS', T114, 'FAHRENHEIT')
1020 FORMAT ('b', T11, I5, T65, F6.2, T116, F6.2)
     C = 0.0
     LINENO = 1
     Q = 9./5.
     WRITE (6,1000)
     WRITE (6,1010)
     WHILE (C .LE. 100.)
         F = Q*C + 32.
         WRITE (6,1020) LINENO, C, F
         C = C + 0.1
         LINENO = LINENO + 1
     ENDWHILE
     STOP
     END
```

Computer output for this program is given in Figure 7.1. The output contains a surprise—the printing stops with a value of 99.90 for Celsius instead of 100.00. The reason for this will be discussed in Chapter 8.

Changes that are considered trivial by users of reports sometimes require extensive changes in the program. As a simple illustration, suppose that the user later de-

```
 1 C
 2 C           TEMPERATURE CONVERSION TABLE
 3 C           CELSIUS TO FAHRENHEIT
 4 C
 5  1000 FORMAT('1',T54,'TEMPERATURE CONVERSION TABLE')
 6  1010 FORMAT('0',T12,'LINE',T65,'CELSIUS',T114,'FAHRENHEIT')
 7  1020 FORMAT(' ',T11,I5,T65,F6.2,T116,F6.2)
 8       C=0.0
 9       LINENO=1
10       Q=9./5.
11       WRITE(6,1000)
12       WRITE(6,1010)
13       WHILE( C .LE. 100.)
14          F=Q*C+32.
15          WRITE(6,1020)LINENO,C,F
16          C=C+0.1
17          LINENO=LINENO+1
18       ENDWHILE
19       STOP
20       END
```

TEMPERATURE CONVERSION TABLE

LINE	CELSIUS	FAHRENHEIT
1	.00	32.00
2	.10	32.18
3	.20	32.36
4	.30	32.54
5	.40	32.72
6	.50	32.90
7	.60	33.08
8	.70	33.26
9	.80	33.44
10	.90	33.62
11	1.00	33.80
12	1.10	33.98
13	1.20	34.16
14	1.30	34.34
.	.	.
.	.	.
.	.	.
.	.	.
987	98.60	209.48
988	98.70	209.66
989	98.80	209.84
990	98.90	210.02
991	99.00	210.20
992	99.10	210.38
993	99.20	210.56
994	99.30	210.74
995	99.40	210.92
996	99.50	211.10
997	99.60	211.28
998	99.70	211.46
999	99.80	211.64
1000	99.90	211.82

FIGURE 7.1   *Temperature conversion table*

cides that he or she wants the headings printed at the top of every page. To accomplish this, the number of lines printed on a page must be counted. An IF statement must be inserted before the printing of values to test the count for completion of the page.

.
.
.

```
IF (count of lines on page indicates a complete page) THEN
    skip to a new page
    write headings
    reset count of lines on a page
ENDIF
```

If we assume that 55 data lines should be written on a page, a suitable program would be

```
1000 FORMAT ('1', T54, 'TEMPERATURE CONVERSION TABLE')
1010 FORMAT ('0', T12, 'LINE', T65, 'CELSIUS', T114, 'FAHRENHEIT')
1020 FORMAT ('b', T11, I5, T65, F6.2, T116, F6.2)
1030 FORMAT ('1')
     C = 0.0
     LINENO = 1
     LPAGE = 1
     Q = 9./5.
     WRITE (6,1000)
     WRITE (6,1010)
     WHILE (C .LE. 100.)
        F = Q*C + 32.
        IF (LPAGE .GT. 55) THEN
            WRITE (6,1030)
            WRITE (6,1010)
            LPAGE = 1
        ENDIF
        WRITE (6,1020) LINENO, C, F
        C = C + 0.1
        LPAGE = LPAGE + 1
        LINENO = LINENO + 1
     ENDWHILE
     STOP
     END
```

Making this modification in the program required the addition of eight lines to the program.

How could the program be modified to print TEMPERATURE CONVERSION TABLE–CONTINUED at the top of each page? See if you can generalize the program to print the data lines single-spaced, double-spaced, or triple-spaced, depending upon the value of an indicator read at the beginning of program execution. You can also generalize the program to work for any interval of degrees Celsius, not just 0.10°C.

The output of the payroll report program discussed in Chapter 6 can be significantly improved by including statements to print a title and headings. For the report we need:

1. *Title*

PAYROLL REPORT

2. *Headings*

EMPLOYEE NUMBER
HOURS
RATE
DEDUCTION
GROSS PAY
NET PAY
OVERTIME PAY

The spacing between the headings must be determined (usually finding a reasonable spacing involves some trial and error). Using the same number of columns for each heading is often a good first guess. Using 15 columns for each heading appears to be satisfactory in this case, since $7 \times 15 = 105$, leaving $132 - 105 = 27$ columns to be divided between the left and right margins. We will arbitrarily use 15 of the spaces for the left margin, leaving 12 for the right margin. Each heading will be assumed to occupy a 15-column field with the leftmost field beginning in column 16 and ending in column 30. (Subsequent fields will begin in columns 31, 46, 61, 76, 91, and 106.) Each heading will be right-justified in its field, and two-word headings such as EMPLOYEE NUMBER will be written on two lines. The title will be centered over the field used for the headings. These guesses give the following tentative design:

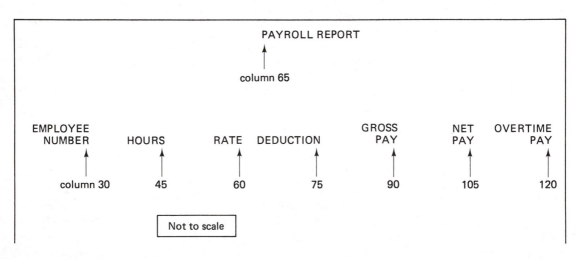

Statements to print the title, headings, and data are:

1. *Title*

```
      WRITE (6,1000)
1000  FORMAT ('1', T66, 'PAYROLL REPORT')
```

2. *Headings*

```
      WRITE (6,1010)
1010  FORMAT ('0', T24, 'EMPLOYEE', T87, 'GROSS', T104, 'NET',
   1     T114, 'OVERTIME')
      WRITE (6,1020)
1020  FORMAT ('b', T26, 'NUMBER', T42, 'HOURS', T58, 'RATE', T68,
   1     'DEDUCTION', T89, 'PAY', T104, 'PAY', T119, 'PAY')
```

3. *Data* (EMPNUM is to be integer mode, and NET is to be real mode)

```
      WRITE (6,1030) EMPNUM, HOURS, RATE, DEDUCT, GROSS, NET
1030  FORMAT ('b', T17, I15, F15.1, F15.2, F15.2, F15.2, F15.2, F15.2)
      WRITE (6,1030) EMPNUM, HOURS, RATE, DEDUCT, GROSS, NET,
   1 OVPAY
```

Note: When a specification appears repeatedly as does F15.2 (5 times) at the end of FORMAT statement 1030, the sequence can be abbreviated by inserting a *repetition factor* before the specification. This allows the statement to be written in its equivalent form

```
1030  FORMAT ('b', T17, I15, F15.1, 5F15.2)
```

repetition factor

A program for this report is shown in Fig. 7.2.

A report layout for the Manhattan Island problem is shown below, and the computer program to produce it is given in Figure 7.3. In interpreting the table, recall that only the leftmost seven digits (approximately) of a given value are correct.

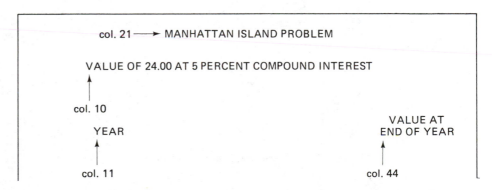

```
1 C
2 C              PAYROLL REPORT
3 C
4         REAL NET
5 1000    FORMAT('1',T66,'PAYROLL REPORT')
6 1010    FORMAT('0',T24,'EMPLOYEE',T87,'GROSS',T104,'NET',T114,'OVERTIME')
7 1020    FORMAT(' ',T26,'NUMBER',T42,'HOURS',T58,'RATE',T68,'DEDUCTION',
8       *        T89,'PAY',T104,'PAY',T119,'PAY')
9 1030    FORMAT(' ',T17,I15,F15.1,5F15.2)
10 1040   FORMAT(I10,3F10.2)
11        WRITE(6,1000)
12        WRITE(6,1010)
13        WRITE(6,1020)
14        READ(5,1040)EMPNUM,HOURS,RATE,DEDUCT
15        WHILE( EMPNUM .GE. 0)
16            IF( HOURS .LE. 40.0) THEN
17                GROSS=HOURS*RATE
18                NET=GROSS-DEDUCT
19                WRITE(6,1030)EMPNUM,HOURS,RATE,DEDUCT,GROSS,NET
20            ELSE
21                OVPAY=1.5*(HOURS-40.0)*RATE
22                GROSS=40.0*RATE+OVPAY
23                NET=GROSS-DEDUCT
24                WRITE(6,1030)EMPNUM,HOURS,RATE,DEDUCT,GROSS,NET,OVPAY
25            ENDIF
26            READ(5,1040)EMPNUM,HOURS,RATE,DEDUCT
27        ENDWHILE
28        STOP
29        END
```

PAYROLL REPORT

EMPLOYEE NUMBER	HOURS	RATE	DEDUCTION	GROSS PAY	NET PAY	OVERTIME PAY
1001	38.0	2.75	26.10	104.50	78.40	
1002	42.0	2.75	27.45	118.25	90.80	8.25
1003	36.0	3.25	25.37	117.00	91.63	
1004	39.5	3.10	28.40	122.45	94.05	
1005	46.5	3.35	31.70	166.66	134.96	32.66
1006	43.0	3.20	29.60	142.40	112.80	14.40
1007	40.0	3.00	30.00	120.00	90.00	
1008	51.5	2.75	29.50	157.44	127.94	47.44

FIGURE 7.2 *Payroll report*

```
1 C
2 C              MANHATTAN ISLAND PROBLEM
3 C
4         INTEGER YEAR,THISYR
5 1000    FORMAT('1',T22,'MANHATTAN ISLAND PROBLEM')
6 1005    FORMAT(' ',T11,'VALUE OF 24.00 AT 5 PERCENT COMPOUND INTEREST')
7 1010    FORMAT('0',T45,'VALUE AT')
8 1020    FORMAT(' ',T12,'YEAR',T45,'END OF YEAR')
9 1030    FORMAT(I4)
10 1040   FORMAT(' ',T12,I4,T36,F20.0)
11        YEAR=1626
12        VALUE=24.00
13        WRITE(6,1000)
14        WRITE(6,1005)
```

FIGURE 7.3 *Manhattan Island problem*

150

```
15      WRITE(6,1010)
16      WRITE(6,1020)
17      READ(5,1030)THISYR
18      WHILE( YEAR .LE. THISYR)
19         VALUE=VALUE+0.05*VALUE
20         IF( (YEAR-(YEAR/10)*10) .EQ. 0 ) THEN
21            WRITE(6,1040)YEAR,VALUE
22         ENDIF
23         YEAR=YEAR+1
24      ENDWHILE
25      YEAR=YEAR-1
26      IF( (YEAR-(YEAR/10)*10) .NE. 0) THEN
27         WRITE(6,1040)YEAR,VALUE
28      ENDIF
29      STOP
30      END
```

MANHATTAN ISLAND PROBLEM
VALUE OF 24.00 AT 5 PERCENT COMPOUND INTEREST

YEAR	VALUE AT END OF YEAR
1630	31.
1640	50.
1650	81.
1660	132.
1670	216.
1680	351.
1690	572.
1700	932.
1710	1518.
1720	2473.
1730	4028.
1740	6561.
1750	10687.
1760	17409.
1770	28357.
1780	46191.
1790	75240.
1800	122557.
1810	199633.
1820	325181.
1830	529686.
1840	862802.
1850	1405414.
1860	2289271.
1870	3728981.
1880	6074117.
1890	9894096.
1900	16116438.
1910	26251984.
1920	42761712.
1930	69654336.
1940	113459552.
1950	184813664.
1960	301041984.
1970	490365824.
1980	798754304.
1981	838691968.

FIGURE 7.3 *(cont.)*

REVIEW QUESTIONS

1. Give several reasons why it is important to be able to specify the format of input/output data.

2. Where in a READ or WRITE statement does the FORMAT statement number appear? Can this statement number be replaced by a variable?

3. Where in their fields should integer data be punched? Explain your answer.

4. In the reading of formatted real-mode values, how is the location of the decimal determined?

5. List the rules for forming specifications of the integer- and real-mode types.

6. If both integer and real values are to be read from the same card, what restriction is placed on the corresponding READ and FORMAT statements?

7. Why is the FORMAT statement a nonexecutable statement? What is the purpose of the statement?

8. Where may FORMAT statements be placed in a program? Is it necessary for a FORMAT statement to be adjacent to the READ or WRITE statement that references it?

9. Why may a FORMAT statement be referenced by more than one READ or WRITE statement?

10. What is the primary difference in FORMAT statements used with READ statements and FORMAT statements used with WRITE statements?

11. List the carriage control indicators and their interpretations.

12. Give three ways of supplying the appropriate carriage control character to cause the printer to skip to the next line.

13. Describe the "print buffer" model for the setting up of a line to be printed.

14. What is the normal number of characters that can be printed on a line?

15. Where are values printed in their fields? When is a decimal printed?

16. A WRITE statement appears without a list of variables. What will happen?

17. Within a FORMAT statement, how are literal data identified? Give two methods.

18. What is the purpose of the X specification? Does the integer in the specification appear in the same relative position as it does in the specifying of an integer field?

19. What is the purpose of the T specification?

20. What is the purpose of the H specification? Describe an error that tends to occur in using this specification.

REVIEW QUIZ

1. A valid statement is:
   (A) Integers must be right-justified in their fields.
   (B) Real numbers must be right-justified in their fields.
   (C) The size of an integer field is given by its READ statement.
   (D) All specifications within a FORMAT statement must have a corresponding variable.
   (E) READ statements must have an associated FORMAT statement.

2. An example of an integer field that is specified to be exactly 10 columns wide is (A) F10, (B) 2I5. (C) I10.2 (D) I10, (E) two of the previous answers.

3. An example of a valid specification is (A) -I5, (B) F10.0, (C) F6.8, (D) R10.2, (E) two of the previous answers.

4. An example of a FORMAT statement that is suitable for use with the statement READ(5,2)A,N,B is (A) 2 FORMAT(I7, I7, I7); (B) 2 FORMAT(F5.2,I3,F4.3); (C) 2 FORMAT(F9.4,I6,I2); (D) 5 FORMAT(F10.2,I6,F12.1); (E) two of the previous answers.

5. An *invalid* statement is:
   (A) FORMAT statements must immediately follow the statement that references them.
   (B) FORMAT statements are nonexecutable.
   (C) More than one READ statement may reference a given FORMAT statement.
   (D) A FORMAT statement number must be in the integer mode.
   (E) Both real and integer specifications may appear in the same FORMAT statement.

6. A valid statement is:
   (A) A given FORMAT statement may be used in a single program for both reading and writing.
   (B) A FORMAT statement may contain specifications for more than one card.
   (C) A FORMAT statement may indicate the skipping of card columns.
   (D) A FORMAT statement does not have to be immediately adjacent to a statement that references it.
   (E) All the previous answers.

7. A "blank" when used for carriage control causes (A) double spacing, (B) single spacing, (C) a skip to a new page, (D) suppress space before printing, (E) sheet eject before printing.

8. The specification that is used to cause double spacing is (A) '1', (B) '0', (C) '+', (D) 2X, (E) two of the previous answers.

9. A valid statement is:
   (A) FORMAT statements used with READ must have carriage control information.
   (B) In FORMAT statements the specifications are separated by blanks.
   (C) 10 FORMAT(I12) can be used for the output of an integer value.
   (D) Two or more FORMAT statements can have the same statement number.
   (E) Two of the previous answers.

10. A valid pair of statements is:
    (A) READ(5,2)N   2 FORMAT(I4)
    (B) READ(5,1)N   1 FORMAT(F10.6)
    (C) READ(5,1)X   1 FORMAT(I4, F8.2)
    (D) READ(5,1)X   5 FORMAT(F10.2)
    (E) READ(5,2)X   2 FORMAT(' ',I10.2)

11. An example of a FORMAT statement that is suitable for use with the statement READ(5,10)A,B,C is (A) 10 FORMAT (3I4); (B) 5 FORMAT(3F10.2); (C) 10 FORMAT(F10.2,I3,F8.1); (D) 5 FORMAT(3I2); (E) 10 FORMAT(12F7.2).

12. An example of an invalid FORMAT statement is:
    (A) 10 FORMAT(I15).
    (B) 1500 FORMAT('+',F8.2,I6).
    (C) 1000 FORMAT(I6,I6,F10.2).
    (D) 1210 FORMAT('0', '00012',F12.2, 'X=',F10.1).
    (E) 1150 FORMAT('1'I10,F5.6).

13. A specification that could be successfully used to print the value −14782 is (A) I6, (B) F10.2, (C) I5, (D) F10, (E) two (or more) of the previous answers.

14. A number that cannot be printed using the specification F8.3 is (A) 100.25, (B) -12.123, (C) 123.123, (D) 51123.123, (E) -102.

15. The number of cards that will be read by the statements

$$READ(5,1000)A,B,C,E,D,F$$
$$1000\ FORMAT(F10.4,F10.4,F10.1)$$

is (A) 0, (B) 1, (C) 2, (D) 3, (E) none of the previous answers.

16. The number of values that will be read as a result of the execution of the statement

$$1050\ FORMAT(F10.2,I2,I6,F8.1)$$

is (A) 1, (B) 2, (C) 3, (D) 4, (E) none of the previous answers.

17. An example of a FORMAT statement that could be used with

$$WRITE(6,1300)I,J,X,K$$

is:
(A) 1300 FORMAT('0',I6,I6,F10.2,F10.2).
(B) 1300 FORMAT(I10,I10,I10,I10).
(C) 1300 FORMAT('1',I6,I2,F7.0,I12).
(D) 1300 FORMAT('0',I10,T20,I6,T30,F10.2,T60,I6).
(E) two of the previous answers.

18. Which of the FORMAT statements could be used to read the data

$$13\quad 1703.21\quad 45\quad 19.607$$

from a single card?
(A) 1000 FORMAT(I3,F10.2,F10.2,I4,I4,I4,I4).
(B) 1000 FORMAT(I2,F12.4,I2,F12.4).
(C) 1000 FORMAT(F10.2,F10.2,F8.1).
(D) 1000 FORMAT(I4,F9.1,I2,I2).
(E) 1000 FORMAT(I4,F7.2).

19. The statement

$$1250\ FORMAT('0','Xb=b',F10.2,10X,'bbYb=b',F10.2)$$

is equivalent to:
(A) 1250 FORMAT('0','Xb=b',F10.2,T10,'bbYb=b',F10.2).
(B) 1250 FORMAT('0','Xb=b',F10.2,T15,'bbYb=b',F10.2).
(C) 1250 FORMAT('0','Xb=b',F10.2,T15,'bbYb=b').
(D) 1250 FORMAT('0','Xb=b',F10.2,T28,'Yb=b',F10.2).
(E) Two of the previous answers.

20. An *invalid* pair of statements is:
(A)　　　WRITE(6,1000)X
　　　1000 FORMAT('0','6Xb=b')
(B)　　　WRITE(6,1000)
　　　1000 FORMAT('1',T50,'GRADE REPORT')

```
(C)        WRITE(6,1000)Y
      1000 FORMAT('+','bYb=b',F10.2)
(D)        WRITE(6,1000)
      1000 FORMAT('0',50X,'GRADE REPORT')
(E)        WRITE(6,1000)MASS
      1000 FORMAT('0','bANSWERb',I10)
```

EXERCISES   1. Find the error(s), if any, in each of the following:

```
a.        READ (5,1000) I,J
     1010 FORMAT (I6, I10)
b.        READ (5,1000) I,J
     1000 FORMAT (I6)
c.        READ (5,1000) NUMBR, INCHES, FEET
     1000 FORMAT (2I6, I10)
d.        READ (5,1000) N,X,Y
     1000 FORMAT (I6, F10.2, F12.3)
e.        READ (5,1000) A,H,B,C
     1000 FORMAT (F8.1, I6, F10.0, F10.1)
f.        READ (5,1000) E,F
     1000 FORMAT (F10.12, F9.3)
g.        WRITE (6,1000) XY,AB
     1000 FORMAT ('b', F9.3, I9)
h.        WRITE (6,1000) XY, IJ, YZ
     1000 FORMAT ('-', F6.1, I6, F7.0)
i.        WRITE (6,1000) LOOP
     1000 FORMAT ('1', 'THE NUMBER OF EXECUTIONS OF THE LOOP IS')
j.        WRITE (6,1000)
     1000 FORMAT ('0', 'THE RESULT IS)
k.        WRITE (6,1000) Q,R
     1000 FORMAT ('b', F10.2, X5, F6.2)
l.        WRITE (6,1000) A,B,C,I,J
     1000 FORMAT (F10.0, F8.2, F12.0, I6, I8, I4)
```

2. Give the output for each of the following program segments. Indicate blanks in the output line by using b.

```
a.        X = 5.5
          Y = 0.27*X
          WRITE (6,1000) X,Y
     1000 FORMAT ('1', F3.0, T10, F8.2, 'ANSWERS')
b.        L = 1797
          M = -5
          N = L/M
          WRITE (6,1000) L,M,N
     1000 FORMAT ('0', T5, I4, T10, I2, T15, I3)
c.        AA = -0.0011
          BB = 5.0296
          CC = AA + BB
          WRITE (6,1000) CC, BB, AA
     1000 FORMAT ('b', T2, 3F7.3)
```

d.   X = 400.3
       Y = 3.1
       Z = X∗Y
       WRITE (6,1000) X,Y,Z
    1000 FORMAT (F4.1, 1X, F3.1, 2X, F7.2)

3. Give the values that would be associated with the variables N, S, and T as a result of the following read operations:

Given:

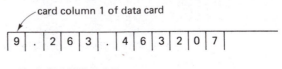

card column 1 of data card

| 9 | . | 2 | 6 | 3 | . | 4 | 6 | 3 | 2 | 0 | 7 | |

READ (5,1000) N,S,T

	Values of:		
	N	S	T

a. 1000 FORMAT (I1, 2X, F3.1, F4.2)
b. 1000 FORMAT (2X, I2, F4.2, F3.1)
c. 1000 FORMAT (3X, I1, F6.2, F4.0)
d. 1000 FORMAT (I1, F7.1, F2.0)
e. 1000 FORMAT (I2, F4.0, F5.1)

PROGRAMMING EXERCISES

1. For the integers 2 through 7, print a table that contains the second, third, fourth, and fifth powers of each integer. The table should have a title, and a heading should be printed for each column.

2. Using an appropriate title and column headings, print a table showing the yearly value over a 10-year period of $1000 compounded annually at rates of 4, 5, 6, 7, and 8 percent. The table should make comparison of values easy.

3. Read a card that contains the height in feet of an object suspended above the ground. This height can have a value up to 10,000 feet. The object, which is initially at rest, is allowed to fall until it strikes the ground. Print a table with an appropriate title and headings giving the number of seconds passed and the corresponding distance from the ground. Printing should be done for 5-second intervals. If during the last interval, the object strikes the ground before the interval is over, print the actual time of impact. Following the table, print the message

    THE TIME REQUIRED TO FALL XXXXX FEET IS XX.X SECONDS

    where the fields containing X's are to be filled with your data.

4. The program in Figure 6.6, which computes the prime numbers less than 1000, prints one prime number per line and therefore requires several pages for its out-

put. Revise the program so that five values are printed on each line. Print an appropriate title.

5. Revise the program of Programming Exercise 3 to print exactly 50 lines on each page. Also print the title on each page. At the top center of each page, print the page number preceded by the word PAGE.

6. Write a program that reads a numerical code for a date in the form

month, day, code for day of week

where the code for the day of the week is

1	Sunday
2	Monday
3	Tuesday
etc.	

translates the month and code for day of week to words, and prints the results. For example,

1,23,7

should be transformed to

JANUARY 23 SATURDAY

7. Write a program to produce bank statements. The input should consist of a set of cards, one number per card, of the following types:

0001	account number
175.21	opening balance
73.62	a deposit (the value is positive)
-16.27	a check (the value is negative)
-5.93	a check
-96.08	a check
.	
.	
.	
	various deposits and checks
-1	last card indicator

Your program should print a report that has all items identified appropriately. Use your imagination in designing the bank statement.

8. Simple designs (or complicated designs, if one is willing to do the work) can be printed by using FORMAT statements containing properly designed literal data. In the technique, a rough draft of the figure is drawn, and it is determined in which row and column each character is to be printed. Then a FORMAT statement is prepared for each line. Using this technique print either of the following. You may wish to expand the technique to print a more interesting design. For example, "Snoopy" calendars found on many college campuses are printed this way.

a.

```
*     *       *         * * *     * * *     *       *       line 1
*     *     *   *       *       *   *   *   *       *       line 2
*     *   *       *     *         *   *   *   *     *       line 3
* * * * *   * * * * *   * * *     * * *         .   *       line 4
*     *   *       *     *         *               *         line 5
*     *   *       *     *         *               *         line 6
*     *   *       *     *         *               *         line 7
```

Note: The grid is not to be printed. It was drawn to help you visualize the locations of the characters.

b.

```
            *
            *
        * * *   * *       * *
          *       *     *       *
          * *       * *         *
          *   *                 *
          *       *             *
          *                     *
            *               *
              *           *
                *       * *
                  * *   *   *
                      * *
                    * * *
```

9. The "change-maker problem" is a classical one in programming. A person makes a purchase and pays with a $1 bill. The change can be anything from nothing to 99¢. Write a program to determine the number of half-dollars, quarters, dimes, nickels, and pennies that a person would receive for a given amount. Note that the number of half-dollars, quarters, and nickels can only be one or zero. Your output should resemble that given below.

Change-maker problem

AMOUNT	HALF-DOLLARS	QUARTERS	DIMES	NICKELS	PENNIES
99	1	1	2	0	4
52	1	0	0	0	2
49	0	1	2	0	4

Change-maker problem

AMOUNT	HALF-DOLLARS	QUARTERS	DIMES	NICKELS	PENNIES
31	0	1	0	1	1
13	0	0	1	0	3
10	0	0	1	0	0
6	0	0	0	1	1
1	0	0	0	0	1

10. Write a computer program that prints the following summary of football statistics.

	FOOTBALL STATISTICS MUSCULAR UNIVERSITY			
GAME	YARDS RUSHING	YARDS PASSING	TOTAL YARDS	TOTAL YARDS BY OPPONENT
1	367	221	588	206
2	401	189	590	182
3	399	271	670	98
.	.	.	.	.
.	.	.	.	.
.	.	.	.	.
AVERAGES				

At the bottom of each column, print the average for the column. (Use the real mode.)

Data are to be punched as follows:

Data element	Mode	Columns
Game	Integer	1–2
Yards rushing	Integer	4–6
Yards passing	Integer	8–10
Yards by opponent	Integer	12–14

Use the following data (one line per card):

1	367	221	206
2	401	189	182
3	399	271	98
4	297	301	296
5	371	142	301
6	342	106	248
7	307	87	319

8	321	119	386
9	411	138	198
10	206	204	216
11	367	147	223

11. The Acme Manufacturing Company has decided to use its computer for inventory control. Write a computer program to print a stock status report for the company. The report has the following form:

STOCK STATUS REPORT
ACME MANUFACTURING COMPANY

PART NUMBER	NUMBER OF ITEMS	VALUE PER ITEM	TOTAL VALUE FOR PART
1001	1705	2.75	4688.75
1002	326	6.05	1972.30
1003	906	3.15	2853.90
etc.			

TOTAL VALUE OF STOCK = XXXXXXX.XX

your answer

12. **WORLD POPULATION**

In 1900 the world's population was approximately 1.65 billion people. The number of births per year has equaled approximately 2.6 percent of the population at the beginning of a given year. The death rate in 1900 was approximately 1.4 percent of the population at the beginning of the year. The death rate has been increasing at an annual rate of 0.01 percent (1.4% in 1900, 1.41% in 1901, 1.42% in 1902, etc.) because the food supply has not been increasing fast enough, natural resources are being depleted, and pollution is increasing. Assuming these trends continue, print a table showing annual population figures from 1900 until 2100.

WORLD POPULATION

YEAR	POPULATION (BILLIONS)	BIRTHS (BILLIONS)	DEATHS (BILLIONS)
1900	1.6500	0.04290	0.02310
1901	1.6698	0.04341	0.02354
1902	1.6897	0.04390	0.02399
.	.	.	.
.	.	.	.
.	.	.	.

CHAPTER 8 ARITHMETIC

Arithmetic is performed in FORTRAN by assignment statements, in which the calculation corresponds to the expression to the right of the equals sign and the result is assigned to the variable on the left. The rules for forming assignment statements will be made explicit in this chapter, and the range of possible arithmetic operations will be extended by the introduction of the topic of intrinsic functions. Brief general discussions of computational errors and of evaluation of expressions will conclude the chapter.

8.1 ASSIGNMENT STATEMENTS

The syntax of the assignment statement is

$$\langle \text{variable} \rangle = \langle \text{arithmetic expression} \rangle$$

where ⟨variable⟩ is the name of any FORTRAN variable

⟨arithmetic expression⟩ is an allowed combination of one or more constants, variables, arithmetic operators, parentheses, and functions

Note: The term "statement" refers to the entire unit consisting of the variable, equals sign, and arithmetic expression. The term "expression" refers to the arithmetic expression that appears to the right of the equals sign.

The *arithmetic operators* are:

+	addition
–	subtraction
*	multiplication
/	division
**	exponentiation

The following rules apply to the formation of expressions:

1. All operations must be stated explicitly; no operation can be implied.

Valid examples:

A+B
A*B

$$A/B$$
$$A*(B/C)$$
$$5.*A$$
$$(2.*X - 4.*B)/(A + 3.*Y**3)$$

Invalid examples:

5.A	An operator is omitted or the name of the variable is invalid.
A(B/C)	An operator should follow the A.
(A)(B)	An operator is needed between (A) and (B).
(A*B)2.C	Two operators are missing, before and after 2.

2. Operators cannot be adjacent to each other.

Invalid examples	Corrected form
A*-B	A*(-B)
A*/B	Unknown:
	1. One of the operators could have accidentally been inserted, so that the correct form is A*B or A/B.
	2. A variable, X, could have been omitted, so that the correct form is A*X/B.
--A	-(-A)

3. Mixed-mode expressions are allowed; that is, not all the constants, variables, and functions have to be of the same type. The implications of this rule will be discussed in detail in Section 8.3.

4. Any expression may be enclosed in parentheses. This does not affect either the mode or the value of the expression.

Valid examples:

$$2.$$
$$(2.)$$
$$A$$
$$(A)$$
$$((A))$$
$$2.*A - B$$
$$(2.*A - B)$$
$$(2.*A) - B$$
$$((2.*A) - B)$$
$$(((2.)*A) - (B))$$

5. The expression A**B**C is permitted and is evaluated as A**(B**C).

A common error not mentioned in the rules is the failure to balance parentheses in long expressions. The following are typical:

$$((-B - 4.*A*C)/(2.*A) \longleftarrow \text{missing parenthesis}$$

$$(X**2 - B*X + C/(B*C)$$

    no parenthesis corresponding to this one

$$1./(2.*PI)*(SQRT(A/B)$$

    no parenthesis corresponding to this one

$$0.1753*X**2 - 97.3X/(A - B)*C)/(75.*(X - C))$$

    no parenthesis corresponding to this one

Whenever you write an expression using parentheses, count the number of left and right parentheses—if the counts do not agree, there must be an error.

Another frequently occurring error is the use of an undefined variable in an expression. Consider the expression

$$HOURS*RATE-TAX-DEDUCT$$

The syntax is valid as an isolated expression, but in the context of a program all the variables must have values assigned to them before the expression can be evaluated. A variable is defined (i.e., has a value) if before it is used in an expression, the variable:

1. Appears to the left of the equals sign in an assignment statement; or
2. Appears in a READ statement as a quantity whose value is to be input.

A variable that does not satisfy one of these rules is an undefined variable. Thus expressions must obey the following rule:

In a program, all variables appearing in an expression must be defined prior to their appearance in the expression.

Find the error(s) in each of the following:

1. Z = W*CORRECT - 5.0
2. LAST = (FIRST**3 - 5(LAST**2)
3. -X = I + J
4. RATE = $2.75 + OVRATE
5. X - Y = A*(B-C) + 37.8
6. FREQ**2 = 4.*PI*MASS

7. $X = 7.Y/((A-B)*(C+D))$
8. $QES = 2.075*(X**2 - Y)/(3.9*R**-2)$
9. $ANS = (7.71*X + 3.26*Y)/-2.*(X-5.1*A*(B-C))$
10. $X1 = ((A+B)/C)**2 - (A-B)/C)**2)$

Answers:

1. CORRECT has too many characters.
2. a. Unbalanced parentheses.
   b. Arithmetic operator needed after 5.
3. $-X$ is not a legitimate name for a variable. Minus sign not allowed. (The only thing that can appear to the left of an equals sign is the name of a variable.)
4. $ in $2.75 is not allowed.
5. X-Y cannot appear to the left of the equals sign. It is an expression, not the name of a variable.
6. FREQ**2 is an expression, not the name of a variable.
7. An arithmetic operator is needed after 7.
8. Adjacent arithmetic operators appear in R**-2.
9. Adjacent arithmetic operators /- appear before 2.
10. Unbalanced parentheses.

8.2   HIERARCHY OF OPERATIONS

The rules presented so far for assignment statements fail to indicate the order of evaluation of operations, and they are in this sense ambiguous. Does A/B*C mean

$$\left(\frac{A}{B}\right)C \quad \text{or} \quad \frac{A}{(B)(C)} \quad ?$$

Does A-B/C mean

$$\frac{A-B}{C} \quad \text{or} \quad A - \frac{B}{C} \quad ?$$

Such ambiguities must be eliminated to allow the compiler to generate the proper machine-language instructions. FORTRAN solves the problem by evaluating operations in a priority sequence called the hierarchy of operations. The hierarchy is summarized in Table 8.1. Notice that multiplication and division have the same priority, and addition and subtraction have the same priority. When the hierarchy table is inadequate to determine the next operation to be performed, the computed value is the same as that which would be obtained by execution of the operations in order of their left-to-right appearance in the expression (left-to-right rule).[†] Thus the order of

---

[†] A**B**C is an exception that is evaluated as if it were A**(B**C).

TABLE 8.1 *Hierarchy of FORTRAN arithmetic operations*

Operation	Priority[a]
**	Highest (evaluate first)
* /	Intermediate
+ −	Lowest (evaluate last)

[a]Operations within parentheses are evaluated *before* operations not enclosed in parentheses.

evaluation of operations in A/B∗C is

$$\begin{array}{cc} A\ /\ B\ *\ C \\ \uparrow\quad\uparrow \\ \text{1st}\quad\text{2nd} \end{array}$$ Both operations have the same priority, so the left-to-right rule applies.

For A−B/C the operations have different properties, so

$$\begin{array}{cc} A\ -\ B\ /\ C \\ \ \uparrow\quad\uparrow \\ \text{2nd}\quad\text{1st} \end{array}$$ which is equivalent to $A - \left(\dfrac{B}{C}\right)$

The order of evaluation can be changed at will by enclosing operations in parentheses. For example,

$$\begin{array}{cc} (A\ -\ B)\ /\ C \\ \ \uparrow\quad\quad\uparrow \\ \text{1st}\quad\ \text{2nd} \end{array}$$

Consider the following more complex examples:

$$\begin{array}{ccccc} (A\ -\ B)\ /\ (C\ -\ D)\ *\ E \\ \ \uparrow\quad\quad\uparrow\quad\ \uparrow\quad\ \uparrow \\ \text{1st}\quad\text{3rd}\quad\text{2nd}\quad\text{4th} \end{array}$$

$$\begin{array}{ccccc} 5.6\ *\ X\ **\ 2\ -\ 10.6\ *\ X\ +\ 27.3 \\ \ \uparrow\quad\ \uparrow\quad\quad\uparrow\quad\quad\ \uparrow\quad\ \uparrow \\ \text{2nd}\quad\text{1st}\quad\text{4th}\quad\ \text{3rd}\quad\text{5th} \end{array}$$

$$\begin{array}{ccccc} (X\ -\ Y)\ **\ 2\ +\ (A\ +\ B)\ /\ C \\ \ \uparrow\quad\quad\uparrow\quad\ \uparrow\quad\quad\uparrow\quad\quad\uparrow \\ \text{1st}\quad\text{3rd}\quad\text{5th}\quad\ \text{2nd}\quad\text{4th} \end{array}$$

$$(C - (A + B)) \; / \; D \; * \; E \; / \; F$$

$$\uparrow \qquad \uparrow \qquad \uparrow \qquad \uparrow \qquad \uparrow$$

$$\text{2nd} \quad \text{1st} \quad \text{3rd} \quad \text{4th} \quad \text{5th}$$

You must consciously think about the rules of hierarchy and the order of evaluation of operations in changing algebraic statements to FORTRAN. Otherwise, you will probably make an error. For example,

$$R = \frac{ax^2 + bx + c}{a - b}$$

must be written in FORTRAN as

$$R = (A*X**2 + B*X + C)/(A-B)$$

Omission of either pair of parentheses would produce a statement that does not correspond to the algebraic statement. The FORTRAN statement

$$R = (A*X**2 + B*X + C)/A-B$$

$$\text{no parentheses}$$

is equivalent to

$$R = \frac{ax^2 + bx + c}{a} - b$$

Familiarity with an algebraic statement tends to encourage carelessness in writing the statement in FORTRAN. Most college students have encountered, for example, the solution for roots of a quadratic equation

$$\text{root } 1 = \frac{-b + \sqrt{b^2 - 4ac}}{2a}$$

$$\text{root } 2 = \frac{-b - \sqrt{b^2 - 4ac}}{2a}$$

In FORTRAN, the solution for root 1 must be written as

$$R1 = (-B + SQRT (B**2 - 4.*A*C))/(2.*A)$$

Yet, many individuals will write the statement incorrectly by omitting one or more of the required pairs of parentheses. Do not hesitate to use extra parentheses whenever they make a statement easier for you to understand. Unnecessary parentheses will not change the instructions produced by the compiler, but a missing pair of parentheses may cause an unanticipated result.

8.3   MIXED-MODE STATEMENTS

FORTRAN syntax allows constants and variables of either the real or the integer mode to be intermixed freely in forming assignment statements. If both modes appear in an assignment statement, it is called a mixed-mode statement. Mixing modes can have a significant effect upon the performing of the computations for a statement and upon the answer.

The representation in computer memory of integer- and real-mode values is quite different. Integers are stored as binary integers, but real-mode values are stored as binary numbers in exponential form. The actual representation for the two modes depends upon the computer. For example, for the IBM 370 series of computers using 32 bits for representation of values, the appearance of 517 is

517 (integer) 0000 0000 0000 0000 0000 0010 0000 0101

517.   (real) 0100 0011 0010 0000 0101 0000 0000 0000

The two representations are significantly different, and similar differences in representation would be observed for any computer.

Computer circuitry can perform arithmetic on two integers or on two real values, but not on values of mixed mode—their representation is too different. If a program contains the expression

$$X + I$$

the compiler will generate instructions to translate the value of I from integer mode to real mode before the calculation is made. (The original value of I is not changed.) In general,

Mixed-mode FORTRAN computations are performed as real-mode computations.

The variable to the left of the equals sign in an assignment statement may have a different mode from the expression in the statement. This allows changing the mode of a value and assigning it to a new variable. The statement

$$IX = X$$

takes the real-mode value of X and assigns its corresponding integer value to the variable IX. For

$$X = 2.073$$

execution of IX = X gives

$$IX = 2$$

For

$$X = 0.9783$$

execution of IX = X gives

$$IX = 0$$

These examples are illustrations of the general rule:

> Assignment of a real-mode value to an integer variable results in elim-
> inating all digits to the right of the decimal with no rounding (i.e., trunca-
> tion occurs).

The assignment of an integer value to a real-mode variable is also legitimate. The statement

$$X = IX$$

assigns the real-mode form of the value of IX as the value of X.

Now several examples will be presented to illustrate the points made about mixed-mode computations. You should test your understanding by calculating the answer before examining the solution.

Example 1

What is the value of X after the execution of the following sequence of statements?

$$K = 5$$
$$L = 3$$
$$M = K/L$$
$$X = M$$

Solution

$$M = 5/3 = 1 \qquad \text{truncation occurs}$$
$$X = 1.0$$

Example 2

What is the value of X after the execution of the following sequence of statements?

$$K = 5$$
$$L = 3$$
$$X = K/L$$

Solution

$$K/L = 5/3 = 1$$
$$X = 1.0$$

The statement $X = K/L$ is tricky. The expression K/L refers only to integer values, so the computation is made in integer mode. The integer result, 1, is then converted to the real mode and assigned as the value of X. The sequence of operations is critical.

Example 3

For the following sequence, are the values of IP and IQ the same?

$$K = 8$$
$$IP = K - K/3*3$$
$$IQ = K - K/3.*3$$

Solution

All values associated with the computation of IP are integer mode. This gives

$$IP = 8 - 8/3 * 3 = 8 - 2 * 3 = 2$$

$$\nearrow \quad \uparrow \quad \uparrow$$
$$\text{3rd} \quad \text{1st} \quad \text{2nd}$$

For the computation of IQ, 8/3. is in mixed mode. This gives

$$IQ = 8 - 8/3. * 3$$
$$= 8 - 2.6666666 * 3.$$
$$= 8 - 7.9999998$$
$$= 0.$$
$$= 0$$

→ At each stage computations are done in real mode.

Note: With some computers the answer will be a small (e.g., 0.0000002) non-zero value.

Example 4

What is the value of IR for the sequence below?

$$K = 8$$
$$IR = K - K/3 * 3.$$

Solution

In the term K/3*3. the first operation K/3 involves only integer values, but the result will be multiplied by the real constant 3.; does this mean that the operation K/3 will also be done in real mode?

Integer division followed by real multiplication gives

$$8/3*3. = 2*3. = 6. \quad \text{and} \quad IR = 2.$$

Real division followed by real multiplication gives

$$8./3.*3. = 8. \quad \text{and} \quad IR = 0.$$

The answer obtained will depend upon the method used by a particular compiler for handling mixed-mode expressions. According to the standards that define the language, the mode of the answer depends only upon the mode of the operands for a particular operation. This implies that $IR = 2.0$ is the answer, since 8/3 should give an integer-mode result; but you should be careful when using different compilers.

8.4 INTRINSIC FUNCTIONS

Computer circuitry is normally constructed to perform only the arithmetic operations of addition, subtraction, multiplication, and division. More complex operations are not wired into the circuitry because they are costly; instead, they are simulated by sequences of instructions which use the hardwired operations. The additional operations supplied with a compiler are called intrinsic functions (sometimes called library functions).

Each intrinsic function consists of a sequence of instructions based on an algorithm that gives accuracy and machine efficiency. These functions, written by professional programmers, are an intrinsic part of the language (hence, the name) and can be used by giving the name of the function and its arguments. The operation SQRT, for square root, which was mentioned earlier in the discussion of the prime-number problem, is a typical intrinsic function.

8 4.1 Characteristics of Intrinsic Functions

In this section, the general rules that apply to intrinsic functions are listed and illustrated. The rules are:

1. Each intrinsic function has a name (e.g., SQRT) that is used to reference the function. The names resemble those for names of ordinary variables, and in fact, the names were assigned using the rules for naming FORTRAN variables. This is important in determining the mode of the function and will be important later in defining your own FORTRAN functions.

2. The mode of the answer produced by applying a function is determined by the mode of the name of the function. The name of the square-root function is SQRT. Its first character is S, which implies the real mode. Thus the first character of the name of an intrinsic function implies the mode of the answer. Some additional examples are

Function	Mode of answer
COS	Real
SIN	Real
FLOAT	Real
IFIX	Integer
MOD	Integer

3. Application of an intrinsic function to a FORTRAN expression always produces a single answer which, for visualizing the operation of a function, can be considered as being assigned to a variable corresponding to the name of the function. For example, the statement

$$Z = SQRT(X)$$

applies the function SQRT to the argument X to obtain the square root of X. This answer is "assigned" as the value of SQRT, and the value of SQRT is assigned as the value of Z. Actually, a value is not truly assigned to SQRT (or any other function), because no memory cells are ever set aside to receive the value. Instead, the answer is saved temporarily, usually in a register, so the value can be used in subsequent steps. A *register* is a special storage cell normally having the same capacity as a memory cell of the computer concerned and also having special properties for use during arithmetic and logical operations. To make the discussion more concrete, consider the execution of the statements

$$X = 37.9$$
$$Z = SQRT(X)$$

a. The instructions that constitute the intrinsic function SQRT compute 6.156297 as the answer.
b. The answer is saved temporarily as the contents of a computer register. Thus 6.156297 is stored in the register.
c. Contents of the register are assigned to the variable Z.

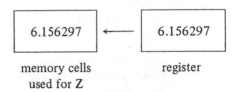

memory cells
used for Z

register

4. The arguments of an intrinsic function are placed in parentheses immediately following the name of the function. If there is more than one argument, the individual arguments must be separated by commas. Examples are

$$SQRT(X)$$

$$COS(Y)$$

$$MOD(M,N)$$

5. For an intrinsic function, the list of actual arguments must agree with the list of dummy arguments used in defining the function. This means that the number of arguments, their mode, and relative positions are all important. A similar situation was encountered previously in defining procedures in MLOGO. The definition of the procedure POLY began

TO POLY   SIDE   ANGLE

Thereafter, to use POLY two arguments were required:

POLY 100 90

Omission of an argument would be a disaster. (What would POLY 50 produce?) Accidentally interchanging the arguments also changed the result (POLY 100 90 is not the same as POLY 90 100). Correspondingly, in FORTRAN

SQRT   must have exactly one argument and it must be real mode

MOD   must have exactly two arguments and they must both be integer mode

To use FORTRAN intrinsic functions properly, you will either have to memorize facts about the argument lists or have to consult a table of functions to obtain the information as it is needed.

6. Provided that arguments are of proper mode, they may be constants, variables, or arithmetic expressions. All of the following are valid:

Example	*Type argument*
SQRT (.37)	Constant
SQRT (1093.68)	Constant
SQRT (X)	Variable
SQRT (VAR)	Variable
SQRT (X**2 + Y**2)	Expression
SQRT ((A−B)/2.5 + 3.6*Z + 5.1)	Expression

If an expression is used as an argument, the expression is evaluated, and the resulting value is operated upon by the function; the value of the expression is not saved and therefore cannot be used elsewhere in the program.

7. Functions can be used in constructing arithmetic expressions. This means that intrinsic functions can include other intrinsic functions or arguments. Valid examples are

$$SQRT\ (COS(X))$$

$$SQRT\ (10.96 + SQRT(X))$$

$$SQRT\ (COS(Z) + SIN(Y))$$

Intrinsic functions can be nested in this fashion to any desired depth. The characteristics of some commonly encountered intrinsic functions are given in Table 8.2.

8.4.2 Examples Using Intrinsic Functions

Example 1: Hypotenuse of Right Triangles

The length of the hypotenuse, h, of a right triangle can be calculated in a number of ways.

a. The Pythagorean theorem gives

$$h^2 = x^2 + y^2 \quad \text{or} \quad h = \sqrt{x^2 + y^2}$$

TABLE 8.2 *FORTRAN intrinsic functions*

Name	Form	
SQRT	SQRT(R)	Compute the square root of R.
SIN	SIN(R)	Compute the sine of R. R must be in radians.
COS	COS(R)	Compute the cosine of R. R must be in radians.
TAN	TAN(R)	Compute the tangent of R. R must be in radians.
EXP	EXP(R)	Compute the Rth power of e.
ALOG	ALOG(R)	Compute the natural logarithm of R.
ALOG10	ALOG10(R)	Compute the base 10 logarithm of R.
FLOAT	FLOAT(I)	Obtain the real-mode equivalent of the value of I.
IFIX	IFIX(R)	Obtain the integer-mode equivalent of the value of R.
MOD	MOD(I,J)	Compute the remainder for division of I by J.
MAX	MAX(I,J)	Choose the larger value.
MIN	MIN(I,J)	Choose the smaller value.
IABS	IABS(I)	Take the absolute value.
ABS	ABS(R)	Take the absolute value.

where R is a real-mode arithmetic expression.

I, J are integer-mode expressions.

where x and y are the other sides.

b. Trigonometry gives

$$\cos\theta = \frac{x}{h} \quad \text{or} \quad h = \frac{x}{\cos\theta}$$

c. Trigonometry gives

$$\sin\theta = \frac{y}{h} \quad \text{or} \quad h = \frac{y}{\sin\theta}$$

Write a program that uses these three methods to compute the value of h for several triangles. For each triangle, the input consists of the values for x, y, and the angle in degrees. Examine the output—do the methods give the same results?

Solution

A computer program for this problem is shown in Figure 8.1. The hypotenuse, h, was easily computed using the intrinsic functions in the statements

$$H1 = SQRT(X**2 + Y**2)$$

$$H2 = X/COS(ANGLE*RAD)$$

$$H3 = Y/SIN(ANGLE*RAD)$$

Notice that the angle which was in degrees was multiplied by RAD (equal to 2*PI/360.) to change the angle to radians. Failure to make this conversion would produce an invalid answer.

Example 2: Roots of the Quadratic Equation

The quadratic equation is

$$ax^2 + bx + c = 0$$

with the solution

$$x = \frac{-b \pm \sqrt{b^2 - 4ac}}{2a}$$

Compute the roots of the quadratic equation for a series of equations.

```
1  C
2  C              COMPUTATION OF THE HYPOTENUSE OF RIGHT TRIANGLES
3  C
4  1000   FORMAT('1',T52,'HYPOTENUSE OF RIGHT TRIANGLES')
5  1010   FORMAT('0',T81,'LENGTH OF HYPOTENUSE')
6  1020   FORMAT(' ',T35,'X',T50,'Y',T61,'ANGLE',T71,'PYTHAGORAS',T90,
7      *          'COSINE',T107,'SINE')
8  1030   FORMAT(' ',T21,2F15.2,T51,F15.1,T66,3F15.5)
9  1040   FORMAT(3F10.0)
10         PI=3.141592
11         RAD=(2*PI)/360.
12         WRITE(6,1000)
13         WRITE(6,1010)
14         WRITE(6,1020)
15         READ(5,1040)X,Y,ANGLE
16         WHILE( X .GE. 0.0)
17            H1=SQRT(X**2+Y**2)
18            H2=X/COS(ANGLE*RAD)
19            H3=Y/SIN(ANGLE*RAD)
20            WRITE(6,1030)X,Y,ANGLE,H1,H2,H3
21            READ(5,1040)X,Y,ANGLE
22         ENDWHILE
23         STOP
24         END
```

HYPOTENUSE OF RIGHT TRIANGLES

| | | | | LENGTH OF HYPOTENUSE | |
X	Y	ANGLE	PYTHAGORAS	COSINE	SINE
15.00	1.31	5.0	15.05709	15.05730	15.03056
15.00	2.64	10.0	15.23055	15.23140	15.20315
15.00	5.76	21.0	16.06791	16.06717	16.07287
15.00	6.99	25.0	16.54872	16.55067	16.53975
15.00	8.66	30.0	17.32038	17.32051	17.32000
15.00	11.72	38.0	19.03571	19.03527	19.03643
15.00	12.59	40.0	19.58336	19.58111	19.58656
15.00	13.51	42.0	20.18713	20.18449	20.19038

FIGURE 8.1   *Computation of the hypotenuse of right triangles*

Solution

A simple computer program to solve the problem is given in Figure 8.2. The program can be improved, but discussion of the improvements will be delayed until Chapter 9, since we are presently interested only in using the intrinsic functions.

Example 3: Prime Numbers—MOD Function

The program for the determination of the prime numbers less than 1000 (in Example 3 of Chapter 6) contained the assignment statements

REMAIN = NUMBER − (NUMBER/2)*2

REMAIN = NUMBER − (NUMBER/INTEGR)*INTEGR

for determining the remainder upon division by 2 and by INTEGR. Using the MOD function to obtain the remainder allows these statements to be

```
1  C
2  C           ROOTS OF THE QUADRATIC EQUATION
3  C
4  1000 FORMAT('1',T51,'ROOTS OF THE QUADRATIC EQUATION')
5  1010 FORMAT('0',T45,'A',T60,'B',T75,'C',T86,'ROOT1',T101,'ROOT2')
6  1030 FORMAT(' ',T31,3F15.3,T76,2F15.4)
7  1040 FORMAT(3F10.0)
8       WRITE(6,1000)
9       WRITE(6,1010)
10      READ(5,1040)A,B,C
11      WHILE( A .GE. 0.)
12         X1=(-B+SQRT(B**2-4.*A*C))/(2.*A)
13         X2=(-B-SQRT(B**2-4.*A*C))/(2.*A)
14         WRITE(6,1030)A,B,C,X1,X2
15         READ(5,1040)A,B,C
16      ENDWHILE
17      STOP
18      END
```

ROOTS OF THE QUADRATIC EQUATION

A	B	C	ROOT1	ROOT2
1.000	3.000	2.000	-1.0000	-2.0000
1.000	.000	-4.000	2.0000	-2.0000
1.000	2.000	-3.000	1.0000	-3.0000
10.000	26.000	12.000	-.6000	-2.0000
24.000	62.000	35.000	-.8333	-1.7500
11.275	40.210	31.000	-1.1273	-2.4390

FIGURE 8.2 *Roots of the quadratic equation*

replaced by

$$REMAIN = MOD(NUMBER,2)$$

$$REMAIN = MOD(NUMBER, INTEGR)$$

Solution

The computer program that results from making these changes is shown in Figure 8.3.

8.5   PROGRAMMER-DEFINED FUNCTIONS

The intrinsic functions exist for commonly encountered mathematical operations, but you may wish to perform repeatedly some operation that is not included in the intrinsic functions. To handle these cases, FORTRAN allows you to define your own functions. User-defined functions are of two types: arithmetic statement functions, and functions (this latter type has no preceding, qualifying words). This section will present the methods for defining and using functions.

```
 1 C
 2 C         PRIME NUMBERS LESS THAN 1000
 3 C         ILLUSTRATION OF MOD FUNCTION
 4 C
 5         INTEGER PRIME,REMAIN
 6         NUMBER=1
 7         WRITE(6,*)NUMBER
 8         NUMBER=2
 9         WRITE(6,*)NUMBER
10         NUMBER=3
11         WHILE( NUMBER .LT. 1000)
12            PRIME=1
13            INTEGR=3
14            REMAIN=MOD(NUMBER,2)
15            IF(REMAIN .EQ. 0) THEN
16               PRIME=0
17            ENDIF
18            LIMIT=SQRT(FLOAT(NUMBER))
19            WHILE( (PRIME .EQ. 1) .AND. (INTEGR .LE. LIMIT))
20               REMAIN=MOD(NUMBER,INTEGR)
21               IF( REMAIN .EQ. 0 ) THEN
22                  PRIME=0
23               ENDIF
24               INTEGR=INTEGR+2
25            ENDWHILE
26            IF( PRIME .EQ. 1 ) THEN
27               WRITE(6,*)NUMBER
28            ENDIF
29            NUMBER=NUMBER+1
30         ENDWHILE
31         STOP
32         END
```

```
        1
        2
        3
        5
        7
       11
       13
       17
       19
       23
       29
       31
       37
       41

        .
        .
        .

      953
      967
      971
      977
      983
      991
      997
```

FIGURE 8.3   *Prime numbers less than 1000: illustration of MOD function*

8.5.1 Arithmetic Statement Functions

The possibility for defining a useful arithmetic statement function arises when some similar computation appears several times in a program or subprogram. For example, suppose that the following statements appear within a program:

.
.
.

$$CALC = A*X**2 - B*X+C$$

.
.

$$ANSR = D*Y**2 - E*Y+F$$

.
.

$$VALU = R*Z**2 - S*Z+T$$

.
.
.

Notice that the arithmetic expression has the same form for the three statements, although the variables used are different. The arithmetic statement function, COMP:

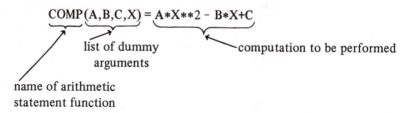

could be used to make the calculations by substituting the actual arguments

.
.
.

$$CALC = COMP(A,B,C,X)$$

.
.

$$ANSR = COMP(D,E,F,Y)$$

.
.

$$VALU = COMP(R,S,T,Z)$$

The syntax of an arithmetic statement function is

name of function (list of dummy arguments) = arithmetic expression

Implicit in this syntax is the limitation that arithmetic statement functions must be definable using a single statement. For example, the computing of the average of N numbers (where N varies from one computation to another) cannot be expressed as an arithmetic statement function, since a loop to add the values and a statement to compute the average are required. The "name of function" may be any legitimate name for a FORTRAN variable, and the mode of the name implies the mode of the answer. The definition must be placed before any executable statements in the program that uses it.

The rules for using an arithmetic statement function are identical to those described earlier for intrinsic functions. For example, constants, variables, or arithmetic expressions can be used as arguments, and arithmetic statement functions can be used as arguments for other functions. The statement

$$X = SQRT(COMP(2.505, 9.1, 3.27, P+5.3))$$

is equivalent to

$$X = SQRT(2.505*(P+5.3)**2 - 9.1*(P+5.3)+3.27)$$

Figure 8.4 shows a modification of the quadratic equation program to use the arithmetic statement function DISC.

8.5.2 Functions

Any program or portion of a program that produces a single value as its result can be changed to a function. The resulting function can then be stored in a library of subprograms and used thereafter as if it were an intrinsic function. The details of a calculation need be considered only during the writing of the function. This is a powerful programming tool.

To define a function, use the form

FUNCTION name of function (list of dummy arguments)
.

.

.

body
name of function = expression
.

.

RETURN
END

```
 1 C
 2 C          ROOTS OF QUADRATIC EQUATION
 3 C          ILLUSTRATION OF AN ARITHMETIC STATEMENT FUNCTION
 4 C
 5 1000    FORMAT(' ',T51,'ROOTS OF THE QUADRATIC EQUATION')
 6 1010    FORMAT('0',T45,'A',T60,'B',T75,'C',T86,'ROOT1',T101,'ROOT2')
 7 1030    FORMAT(' ',T31,3F15.3,T76,2F15.4)
 8 1040    FORMAT(3F10.0)
 9         DISC(A,B,C)=SQRT(B**2 - 4.*A*C)
10         WRITE(6,1000)
11         WRITE(6,1010)
12         READ(5,1040)A,B,C
13         WHILE(A .GE. 0.0 )
14             X1=(-B+DISC(A,B,C))/(2.*A)
15             X2=(-B-DISC(A,B,C))/(2.*A)
16             WRITE(6,1030)A,B,C,X1,X2
17             READ(5,1040)A,B,C
18         ENDWHILE
19         STOP
20         END
```

                    ROOTS OF THE QUADRATIC EQUATION

A	B	C	ROOT1	ROOT2
1.000	3.000	2.000	-1.0000	-2.0000
1.000	.000	-4.000	2.0000	-2.0000
1.000	2.000	-3.000	1.0000	-3.0000
10.000	26.000	12.000	-.6000	-2.0000
24.000	62.000	35.000	-.8333	-1.7500
11.275	40.210	31.000	-1.1273	-2.4390

FIGURE 8.4 *Roots of the quadratic equation: illustration of arithmetic statement functions*

The word "FUNCTION" is the signal that the definition for a function follows. The name of the function can be any legitimate name for a FORTRAN variable. Since the value of the function is assigned to the name of the function, the mode of the name is important. The name of the function must appear to the left of the equals sign in at least one statement. The word "END" signals to the compiler that the definition is complete. The RETURN statement means to stop executing the function and to return to the program that used the function. The RETURN statement can be omitted when it occurs immediately *before* the END statement, but I always use it.

Consider the following function for computing the factorial of an integer. The factorial is computed by multiplying N by the successively smaller integers through integer 1; that is:

$$\text{factorial of } N = N*(N-1)*(N-2)* \ldots *1$$

$$\text{factorial of } 4 = 4*3*2*1 = 24$$

$$\text{factorial of } 7 = 7*6*5*4*3*2*1 = 5040$$

The function is defined as

```
        FUNCTION NFAC(N)                          The name of the function implies an
        NFAC = 1                                  integer mode for the value
        IF (N .LT. 0) THEN                         returned
            WRITE (6,1000)
  1000     FORMAT (' ', 'ERROR IN FACTORIAL. ARGUMENT IS NEGATIVE')
        ELSE
          I = 1
          WHILE (I .LE. N)                          The name of the function must
              NFAC = I*NFAC                          appear at least one time as a
              I = I+1                                variable to which a value is
          ENDWHILE                                  assigned
        ENDIF
        RETURN
        END
```

Variables that appear in the list of dummy arguments, in this case N, are usable outside the function; that is, they are global variables. Any variable that appears in the body of the function but not in the list of dummy arguments is a local variable. In the function NFAC the variable I is a local variable.

As another example, consider the useful function RAND, which generates uniformly distributed random numbers between 0.0 and 1.0. The routine is

```
            FUNCTION RAND(IBEG,ITER)
            ITER = IBEG*899
            IF (ITER .LT. 0) THEN
                ITER = ITER + 32767 + 1
            ENDIF
            RAND = FLOAT(ITER)/32767.
            RETURN
            END
```

The argument IBEG is used to start the calculation, and the value of the argument ITER as computed by RAND must be used as a new value for IBEG on a subsequent execution of RAND. The method is based upon the fact that a computer memory cell can contain numbers only with a particular range (e.g., −32,768 to 32,767 for 16-bit memory cells). The execution of the statement

$$ITER = IBEG*899$$

may produce a value that is too large to fit in a cell, a condition called overflow. When overflow occurs, the result may be a negative value. If this occurs, a positive value is produced by causing another overflow, using

$$ITER = ITER + 32767 + 1$$

Finally, dividing by the largest possible value, 32767, produces a random number in the range 0.0 to 1.0. Figure 8.5 demonstrates the use of RAND to simulate the rolling of dice 10 times. Notice that statements that define RAND are placed immediately after the mainline program. As an alternative, you could store RAND in a subprogram library using the technique that is appropriate for your computer.

```
 1  C
 2  C
 3  C            GENERATION OF RANDOM NUMBERS
 4  C            ILLUSTRATION OF FUNCTION RAND
 5  C
 6             IX=13
 7             I=1
 8             WHILE(I .LE. 10)
 9                RN=RAND(IX,IZ)
10                IRN=6*RN+1
11                IX=IZ
12                RQ=RAND(IX,IZ)
13                IRQ=6*RQ+1
14                IT=IRN+IRQ
15                WRITE(6,1000)RN,IRN,IRQ,IT
16  1000          FORMAT(F10.5,2X,I6,2X,I6,4X,I6)
17                IX=IZ
18                I=I+1
19             ENDWHILE
20             STOP
21             END
22  C
23  C
24  C
25             FUNCTION RAND(IBEG,ITER)
26             ITER=IBEG*899
27             IF(ITER.LT.0)THEN
28                ITER=ITER+32767+1
29             ENDIF
30             RAND=FLOAT(ITER)/32767
31             RETURN
32             END
```

```
.35667        3        4        7
.10837        1        3        4
.06125        1        1        2
.32469        2        6        8
.88305        6        6       12
.59569        4        4        8
.19700        2        1        3
.29637        2        3        5
.37815        3        6        9
.80175        5        5       10
```

FIGURE 8.5 *Simulation of rolling dice: illustration of a user-defined function*

8.6 ARITHMETIC ERRORS*

The computer circuitry almost never fails to perform arithmetic according to design standards. The malfunction would be detected immediately by other circuits, which would stop the processing until repairs are completed. But the computer can produce an inaccurate result, even if the FORTRAN program is correct. This section presents a survey of some sources of inaccuracy to alert you to potential dangers in using the computer. No attempt will be made to be comprehensive in discussing these difficulties.

Arithmetic in FORTRAN is performed on either integers or real numbers. For both types of numbers, the fundamental problem is:

Only a small, finite number of bits are available for storing numbers within the computer.

This fact, which will now be considered in more detail, is of great significance and has a profound effect on program-writing technique in FORTRAN.

8.6.1 Integer Overflow

Consider a computer that uses 16 bits for storing integers. (Any reasonable number of bits could have been selected, since the discussion does not depend on that, but 16 bits are a popular choice for the designing of computers.) Typical positive integers are:

$$0000 \ 0001 \ 0000 \ 0001 = 257_{10}$$
$$0000 \ 1000 \ 0000 \ 0111 = 2055_{10}$$
$$0011 \ 0000 \ 0001 \ 0000 = 12304_{10}$$

A common design decision is to use the leftmost bit to indicate the sign of the integer with the convention that 0 means positive and 1 means negative. For example,

$$0010 \ 1000 \ 0000 \ 0000 = +10240$$

$$\uparrow$$
$$\text{sign bit} \begin{cases} 0 \text{ means } + \\ 1 \text{ means } - \end{cases}$$

The largest positive integer that can be stored in 16 bits using this convention is

$$0111 \ 1111 \ 1111 \ 1111 = 32{,}767$$

---

*The reading of the remainder of this chapter can be delayed or omitted without loss of continuity.

Note: The base 10 value can be obtained by adding $2^{14} + 2^{13} + 2^{12} + \cdots + 2^2 + 2^1 + 2^0$ or by noting that the value is 1 less than

$$1000 \quad 0000 \quad 0000 \quad 0000 = 2^{15} = 32{,}768$$

if such a large positive number were allowed.

If 1 is added to this largest positive integer, a 1 bit is carried into the leftmost bit position:

$$
\begin{array}{r}
0111 \quad 1111 \quad 1111 \quad 1111 \\
+\,0000 \quad 0000 \quad 0000 \quad 0001 \\
\hline
1000 \quad 0000 \quad 0000 \quad 0000
\end{array}
$$

sign bit indicates a negative number

The integer has suddenly gone from being positive to being negative, a phenomenon called *overflow*, which was used earlier in the function called RAND.

Negative integers are usually stored in a representation called *two's-complement notation.* To obtain the two's complement of an integer, invert each bit (change 0 to 1 and 1 to 0) and add 1 to the result. For example, to obtain the two's complement of 3:

$$
\begin{array}{ll}
0000 \quad 0000 \quad 0000 \quad 0011 & = 3_{10} \\
1111 \quad 1111 \quad 1111 \quad 1100 & \text{invert bits} \\
0000 \quad 0000 \quad 0000 \quad 0001 & \text{add 1} \\
\hline
1111 \quad 1111 \quad 1111 \quad 1101 & = -3 \text{ in two's-complement form}
\end{array}
$$

sign bit

Given a negative integer, the corresponding positive integer can be found by reversing the process: (1) subtract 1 from the integer, and (2) invert the bits. (An alternative method is to calculate a value assuming that 0's are significant and then add 1 to the result.)

Using two's-complement notation is probably inconvenient for you, but it is highly satisfactory for computers and can lower the cost of a computer by reducing the amount of circuitry required. The reduction is possible because subtraction of B from A (i.e., $A - B$) is equivalent to taking the two's complement of B and adding the result to A. This allows the circuitry for subtraction to be replaced by simpler circuitry for inverting the bits.

Consider again the example in which 1 was added to 32,767 and overflow occurred. The result was 1000 0000 0000 0000. Let us compute the value of this integer:

1. The sign bit is 1, so the integer is negative.

2. Assuming that two's-complement form has been used:
a. Subtract 1:

```
  1000 0000 0000 0000    original negative integer
- 0000 0000 0000 0001    subtract 1
  ─────────────────────
  0111 1111 1111 1111
```

b. Invert the bits:

```
  0111 1111 1111 1111    invert bits
  1000 0000 0000 0000    magnitude of integer
```

The value of this integer, ignoring the sign bit, is the absolute value of the integer of interest to us. The value, therefore, is -32,768.

The interesting result is that $32,767 + 1 = -32,768$, which is a relatively significant change. Such changes will be disastrous in performing integer arithmetic. Since integer overflow can cause havoc in arithmetic operations, many computers have circuitry to detect overflow and immediately terminate the execution of a program when overflow occurs.

For the 16-bit memory cell that was used to illustrate the representation of integers, the range of possible values is

$$-32,768 \text{ to } 32,767 \quad (16\text{-bit range})$$

Attempts to use integers outside this range produce errors. If the size of a memory cell is expanded to 32 bits, the range becomes

$$-2,147,483,648 \text{ to } 2,147,483,647 \quad (32\text{-bit range})$$

Integers can be much larger for this larger number of bits, but the possibility of overflow still exists. Thus, for integers, the finite size of a memory cell has a significant effect on the arithmetic that can be done.

8.6.2 Overflow and Underflow for Real Numbers

The representation of real numbers within computer memory is more complex than the representation of integers, and in addition there is a considerable variation in the form of the representation between different computers. For these reasons a detailed discussion of the internal form of real numbers will not be presented. The following applies to almost all the different representations:

1. A finite number of bits are available for representing the real number. (This is always true.)
2. A real number is stored in exponential form.

3. More bits are used for storing the mantissa (i.e., fractional part) of the number than are used for the exponent.

As was the case with integers, the finite number of bits available restricts the range of values and makes overflow (and underflow, in which the numbers are too small to be represented) possible. For the IBM 370 series of computers, the number of bits used in real-number representation is

sign	1 bit
mantissa	24 bits
exponent	7 bits
real number	32 bits

The 24 bits available for the mantissa correspond to approximately 7.2 digits in base 10. This fact is responsible for the statement (which has been made several times previously) that the accuracy of real numbers is restricted to approximately seven digits. Only by increasing the number of bits available for the mantissa can the accuracy be increased.

The 7 bits used for the exponent in the IBM 370 representation restricts the range of the exponent to approximately 10^{-78} to 10^{78}. (For other computers the allowed range of exponents will probably be different.) If the number becomes less than 10^{-78} (e.g., 10^{-79}), underflow occurs and the number suddenly becomes zero. If the number becomes greater than 10^{78}, overflow occurs. For a real number, either underflow or overflow will produce an error.

Example: Calculation of Pi

The purpose of this example is to obtain an approximate value for the mathematical constant pi ($\pi = 3.141592653$) and to observe the consequences of underflow. You should note that initially the calculated value of π becomes more accurate as the calculation is repeated. Then the calculated value remains constant despite the fact that Y has a value of zero. For some computers, the value of π becomes less accurate for each computation after Y becomes zero.

The computational procedure is based on the following:

1. The circumference of a circle, C, is given by $C = 2\pi R$, where R is the radius of the circle. For the special case of a circle of unit radius ($R = 1.$), $C = 2\pi$. The value of π is given by $\pi = C/2$.
2. If the value of C can be calculated, the value of π can be calculated. An approximate value for the circumference can be calculated by adding the lengths of the sides of a regular polygon inscribed in the circle. As the number of sides associated with the polygon increases, the perimeter of the polygon approaches the circumference of the circle. Suppose that we start with a hexagon and double the number of sides:

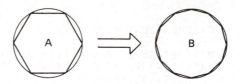

Polygon B gives a much better approximation of a circle than polygon A. Continual doubling the number of sides should give a very good value for the circumference.

3. Determine the perimeter of the polygon by calculating the length of a side and multiplying by the number of sides. Start with a regular hexagon inscribed in the circle (six sides, each of unit length). If we know the number of sides, NS, and the length of a side, **SIDELG**, the same quantities can be obtained for a regular polygon with twice as many sides

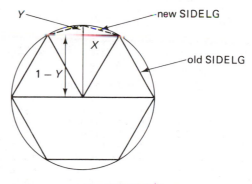

$$X = \text{SIDELG}/2$$
$$1^2 = X^2 + (1 - Y)^2$$

or

$$Y = 1 - \sqrt{1 - X^2}$$

The new **SIDELG** can be obtained

$$\text{SIDELG}^2 = X^2 + Y^2$$

or

$$\text{SIDELG} = \sqrt{X^2 + Y^2}$$

Solution

The program based on this method and its output are given in Figure 8.6. (The number of sides is doubled 100 times.)

```
1 C
2 C          CALCULATION OF PI
3 C
4  1000 FORMAT('1',T59,'CALCULATION OF PI')
5  1010 FORMAT('0',T41,'SIDES',T60,'X',T75,'Y',T85,'SIDELG',T104,'PI')
6  1020 FORMAT(' ',T31,5E15.7)
7       SIDES=6.
8       SIDELG=1.0
9       TIMES=1.0
10      WRITE(6,1000)
11      WRITE(6,1010)
12      WHILE( TIMES .LE. 100. )
13         X=SIDELG/2.
14         Y=1-SQRT(1-X**2)
15         SIDELG=SQRT(X**2+Y**2)
16         SIDES=2*SIDES
17         PI=SIDES*SIDELG/2.0
18         WRITE(6,1020)SIDES,X,Y,SIDELG,PI
19         TIMES=TIMES+1
20      ENDWHILE
21      STOP
22      END
```

CALCULATION OF PI

SIDES	X	Y	SIDELG	PI
.1200000E+02	.5000000E+00	.1339746E+00	.5176381E+00	.3105829E+01
.2400000E+02	.2588190E+00	.3407419E-01	.2610524E+00	.3132628E+01
.4800000E+02	.1305262E+00	.8555055E-02	.1308063E+00	.3139350E+01
.9600000E+02	.6540313E-01	.2140999E-02	.6543818E-01	.3141033E+01
.1920000E+03	.3271909E-01	.5353689E-03	.3272347E-01	.3141453E+01
.3840000E+03	.1636174E-01	.1338720E-03	.1636228E-01	.3141559E+01
.7680000E+03	.8181142E-02	.3337860E-04	.8181211E-02	.3141585E+01
.1536000E+04	.4090605E-02	.8344650E-05	.4090614E-02	.3141592E+01
.3072000E+04	.2045307E-02	.2026558E-05	.2045308E-02	.3141593E+01
.6144000E+04	.1022654E-02	.4768372E-06	.1022654E-02	.3141594E+01
.1228800E+05	.5113272E-03	.0000000E+00	.5113272E-03	.3141594E+01
.2457600E+05	.2556636E-03	.0000000E+00	.2556636E-03	.3141594E+01
.4915200E+05	.1278318E-03	.0000000E+00	.1278318E-03	.3141594E+01
.	.	.	.	.
.	.	.	.	.
.7427640E+28	.8459199E-27	.0000000E+00	.8459199E-27	.3141594E+01
.1485528E+29	.4229599E-27	.0000000E+00	.4229599E-27	.3141594E+01
.2971056E+29	.2114800E-27	.0000000E+00	.2114800E-27	.3141594E+01
.5942112E+29	.1057400E-27	.0000000E+00	.1057400E-27	.3141594E+01
.1188422E+30	.5286999E-28	.0000000E+00	.5286999E-28	.3141594E+01
.2376845E+30	.2643500E-28	.0000000E+00	.2643500E-28	.3141594E+01
.4753690E+30	.1321750E-28	.0000000E+00	.1321750E-28	.3141594E+01
.9507380E+30	.6608749E-29	.0000000E+00	.6608749E-29	.3141594E+01
.1901476E+31	.3304374E-29	.0000000E+00	.3304374E-29	.3141594E+01
.3802952E+31	.1652187E-29	.0000000E+00	.1652187E-29	.3141594E+01
.7605904E+31	.8260936E-30	.0000000E+00	.8260936E-30	.3141594E+01

FIGURE 8.6   *Calculation of pi*

8.6.3 Addition and Subtraction of Real Numbers

The finite number of bits available for storing the mantissa of a real number can introduce errors into a computation. As an example, consider the addition of the three numbers

$$0.5967391E\ 04$$

$$0.2068988E\ 01$$

$$0.3140873E\ 01$$

The order in which the numbers are added affects the answer! In computing the sum, only seven digits can be retained after each addition:

Method 1

$$
\begin{array}{r}
5967.391 \\
+\quad 2.068988 \\
\hline
5969.459 \\
+\quad 3.140873 \\
\hline
5972.599
\end{array}
$$

after chopping off the extra digits (for 5969.459)

after chopping off the extra digits (for 5972.599)

Performing the summation in a different order gives

Method 2

$$
\begin{array}{r}
2.068988 \\
+\quad 3.140873 \\
\hline
5.209861 \\
+\ 5967.391 \\
\hline
5972.600
\end{array}
$$

after chopping off the extra digits

As a result of the roundoff error, the two answers, 5972.599 and 5972.600, are not equal. The error in the answer produced by method 1 is quite small, but in a scientific computation involving hundreds of thousands of calculations, the accumulated error may become disastrously large.

Example: Summation Techniques
For the series

$$\frac{1}{1.^3} + \frac{1}{2.^3} + \frac{1}{3.^3} + \frac{1}{4.^3} + \cdots + \frac{1}{100.^3}$$

is the same answer obtained: (1) when the sum is computed by adding the terms in their left-to-right order of appearance, and (2) when the sum is computed by adding terms in right-to-left order?

Solution

A program that makes the computations is shown in Figure 8.7.

```
 1  C
 2  C           COMPARISON OF SUMMATION TECHNIQUES
 3  C
 4  1000 FORMAT('1','THE VALUE FOR LEFT-TO-RIGHT EVALUATION IS ',F15.10)
 5  1010 FORMAT(' ','THE VALUE FOR RIGHT-TO-LEFT EVALUATION IS ',F15.10)
 6       SUM=0.0
 7       X=1.0
 8       WHILE( X .LE. 100. )
 9          TERM=1.0/X**3
10          SUM=SUM+TERM
11          X=X+1.0
12       ENDWHILE
13       WRITE(6,1000)SUM
14       SUM=0.0
15       X=100.0
16       WHILE( X .GE. 1.0 )
17          TERM=1.0/X**3
18          SUM=SUM+TERM
19          X=X-1.0
20       ENDWHILE
21       WRITE(6,1010)SUM
22       STOP
23       END
```

```
THE VALUE FOR LEFT-TO-RIGHT EVALUATION IS    1.2020080090
THE VALUE FOR RIGHT-TO-LEFT EVALUATION IS    1.2020075321
```

only these digits are significant

FIGURE 8.7 *Comparison of summation techniques*

8.6.4   Inexact Representation of Real Numbers

In base 10 there are many real numbers such as $\frac{1}{3}$ (0.3333 . . .) which cannot be represented exactly. Difficulties of this type arise in every number system. Many simple base 10 real numbers, such as 0.1, 0.2, and 0.3, cannot be represented exactly in the binary-number system. This fact has a profound effect on the outcome of real-number computations.

The value of numbers in the binary-number system is based on a positional notation that resembles the system used for base 10 numbers. Consider the number 5273

5 2 7 3.

units position (10^0)

tens position (10^1)

hundreds position (10^2)

thousands position (10^3)

$$5273._{10} = (5 \times 10^3) + (2 \times 10^2) + (7 \times 10^1) + (3 \times 10^0)$$

Each position moving to the left of the decimal represents a higher power of 10. For binary numbers the situation is similar except that positions represent powers of 2:

1 1 1 1 1.

units position (2^0)

2 position (2^1)

4 position (2^2)

8 position (2^3)

16 position (2^4)

$$11111. = (1 \times 2^4) + (1 \times 2^3) + (1 \times 2^2) + (1 \times 2^1) + (1 \times 2^0) = 31._{10}$$

A convenient way to change a base 10 number ($\geqslant 1.0$) to base 2 is to divide the number repeatedly by 2 until the number is reduced to zero and to note the remainders. The sequence of remainders, with the last being the most significant, is the base 2 equivalent of the number.

$$26._{10} = ?_2$$

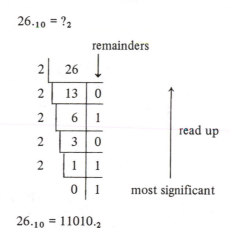

$$26._{10} = 11010._2$$

Check of answer:

$$11010. = (1 \times 2^4) + (1 \times 2^3) + (1 \times 2^1)$$
$$= 16. + 8. + 2.$$
$$= 26._{10}$$

Positions to the right of the decimal in a binary number represent negative powers of 2 $(2^{-1}, 2^{-2}, 2^{-3}$, etc.). The value of 0.1111_2 is

0. 1 1 1 1

.0625 position $(2^{-4} = (\frac{1}{2})^4 = 1/16 = .0625)$
.125 position $(2^{-3} = (\frac{1}{2})^3 = 1/8 = .125)$
.25 position $(2^{-2} = (\frac{1}{2})^2 = 1/4 = .25)$
.5 position $(2^{-1} = (\frac{1}{2})^1 = .5)$

$$0.1111_2 = (1 \times 2^{-1}) + (1 \times 2^{-2}) + (1 \times 2^{-3}) + (1 \times 2^{-4})$$
$$= .5 + .25 + .125 + .0625$$
$$= 0.9375_{10}$$

A convenient way to change a base 10 number (<1.0) to base 2 is to multiply the decimal part of the number repeatedly by 2 until the decimal part becomes zero and to note the carries. The sequence of carries, with the first being most significant, is the base 2 equivalent of the number.

$$0.78125_{10} = ?_2$$

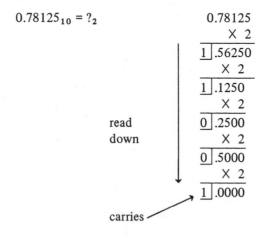

read
down

carries

$$0.78125_{10} = 0.11001_2$$

Check of answer:

$$0.11001_2 = (1 \times 2^{-1}) + (1 \times 2^{-2}) + (1 \times 2^{-5})$$

$$= 0.5 + 0.25 + 0.03125$$

$$= 0.78125_{10}$$

Now convert 0.2_{10} to base 2.

$$0.2_{10} = ?_2$$

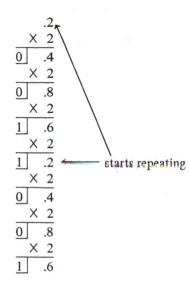

starts repeating

$$0.2_{10} = 0.0011 \ \ 0011 \ \ 0011 \ \ 0011 \ \ 0011 \ \ 0011 \ldots$$

For this conversion the bit pattern 0011 keeps repeating to require an infinite number of bits for the exact representation of 0.2_{10}. If the first 24 bits of this infinite sequence are retained, which is fairly typical of computers, the value is approximately

$$0.0011 \ \ 0011 \ \ 0011 \ \ 0011 \ \ 0011 \ \ 0011 \ \cong 0.19999995_{10} \neq 0.2_{10}$$

This truncation error cannot be avoided in using FORTRAN real-mode values, and errors caused by it can accumulate rapidly. Thus

$$0.2 + 0.2 + 0.2 + 0.2 + 0.2 \neq 1.0$$

$$\cong 0.99999975$$

8.7 ROUNDING

To reduce the error in calculations, some computers perform a rounding opera-tion as part of each real-mode addition or subtraction. The idea is the same as in making a monetary calculation to "the nearest penny." If, for example, a person's federal withholding tax is computed to be \$107.2354, the actual tax is rounded to \$107.24. If the digits to the right of the second decimal position had been less than 5 as in \$107.2348, truncation would have occurred giving \$107.23. For real-mode values expressed as binary numbers in computer computations, the principle is

> Add 1 to the least significant digit if the bit that would be immediately to its right is a 1.

To illustrate the idea with binary numbers, let us assume for simplicity that the computer can store only 8 bits. If the numbers are (recall that they are stored in exponential form)

$$1.100 \quad 1000 \times 2^{-1}$$

and

$$1.001 \quad 1001 \times 2^{-6}$$

then adjusting exponents and adding gives

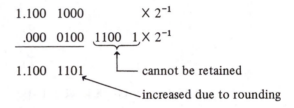

Notice that the rounding can cause the sum to be larger than would actually be the case if all the bits could be retained.

As an example of the effect of rounding, we will reconsider the conversion of Celsius temperatures to Fahrenheit as given in Fig. 7.1. That computation was surprising in that the output stopped earlier than expected. For the loop

```
            .
            .
            .
        WHILE (C .LE. 100.)
            F = Q*C + 32
            WRITE (6,1020) LINENO,C,F
            C = C + 0.1
            LINENO = LINENO + 1
        ENDWHILE
            .
            .
            .
```

```
1  C
2  C                TEMPERATURE CONVERSION TABLE
3  C                CELSIUS TO FAHRENHEIT
4  C                ILLUSTRATION OF ROUNDING AND TRUNCATION
5  C
6  1000 FORMAT('1',T4,'TEMPERATURE CONVERSION TABLE')
7  1010 FORMAT('0',2X,'LINE',5X,'CELSIUS',3X,'FAHRENHEIT')
8  1020 FORMAT(' ',I6,2X,F10.5,2X,F10.5)
9  1030 FORMAT('0','CLIMIT= ',F10.5,6X,'C= ',F10.5,6X,'F= ',
10     *        F10.5)
11       CLIMIT=100.00
12       C=0.0
13       LINENO=1
14       Q=9./5.
15       WRITE(6,1000)
16       WRITE(6,1010)
17       WHILE( C .LE. CLIMIT)
18          F=Q*C+32.
19          WRITE(6,1020)LINENO,C,F
20          C=C+0.1
21          LINENO=LINENO+1
22       ENDWHILE
23       WRITE(6,1030)CLIMIT,C,F
24       STOP
25       END
```

```
              TEMPERATURE CONVERSION TABLE

         LINE      CELSIUS    FAHRENHEIT
            1      .00000      32.00000
            2      .10000      32.18000
            3      .20000      32.36000
            4      .30000      32.54000
            5      .40000      32.72000
            6      .50000      32.90000
             .         .          .
             .         .          .
             .         .          .
          415     41.39966     106.51938
          416     41.49966     106.69939
          417     41.59966     106.87938
          418     41.69965     107.05937
          419     41.79965     107.23936
          420     41.89965     107.41937
          421     41.99965     107.59937
          422     42.09965     107.77936
          423     42.19965     107.95937
          424     42.29964     108.13936
             .         .          .
             .         .          .
             .         .          .
          994     99.30147     210.74265
          995     99.40147     210.92264
          996     99.50148     211.10266
          997     99.60149     211.28268
          998     99.70149     211.46268
          999     99.80150     211.64270
         1000     99.90150     211.82269

     CLIMIT=  100.00000     C=  100.00151     F=  211.82269
```

FIGURE 8.8   *Rounding and truncation*

The last line printed was for C = 99.90 instead of for C = 100.0. The explanation is that the rounding used by the computer causes the value of C to be 100.0015 at the time its value should have been 100.0000 (see Figure 8.8). Actually, the combination of truncation and rounding causes the computed value to oscillate between being too large and too small. You should try this program on your computer.

8.8   OTHER ERRORS

The types of errors described so far can cause serious difficulties in solving mathematical problems with the computer. For example, in the solving of a pair of simultaneous equations, the computed values can be in error by more than 100 percent if the lines described by the equations are nearly parallel. Analysis of the errors in mathematical computations done by computer is part of the field of numerical analysis. In general, you should not trust an answer to a numerical solution of a mathematical model until an analysis of error has been made. Analyzing the error may be more difficult than solving the original problem.

Note: Other computer languages, such as COBOL, which are not used for complex mathematical computations avoid the difficulties associated with real-mode calculations by using a different representation—decimal representation—for numbers. In decimal representation, each digit of a number is encoded and stored individually. Arithmetic is quite different from that described so far, and usually different circuitry is required. Decimal representation is particularly convenient for arithmetic on large monetary values in which the exact answer must be known.

REVIEW QUESTIONS

1. What is an assignment statement? How does it differ from an arithmetic expression?
2. List five syntax rules that apply to the formation of arithmetic expressions.
3. What are the hierarchy rules for FORTRAN operations? How can a programmer cause operations to be executed in a desired order regardless of the hierarchy rules?
4. What restrictions, if any, exist for mixing modes in arithmetic expressions and in assignment statements?
5. What is a FORTRAN intrinsic function? List several examples.
6. How does one determine the mode of an intrinsic function?
7. What items constitute legitimate arguments for intrinsic functions? What restriction exists regarding the mode of arguments for intrinsic functions?
8. What is an arithmetic statement function? How is one defined? How is one used?
9. What are the rules for defining a function? What restrictions, if any, apply to the name of a function?
10. What types of programs can be changed into functions?
11. How are functions used within a program?
12. What is a dummy argument? Where do dummy arguments appear?

13. In a function, which variables are global and which are local?
14. What is integer overflow and why does it occur in computers?
15. Describe two's-complement notation for integers.
16. What is real-number underflow?
17. In complex real-mode computations, why is some error inevitable?

REVIEW QUIZ

1. The algebraic expression

$$\frac{X + Y}{Z + W}$$

would be evaluated by the FORTRAN arithmetic expression (A) X+Y/Z+W, (B) (X+Y)/(Z+W), (C) X+Y/(Z+W), (D) (X)+(Y)/(Z+W), (E) (X+Y/(Z+W).

2. An example of a valid FORTRAN assignment statement is (A) X = 7Y, (B) M2 = N7*L, (C) ZIP = 29613, (D) Y = 5(Z)+4, (E) two of the previous answers.

3. An example of a valid FORTRAN assignment statement is (A) ABCDEFG = B-C, (B) 678 = NJH, (C) IXJ = -76, (D) A-B = 2.*X/(C-D**2), (E) two of the previous answers.

4. An example of a valid FORTRAN assignment statement is (A) -X = 2.303, (B) XY = D*(B-(C+D)+E, (C) PAY = (RATE) (HOURS)-TAX, (D) NEXT = 2*NEXT-5, (E) two of the previous answers.

5. An example of a valid FORTRAN assignment statement is (A) X = X*20. + Y, (B) Y = SQRT(X**2+3X), (C) RATE = DISTANCE/SPEED, (D) LA23 = X/Y*-Z, (E) none of these.

6. An example of a valid mixed-mode arithmetic expression is (A) K**2, (B) A*B-C/210, (C) (X+Y)* 0.75, (D) SQRT(Z-9.7C), (E) two of the previous answers.

7. An example of a valid assignment statement that is not mixed-mode is (A) I = 2.*J-A, (B) JKX = JKX**2.4, (C) HERB = I*K-L, (D) NEXT = 2(I-J)+K, (E) none of the previous answers.

8. In the FORTRAN expression A-B + 6.2/C**3*D, the second operation performed will be (A) addition, (B) subtraction, (C) multiplication, (D) division, (E) exponentiation.

9. For the statement ANS = 3.*A**AA + C/2-B, the second arithmetic operation performed will be (A) addition, (B) subtraction, (C) multiplication, (D) division, (E) exponentiation.

10. In the statement A = X*Y**C-U/W + 5.0, the last operation done will be (A) multiplication, (B) subtraction, (C) addition, (D) division, (E) exponentiation.

11. An example of *invalid* use of a library function is (A) NEXT = SQRT(X), (B) NEXT = SQRT(JX), (C) NEXT = IFIX(XJ), (D) NEXT = SQRT(FLOAT(NEXT)), (E) none of the previous answers.

12. The statement Z = X*Y + 2.*C**2 + 0.05 (A) contains a grammar error, (B) is real mode, (C) is integer mode, (D) will be evaluated with the integer mode dominating, (E) will be evaluated with multiplication being the first arithmetic operation performed.

13. An example of an equivalent pair of statements is (A) I = J/(2∗2) and I = J/2∗2, (B) A = B/B∗C and A = (B)/(B∗C), (C) A = X/Y/Z and A = X/(Y/Z), (D) A = A+B∗C+D and A = (A+B)∗C+D, (E) A = A−B/C−D and A = A−(B/C)−D.

14. Given I = 2, J = 5, K = 8. The value of L as a result of executing L = I∗J/K will be (A) 0, (B) 1, (C) 2, (D) 1.2, (E) none of the previous answers.

15. Given K = 5, L = 2, A = K/L, the value of A is (A) 2.5, (B) 2, (C) 2.0, (D) 0.4, (E) none of the previous answers.

Use the following values to answer questions 16 to 18.

$$K = 2$$
$$L = 3$$
$$M = 5$$

16. The value of I after executing I = K/L + M/L will be (A) 0, (B) 1, (C) 2, (D) 3, (E) none of the previous answers.

17. The value of X after executing X = K/L + M/L will be (A) 0, (B) 0.0, (C) 1.33, (D) 2.33, (E) none of the previous answers.

18. The value of I after executing I = (2.0/K)∗(6.0/L) will be (A) 0, (B) 1, (C) 1.0, (D) 2.0, (E) 2.

Use the following statements which are executed in sequence in answering questions 19 and 20.

$$X = X+Y$$
$$Y = (X+Y)∗∗2$$
$$I = Y+0.25$$
$$SUM = I+Y+X$$

19. Given X = 6. and Y = 5., the number that will be stored in I is (A) 256., (B) 5.25, (C) 256.25., (D) 256, (E) none of these.

20. Given X = 6. and Y = 5., the number that will be stored in SUM is (A) 523., (B) 523, (C) 42.25, (D) 16.25, (E) 16.

21. Given:

$$A = 4.0$$
$$B = 2.0$$
$$X = A∗B−2.0$$
$$WHILE(X.GE.3.0)$$
$$X = X−2.0$$
$$ENDWHILE$$

The number of times the statement X = X−2.0 is executed is (A) 0, (B) 1, (C) 2, (D) 3, (E) none of the previous answers.

22. An *invalid* statement is:
(A) Overflow is limited to input/output operations.
(B) Overflow results from the finite size of memory cells.
(C) Overflow may occur when arithmetic operations are performed.

(D) Overflow produces an invalid arithmetic result.

(E) Overflow can be used as a signal to terminate the execution of a loop.

23. The base 10 number 0.4 (A) would normally be stored in a computer using integer mode, (B) has an exact representation in the binary number system, (C) requires an infinite number of bits for its representation, (D) will have an exponent of 1 when stored as a real number, (E) two of the previous answers.

24. Given:

$$X = 0.1$$
$$\text{WHILE}(X \text{ .LT. } 10.0)$$
$$X = X+0.1$$
$$\text{ENDWHILE}$$

(A) When the loop terminates, X will have a value of 10.0.

(B) In the statement X = X+0.1, the amount added to X is slightly larger than 0.1.

(C) The loop will not terminate.

(D) When the loop terminates, the value of X will be approximately 10.1.

(E) Two of the previous answers.

25. Real-number overflow (A) is a property of the exponential part of the number, (B) involves both the fractional and exponential part, (C) never causes errors, (D) can be avoided by using exponential notation, (E) none of the previous answers.

26. The arguments in the definition of a function are called "dummy arguments" or "dummy variables" because (A) they indicate the number and mode of the actual arguments; (B) they do not give the actual storage locations; (C) in the definition, they do not cause any values to be transferred; (D) in using the function, different variables can be used in the argument list; (E) all the previous answers.

27. Assume that a valid function has been defined using the statement FUNCTION CALC (X,Y,I). An example of valid use of the function is (A) X = CALC (Y,X,I); (B) CALL CALC (X,Y,I); (C) Z = CALC (BLOCK,KOUNT,TEMP); (D) FINAL = CALC (VECTOR,Y); (E) two of the previous answers.

28. An *invalid* statement is:

(A) A definition of a function must use the FUNCTION statement.

(B) Local variables in a function may have the same names as variables in the calling program.

(C) The last statement in a function must be END.

(D) The mode of the answer is determined by the mode of the name of the function.

(E) The END statement can appear more than one time in a function.

EXERCISES

1. Find the syntax error(s), if any, in the following:

   a. INIT = L(2K+7)
   b. X/Y*0.5*C**2
   c. X = 1./-2*Y
   d. I+J = X

   e. PAY = $2.30*HOURS−TAX

   f. J(A) = A−10.0*I

   g. CORRECT = CORRECT + 1

   h. XYZ = XYZ**2 − 2.0

   i. X = 2.5*R/(P−5) (A7−3)

   j. X = (4.2*Y*(Z−5.1) + Y/2*3.5

   k. DEDUCTION = 0.18*EXEMPT*PAY − 1,600.00

   l. X = SQRT(XTEST + Y/(A+B)

   m. K = (3I/4M)**2 + 3(J+K)/M

   n. NEXT = MOD(I/2.5,X) + 10

2. Write algebraic expressions that correspond to the following:

   a. G = X*(X**2 + Y**2)/(X**2 − Y**2 + 2.0)

   b. X = E*H/A/B

   c. X = Y−Y/Z + Y+1.0

   d. ROOT = (B**2 − 4.0*A*C)/2.0*A

   e. R = A+B/(C+D)*E

3. What is the order of execution of operations in the following?

   a. N = I−J*K/M−N

   b. P = (X*Y+A+B)*Z

   c. A = X**2 + X*Y/(A−B)

   d. EXTRA = (A−2.0*(A−B))/(X*Y)

   e. PAY = 2.85*HOURS − FICA − FED − DEDUCT

4. Give the calculated value of the variable J, or XJ, as it would be stored in the memory of the computer.

   a. J = 20*(19/20)

   b. J = 20*(20/19)

   c. J = (20*19)/20

   d. J = 20*19/20

   e. J = 4*3/2 + 3/2*2

   f. J = 20*(19.0/20)

   g. XJ = 20*(19/20)

   h. XJ = 20*(19/20.0)

5. Give the binary equivalent of the following:

   a. 57

   b. −57 (two's complement)

   c. 0.75

   d. 0.1

6. Given the following portion of a program, what is the value of N immediately after completion of the loop?

```
N = 0
I = 4
J = 1
WHILE (J .LE. I)
    N = N + I*J
    J = J+1
ENDWHILE
```

PROGRAMMING
EXERCISES

1. As a marketing ploy, some banks emphasize in their advertising the total money the customer would have at the end of 5, 10, and 20 years if he invested $10 weekly at a nominal interest rate of 5 percent. Compute the value of the investment at the end of these times. Compare them with the values that would result from investing the same funds in a savings and loan account at a nominal interest rate of 5.5 percent. The value of regular deposits is given by

$$V = D* \left[\frac{(1 + i/N)^{N*Y} - 1}{i/N} \right]$$

where V = total value after Y years
Y = number of years
D = amount of regular deposit
i = nominal interest rate (6% is expressed as 0.06)
N = number of deposits per year

2. You wish to buy an automobile and want to investigate the effect of making different down payments and of paying for different numbers of months. Assume that the nominal interest rate is 10 percent. Compute the monthly payment and total amount paid for the following cases:

$3000 borrowed for 36 months
$3000 borrowed for 48 months
$4000 borrowed for 36 months
$4000 borrowed for 48 months

The amount required as a monthly payment is given by

$$M = \left[\frac{i*A/N}{1 - (i/N + 1)^{-N*Y}} \right]$$

where M = monthly payment
A = amount borrowed
i = nominal interest rate
N = number of payments per year
Y = number of years

3. Theoretically, the value of pi (3.141592 . . .) can be computed using the infinite series

$$\frac{\pi}{4} = 1 - \frac{1}{3} + \frac{1}{5} - \frac{1}{7} + \frac{1}{9} - \frac{1}{11} + \cdots$$

But the series converges very slowly and requires the use of many terms to obtain accuracy. Use the series to compute pi to an accuracy of six significant figures. Print the computed value after every 500th value, as well as the final value. To prevent a possible "runaway" program, stop the computation, in any case, after the 10,000 term. Do *not* use the known value of pi in your program.

4. The growth of bacteria in a highly favorable environment is crudely approximated by the equation

$$N = N_0 e^{rt}$$

where N_0 = initial population
e = 2.71828
r = rate constant
t = time
N = population at time t

Assuming a rate constant of 0.15 and an initial population of 1000 bacteria, compute and print the population for 100 time intervals.

5. A perfect number is one that equals the sum of its exact divisors (excluding the number itself). For example, 6 is a perfect number:

$$6 = 1 + 2 + 3$$

Find and print all the perfect numbers less than or equal to 1000.

6. Bohr's theory of the hydrogen atom predicts that the wave numbers of the spectral lines are given by

$$\bar{v} = 109{,}677 \left(\frac{1}{2^2} - \frac{1}{n^2} \right)$$

where n = 3, 4, 5, ... Compute and print the first 20 spectral lines predicted by the model.

7. The day of the week, Sunday, Monday, etc., can be calculated using the formula known as Zeller's congruence:

$$\text{day} = \left[\langle 2.6M - 0.19 \rangle + K + D + \frac{D}{4} + \frac{C}{4} - 2C \right] \bmod 7$$

where M = month number with January and February taken as months 11 and 12 of the *preceding year*; March is 1, April is 2, . . . , December is 10
K = day of the month
C = century
D = year in century
Day will have values in the range 0 to 6, where Sunday is 0, Monday is 1, etc.
All variables are integer mode.
The $\langle \; \rangle$ around $2.6M - 0.19$ means: take the largest integer in the computed value.

For example:

    1. July 4, 1953

$$M = 5$$
$$K = 4$$
$$C = 19$$
$$D = 53$$

The day computed is 6, Saturday.

    2. January 23, 1954

$$M = 11$$
$$K = 23$$
$$C = 19$$
$$D = 53$$

The day computed is 6, Saturday.

Compute and print the day of the week for the following dates, which are in standard notation. (The program will have to change them.)

Month	Day	Century	Year
07	20	19	46
04	14	19	68
02	29	19	68
02	10	21	00
02	12	19	33
04	21	19	31
06	18	19	56
11	07	19	58
07	20	19	48
12	07	19	42
01	03	19	78
08	01	19	79

8. Using the technique described in Section 8.6.4, convert a series of decimal numbers to the binary-number system. Try to find a method of printing the bits for a given conversion on a single line.

9. For the following portion of a simple electrical circuit:

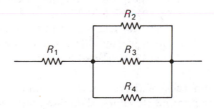

The total resistance R_T is given by

$$R_T = R_1 + 1/(1/R_2 + 1/R_3 + 1/R_4)$$

Write a program that computes R_T for the following values:

R_1	R_2	R_3	R_4
2.02	9.6	4.017	3.921
0.001752	4.99	0.1236	3.094
0.001752	0.483	0.1236	0.0663
93.143	0.0571	0.9434	1.7542

10. For the pair of simultaneous equations

$$ax + by = c$$
$$dx + ey = f$$

write a program that will compute the solutions for x and y. Test the program with the input:

a	b	c	d	e	f
0.667	-1.0	2.0	1.0	0.50	7.0
1.0	-1.0	1.0	1.0	1.0	5.0
0.667	-1.0	4.0	1.0	0.75	6.0
0.333	-0.667	2.0	1.0	-2.0	6.0
0.25	-0.333	-0.416667	0.10	0.20	0.50

11. The purpose of this program is to compare the accuracy of two methods of computing square roots. (The accuracy will vary from computer to computer.) Starting with 10.0 and increasing in steps of 0.05 unit until the number exceeds 20.0:

1. Compute the square of the number ($X \equiv$ number, $Y \equiv$ square of X).
2. Take the square root of the square produced in (1) using SQRT(Y).
3. Compute the difference in the original number and the result produced by (2), X - SQRT(Y).
4. Take the square root of the square produced in (1) using Y**0.5.
5. Compute the difference in the original number and the result produced by (4), X - Y**0.5.

Print each of these results in a suitable table such as that given below. Use F8.4 for printing all values. Examine the table to determine how accurately your computer makes these calculations.

SQUARE-ROOT CALCULATION

X	Y = X**2	SQRT(Y)	X-SQRT(Y)	Y**0.5	X-Y**0.5
10.0000	100.0000	10.0000	0.0000	10.0000	0.0000
10.0500	101.0025	10.0500	0.0000	10.0500	0.0000
10.1000	102.0100	10.1000	0.0000	10.1000	0.0000
.	.	.	.	.	.
.	.	.	.	.	.
.	.	.	.	.	.

12. In a computer science course the overall grade average is computed using the following scheme:

four quizzes	50%
programs	30%
final exam	20%
	100%

For each member of the class, read four quiz grades, a numerical grade based on the programs, and the final examination grade. Compute the overall grade average for each class member, and print it with the input data in a report of your own design.

13. As a demonstration of the difficulty of obtaining accurate measurements, the members of a physics class have measured the sides of a set of right triangles. For each set of measurements, use the observed values of sides A and B to compute an expected value for side C. Compare the expected and observed values for C. ($C = \sqrt{A^2 + B^2}$.) Input data are:

A	B	C
5.01	5.02	7.09
5.03	6.63	8.30
5.03	6.62	8.25
4.96	7.21	8.75
9.00	9.00	12.60
7.25	8.46	11.35
6.24	10.09	11.86
10.00	10.25	14.30
11.75	5.95	13.07
8.09	10.81	13.51

14. This problem is an extension of the world population problem (Programming Exercise 12) of Chapter 7, and all the assumptions made there apply here also. In addition, we wish to consider the effect of crowding. Assume that every increase of 100,000,000 people increases the death rate by 0.01%. Print a table showing the annual population from 1900 until 2100.

9 DECISION MAKING

The IF statement is by far the most important type of statement in FORTRAN for making decisions. In practically all of the programs written so far, one or more IF statements has been essential. This chapter reviews the IF . . . THEN . . . ELSE . . . ENDIF statement, expands some concepts, and presents another form of the IF statement, the ELSEIF statement. Standard FORTRAN logical IF statements and arithmetic IF statements are presented and discussed. The ability to use these statements and the techniques associated with them provide powerful tools for organizing the logic of a program.

9.1   IF . . . THEN . . . ELSE . . . ENDIF STATEMENT (BLOCK IF)

The IF . . . THEN . . . ELSE . . . ENDIF statement of FORTRAN, known as the block IF statement, is essential for writing structured programs, and it is, consequently, very important. Fortunately, you already know a significant amount about this form of IF, but for completeness and convenience the information will be repeated in this section. The block IF statement has the syntax

IF (condition) THEN

(1st block of statements)

ELSE

(2nd block of statements)

ENDIF

where condition   is any expression that always evaluates to a value of true or false
     1st block of   is a block of one or more statements that are to be executed if
      statements   the condition has the value TRUE
     2nd block of   is a block of one or more statements that are to be executed if
      statements   the condition has the value FALSE

An alternative valid form omits the ELSE clause:

IF (condition) THEN

(1st block of statements)

ENDIF

For either form of the IF statement, the statement immediately following the keyword ENDIF is executed after the appropriate block of statements has been executed. These two forms of the IF statement are shown below in flowchart form.

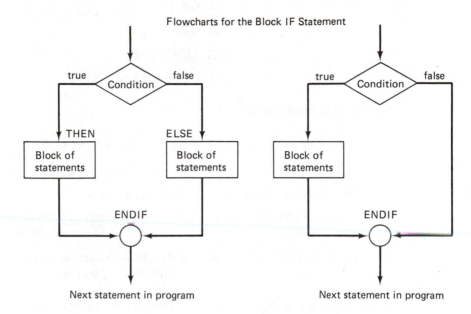

Flowcharts for the Block IF Statement

The condition, which must be enclosed in parentheses immediately following the keyword IF, may be simple or complex, but it must always give a value of TRUE or FALSE. In our previous work the condition was formed by comparing two arithmetic expressions using a relational operator:

$$\langle \text{condition} \rangle = \left\langle \begin{matrix} \text{arithmetic} \\ \text{expression} \end{matrix} \right\rangle \langle \text{relational operator} \rangle \left\langle \begin{matrix} \text{arithmetic} \\ \text{expression} \end{matrix} \right\rangle$$

The relational operators are

.EQ.	equal
.NE.	not equal
.LT.	less than
.LE.	less than or equal
.GT.	greater than
.GE.	greater than or equal

The arithmetic expressions that are compared may be as simple or complex as needed for a particular problem. Examples of valid conditions are

$$X \text{ .EQ. } Y$$

$$X \text{ .GT. } Y$$

$$X + 1.0 \text{ .GT. } Y$$

$$(X + 1.0) \text{ .GT. } Y$$

$$(X + 1.0) \text{ .LE. } (Y + 2.*B)$$

$$2.*A \text{ .GE. SQRT (ABS } (X-Y))$$

Some invalid conditions are

X	does not evaluate to T or F
A .ET. B	invalid relational operator
(X+1.0 .NE. (5.*Y+1.0)	missing parenthesis
R = SQRT (X**2 + Y**2)	an arithmetic statement, not an arithmetic expression used in a condition
(Y=Y+1.0) .EQ. (R=R-2.0)	arithmetic statements are used instead of arithmetic expressions

The comparison of expressions of different mode is syntactically valid but should be avoided if possible. For example, the conditions

$$X \text{ .EQ. } 1 \quad \text{different modes}$$

$$Y \text{ .GT. } N \quad \text{different modes}$$

will be accepted by the compiler, but the comparisons may not behave as you have planned since integer mode values will have to be transformed to real mode before the comparison can be made.

The IF . . . THEN . . . ELSE . . . ENDIF statement has been used throughout the book in writing programs. Consequently, you should be quite familiar with the use of the IF statement. All of the programs have, however, been relatively simple (remember Yourdon's classification of program complexity in Chapter 5). If the programs seemed complex, it was probably because of a lack of experience in using computers—solving problems in a "foreign" language that you are just learning is not easy. As IF statements become nested within IF statements, the logic becomes more difficult to handle properly, and the programming takes much more effort. This point will now be illustrated by several examples.

Example 1: Calculation of the Roots of the Quadratic Equation
Write a program that will find the roots of an arbitrary number of quadratic equations, $ax^2 + bx + c = 0$. The coefficients will be allowed to have

any value, including zero. A value of -9999. for the coefficient *a* will indicate that execution of the program is to be terminated.

A very simple version of this program was given in Chapter 8 to illustrate the use of the intrinsic function SQRT. That program would have failed to operate properly under the following conditions:

1. In using the quadratic formula

$$x = \frac{-b \pm \sqrt{b^2 - 4ac}}{2a}$$

the coefficient *a* is not allowed to be zero, to avoid division by zero.

2. The square root of a negative number cannot be obtained using SQRT. That is, the discriminant (called DISC in the program) $b^2 - 4ac$ must be positive. If the discriminant is negative, the roots of the equation are imaginary.

The program for the roots of a quadratic equation must be modified to prevent these catastrophes and to obtain valid answers for these cases. An important principle is being illustrated:

Input data for a program should be checked for validity as the data are being read. The program should be able to take appropriate actions for all data.

Not all programs make use of this principle, and many of the programs presented here will be deficient in this respect, since our goal will be to present other concepts and ideas. Yet, any professional programmer (interpret this as any person writing a program for some important reason) in science or business who ignores this principle is placing his or her job in jeopardy. I have written business programs in which most of the statements checked the validity of the input data.

A. *Level 1 Solution*

```
read coefficients
WHILE (not last card indicator)
        IF (A equal 0) THEN
                make appropriate calculation
                write answer
        ELSE
                calculate discriminant
                IF (discriminant is positive) THEN
                        calculate roots
                        write answers
```

ELSE

calculate roots

write answers

ENDIF

ENDIF

read coefficients

ENDWHILE

STOP

END

Notice that an IF statement is nested within the ELSE clause of another IF statement.

B. Level 2 Solution

What are the appropriate calculations for the different cases?

1. For the case $A = 0$,

$$AX^2 + BX + C = 0 \quad \text{becomes} \quad BX + C = 0$$

The answer is

$$X = -C/B$$

and the equation is no longer a quadratic equation.

2. For the case DISC = B**2 - 4.*A*C = a positive value, the roots are

$$X1 = (-B + SQRT(DISC))/(2.*A)$$

and

$$X2 = (-B - SQRT(DISC))/(2.*A)$$

3. For the case DISC = B**2 - 4.*A*C = a negative value, the roots are

$$X1 = -B/(2.*A) + (SQRT(ABS(DISC))/(2.*A))i$$

Note: ABS(X) denotes taking the absolute value of X.

and

$$X2 = -B/(2.*A) - (SQRT(ABS(DISC))/(2.*A))i$$

where the i designates the imaginary component of the root. In making the calculations, the i will be ignored, but it will be printed with the answers by using an appropriate FORMAT statement.

Incorporating these statements into the program, but ignoring details of input/output, gives

```
read A,B,C
WHILE (A .NE. -9999.)
    IF (A .EQ. 0.) THEN
        X1 = -C/B
        write A,B,C,X1
    ELSE
        DISC = B**2 - 4.*A*C
        IF (DISC .GE. 0.) THEN
            X1 = (-B + SQRT(DISC))/(2.*A)
            X2 = (-B - SQRT(DISC))/(2.*A)
            write A,B,C,X1,X2
        ELSE
            X1  = -B/(2.*A)
            X11 = -SQRT(ABS(DISC))/(2.*A)
            X2  = -B/(2.*A)
            X22 = + SQRT(ABS(DISC))/(2.*A)
            write A,B,C,X1,X11,X2,X22
        ENDIF
    ENDIF
    read A,B,C
ENDWHILE
STOP
END
```

C. Level 3 Solution

The equations used to compute the roots do not perform the arithmetic in an efficient way. For example, the square root of DISC will be computed more than once, and (2.*A) will be computed four times for the case of imaginary roots. Each of these calculations takes computer time and costs money. Thus there is something to be gained by eliminating repetitious computations, although doing so may reduce the clarity of the program. The trade-off between computer time and program clarity poses a dilemma in many programs. There is no easy answer to the question of which should be emphasized. Generally, if the logic is very complicated, and the program is likely to be modified, I emphasize clarity. If the instructions are part of a subprocedure that will be used frequently by many different programs, I emphasize speed of execution. For this program a middle stance will be taken with some repetitive calculations being eliminated but with reasonable clarity being maintained.

```
read A,B,C
WHILE (A .NE. -9999.)
    IF (A .EQ. 0.) THEN
        X1 = -C/B
        write A,B,C,X1
    ELSE
        D = 2.*A
        DISC = B**2 - 4.*A*C
        IF (DISC .GE. 0.) THEN
            SQ = SQRT(DISC)
            X1 = (-B+SQ)/D
            X2 = (-B-SQ)/D
            write A,B,C,X1,X2
        ELSE
            SQABS = SQRT (ABS(DISC))
            X1 = -B/D
            X11 = SQABS/D
            X2 = X1
            X22 = -X11
            write A,B,C,X1,X11,X2,X22
        ENDIF
    ENDIF
    read A,B,C
ENDWHILE
STOP
END
```

D. Level 4 Solution

Adding the details for the input and the output report gives the final program. Figure 9.1 shows the computer output for the program.

Example 2: Scoring of Bowling

Write a program to determine scores for the game of bowling and print the scoring for each frame in the game, indicating whether a strike, spare, or open frame occurred. The program should work for an arbitrary number of games.

In case you do not know the rules of the game, a brief summary follows. The object of bowling is to knock down 10 wooden pins with a ball. The game is divided into 10 frames, with either one or two balls being rolled in a frame. The possibilities for scoring are:

```
 1  C
 2  C                 CALCULATION OF THE ROOTS OF THE QUADRATIC EQUATION
 3  C
 4  1000 FORMAT('1',T53,'ROOTS OF QUADRATIC EQUATION')
 5  1010 FORMAT('0',T30,'A',T45,'B',T65,'C',T75,'ROOT1',T95,'ROOT2')
 6  1020 FORMAT(' ')
 7  1030 FORMAT(' ',T21,3F15.4,T71,F10.4)
 8  1040 FORMAT(' ',T21,3F15.4,T71,F10.4,T91,F10.4)
 9  1050 FORMAT(' ',T21,3F15.4,F8.4,'+',F8.4,'I',T86,F8.4,'-',F8.4,'I')
10  1060 FORMAT(3F10.4)
11       WRITE(6,1000)
12       WRITE(6,1020)
13       WRITE(6,1010)
14       WRITE(6,1020)
15       READ(5,1060)A,B,C
16       WHILE( A .NE. -9999.)
17         IF ( A .EQ. 0.) THEN
18            X1=-C/B
19            WRITE(6,1030)A,B,C,X1
20         ELSE
21            D=2.*A
22            DISC=B**2-4.*A*C
23            IF( DISC .GE. 0.) THEN
24               SQ=SQRT(DISC)
25               X1=(-B+SQ)/D
26               X2=(-B-SQ)/D
27               WRITE(6,1040)A,B,C,X1,X2
28            ELSE
29               SQABS=SQRT(ABS(DISC))
30               X1=-B/D
31               X11=SQABS/D
32               X2=X1
33               X22=-X11
34               WRITE(6,1050)A,B,C,X1,X11,X2,X22
35            ENDIF
36         ENDIF
37         READ(5,1060)A,B,C
38       ENDWHILE
39       STOP
40       END
```

```
                   ROOTS OF QUADRATIC EQUATION

 A          B              C             ROOT1              ROOT2


  1.0000     3.0000         2.0000        -1.0000            -2.0000
  1.0000      .0000        -4.0000         2.0000            -2.0000
  1.0000     2.0000        -3.0000         1.0000            -3.0000
 10.0000    26.0000        12.0000         -.6000            -2.0000
 24.0000    62.0000        35.0000         -.8333            -1.7500
 11.2750    40.2100        31.0000        -1.1273            -2.4390
   .0000    30.0000        60.0000        -2.0000
   .0000    15.0000        75.0000        -5.0000
 10.0000    -5.0000         5.0000         .2500+    .6614I     .2500-   -.6614I
  1.0000     1.0000         4.0000        -.5000+   1.9365I    -.5000-  -1.9365I
  1.0000      .0000        25.0000         .0000+   5.0000I     .0000-  -5.0000I
  1.0000      .0000        49.9000         .0000+   7.0640I     .0000-  -7.0640I
```

FIGURE 9.1   *Calculation of the roots of the quadratic equation*

1. The first ball rolled in the frame knocks down all 10 pins—a strike. No more balls are rolled in that frame. The score for the frame is the number of pins knocked down plus the sum of the number of pins knocked down by the next two balls rolled [in the next frame(s)] .
2. The first ball rolled in the frame fails to knock down all the pins, but the second ball knocks down the remaining pins. This is called a spare. The score for the frame is the sum of the number of pins knocked down by these two balls plus the number of pins knocked down by the first ball in the next frame.
3. The two balls rolled in a frame may fail to knock down all 10 pins. This is called an open frame. The score for the frame is the number of pins knocked down by the two balls rolled in the frame.

Notice that for a strike, the pins knocked down by the second and third balls are counted in the scoring of more than one frame. For a spare, the number of pins knocked down by the third ball is counted in the scoring of two frames. Thus sequences of strikes and spares cause a rapid increase in score. The tenth frame is exceptional in that three balls may be rolled, instead of the normal maximum of two, if a strike or spare is made in the tenth frame. This exception about the number of balls rolled was introduced to make the scoring rules given above apply to the tenth frame. As the game proceeds, players maintain a cumulative score by adding the score for the current frame to the cumulative score up to that frame.

To illustrate the scoring rules and to give a sample of the output wanted, a sample game is shown below.

FRAME	BALL 1	BALL 2	SCORE	
1	6	4	20	SPARE
2	10		39	STRIKE
3	3	6	48	OPEN
4	5	5	68	SPARE
5	10		95	STRIKE
6	10		115	STRIKE
7	7	3	135	SPARE
8	10		150	STRIKE
9	5	0	155	OPEN
10	6	4	174	SPARE
10	9			

Some sample score computations are

Frame 1: a spare $SCORE = 0 + \underbrace{6 + 4} + 10 = 20$

previous   frame   from frame
score   1   2

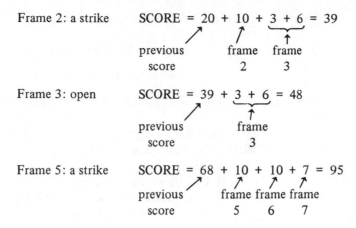

Frame 2: a strike   SCORE = 20 + 10 + 3 + 6 = 39

previous   frame   frame
score   2   3

Frame 3: open   SCORE = 39 + 3 + 6 = 48

previous   frame
score   3

Frame 5: a strike   SCORE = 68 + 10 + 10 + 7 = 95

previous   frame frame frame
score   5   6   7

This is an extremely interesting problem for computer solution for two reasons: (1) almost everyone learns to score the game of bowling after a few games, and (2) almost everyone has a very difficult time writing a computer program to do the scoring. Usually, many hours (even days) are required by the typical student to write a successful program. Why? The arithmetic is trivial, and the final program does not have many more steps than programs considered previously. But the required nesting of decisions makes organizing the program logic very difficult. Using structured programming and stepwise refinement can be quite helpful in writing the program. To emphasize the value of structured programming, a nonstructured solution will be given in a later section—it will be a challenge to understand the nonstructured program. Before reading the proposed solution, you can give your programming skills a rigorous test by writing the program for yourself.

I wrote several programs which worked satisfactorily—they gave correct scores—before I selected the one that is presented here. Each of the discarded programs has one or more features that was not aesthetically pleasing, and I am confident that there must be a better method than the one presented. It is fairly easy to write a more satisfying program using subscripted variables (to be discussed in detail later). Stepwise refinement was used in all my attempts.

A. Level 1 Solution

This design for the program is based on the following observations:

1. The first 9 frames are different from the tenth frame in that:
   a. A maximum of two balls are rolled in any frame through frame 9.
   b. Either two or three balls may be rolled in frame 10.
2. The scores for both strikes and spares are computed by adding the pins knocked down by three consecutive balls.

Thus the program will be organized in the form

score the first nine frames

score the tenth frame

After some work, the following tentative solution is obtained:

```
read first ball of first game
WHILE (there are games to be played)
     initialize
     WHILE (it is frame 1 through 9)
          IF (a strike or spare occurs) THEN
               compute score
               write score
               rename balls used to compute score
          ELSE
               compute score
               write score
               read next ball
          ENDIF
          increase frame
     ENDWHILE
     IF (strike or spare in tenth frame) THEN
          read last ball
          compute score
          write score
     ELSE
          compute score
          write score
     ENDIF
     read first ball of next game
ENDWHILE
STOP
END
```

B. Level 2 Solution

A value of 99 for the first ball of a game will be used to indicate that no more games are to be played. (This value could never occur in a real game.) All computations should be in the integer mode, since it is not possible to knock down a fraction of a pin. In computing the score for a frame, it may be necessary to know the number of pins knocked down by three balls. The variables BALL1, BALL2, and BALL3 will be used for these values with the last character in the name 1, 2, or 3 serving to indicate the sequence for rolling the balls. The revised solution is

```
read BALL1
WHILE (BALL1 .NE. 99)
    initialize                                              (1)
    WHILE (FRAME .LE. 9)
        IF (BALL1 + BALL2 .GE. 10) THEN                     (2)
            SCORE = SCORE + BALL1 + BALL2 + BALL3  (3)
            write score                                     (4)
            rename balls used to compute score              (5)
        ELSE
            SCORE = SCORE + BALL1 + BALL2
            write score
            read next ball                                  (6)
        ENDIF
        FRAME = FRAME + 1
    ENDWHILE
    IF (BALL1 + BALL2 .GE. 10) THEN
        read BALL3
        SCORE = SCORE + BALL1 + BALL2 + BALL3
        write score                                         (7)
    ELSE
        SCORE = SCORE + BALL1 + BALL2
        write score
    ENDIF
    read BALL1
ENDWHILE
STOP
END
```

C. Level 3 Solution

There are still many problems associated with obtaining a complete solution. In the line identified as (1), we know part of what is required:

(1) initialize $\Longrightarrow$ SCORE = 0

FRAME = 1

initialize   (for things not discovered yet)

At line (2) the value of BALL2 is used, but the value has not been read. Should the READ statement be placed before or after WHILE? (It could be done either way, but the choice will affect the rest of the program.) As a guess, the READ statement will be placed before the WHILE. Line (3) is a problem because the value of BALL3 is not known. A READ statement will be placed immediately before line (3). Lines (4) and (5) are a problem to expand. The way the score is written, line (4) will depend upon whether a strike or spare was rolled. The same problem exists for line (7). The renaming of balls in line (5) will depend upon the technique used to handle line (4). To avoid getting lost in details, the expansion of lines (4), (5), and (7) will be delayed until the next level. The solution at this stage is

```
read BALL1
WHILE (BALL1 .NE. 99)
    SCORE = 0
    FRAME = 1
    initialize                                          (8)
    read BALL2
    WHILE (FRAME .LE. 9)
        IF (BALL1 + BALL2 .GE. 10) THEN
            read BALL3
            SCORE = SCORE + BALL1 + BALL2 + BALL3
            write score                                 (9)
            rename balls used to compute score          (10)
        ELSE
            SCORE = SCORE + BALL1 + BALL2
            write score                                 (11)
            read BALL1, BALL2
        ENDIF
        FRAME = FRAME + 1
    ENDWHILE
    IF (BALL1 + BALL2 .GE. 10) THEN
        read BALL3
        SCORE = SCORE + BALL1 + BALL2 + BALL3
        write score                                     (12)
    ELSE
        SCORE = SCORE + BALL1 + BALL2
        write score
    ENDIF
    read BALL1
ENDWHILE
STOP
END
```

4. Level 4 Solution

The remaining problems at lines (9), (11), and (12) involve the writing of scores. Lines (9) and (12) are both embedded in an IF statement which guarantees that a strike or spare is made before the WRITE statement is reached. Since the writing to be done depends upon whether a strike or a spare has been made, an additional IF statement must be inserted. The renaming of balls at line (10) also depends on whether a strike or a spare is made, and thus the renaming statements are included in the new IF statement. For lines (9) and (10) we shall insert (ignoring the FORMAT statements for now)

```
IF (BALL1 .EQ. 10) THEN
      WRITE (6,  ) FRAME, BALL1, SCORE
      BALL1 = BALL2
      BALL2 = BALL3
ELSE
      WRITE (6,  ) FRAME, BALL1, BALL2, SCORE
      BALL1 = BALL3
      READ (5,  ) BALL2
ENDIF
```

In the section for a strike, the statements

```
BALL1 = BALL2
BALL2 = BALL3
```

recognize that in the case of a strike, the second and third balls used in the scoring are the first and second balls for the next frame. In the section for a spare (ELSE clause), the statements

```
BALL1 = BALL3
READ (5,  ) BALL2
```

recognize that the third ball used in the scoring is the first ball of the next frame and that the second ball of the frame needs to be read before beginning processing for the next frame. A similar IF statement without the renaming of balls and with appropriate WRITE statements needs to be inserted at line (12). No further initialization appears to be needed at line (8), so that line will be dropped. The WRITE statement at (11) does not involve further decisions and is included as (ignoring the FORMAT statement)

```
WRITE (6,  ) FRAME, BALL1, BALL2, SCORE
```

The computer printout for the final solution is shown in Figure 9.2.

9.2   LOGICAL VARIABLES, EXPRESSIONS, AND STATEMENTS

The component of an IF statement called the "condition" is an example of a logical expression. A *logical expression* is defined as any expression that always gives a

```
 1 C
 2 C          SCORING OF BOWLING
 3 C
 4           INTEGER BALL1,BALL2,BALL3,FRAME,SCORE
 5 1000 FORMAT('1')
 6 1010 FORMAT('0','FRAME',4X,'BALL 1',4X,'BALL 2',4X,'SCORE')
 7 1020 FORMAT(' ',I3,7X,I2,18X,I3,6X,'STRIKE')
 8 1030 FORMAT(' ',I3,7X,I2,8X,I2,8X,I3,6X,'SPARE')
 9 1040 FORMAT(' ',I3,7X,I2,8X,I2,8X,I3,6X,'OPEN')
10 1050 FORMAT(' ',I3,7X,I2)
11 1060 FORMAT(' ',I3,7X,I2,8X,I2)
12 1070 FORMAT(I2)
13      WRITE(6,1000)
14      READ(5,1070)BALL1
15      WHILE( BALL1 .NE. 99)
16         SCORE=0
17         FRAME=1
18         WRITE(6,1010)
19         READ(5,1070)BALL2
20         WHILE( FRAME .LE. 9)
21            IF( BALL1+BALL2 .GE. 10) THEN
22               READ(5,1070)BALL3
23               SCORE=SCORE+BALL1+BALL2+BALL3
24               IF( BALL1 .EQ. 10) THEN
25                  WRITE(6,1020)FRAME,BALL1,SCORE
26                  BALL1=BALL2
27                  BALL2=BALL3
28               ELSE
29                  WRITE(6,1030)FRAME,BALL1,BALL2,SCORE
30                  BALL1=BALL3
31                  READ(5,1070)BALL2
32               ENDIF
33            ELSE
34               SCORE=SCORE+BALL1+BALL2
35               WRITE(6,1040)FRAME,BALL1,BALL2,SCORE
36               READ(5,1070)BALL1,BALL2
37            ENDIF
38            FRAME=FRAME+1
39         ENDWHILE
40         IF( BALL1+BALL2 .GE. 10) THEN
41            READ(5,1070)BALL3
42            SCORE=SCORE+BALL1+BALL2+BALL3
43            IF( BALL1 .EQ. 10) THEN
44               WRITE(6,1020)FRAME,BALL1,SCORE
45               WRITE(6,1050)FRAME,BALL2
46               WRITE(6,1050)FRAME,BALL3
47            ELSE
48               WRITE(6,1030)FRAME,BALL1,BALL2,SCORE
49               WRITE(6,1050)FRAME,BALL3
50            ENDIF
51         ELSE
52            SCORE=SCORE+BALL1+BALL2
53            WRITE(6,1040)FRAME,BALL1,BALL2,SCORE
54         ENDIF
55         READ(5,1070)BALL1
```

FIGURE 9.2 *Scoring of bowling*

```
56        ENDWHILE
57        STOP
58        END
```

FRAME	BALL 1	BALL 2	SCORE	
1	10		30	STRIKE
2	10		60	STRIKE
3	10		90	STRIKE
4	10		120	STRIKE
5	10		150	STRIKE
6	10		180	STRIKE
7	10		210	STRIKE
8	10		240	STRIKE
9	10		270	STRIKE
10	10		300	STRIKE
10	10			
10	10			

FRAME	BALL 1	BALL 2	SCORE	
1	10		30	STRIKE
2	10		60	STRIKE
3	10		90	STRIKE
4	10		120	STRIKE
5	10		150	STRIKE
6	10		180	STRIKE
7	10		210	STRIKE
8	10		240	STRIKE
9	10		268	STRIKE
10	10		287	STRIKE
10	8	1		

FRAME	BALL 1	BALL 2	SCORE	
1	10		30	STRIKE
2	10		60	STRIKE
3	10		90	STRIKE
4	10		120	STRIKE
5	10		150	STRIKE
6	10		180	STRIKE
7	10		201	STRIKE
8	10		215	STRIKE
9	1	3	219	OPEN
10	10		239	STRIKE
10	8	2		

FRAME	BALL 1	BALL 2	SCORE	
1	10		30	STRIKE
2	10		51	STRIKE
3	10		71	STRIKE
4	1	9	83	SPARE
5	2	8	96	SPARE
6	3	7	110	SPARE
7	4	6	125	SPARE
8	5	5	145	SPARE
9	10		156	STRIKE
10	0	1	157	OPEN

FIGURE 9.2 *(cont.)*

value of TRUE or FALSE. Examples of logical expressions in the bowling problem are

$$BALL1 .NE. 99$$
$$FRAME .LE. 9$$
$$BALL1 + BALL2 .GE. 10$$
$$BALL1 .EQ. 10$$

Expressions such as these which are constructed using the relational operators constitute one class of logical expressions.

The value of a logical expression can be assigned to a logical variable. Suppose that STRIKE is a *logical variable*, that is, a variable whose only allowed values are TRUE or FALSE. Then the statement

$$STRIKE = BALL1 .EQ. 10$$

will assign the value TRUE to STRIKE if BALL1 equals 10, and otherwise will assign the value FALSE. In order for a variable to be used in this manner, it must be specified as a logical variable in a declaration statement at the beginning of the program:

$$LOGICAL STRIKE$$

The use of the LOGICAL declaration statement is similar to that of the REAL and the INTEGER statements.

Initial values can be assigned to logical variables using the logical constants

$$.TRUE.$$
$$.FALSE.$$

(The periods on each side of these words are required.) For example,

LOGICAL EOF, STRIKE, SPARE
.
.
.
.
EOF = .FALSE.
STRIKE = .FALSE.
SPARE = .TRUE.

are valid FORTRAN statements.

Logical variables can be combined in expressions using the FORTRAN *logical operators* .AND. , .OR. , .NOT. , .EQU. , and .NEQU. which obey the normal rules for logic. The following are valid logical expressions:

$$OP1 .AND. OP2$$

OP1 .OR. OP2

OP1 .EQU. OP2

OP1 .NEQU. OP2

.NOT. OP1

where OP1 and OP2 are variables that have been defined as LOGICAL or are expressions that evaluate to .TRUE. or .FALSE.

The application of the .AND. operation gives a value of .TRUE. if and only if both its operands have the value .TRUE.; otherwise, the value is .FALSE. (see Table 9.1).

TABLE 9.1 *Definition of the logical operators*

		OP2	
	.AND.	.FALSE.	.TRUE.
OP1	.FALSE.	.FALSE.	.FALSE.
	.TRUE.	.FALSE.	.TRUE.

		OP2	
	.OR.	.FALSE.	.TRUE.
OP1	.FALSE.	.FALSE.	.TRUE.
	.TRUE.	.TRUE.	.TRUE.

		OP2	
	.EQU.	.FALSE.	.TRUE.
OP1	.FALSE.	.TRUE.	.FALSE.
	.TRUE.	.FALSE.	.TRUE.

		OP2	
	.NEQU.	.FALSE.	.TRUE.
OP1	.FALSE.	.FALSE.	.TRUE.
	.TRUE.	.TRUE.	.FALSE.

	.NOT.	
OP1	.FALSE.	.TRUE.
	.TRUE.	.FALSE.

Application of the .OR. operation gives a value of .TRUE. if either of the operands has the value .TRUE. The equivalence operator .EQU. produces a value of .TRUE., if both its operands are true or both are false. The nonequivalence operator .NEQU. produces a value of .TRUE. only if its operands have different values. The operation .NOT. produces a value that is the opposite of the value of its operand.

To illustrate the application of these operators, let us assume that

LOGICAL LX, LY, LZ
LX = .TRUE.
LY = .TRUE.
LZ = .FALSE.

Then

Logical expression	Value
LX .AND. LY	.TRUE.
LX .AND. LZ	.FALSE.
LZ .AND. LX	.FALSE.
LZ .AND. LY	.FALSE.
LX .OR. LY	.TRUE.
LX .OR. LZ	.TRUE.
LY .OR. LZ	.TRUE.
LX .EQU. LY	.TRUE.
LX .EQU. LZ	.FALSE.
LX .NEQU. LY	.FALSE.
LX .NEQU. LZ	.TRUE.
.NOT. LX	.FALSE.
.NOT. LY	.FALSE.
.NOT. LZ	.TRUE.

Logical expressions can be combined to form larger logical expressions of arbitrary complexity. Using the same values for LX, LY, and LZ gives, for example, the following:

Logical expression	Value
(LX .OR. LZ) .AND. LY	.TRUE.
(LX .OR. LY) .AND. (.NOT. LZ)	.TRUE.
(.NOT. (LX .OR. LY)) .AND. LY	.FALSE.
(LX .AND. LY) .OR. (LX .AND. LZ)	.TRUE.
(LX .EQU. LY) .OR. (LX .AND. LZ)	.TRUE.

where the expressions in parentheses have been evaluated first

To resolve ambiguities in the order of application of logical operations, the hierarchy in Table 9.2 is assumed.

TABLE 9.2 *Hierarchy of logical operations*

Operation	Hierarchy[a]
.NOT.	Highest (apply first)
.AND.	Intermediate 1
.OR.	Intermediate 2
.EQU. or .NEQU.	Lowest (apply last)

[a]Parentheses can be used to change the order of evaluation.

The hierarchy rules imply the order of evaluation in the following expressions to be:

1. LX .OR. LY .AND. .NOT. LZ
          ↑   ↑   ↑
        3rd   2nd   1st

   which is equivalent to

   LX .OR. (LY .AND. (.NOT. LZ))

2. (LX .OR. LY) .AND. (.NOT. LZ)
           ↑   ↑   ↑
          1st   3rd   2nd

3. LX .AND. LY .OR. LZ
            ↑   ↑
          1st   2nd

4. LX .OR. LY .AND. LZ
           ↑   ↑
         2nd   1st

The most complicated logical expressions contain arithmetic operators, relational operators, and logical operators, as in

A + B .GT. 99. .OR. A - B .LT. 50.

What is the order of evaluation in this expression? The rule is:

In logical expressions, evaluate operations in the order

arithmetic operations	first
relational operations	second
logical operations	third

except as modified by parentheses.

Thus the evaluation of the previous expression is

$$A + B \text{ .GT. } 99. \text{ .OR. } A - B \text{ .LT. } 50.$$
$$\uparrow \qquad \uparrow \qquad \uparrow \qquad \uparrow \qquad \uparrow$$
$$\text{1st} \qquad \text{3rd} \qquad \text{5th} \qquad \text{2nd} \qquad \text{4th}$$

which is equivalent to

$$((A+B) \text{ .GT. } 99.) \text{ .OR. } ((A-B) \text{ .LT. } 50.)$$

You should make liberal use of parentheses whenever you have doubts about the evaluation of an expression. Use of parentheses may make the expression easier to read even when you have no doubts about the order of evaluation.

Logical variables are used in programs:

1. To avoid multiple evaluations of logical expressions.
2. To improve program clarity.
3. To serve as indicators, called *flags*, of program states.

Suppose that a program has three occurrences of IF statements of the form

IF (X .EQ. Y) THEN
.
.
.
ENDIF

The condition X. EQ. Y would have to be evaluated each time that it is encountered. The multiple evaluation could be avoided by inserting in the program

LOGICAL LVALUE
.
.
.
LVALUE = X .EQ. Y

with the IF statements then having the form

IF (LVALUE) THEN
.
.
.
ENDIF

If you use this technique, be sure the logical statement appears as many times as necessary—it may not be sufficient to insert the logical statement a single time. Again, consider the bowling program. The condition BALL1 + BALL2 .GE. 10 appears in two IF statements

```
            .
            .
            .

        WHILE (FRAME .LE. 9)
            IF (BALL1 + BALL2 .GE. 10) THEN
            .
            .
            .

        ENDWHILE
        IF (BALL1 + BALL2 .GE. 10) THEN
            .
            .
            .
```

which could be changed to

```
        LOGICAL ALLPIN
            .
            .
            .

        WHILE (FRAME .LE. 9)
            ALLPIN = BALL1 + BALL2 .GE. 10              (1)
            IF (ALLPIN) THEN
            .
            .
            .

        ENDWHILE
        ALLPIN = BALL1 + BALL2 .GE. 10                  (2)
        IF (ALLPIN) THEN
            .
            .
            .
```

The statement marked (2) is essential because the values of BALL1 and BALL2 change between the two statements (1) and (2).

The use of logical variables to improve program clarity is highly desirable, but it is not always obvious what constitutes improved readability and clarity. For example, the bowling example includes the statement

IF (BALL1 + BALL2 .GE. 10) THEN
.
.

.

ENDIF

which tests for a possible strike or spare. The statement can be rewritten using the logical operator .OR.

IF ((BALL1.EQ. 10) .OR. ((BALL1 + BALL2) .EQ. 10)) THEN
.
.
.

.

ENDIF

Which is clearer? A third possibility is to redefine the statement using logical variables.

LOGICAL STRIKE, SPARE
.

.

.

.

STRIKE = BALL1 .EQ. 10
SPARE = BALL1 + BALL2 .EQ. 10
IF (STRIKE .OR. SPARE) THEN
.

.

.

ENDIF

Which of the three methods is clearest? The answer depends upon the person. My guess is that the last method will be clearest to a person who is studying the program for the first time. Figure 9.3 gives the bowling program using logical variables.

In the program of Figure 9.3, the variable PLAY is an example of a flag used to signal whether or not a new game is to be played. Flags can be used whenever you need to pass program status information from one part of a program to another. PLAY is not, however, a particularly good example of a flag, since it is used in only one decision statement in the program. Normally, a flag is introduced when the information is used in several decisions. For example, suppose that in printing a long, complex report, there are several places at which a particular explanation line may or may not be printed, depending upon what has happened so far in the program. The status for printing the line may be conveniently saved as the value of a flag.

```
1   C
2   C           SCORING OF BOWLING
3   C           ILLUSTRATION OF LOGICAL VARIABLES
4   C
5           INTEGER BALL1,BALL2,BALL3,FRAME,SCORE
6           LOGICAL PLAY,STRIKE,SPARE
7   1000 FORMAT('1')
8   1010 FORMAT('0','FRAME',4X,'BALL 1',4X,'BALL 2',4X,'SCORE')
9   1020 FORMAT(' ',I3,7X,I2,18X,I3,6X,'STRIKE')
10  1030 FORMAT(' ',I3,7X,I2,8X,I2,8X,I3,6X,'SPARE')
11  1040 FORMAT(' ',I3,7X,I2,8X,I2,8X,I3,6X,'OPEN')
12  1050 FORMAT(' ',I3,7X,I2)
13  1060 FORMAT(' ',I3,7X,I2,8X,I2)
14  1070 FORMAT(I2)
15         WRITE(6,1000)
16         READ(5,1070)BALL1
17         PLAY=BALL1 .NE. 99
18         WHILE(PLAY)
19            SCORE=0
20            FRAME=1
21            WRITE(6,1010)
22            READ(5,1070)BALL2
23            STRIKE=BALL1 .EQ. 10
24            SPARE= BALL1+BALL2 .EQ. 10
25            WHILE( FRAME .LE. 9)
26               IF(STRIKE .OR. SPARE) THEN
27                  READ(5,1070)BALL3
28                  SCORE=SCORE+BALL1+BALL2+BALL3
29                  IF(STRIKE) THEN
30                     WRITE(6,1020)FRAME,BALL1,SCORE
31                     BALL1=BALL2
32                     BALL2=BALL3
33                  ELSE
34                     WRITE(6,1030)FRAME,BALL1,BALL2,SCORE
35                     BALL1=BALL3
36                     READ(5,1070)BALL2
37                  ENDIF
38               ELSE
39                  SCORE=SCORE+BALL1+BALL2
40                  WRITE(6,1040)FRAME,BALL1,BALL2,SCORE
41                  READ(5,1070)BALL1,BALL2
42               ENDIF
43               FRAME=FRAME+1
44               STRIKE= BALL1 .EQ. 10
45               SPARE= BALL1+BALL2 .EQ. 10
46            ENDWHILE
47            IF(STRIKE .OR. SPARE) THEN
48               READ(5,1070)BALL3
49               SCORE=SCORE+BALL1+BALL2+BALL3
50               IF(STRIKE) THEN
51                  WRITE(6,1020)FRAME,BALL1,SCORE
```

FIGURE 9.3 *Scoring of bowling: illustration of logical variables*

```
52              WRITE(6,1050)FRAME,BALL2
53              WRITE(6,1050)FRAME,BALL3
54          ELSE
55              WRITE(6,1030)FRAME,BALL1,BALL2,SCORE
56              WRITE(6,1050)FRAME,BALL3
57          ENDIF
58       ELSE
59          SCORE=SCORE+BALL1+BALL2
60          WRITE(6,1040)FRAME,BALL1,BALL2,SCORE
61       ENDIF
62       READ(5,1070)BALL1
63       PLAY= BALL1 .NE. 99
64    ENDWHILE
65    STOP
66    END
```

FRAME	BALL 1	BALL 2	SCORE	
1	10		30	STRIKE
2	10		60	STRIKE
3	10		90	STRIKE
4	10		120	STRIKE
5	10		150	STRIKE
6	10		180	STRIKE
7	10		210	STRIKE
8	10		240	STRIKE
9	10		270	STRIKE
10	10		300	STRIKE
10	10			
10	10			

FRAME	BALL 1	BALL 2	SCORE	
1	10		30	STRIKE
2	10		60	STRIKE
3	10		90	STRIKE
4	10		120	STRIKE
5	10		150	STRIKE
6	10		180	STRIKE
7	10		210	STRIKE
8	10		240	STRIKE
9	10		268	STRIKE
10	10		287	STRIKE
10	8			
10	1			

FRAME	BALL 1	BALL 2	SCORE	
1	10		30	STRIKE
2	10		60	STRIKE
3	10		90	STRIKE
4	10		120	STRIKE
5	10		150	STRIKE
6	10		180	STRIKE

FIGURE 9.3   *(cont.)*

230

7	10		201	STRIKE
8	10		215	STRIKE
9	1	3	219	OPEN
10	10		239	STRIKE
10	8			
10	2			

FRAME	BALL 1	BALL 2	SCORE	
1	10		30	STRIKE
2	10		51	STRIKE
3	10		71	STRIKE
4	1	9	83	SPARE
5	2	8	96	SPARE
6	3	7	110	SPARE
7	4	6	125	SPARE
8	5	5	145	SPARE
9	10		156	STRIKE
10	0	1	157	OPEN

FIGURE 9.3 (*cont.*)

The values of logical variables may be read or printed using a technique similar to that used for integers. The form of the specification for use in FORMAT statements is

Lw   where w is the field width

The following statements read logical values entered as T or F and prints them as T or F.

LOGICAL L,M,N
.
.
.

READ (5,1000) L,M,N
1000 FORMAT (3L5)
WRITE (6,1010) L,M,N
1010 FORMAT (' ', 3L10)

Input values should be right-justified within their fields.

9.3   ELSEIF STATEMENT

As the nesting of IF statements becomes deeper, it becomes more difficult for us to remember the details that will lead to the execution of a particular deeply nested block of statements. (Remember George Miller's work on short-term memory.) You can experience this difficulty directly by deciding upon the conditions that will lead to the execution of the statements called "block X" in the following:

```
            IF (A .EQ. B) THEN
            .
            .
            .
            IF (C .GT. D) THEN
            .
            .
            .
            ELSE
                .
                .
                .
                IF (E .LE. F) THEN
                .
                .
                .
                IF (G .GE. H) THEN
                .
                .
                .
                ELSE
                    .
                    .
                    .
                    IF (P .LT. R) THEN
                    .
                    .
                    .
                    ELSE
                        .
                        .
                        .
                        IF (R .EQ. Q) THEN
                        .
                        .
                        .
                        block X
                        .
                        .
                        .
                        ENDIF
                    ENDIF
                ENDIF
                ENDIF
            ENDIF
        ENDIF
```

Block X will be executed when all of the following are true simultaneously:

1. A is equal to B.
2. C is not greater than D.
3. E is less than or equal to F.
4. G is not greater than or equal to H.
5. P is not less than R.
6. R is equal to Q.

Did you reach the same conclusion given here? Are you certain that the answer given here is correct? Could you have remembered all these details if you had to modify the program to include another situation? Would modification be more difficult if there were more IF statements? Consideration of this example and others leads to the conclusion:

> Deeply nested IF statements should be avoided in writing computer programs.

A corollary of this conclusion is

> Structured programs can be made incomprehensible by using deeply nested IF statements.

In writing programs, circumstances may arise in which it is extremely difficult to avoid using deeply nested IF statements—you should, however, make the attempt to avoid them. A programming construct that can sometimes be used to clarify the program logic is the ELSEIF statement.

```
IF (condition 1) THEN
    .
    .
    .

ELSEIF (condition 2) THEN
    .
    .
    .

ELSEIF (condition 3) THEN
    .
    .
    .

ELSEIF (condition n) THEN
    .
    .
    .

ENDIF    Note: Else can occur after last ELSEIF.
```

There can be an arbitrary number of ELSEIF clauses in the statement. Execution proceeds by testing of the conditions until a condition is found that is true; then the block of statements following the ELSEIF (or IF) up to the next ELSEIF (or ENDIF) is executed; and then the statement immediately following the ENDIF is executed. Notice that (1) if none of the conditions is true, no block of statements is executed within the IF statement, and (2) only one block of statements is executed. These ideas are illustrated by the following simple example.

Example 3:   Quiz Grades—Illustration of ELSEIF statement
Write a program that reads a student ID number and quiz score and prints a letter grade according to the scale

A	above 90
B	80–89
C	70–79
D	60–69
F	less than 60

The program should work for an arbitrary number of scores. A negative score is the last card indicator.

Solution

A solution using the ELSEIF statement is given in Figure 9.4, and another solution using the standard IF statement is given in Figure 9.5.

The heart of the program that uses the ELSEIF statement is the ELSEIF statement itself:

```
IF (SCORE .GE. 90) THEN                    (1)
    WRITE (6,1020) IDNUM, SCORE            (2)
ELSEIF (SCORE .GE. 80) THEN                (3)
    WRITE (6,1030) IDNUM, SCORE            (4)
ELSEIF (SCORE .GE. 70) THEN                (5)
    WRITE (6,1040) IDNUM, SCORE            (6)
ELSEIF (SCORE .GE. 60) THEN                (7)
    WRITE (6,1050) IDNUM, SCORE            (8)
ELSEIF (SCORE .LT. 60) THEN                (9)
    WRITE (6,1060) IDNUM, SCORE           (10)
ENDIF                                      (11)
```

Suppose that a SCORE of 64 is read. Then:

1. Conditions (1), (3), and (5) will be tested in succession, and all will evaluate to false.

```
 1 C
 2 C           QUIZ GRADES     ILLUSTRATION OF ELSEIF STATEMENT
 3 C
 4           INTEGER SCORE
 5 1000     FORMAT('1',T20,'QUIZ SCORES')
 6 1010     FORMAT('0',T10,'ID NUMBER',T25,'SCORE',T36,'GRADE')
 7 1020     FORMAT(' ',T14,I4,T26,I3,T38,'A')
 8 1030     FORMAT(' ',T14,I4,T26,I3,T38,'B')
 9 1040     FORMAT(' ',T14,I4,T26,I3,T38,'C')
10 1050     FORMAT(' ',T14,I4,T26,I3,T38,'D')
11 1060     FORMAT(' ',T14,I4,T26,I3,T38,'F')
12 1070     FORMAT(2I5)
13          WRITE(6,1000)
14          WRITE(6,1010)
15          READ(5,1070)IDNUM,SCORE
16          WHILE( SCORE .GE. 0)
17             IF( SCORE .GE. 90) THEN
18                WRITE(6,1020)IDNUM,SCORE
19             ELSEIF( SCORE .GE. 80) THEN
20                WRITE(6,1030)IDNUM,SCORE
21             ELSEIF( SCORE .GE. 70) THEN
22                WRITE(6,1040)IDNUM,SCORE
23             ELSEIF( SCORE .GE. 60) THEN
24                WRITE(6,1050)IDNUM,SCORE
25             ELSEIF( SCORE .LT. 60) THEN
26                WRITE(6,1060)IDNUM,SCORE
27             ENDIF
28             READ(5,1070)IDNUM,SCORE
29          ENDWHILE
30          STOP
31          END
```

```
                              QUIZ SCORES

         ID NUMBER          SCORE          GRADE
              1001            83             B
              1002            92             A
              1003            76             C
              1004            54             F
              1005            73             C
              1006            61             D
              1007            73             C
              1008            77             C
              1009            78             C
              1010            82             B
              1011            84             B
              1012            79             C
              1013            87             B
              1014            64             D
              1015            54             F
              1016            71             C
              1017            91             A
              1018            58             F
              1019            88             B
              1020            97             A
```

FIGURE 9.4   *Quiz grades: illustration of ELSEIF statement*

```
1 C
2 C              QUIZ GRADES          IF...ELSE...ENDIF STATEMENTS
3 C
4        INTEGER SCORE
5 1000 FORMAT('1',T20,'QUIZ GRADES')
6 1010 FORMAT('0',T10,'ID NUMBER',T25,'SCORE',T36,'GRADE')
7 1020 FORMAT(' ',T14,I4,T26,I3,T38,'A')
8 1030 FORMAT(' ',T14,I4,T26,I3,T38,'B')
9 1040 FORMAT(' ',T14,I4,T26,I3,T38,'C')
10 1050 FORMAT(' ',T14,I4,T26,I3,T38,'D')
11 1060 FORMAT(' ',T14,I4,T26,I3,T38,'F')
12 1070 FORMAT(2I5)
13      WRITE(6,1000)
14      WRITE(6,1010)
15      READ(5,1070)IDNUM,SCORE
16      WHILE( SCORE .GE. 0)
17        IF( SCORE .GE. 90) THEN
18            WRITE(6,1020)IDNUM,SCORE
19        ELSE
20          IF(SCORE .GE. 80) THEN
21              WRITE(6,1030)IDNUM,SCORE
22          ELSE
23            IF( SCORE .GE. 70) THEN
24                WRITE(6,1040)IDNUM,SCORE
25            ELSE
26              IF( SCORE .GE. 60) THEN
27                  WRITE(6,1050)IDNUM,SCORE
28              ELSE
29                  WRITE(6,1060)IDNUM,SCORE
30              ENDIF
31            ENDIF
32          ENDIF
33        ENDIF
34        READ(5,1070)IDNUM,SCORE
35      ENDWHILE
36      STOP
37      END
```

                          QUIZ GRADES

ID NUMBER	SCORE	GRADE
1001	83	B
1002	92	A
1003	76	C
1004	54	F
1005	73	C
1006	61	D
1007	73	C
1008	77	C
1009	78	C

FIGURE 9.5 *Quiz grades: using standard IF statements*

236

1010	62	B
1011	84	B
1012	79	C
1013	87	B
1014	64	D
1015	54	F
1016	71	C
1017	91	A
1018	58	F
1019	88	B
1020	97	A

FIGURE 9.5   (*cont.*)

2. Condition (7) is tested and found to be true. Thus the statement (8)

$$\text{WRITE (6,1050) IDNUM, SCORE}$$

is executed. (If there had been more than one statement in the block, additional statements would have been executed.)
3. The program executes next the statement that follows ENDIF.

Suppose that a SCORE of 90 is read. Then:

1. Condition (1) is tested and found to be true. Thus the statement (2)

$$\text{WRITE (6,1020) IDNUM, SCORE}$$

is executed.
2. The program executes next the statement that follows ENDIF.

The order of occurrence of the ELSEIF conditions is critical for the program as it is written. If the conditions were accidentally interchanged to give

```
IF (SCORE .GE. 70) THEN
    WRITE (6,1040) IDNUM, SCORE
ELSEIF (SCORE .GE. 80) THEN
    WRITE (6,1030) IDNUM, SCORE
ELSEIF (SCORE .GE. 90) THEN
    WRITE (6,1020) IDNUM, SCORE
ELSEIF (SCORE .GE. 60) THEN
    WRITE (6,1050) IDNUM, SCORE
ELSEIF (SCORE .LT. 60) THEN
    WRITE (6,1060) IDNUM, SCORE
ENDIF
```

a score of 93 would print a grade of C (93 is greater than or equal to 70). In fact, all scores of 70 or above would print a grade of C. The statements

ELSEIF (SCORE .GE. 80) THEN

ELSEIF (SCORE .GE. 90) THEN

would never be executed, since any score that would satisfy them would satisfy IF (SCORE .GE. 70) earlier in the program.

The danger of obtaining invalid results from ELSEIF statements out of proper sequence can be eliminated (or at least reduced) by using more explicit conditions. In the program a grade of C is printed if the score is 70 or above and the grade is not A or B; that is, the score is less than 80. Using the grading scale as given in the statement of the problem would produce

```
IF (SCORE .GE. 90) THEN
    WRITE (6,1020) IDNUM, SCORE
ELSEIF ((SCORE .LE. 89) .AND. (SCORE .GE. 80)) THEN
    WRITE (6,1030) IDNUM, SCORE
ELSEIF ((SCORE .LE. 79) .AND. (SCORE .GE. 70)) THEN
    WRITE (6,1040) IDNUM, SCORE
ELSEIF ((SCORE .LE. 69) .AND. (SCORE .GE. 60)) THEN
    WRITE (6,1050) IDNUM, SCORE
ELSEIF (SCORE .LT. 60) THEN
    WRITE (6,1060) IDNUM, SCORE
ENDIF
```

This technique for forming the statement is more difficult to write, but in addition to being safer, it can make the program logic more explicit and easier to follow.

Compare the ELSEIF and standard IF statement approaches to writing quiz grades, as given in Figures 9.4 and 9.5. It is easier for me to follow the logic of the ELSEIF program, although the reverse may be true for you. Figure 9.6 gives a solution to the bowling problem using the ELSEIF statement. You have thus seen two solutions for the quiz-grading problem and three solutions for the bowling problem, and you will see another program for each problem later. From these examples, I hope you will become convinced that:

1. There are many computer programs that will correctly solve a given problem.
2. All programs that solve a given problem are not equally clear.

Some programs will obviously be much closer to being "logic poems" than other programs that solve the same problem. The challenge is to find a better solution.

```
 1  C
 2  C           SCORING OF BOWLING
 3  C           ILLUSTRATION OF ELSEIF STATEMENT
 4  C
 5         INTEGER BALL1,BALL2,BALL3,FRAME,SCORE
 6         LOGICAL PLAY,STRIKE,SPARE,OPEN
 7  1000 FORMAT('1')
 8  1010 FORMAT('0','FRAME',4X,'BALL 1',4X,'BALL 2',4X,'SCORE')
 9  1020 FORMAT(' ',I3,7X,I2,18X,I3,6X,'STRIKE')
10  1030 FORMAT(' ',I3,7X,I2,8X,I2,8X,I3,6X,'SPARE')
11  1040 FORMAT(' ',I3,7X,I2,8X,I2,8X,I3,6X,'OPEN')
12  1050 FORMAT(' ',I3,7X,I2)
13  1060 FORMAT(' ',I3,7X,I2,8X,I2)
14  1070 FORMAT(I2)
15         WRITE(6,1000)
16         READ(5,1070)BALL1
17         PLAY=BALL1 .NE. 99
18         WHILE(PLAY)
19             SCORE=0
20             FRAME=1
21             WRITE(6,1010)
22             READ(5,1070)BALL2
23             STRIKE=BALL1 .EQ. 10
24             SPARE= BALL1+BALL2 .EQ. 10
25             OPEN=BALL1+BALL2 .LT. 10
26             WHILE(FRAME .LE. 9)
27                 IF(STRIKE) THEN
28                     READ(5,1070)BALL3
29                     SCORE=SCORE+BALL1+BALL2+BALL3
30                     WRITE(6,1020)FRAME,BALL1,SCORE
31                     BALL1=BALL2
32                     BALL2=BALL3
33                 ELSEIF(SPARE) THEN
34                     READ(5,1070)BALL3
35                     SCORE=SCORE+BALL1+BALL2+BALL3
36                     WRITE(6,1030)FRAME,BALL1,BALL2,SCORE
37                     BALL1=BALL3
38                     READ(5,1070)BALL2
39                 ELSEIF(OPEN) THEN
40                     SCORE=SCORE+BALL1+BALL2
41                     WRITE(6,1040)FRAME,BALL1,BALL2,SCORE
42                     READ(5,1070)BALL1,BALL2
43                 ENDIF
44                 FRAME=FRAME+1
45                 STRIKE=BALL1 .EQ. 10
46                 SPARE= BALL1+BALL2 .EQ. 10
47                 OPEN= BALL1+BALL2 .LT. 10
48             ENDWHILE
49             IF(STRIKE) THEN
50                 READ(5,1070)BALL3
51                 SCORE=SCORE+BALL1+BALL2+BALL3
52                 WRITE(6,1020)FRAME,BALL1,SCORE
```

FIGURE 9.6   *Scoring of bowling: illustration of the ELSEIF statement*

```
53              WRITE(6,1050)FRAME,BALL2
54              WRITE(6,1050)FRAME,BALL3
55          ELSEIF(SPARE) THEN
56              READ(5,1070)BALL3
57              SCORE=SCORE+BALL1+BALL2+BALL3
58              WRITE(6,1030)FRAME,BALL1,BALL2,SCORE
59              WRITE(6,1050)FRAME,BALL3
60          ELSEIF(OPEN) THEN
61              SCORE=SCORE+BALL1+BALL2
62              WRITE(6,1040)FRAME,BALL1,BALL2,SCORE
63          ENDIF
64          READ(5,1070)BALL1
65          PLAY= BALL1 .NE. 99
66      ENDWHILE
67      STOP
68      END
```

FRAME	BALL 1	BALL 2	SCORE	
1	10		30	STRIKE
2	10		60	STRIKE
3	10		90	STRIKE
4	10		120	STRIKE
5	10		150	STRIKE
6	10		180	STRIKE
7	10		210	STRIKE
8	10		240	STRIKE
9	10		270	STRIKE
10	10		300	STRIKE
10	10			
10	10			

FRAME	BALL 1	BALL 2	SCORE	
1	10		30	STRIKE
2	10		60	STRIKE
3	10		90	STRIKE
4	10		120	STRIKE
5	10		150	STRIKE
6	10		180	STRIKE
7	10		210	STRIKE
8	10		240	STRIKE
9	10		268	STRIKE
10	10		287	STRIKE
10	8			
10	1			

FRAME	BALL 1	BALL 2	SCORE	
1	10		30	STRIKE
2	10		60	STRIKE
3	10		90	STRIKE
4	10		120	STRIKE
5	10		150	STRIKE
6	10		180	STRIKE
7	10		201	STRIKE
8	10		215	STRIKE

FIGURE 9.6   (*cont.*)

9	1	3	219	OPEN
10	10		239	STRIKE
10	8			
10	2			

FRAME	BALL 1	BALL 2	SCORE	
1	10		30	STRIKE
2	10		51	STRIKE
3	10		71	STRIKE
4	1	9	83	SPARE
5	2	8	96	SPARE
6	3	7	110	SPARE
7	4	6	125	SPARE
8	5	5	145	SPARE
9	10		156	STRIKE
10	0	1	157	OPEN

FIGURE 9.6 (*cont.*)

9.4 FORTRAN LOGICAL IF STATEMENT

FORTRAN has two additional types of IF statements—a "logical IF," which is discussed in this section, and an "arithmetic IF," which is treated in the next section. Both types can be used, if you wish, in any program. The logical IF statement receives its name from the fact that it uses a logical expression as a condition. The form of the statement is

IF (condition) statement 1
statement 2

where 1. Condition is any logical expression.
2. Statement 1 and 2 are executable statements.
3. Statement 1 is executed if the condition is true.
4. Statement 2 is executed if the condition is false.
5. If statement 1 does not branch to another location in the program, statement 2 is executed after statement 1.

In a flowchart form the statement is

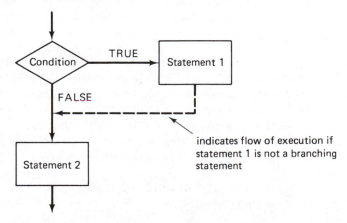

indicates flow of execution if statement 1 is not a branching statement

Some typical logical IF statements and the nature of their operation are

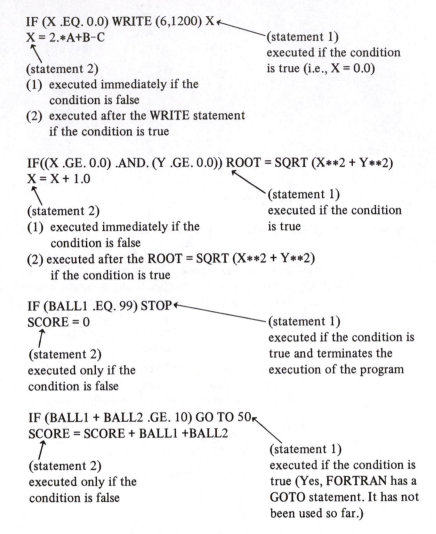

IF (X .EQ. 0.0) WRITE (6,1200) X
X = 2.*A+B−C

(statement 1)
executed if the condition
is true (i.e., X = 0.0)

(statement 2)
(1) executed immediately if the
    condition is false
(2) executed after the WRITE statement
    if the condition is true

IF((X .GE. 0.0) .AND. (Y .GE. 0.0)) ROOT = SQRT (X**2 + Y**2)
X = X + 1.0

(statement 1)
executed if the condition
is true

(statement 2)
(1) executed immediately if the
    condition is false
(2) executed after the ROOT = SQRT (X**2 + Y**2)
    if the condition is true

IF (BALL1 .EQ. 99) STOP
SCORE = 0

(statement 1)
executed if the condition is
true and terminates the
execution of the program

(statement 2)
executed only if the
condition is false

IF (BALL1 + BALL2 .GE. 10) GO TO 50
SCORE = SCORE + BALL1 +BALL2

(statement 1)
executed if the condition is
true (Yes, FORTRAN has a
GOTO statement. It has not
been used so far.)

(statement 2)
executed only if the
condition is false

One restriction in using the logical IF statement has been stated explicitly: statements 1 and 2 must both be executable. (Actually, if statement 2 is a FORMAT statement, it is ignored and the next statement is used—recall that the compiler moves all FORMAT statements to the beginning of the program.) A second restriction is imposed on statement 1 by FORTRAN: statement 1 cannot be another logical IF statement (or a DO statement, which will be discussed in Chapter 10). Examine the following statements and determine which are valid:

1. IF (A .GT. B) WRITE (6, 1357) A,B,C
   WRITE (6,1358)

2. IF (A .LG. X) A = X
   X = Y+1

3. IF (Q .NE. R) STOP
   STOP

4. IF (GROSS-TAX) NET = GROSS
   WRITE (6,1050) GROSS

5. IF (X-Y .LT. A+B) Z = A+B-Y
   X = Y+A

6. IF (A .GT. 100.0) END
   A = A + 5.0

7. IF (NEXT .LT. 0) GO TO 10
   IF (NEXT .LT. 10) GO TO 20
   READ (5,1065) I,J

8. IF (M .EQ. N) FORMAT (2I5)
   READ (5,1000) K,L

9. IF (K+L .GT. 55) IF (N .NE. I1)
   M = K+2*N-L

10. IF (OPEN) GO TO 100
    SCORE = SCORE + BALL1 + BALL2 + BALL3

Answers:

1. Valid		
2. Invalid	.LG. is not a valid relational operator.	
3. Valid (?)	The syntax is valid, but the statement guarantees that execution of the program will be terminated.	
4. Invalid	GROSS-TAX is an arithmetic expression, not a logical expression.	
5. Valid		
6. Invalid	END can appear only at the end of a program.	
7. Valid		
8. Invalid	FORMAT is not an executable statement. In addition, it is missing a statement number.	
9. Invalid	Another logical IF statement, IF (N .NE. I1), is not allowed as statement 1.	
10. Indeterminate	Valid if OPEN is a logical variable; otherwise, invalid.	

A logical IF statement can have a statement number, and this allows it to be referenced in other statements. The following is legitimate:

.
.
.

IF (BALL1 + BALL2 .GE. 10) GO TO 75
.

.

.

75 IF (BALL1 .EQ. 10) GO TO 80
.

.

.

An example that is syntactically valid, but which should be avoided, is

.
.
.

100 IF (X .GT. 0.0) GO TO 100
.

.

.

If X is positive, a jump to statement 100 will be made where a test will be made to determine if X is positive, causing a branch to statement 100 where. . . . An infinite loop results.

To illustrate one method of using the logical IF statement, the quiz-grade program has been revised and is shown in Figure 9.7. The logic of the program seems clear (to me):

1. When a condition is true, an appropriate WRITE statement is executed.
2. Only one of the conditions will ever be true for a legitimate score.
3. Only one line, the appropriate one, will be printed for each score.

The program is different from the earlier versions in that all five IF statements will always be executed, although only one of them will result in a line being printed. For example, if the score being tested is 93, the first IF statement causes a line to be printed, but four other conditions are also tested. For the previous versions of the program, testing is concluded as soon as a condition is found to be true. Excess testing could be eliminated in the logical IF version by reorganizing the program and using GO TO statements. Unfortunately, for most people, the use of GO TO statements makes the logic less clear.

9.5 FORTRAN ARITHMETIC IF STATEMENT

The FORTRAN arithmetic IF statement is fundamentally different from the other types of IF statements in that it uses the value of an arithmetic expression rather

```
 1 C
 2 C          QUIZ GRADES          LOGICAL IF STATEMENT
 3 C
 4      INTEGER SCORE
 5 1000 FORMAT('1',T20,'QUIZ GRADES')
 6 1010 FORMAT('0',T10,'ID NUMBER',T25,'SCORE',T36,'GRADE')
 7 1020 FORMAT(' ',T14,I4,T26,I3,T38,'A')
 8 1030 FORMAT(' ',T14,I4,T26,I3,T38,'B')
 9 1040 FORMAT(' ',T14,I4,T26,I3,T38,'C')
10 1050 FORMAT(' ',T14,I4,T26,I3,T38,'D')
11 1060 FORMAT(' ',T14,I4,T26,I3,T38,'F')
12 1070 FORMAT(2I5)
13      WRITE(6,1000)
14      WRITE(6,1010)
15      READ(5,1070)IDNUM,SCORE
16      WHILE( SCORE .GE. 0)
17         IF( SCORE .GE. 90) WRITE(6,1020)IDNUM,SCORE
18         IF( (SCORE .LE. 89) .AND.(SCORE .GE.80)) WRITE(6,1030)IDNUM,SCO
19   *RE
20         IF( (SCORE .LE. 79) .AND.(SCORE .GE.70)) WRITE(6,1040)IDNUM,SCO
21   *RE
22         IF( (SCORE .LE. 69) .AND.(SCORE .GE.60)) WRITE(6,1050)IDNUM,SCO
23   *RE
24         IF(SCORE .LT. 60) WRITE(6,1060)IDNUM,SCORE
25         READ(5,1070)IDNUM,SCORE
26      ENDWHILE
27      STOP
28      END
```

QUIZ GRADES

ID NUMBER	SCORE	GRADE
1001	83	B
1002	92	A
1003	76	C
1004	54	F
1005	73	C
1006	61	D
1007	73	C
1008	77	C
1009	78	C
1010	82	B
1011	84	B
1012	79	C
1013	87	B
1014	64	D
1015	54	F
1016	71	C
1017	91	A
1018	58	F
1019	88	B
1020	97	A

FIGURE 9.7   *Quiz grades: illustration of FORTRAN logical IF statement*

than the value of a logical expression to determine what statement will be executed next. The form of the statement is

IF (arithmetic expression) N1, N2, N3

where 1. N1, N2, and N3 represent the statement numbers of executable FORTRAN statements.
2. N1, N2, and N3 need not be distinct.
3. If the value of the arithmetic expression is
   (a) negative, branch to statement N1.
   (b) zero, branch to statement N2.
   (c) positive, branch to statement N3.

Examples of valid arithmetic IF statements and their interpretation are

1. IF (X) 10, 20, 30
   execute next if X is +
   execute next if X is 0
   execute next if X is −

2. IF (2.*A−B/C) 50, 30, 40
   execute next if expression is +
   execute next if expression is 0
   execute next if expression is −

3.

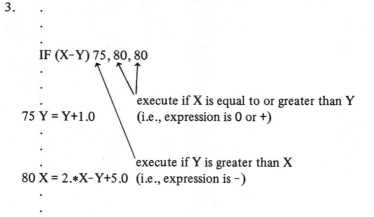

IF (X−Y) 75, 80, 80

75 Y = Y+1.0

execute if X is equal to or greater than Y (i.e., expression is 0 or +)

execute if Y is greater than X

80 X = 2.*X−Y+5.0 (i.e., expression is −)

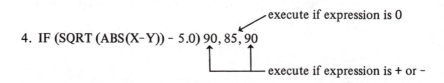

4. IF (SQRT (ABS(X−Y)) − 5.0) 90, 85, 90

execute if expression is 0

execute if expression is + or −

For each of the examples, notice that:

1. Actual statement numbers must be used following the arithmetic expression— variables are not allowed.
2. It is the position of the statement number, not its numerical magnitude, that is important.

A portion of the quiz-grading program is given below to show how a sequence of arithmetic IF statements can be used in solving a problem.

```
            .
            .
            .
     IF (SCORE-90) 20, 10, 10
  10 WRITE (6, 1020) IDNUM, SCORE
     GO TO 90
  20 IF (SCORE-80) 40, 30, 30
  30 WRITE (6, 1030) IDNUM, SCORE
     GO TO 90
  40 IF (SCORE-70) 60, 50, 50
  50 WRITE (6, 1040) IDNUM, SCORE
     GO TO 90
  60 IF (SCORE-60) 80, 70, 70
  70 WRITE (6, 1050) IDNUM, SCORE
     GO TO 90
  80 WRITE (6, 1060) IDNUM, SCORE
  90 READ (5, 1070) IDNUM, SCORE
            .
            .
            .
```

This portion of a program is fairly easy to read, partly because the statement numbers occur in increasing sequence. There is no requirement, however, that statement numbers convey any information about the location of a statement in a program, and programs using arithmetic IF statements can be very difficult to understand. Another difficulty arises in converting the logical expression you wish to test into an appropriate arithmetic expression—this process is highly susceptible to error.

Examine the following statements and determine which are valid:

1. IF (X-2.*Y) 10, 10, 20
2. IF (X = Y+1.0) 25, 35, 40
3. IF (X-Y) 25 30, 50
4. IF (X/Y) 15, 20, 25.5
5. IF (A .LT. B) 70, 90, 80
6. IF (A+B) GO TO 5

  7. IF (ABS(A-B) - 100.0) 100, 90, 80
  8. IF (M) 40, 40, 1
  9. 10 IF (L) 10,20,30
 10. IF (K+L-J) 50, 50, 50

Answers:

  1. Valid
  2. Invalid   X = Y+1.0 is a statement, not an expression.
  3. Invalid   A comma is missing between 25 and 30.
  4. Invalid   25.5 is a real number and thus cannot be a statement number.
  5. Invalid   A .LT. B is a logical expression, not an arithmetic expression.
  6. Invalid   GO TO 5 is a statement, not a set of three statement numbers.
  7. Valid
  8. Valid
  9. Valid (?)   The syntax is valid, but if L is negative, an infinite loop will result.
 10. Valid (?)   The syntax is valid, but the use of an IF statement is unnecessary—the statement is equivalent to GO TO 50.

The arithmetic IF statement gives a programmer much flexibility, as it allows branching to any three locations in the program. The branching can be to locations that precede or follow the IF statement. The trouble with the arithmetic IF statement is that it provides too much flexibility—undisciplined use of the statement leads to programs that are very difficult to understand and to modify. The flow of the program logic can become very convoluted. Advocates of structured programming refer to such programs as "spaghetti bowl" programs. In this metaphor, a long piece of spaghetti represents the flow of logic starting at some statement in the program and moving through other statements and other decisions. The end of the piece of spaghetti can be anywhere, and it is quite difficult to discover how one piece of spaghetti is related to another.

To illustrate the effort required to understand a program that uses arithmetic IF statements, Figure 9.8 gives a solution to the bowling problem. (After this, bowling will not be mentioned again!) The program was written several years ago for a compiler that did not allow IF statements other than arithmetic IF statements. To make the program more readable, statement numbers were maintained in an orderly sequence, and with few exceptions IF statements branch to statements that come later in the program. An even more striking example of the difficulty of understanding nonstructured programs is given later for the eight-queens problem.

You should rarely, if ever, use the arithmetic IF statement.

9.6   COMPUTED GO TO STATEMENT

FORTRAN has an additional decision statement, the computed GO TO statement, which allows branching to many different locations within a program. The form

```
 1 C
 2 C                SCORING OF BOWLING
 3 C                ILLUSTRATION OF ARITHMETIC IF
 4 C
 5         INTEGER FRAME,SCORE,BALL1,BALL2,BALL3
 6  1000 FORMAT('1')
 7  1001 FORMAT(I2)
 8  1002 FORMAT('0','FRAME',4X,'BALL 1',4X,'BALL 2',4X,'SCORE')
 9  1003 FORMAT(' ',I3,7X,I2,18X,I3,6X,'STRIKE')
10  1004 FORMAT(' ',I3,7X,I2)
11  1005 FORMAT(' ',I3,7X,I2,8X,I2)
12  1006 FORMAT(' ',I3,7X,I2,8X,I2,8X,I3,6X,'SPARE')
13  1007 FORMAT(' ',I3,7X,I2,8X,I2,8X,I3,6X,'OPEN')
14  1008 FORMAT(' ','ILLEGAL DATA')
15        WRITE(6,1000)
16  2     FRAME=1
17        SCORE=0
18        READ(5,1001)BALL1,BALL2
19        IF(BALL1-99)5,35,5
20  5     WRITE(6,1002)
21  7     IF(BALL1)32,8,8
22  8     IF(BALL2)32,9,9
23  9     IF(BALL1-10)10,10,32
24  10    IF(BALL2-10)11,11,32
25  11    IF(BALL1+BALL2 - 10)28,12,12
26  12    READ(5,1001)BALL3
27        IF(BALL3)32,14,13
28  13    IF(BALL3-10)14,14,32
29  14    SCORE=SCORE+BALL1+BALL2+BALL3
30        IF(BALL1-10)23,15,23
31  15    WRITE(6,1003)FRAME,BALL1,SCORE
32        BALL1=BALL2
33        BALL2=BALL3
34        IF(FRAME-10)34,17,17
35  17    IF(BALL1-10)20,18,20
36  18    WRITE(6,1004)FRAME,BALL1
37        WRITE(6,1004)FRAME,BALL2
38        GO TO 2
39  20    IF(BALL1+BALL2 - 10)21,21,32
40  21    WRITE(6,1005)FRAME,BALL1,BALL2
41        GO TO 2
42  23    IF(BALL1+BALL2 - 10) 24,24,32
43  24    WRITE(6,1006)FRAME,BALL1,BALL2,SCORE
44        BALL1=BALL3
45        IF(FRAME - 10)31,26,26
46  26    WRITE(6,1004)FRAME,BALL1
47        GO TO 2
48  28    SCORE=SCORE+BALL1+BALL2
49        WRITE(6,1007)FRAME,BALL1,BALL2,SCORE
50        IF(FRAME - 10)30,2,30
51  30    READ(5,1001)BALL1
52  31    READ(5,1001)BALL2
53  34    FRAME=FRAME+1
54        GO TO 7
55  32    WRITE(6,1008)
```

FIGURE 9.8 *Scoring of bowling: illustration of arithmetic IF statement*

```
56  35    STOP
57        END
```

FRAME	BALL 1	BALL 2	SCORE	
1	10		30	STRIKE
2	10		60	STRIKE
3	10		90	STRIKE
4	10		120	STRIKE
5	10		150	STRIKE
6	10		180	STRIKE
7	10		210	STRIKE
8	10		240	STRIKE
9	10		270	STRIKE
10	10		300	STRIKE
10	10			
10	10			

FRAME	BALL 1	BALL 2	SCORE	
1	10		30	STRIKE
2	10		60	STRIKE
3	10		90	STRIKE
4	10		120	STRIKE
5	10		150	STRIKE
6	10		180	STRIKE
7	10		210	STRIKE
8	10		240	STRIKE
9	10		268	STRIKE
10	10		287	STRIKE
10	8			
10	1			

FRAME	BALL 1	BALL 2	SCORE	
1	10		30	STRIKE
2	10		60	STRIKE
3	10		90	STRIKE
4	10		120	STRIKE
5	10		150	STRIKE
6	10		180	STRIKE
7	10		201	STRIKE
8	10		215	STRIKE
9	1	3	219	OPEN
10	10		239	STRIKE
10	8			
10	2			

FRAME	BALL 1	BALL 2	SCORE	
1	10		30	STRIKE
2	10		51	STRIKE
3	10		71	STRIKE
4	1	9	83	SPARE
5	2	8	96	SPARE
6	3	7	110	SPARE
7	4	6	125	SPARE
8	5	5	145	SPARE
9	10		156	STRIKE
10	0	1	157	OPEN

FIGURE 9.8   *(cont.)*

of the statement is

GO TO (sequence of statement numbers), integer variable

required

Some valid examples are

GO TO (10, 20, 30), N

GO TO (20, 10, 30), NVAR

GO TO (99, 100, 52, 21, 37, 43, 16, 4), LL

The integer variable that appears at the end of the statement is allowed to have values 1, 2, 3, ... to a maximum value corresponding to the count of the number of statement numbers within the parentheses. For the statement GO TO (10, 20, 30), N, the allowed values of N are 1, 2, and 3. For the statement GO TO (99, 100, 52, 21, 37, 43, 16, 4), LL, the allowed values of LL are 1, 2, 3, 4, 5, 6, 7, and 8. The value of the integer variable, LL, is the position in the list of statement numbers of the statement that is to be executed next. Thus for

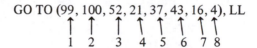

GO TO (99, 100, 52, 21, 37, 43, 16, 4), LL

if the value of LL is less than 1 or greater than the number of statement numbers, the program will compile but will behave unpredictably.

The statements referenced within the computed GO TO statement can be any-where in the program, and undisciplined use of the computed GO TO can produce incomprehensible programs. Furthermore, programs that use computed GO TO state-ments are not structured programs. For these reasons this text will rarely use com-puted GO TO statements. Programming situations arise, however, in which it would be convenient to have a structured programming form of computed GO TO statement. Some languages have such a statement, normally called the CASE statement.

REVIEW QUESTIONS

1. What are the three types of FORTRAN IF statements? Which type is most useful for structured programming?
2. In the block IF statement, how many statements can go in a block? How many blocks are there?
3. How many exit points are there for a block IF statement?
4. What are the relational operators, and how are they used in forming conditions? What values are possible for valid conditions?
5. When is the ELSE clause executed in a block IF statement? Is an ELSE clause required in the block IF?
6. Define the terms "logical variable," "logical constant," "logical expression," and "logical statement."

7. How are logical expressions used in IF statements?

8. List the logical operators, and give the hierarchy of their use.

9. What three types of operators can appear in conditions? What is the order of evaluation of these types?

10. Explain the operation of the ELSEIF statement. How many ELSEIF clauses may appear in a block IF statement?

11. Assume that a block IF statement uses ELSEIF clauses. When can an ELSE clause be included?

12. Following the condition in a logical IF statement, there are two other statements. Under what circumstances are statements 1 and 2 executed?

13. In an arithmetic IF statement, what appears in parentheses immediately after the word IF? How is this item used in making decisions?

14. Consider the three statement numbers at the end of an arithmetic IF statement. How does the relative position of a number affect the outcome? What restrictions, if any, are placed on these numbers?

15. In the computed GO TO statement, why is the relative position of the statement numbers important? What happens if the variable has a value greater than the number of statement numbers?

REVIEW QUIZ

1. An example of a valid block IF statement is

   (A) IF (A .LE. B) THEN

         X = 2.0*A+5.5

      ELSE

         X = 2.0*A+3.2

         A = B

      ENDIF

   (B) IF (A−B) THEN

         X = 2.0*A+5.5

      ELSE

         X = 2.0*A+3.2

         A = B

      ENDIF

   (C) IF (X+Y−12.5) THEN

         X = Y + 10.1

      ENDIF

   (D) IF (C−1.0) 10, 15, 5

   (E) Two of the previous answers

2. A statement that is not particularly useful in writing structured programs is (A) IF ... THEN ... ELSE ... ENDIF, (B) logical IF, (C) block IF, (D) IF ... THEN ... ELSEIF ... ELSEIF ... ENDIF, (E) arithmetic IF.

3. An example of an *invalid* relational operator is (A) OR, (B) .NE., (C) .GT., (D) LE, (E) two of the previous answers.

4. An example of a logical constant is (A) LOGICAL X, (B) .FALSE., (C) X .AND. Y, (D) Z = X .AND. Y, (E) two of the previous answers.

5. Given A = .FALSE., B = .TRUE., C = .TRUE. . The value of A .OR. B .AND. C is (A) .TRUE. and .FALSE., (B) .TRUE., (C) .FALSE., (D) undetermined since the order of application of operators is unknown, (E) the same as the value of (A .OR. B) .AND. A.

6. An example of an *invalid* logical expression is (A) X .LE. Y+15.1; (B) (A .AND. B) .GT. (B .OR. C); (C) X .OR. Y; (D) (A .AND. B) .OR. (B .OR. C); (E) .NOT. (C .OR. D).

7. An example of a valid logical IF statement is (A) IF (X−Y) 5, 10, 15; (B) IF (X = 2.5*A−B) 5, 15, 10; (C) IF (X − 2.3*Y) 10, 10, 5; (D) IF (X) 10, 5, 10; (E) IF (X .GT. Y) WRITE (6, 1000) X.

8. An example of an *invalid* arithmetic IF statement is (A) IF (X−Y) 5, 10, 15; (B) IF (X = 2.5∗A−B) 5, 15, 10; (C) IF (X−2.3∗5) 10, 10, 5; (D) IF(X) 10, 5, 10; (E) IF (X .GT. Y) WRITE (6, 1000) X.

9. Given:

$$X = 2.1$$
$$Y = 9.3$$
$$IF (X−Y+5.5) \ 12, 5, 20$$

The next statement executed is (A) 12, (B) 5, (C) 20, (D) none of the previous answers because the statements contain a syntax error.

10. Given:

$$N = 0$$
$$I = 2$$
$$J = 4$$

```
      IF (I .LE. J) THEN
          N = N+I+J
          WRITE (6, 100)N
100       FORMAT (' ', I10)
      ELSE
          N = N+1
      ENDIF
```

The final value of N is (A) 0, (B) 1, (C) 6, (D) 8, (E) none of the previous answers.

11. Given:

```
      SCORE = 75
      IF (SCORE .GE. 60) THEN
          WRITE (6, 1)
1         FORMAT (' ', 'GRADE = D')
      ELSEIF (SCORE .GE. 70) THEN
          WRITE (6, 2)
2         FORMAT (' ', 'GRADE = C')
      ELSEIF (SCORE .GE. 80) THEN
          WRITE (6, 3)
3         FORMAT (' ', 'GRADE = B')
      ELSEIF (SCORE .GE. 90) THEN
          WRITE (6, 4)
4         FORMAT (' ', 'GRADE = A')
      ENDIF
```

The grade printed will be (A) A, (B) B, (C) C, (D) D, (E) none of the previous answers.

12. Given the following sequence of statements within a program:

```
      X = 63
      IF (X .LE. 50) GO TO 10
      IF (X .LE. 60) GO TO 20
```

IF (X .LE. 70) GO TO 30
IF (X .LE. 80) GO TO 40
IF (X .LE. 90) GO TO 50
GO TO 60

The next statement to be executed will be (A) 10, (B) 20, (C) 30, (D) 40, (E) 50.

13. Given:

$$L = -2$$
20 IF (L+2) 20,20,30
30 L = 2*L+10

The number of times statement 20 is executed is (A) 0, (B) 1, (C) 2, (D) 3, (E) none of the previous answers.

14. A valid statement is:
    (A) IF (A .EQ. B) 5,10,20.
    (B) IF (X+Y−10.5) WRITE (6,1000) X.
    (C) IF (I = 2*K) 10,30,5.
    (D) IF (X .GE. 0.0) FORMAT (F12.1).
    (E) IF (X**2 .LT. 10.1) WRITE (6,100) X.

15. Given:

$$I = 3$$
GO TO (90, 45, 10, 3, 2, 1), I

The next statement executed will be (A) 90, (B) 45, (C) 10, (D) 3, (E) 2.

EXERCISES

1. Correct the syntax errors in the following:
   a. IF (RATE = STDRATE) THEN
          GROSS = STDRATE*HOURS−TAX
          WRITE (6,1000) STDRAT, HOURS, TAX, GROSS
      ENDIF
   b. IF (X .LT. Y)
          X = 2.0*X+12.1
          WRITE (6,1000) X
      ELSE
          X = Y
      ENDIF
   c. IF (X.EQ.Y .AND. A.EQ.B) THEN
          X = X+1.0
          A = A+2.0
          WRITE (6,100) X
      ELSE
          X = X−1.0
          A = 2.1*A
          WRITE (6, 100) A
   d. IF (.NOT. (A .EQ. B) THEN
          A = A+B
          B = B+5.0
      ENDIF

   e. IF (GRADE .GE. 0) THEN
       SUM = 0.0
       I = 1
       WHILE (I .LE. 4)
          SUM = SUM + GRADE
          I = I+1
       ENDIF
   f. IF (R .LQ. Q) 1000 FORMAT (3F6.1)
   g. IF (X−SQRT(Y)) STOP
   h. IF (C − 100.0) F = 9./5.*C+32.
   i. IF (X .GT. Y) 10,20,30
   j. IF (IDNUM .EQ. IDSAVE) THEN
       IF (GRADE .GE. 0) THEN
          SUM = SUM + GRADE
          READ (5,1000) IDNUM, GRADE
     ELSE
       IDSAVE = GRADE
     ENDIF

2. Find the logic errors in each of the following:
   a. READ (5,1000) IDNUM, GRADE
     IF (IDNUM .EQ. IDSAVE) THEN
       NUM = 1
       SUM = 0.0
       WHILE (GRADE .GE. 0)
          SUM = SUM + GRADE
          NUM = NUM + 1
       ENDWHILE
     ELSE
       IDSAVE = IDNUM
     ENDIF
   b. IF (X .LT. Y) ANS = X
     ANS = Y
   c. 15 IF (X−Y) 10,15,20

3. Convert the following into equivalent block IF statements:
   a.   IF (X .GT. Y) GO TO 10
       X = Y**2
       WRITE (6,100) X,Y
       GO TO 15
     10 X = 2*Y
     15 WRITE (6, 101) X
   b.   IF (.NOT. (A .EQ. 0)) GO TO 5
       A = A+1.0
       B = A
       GO TO 10
     5 A = B
       B = 2*(A+B)
    10 WRITE (6,100) A,B
   c.   IF (X−Y) 10,10,20
     10 WRITE (6,50) X
       WRITE (6,60) Y

```
        X = X+Y
        GO TO 30
     20 WRITE (6,70) X,Y
        X = X-Y
     30 Z = SQRT(X)
```

PROGRAMMING EXERCISES

1. Computers often store the day of the year as a running count of the number of days since the beginning of the year. For example, in a non-leap year, February 1 = 32, April 30 = 120, May 1 = 121, and December 31 = 365. Write a program that reads a date in standard format (04 30 = April 30) and prints the day of the year.

2. For people engaged in moderate activities, the recommended daily caloric intake is

> males: 21 cal per pound of body weight
> females: 18 cal per pound of body weight

Actual intakes within ±50 calories of the recommended levels are considered "normal." Other intakes are "high" or "low." Read a set of cards each containing a code for the sex of an individual and the individual's weight and daily caloric intake. Print these data and a message indicating low, normal, or high caloric intake for each individual.

3. This problem is an extension of the previous one. Rewrite your program to consider also different metabolic rates.

	Daily calorie requirements (calories per pound of body weight)	
Metabolic rate	Men	Women
Sedentary	16	14
Light	19	16
Moderate	21	18
Heavy	26	22

4. Write a program that computes the number of days between two dates, and test it on a number of examples. Ordinary years contain 365 days, and leap years, all years that are exactly divisible by 4, contain 366 days (*except* centesimal years, which are those divisible by 400, which have 365 days).

5. For the integers less than or equal to 1000, write a program that finds the prime factors of each integer. For example, the prime factors of 40 are 2 and 5, and the prime factors of 105 are 3, 5, and 7.

6. In the very few days between the end of spring term and the day of graduation, a university registrar has a difficult time examining the records of seniors to determine eligibility for graduation and honors at graduation. The computer can be of great assistance with this problem when the appropriate information has been previously stored in machine-readable form. You are to simulate the operation of such a program to help the registrar. Input is a deck of cards each containing:

> 1. Student ID number (four-digit integer).

2. Number of semester hours earned (three-digit integer).
3. Grade-point average (F4.2).

The rules are:

1. Eligibility for graduation:
   a. At least 126 semester hours earned.
   b. A grade-point average of at least 2.00.
2. Honors at graduation:
   a. Must be eligible to graduate.
   b. Grade-point average of 3.9 or greater: summa cum laude.
   c. Grade-point average between 3.50 and 3.89: magna cum laude.
   d. Grade-point average between 3.20 and 3.49: cum laude.

Write a program that prints an appropriate table for the registrar. Make your own test data.

7. Not surprisingly, FORTRAN logical variables can be used to solve problems in logic. Write a program that prints a truth table for

$$(P \text{ OR NOT } Q) \text{ AND NOT } P$$

Output should have the following form:

TRUTH TABLE FOR (P OR NOT Q) AND NOT P					
P	Q	NOT P	NOT Q	P OR NOT Q	ANS
T	T	F	F	T	F
T	F	F	T	T	F
etc.					

8. Write a program to convert a decimal number to a binary number. The decimal number may be greater or smaller than 1, but none of the numbers greater than 1 will have a fractional part.

9. Thomas H. Holmes and R. H. Rahe developed a Social Readjustment Rating Scale of 43 items that they feel measure the effect of stress on mental and physical health. Of those people with over 300 life change units for the past year, almost 80 percent get sick in the near future; with 150 to 299 units, about 50 percent get sick in the near future; and with fewer than 150 units, only about 30 percent get sick.

Life event	Mean value
1. Death of spouse	100
2. Divorce	73
3. Marital separation	65
4. Jail term	63
5. Death of close family member	63

Life event	Mean value
6. Personal injury or illness	53
7. Marriage	50
8. Fired at work	47
9. Marital reconciliation	45
10. Retirement	45
11. Change in health of family member	44
12. Pregnancy	40
13. Sex difficulties	39
14. Gain of new family member	39
15. Business readjustment	39
16. Change in financial state	38
17. Death of close friend	37
18. Change to different line of work	36
19. Change in number of arguments with spouse	35
20. Mortgage over $10,000	31
21. Foreclosure of mortgage or loan	30
22. Change in responsibilities at work	29
23. Son or daughter leaving home	29
24. Trouble with in-laws	29
25. Outstanding personal achievement	28
26. Spouse begin or stop work	26
27. Begin or end school	26
28. Change in living conditions	25
29. Revision of personal habits	24
30. Trouble with boss	23
31. Change in work hours or conditions	20
32. Change in residence	20
33. Change in schools	20
34. Change in recreation	19
35. Change in church activities	19
36. Change in social activities	18
37. Mortgage or loan less than $10,000	17
38. Change in sleeping habits	16
39. Change in number of family get-togethers	15
40. Change in eating habits	15
41. Vacation	13
42. Christmas	12
43. Minor violations of the law	11

Source: Reproduced by permission of Thomas H. Holmes, M.D., Professor of Psychiatry and Behavioral Sciences, University of Washington, Seattle, and Pergamon Press, Inc., in whose *Journal of Psychosomatic Research* the scale was first published.

Write a program that computes the approximate susceptibility of an individual to illness or depression based on this model. To simplify programming you may wish to restrict your program to the first five life events. (*Note:* Using only the first five items invalidates the model. Programming Exercise 13 in Chapter 11 requires that you use all 43 items.) A convenient method of entering data is to use a card for each individual. Each card column contains an indicator, 0 or 1, for that numbered factor. For example, a 1 in column 4 would indicate a jail term.

10. The overall grade average in a course is computed using the following scheme:

quizzes	50%
programs	30%
final examination	20%

For each class member, read four quiz grades, a numerical grade based on the programs, and the final examination grade. The lowest quiz grade for each student is not to be counted in computing the average. Design and print a report that includes for each student the input data and the overall grade average.

11. In working with its computer printed stock status report, officials have learned that more detail is needed than was given in the previous report (see Chapter 7, Programming Exercise 11). Input will now consist of an arbitrary number of cards for a given item. For a given item the first printed line is to contain the value of the item, but this information is to be omitted from subsequent lines. A subtotal line is to be printed for each item. Otherwise, the report is similar to the earlier one.

STOCK STATUS REPORT
ACME MANUFACTURING COMPANY

PART NUMBER	NUMBER OF ITEMS	VALUE PER ITEM	TOTAL VALUE FOR PART
1001	1705	2.75	4688.75
1001	392		1078.00
1001	409		1124.75
1001	35		96.25
SUBTOTAL	2541		6987.75
1002	326	6.05	1972.30
1002	435		2631.75
etc.			

TOTAL VALUE OF STOCK = XXXXXX.XX

your answer

---

12. Members of the physics class have repeated the experimental measurements of parts of a right triangle (see Chapter 8, Programming Exercise 13), but some students have measured the angle between sides A and C instead of measuring the length of side B.

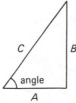

For each set of measurements, whether on sides A and B or on side A and the angle between A and C, compute an expected value for side C. Compare the expected and observed values for C. The program should work for an arbitrary number of measurements. Typical input data are:

Length of A	Length of B	Angle	Length of C
5.01		45°	7.09
5.03		53°40′	8.30
5.03	6.62		8.25
4.96	7.21		8.75
9.00	9.00		12.60
7.25	8.46		11.35
6.24		59°20′	11.86
11.75		27°	13.07
8.09	10.81		13.51

CHAPTER 10 LOOPS

Nearly all the programs considered so far contain one or more loops. This reflects the fact that FORTRAN, in fact most computer languages, are designed to solve problems that involve repetitions of sets of instructions. If a problem does not involve loops, it is probably not worth the effort to write a FORTRAN program to solve it—the problem is likely to be too trivial for using the computer or to involve processes (such as recursion) that are not normally a part of FORTRAN. In this chapter, we review our already extensive experience with WHILE loops and study a new control statement, the DO statement.

10.1   THE STRUCTURE OF LOOPS

All the programs we have studied involving WHILE statements have a similar structure. Consider the FORTRAN program

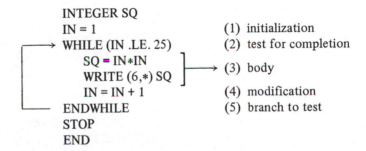

```
        INTEGER SQ
        IN = 1                    (1) initialization
        WHILE (IN .LE. 25)        (2) test for completion
            SQ = IN*IN
            WRITE (6,*) SQ        (3) body
            IN = IN + 1           (4) modification
        ENDWHILE                  (5) branch to test
        STOP
        END
```

The loop has as components: (1) initialization of the loop-controlling variable, (2) test for completion of the loop, (3) body of the loop (the statements we want repeated), (4) modification of the loop-controlling variable, and (5) branch to test for completion of the loop. In general, loops will have these components.

Notice that for this program, the variable used to control the loop was modified within the loop. This is essential with WHILE loops, to avoid infinite loops. A fairly common bug, especially in more complex programs, is to omit the modifying of the variable used to control the loop.

The variable IN in the program for calculating squares of integers is an example of a class of variables called *counters*. These variables count the number of times a loop has been executed and cause an exit from a loop when a limiting value of the counter has been exceeded. A counter always has an initial value, an amount by which it is incremented, and a limiting value. For IN:

1. The initial value was 1:

$$IN = 1$$

2. The increment amount was 1:

$$IN = IN + 1$$

3. The limiting value was 25:

WHILE (IN .LE. 25)

The use of counters is so common in programming that a special statement, the DO statement, has been included in FORTRAN to handle automatically the initializing, incrementing, and testing for the limiting value of a counter. The DO statement is the subject of a later section.

Another method that we have used to control loops involves using the value of an input variable to signal completion of the loop. The averaging of a set of class grades uses this technique:

```
                    .

                    .

                    .

            READ (5,*) GRADE
            WHILE (GRADE .GE. 0.)
                    .

                    .

                    .

                READ (5,*) GRADE
            ENDWHILE
                    .

                    .

                    .
```

The value of GRADE controls the execution of the loop. GRADE is initialized outside the loop by reading a value, and GRADE is modified within the loop by reading a new value. Thus, such loops also have the features of initialization, test for completion, body of the loop, modification of the loop-controlling variable, and branch to the test. Loops of this type are called *indefinite loops* because there is no fixed number of times the loop will be executed.

For the WHILE statement the test for completion of the loop is performed at the beginning of the loop. The location of the test, however, depends upon the loop-controlling statement. For the DO statement the test is at the bottom of the loop. The position of the test can affect the logic of the program.

10.2 DO...ENDDO STATEMENT

The DO...ENDDO Statement is a modified version of the ordinary FORTRAN DO statement; consequently, almost everything said about DO...ENDDO will transfer with little or no modification to the standard FORTRAN DO statement. Notice that DO...ENDDO is a nonstandard statement, not a FORTRAN statement. The purpose of the statement is to facilitate the handling of loops controlled by a counter. The initialization, incrementing, and testing for the limiting value of a counter are all done for the programmer. For example, the program for computing the squares of the first 25 integers can be written as

```
INTEGER SQ
DO IN = 1, 25
    SQ = IN*IN
    WRITE (6,*) SQ
ENDDO
STOP
END
```

In this program, the statement DO IN = 1, 25 is interpreted as

Starting with IN = 1, repeatedly execute the statements between DO and ENDDO. Increase IN by one for each execution of the block of statements, and exit from the loop when IN exceeds 25.

The usefulness of the DO statement should be apparent.

10.2.1 Syntax of the DO...ENDDO Statement

The form of the DO...ENDDO statement is

```
DO I1 = I2, I3, I4
        .
        .
        .
    block of statements
        .
        .
        .
    ENDDO
```

where I1 must be a variable, either integer or real mode

    I2, I3, I4 (a) may be constants, variables, or expressions of either integer or real mode

          (b) I2 and I3 must appear, but I4 is optional

    I1 is a counter called the Do-variable, whose value is to be incremented for each execution of the block of statements

    I2 is the initial value of I1, called the initial parameter

    I3 is the limiting value of I1, called the terminal parameter

    I4 is the increment in I1, called the incrementation parameter, for each execution of the block of statements; if I4 is omitted from the statement, it is assumed to have the value 1; I4 can be negative, but it cannot be zero

Thus we would interpret the following statements as shown:

1.   DO K = 1, 100, 1

        initial value   increment in K
           of K   limiting value of K

The loop will be repeated 100 times.

2.   DO K = 1, 100

      initial   final value of K
  value of K

Since no increment value is given explicitly, it is assumed that I4 has the value 1. The loop will be repeated 100 times.

3.   DO IVAR = 2, 10, 3

      initial   increment in IVAR
    value of   limiting value of IVAR
    IVAR

What will be the value of IVAR during the last execution of the loop? Since

        IVAR = 2   is the initial value, and
        IVAR = IVAR + 3   gives the incremented value,

the sequence of values for IVAR during the execution of the loop is

$$2, 5, 8$$

When IVAR is increased from 8 to 11, the value of IVAR exceeds the limiting value of 10, so an exit is made from the loop. The value of IVAR during the last execution of the loop is, thus, 8. The loop is executed three times.

4. DO NEXT = 1, N

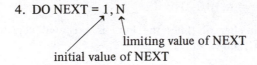

                    limiting value of NEXT

     initial value of NEXT

The number of times the loop will be executed depends upon the value of N. If N = 25, the loop will be repeated 25 times. If N = 1000, the loop will be repeated 1000 times.

5. DO LP = J, M

                 limiting value of LP

     initial value of LP

The number of times the loop is repeated depends on both the value of J and the value of M.

6. DO IOOPS = 1, 75, KK

                        increment to IOOPS

                  limiting value of IOOPS

        initial value of IOOPS

The number of times the loop will be repeated depends on the value of KK. If KK = 1, the loop is repeated 75 times. If KK = 10, the loop is repeated 8 times:

$$IOOPS = IOOPS + KK$$

with successive values of IOOPS: 1, 11, 21, 31, 41, 51, 61, and 71.

7. DO IX3 = 1, 95.6

The loop is executed 95 times.

8. DO LP = 80, 1, -1

The initial value of LP is 80. LP is decremented by 1 for each pass through the loop. The loop is executed 80 times, with the value of LP being 0 upon exit from the loop.

9. DO NUM = 0, 9

The loop is executed 10 times.

10. DO EXPL = 1, 10, 0.2

EXPL is incremented by 0.2 for each pass through the loop.

11. DO XY = A, B+C, D−E

The number of times the loop is executed depends upon the values of A, B+C, and D−E.

10.2.2   Semantics of the DO. . .ENDDO Statement

You may have assumed that the operation of the DO. . .ENDDO statement was similar to the operation of the WHILE. . .ENDWHILE statement. If you made this assumption, you probably would misinterpret the statements

$$DO \ NEXT = 1,10,20$$

and

$$DO \ LM = 2,6,5$$

which have valid syntax and which control loops that are executed one time. The loop controlled by

$$DO \ LP = 100,10$$

is executed zero times. It is important to understand the difference in these cases.

The structure of DO loops and WHILE loops are compared in Figure 10.1. In the DO loop structure, there are two tests for the completion of the loop. The first test is made before the loop is entered, and the second test is made at the bottom of the loop. The test for completion is made by comparing an iteration count (i.e., a count of the number of times the loop should be executed) with zero. If the value of the iteration count is zero, the loop is not to be executed.

When a DO statement is encountered, the following sequence occurs:

1. Any expressions in the parameter list are evaluated, and values are assigned to the initial, terminal, and incrementation parameters.
2. The initial value is assigned to the Do-variable.
3. A value is computed for the iteration count using

$$\text{iteration count} = MAX \ (INT((I3-I2+I4)/I4),0)$$

where INT is a function that computes the largest integer in its argument
MAX is a function that selects the larger of its two arguments

Note: For loops having a positive incrementation parameter, the iteration count will be the number of values that the Do-variable will have before it exceeds its upper limit during execution of the loop. This fact often allows us to determine the number of times a loop will be executed without having to use the foregoing formula. The compiler uses the formula.

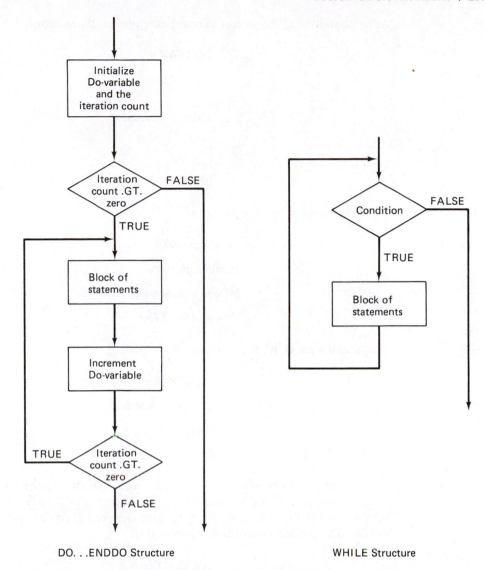

DO. . .ENDDO Structure

WHILE Structure

FIGURE 10.1 *Comparison of DO and WHILE structures*

4. The value of the iteration count is tested to determine whether the loop should be executed.
5. If the iteration count is greater than zero, the statements in the body of the loop are executed.
6. The Do-variable is incremented by an amount equal to the incrementation parameter, and the iteration counter is decremented by one.
7. The iteration counter is tested to determine if additional executions of the loop are required.

As an illustration of the process, consider execution of the structure

$$DO\ IVAR = 2,10,3$$

.

.

.

block of statements

.

.

.

$$ENDDO$$

Values are assigned to the parameters

initial parameter	= 2
terminal parameter	= 10
incrementation parameter	= 3
Do-variable = IVAR	= 2

The iteration count, IC, is computed

$$IC = MAX(INT((10-2+3)/3),0)$$
$$= MAX(INT(3.666666),0)$$
$$= MAX(3,0)$$
$$= 3$$

Thus the loop is to be executed three times. Note that the Do-variable will have successive values of 2, 5, and 8 before it exceeds its upper limit. This fact could have been used to predict the number of times the loop is repeated. At the bottom of the loop the compiler produces instructions equivalent to

$$IVAR = IVAR + 3$$

and

$$IC = IC - 1$$

Finally, a test is made to see if IC has become zero. This DO structure is translated into a series of statements that are equivalent to the sequence

```
IVAR = 2
IC = MAX(INT(10-2+3)/3),0)
IF (IC .GT. 0) THEN
```

```
100      first statement in block
         remaining statements in block
         .
         .
         .
         IVAR = IVAR+3
         IC = IC-1
         IF(IC .GT. 0) GOTO 100
    ENDIF
```

Take particular note of the fact that initialization of the Do-variable is done automatically before the beginning of the loop. If you write a nonstructured program, you can branch into the loop itself. (You should have a very good reason before you depart from using structured techniques.) This would be a disaster, as the iteration count and Do-variable would not be set to their intended initial values. The number of times the loop will be executed would then be unpredictable. Also notice that the incrementing of the Do-variable is done automatically at the end of the loop. You should not explicitly change the value of the Do-variable within the loop.

The use of the Do-variable of a Do statement within the loop is optional. In the following simple program, it is used:

```
ISUM = 0
DO IND = 1,10,3
    ISUM = ISUM + IND
ENDDO
WRITE (6,*) ISUM
STOP
END
```

What value will be printed for ISUM? (Try it.) The answer is 22. In computing the value of ISUM, you must remember that IND is automatically incremented by 3 at the end of the loop.

There is no requirement that the Do-variable be used within the loop. For example, suppose that a class has 31 students, all of whom have taken a quiz, and the average grade is to be computed. In the following program, the Do-variable, I, is not used in the loop.

```
SUM = 0.0
DO I = 1, 31
    READ (5,*) GRADE
    SUM = SUM + GRADE
ENDDO
AVG = SUM/31.0
WRITE (6,*) AVG
STOP
END
```

DO statements can be nested, as needed, within a program. Each FORTRAN compiler imposes an upper limit to the depth of nesting, but for practical purposes the limit is normally so great that you will never reach it. It is important to understand the execution of nested DO statements. Consider the program fragment

```
               .
               .
               .
        DO I = 1,10
           DO J = 1,5
              READ (5,*)Y
              X = X+Y
           ENDDO
        ENDDO
               .
               .
               .
```

The execution sequence is as follows:

1. The statement DO I = 1,10 is executed. This causes I to be set to its initial value of 1 and the iteration count to be set to its initial value of 10.
2. The iteration count is tested, found to be greater than zero, and the body of the loop is entered.
3. The statement DO J = 1,5 is executed. This causes J to be set to its initial value of 1 and the iteration count to be set to its initial value of 5.
4. The iteration count for the inner loop is tested, found to be greater than zero, and the body of its loop is entered.
5. At the bottom of the inner loop, the value of J is incremented, the iteration count for the loop is decremented, and a test is made for completion of the loop.
6. As long as iteration count is greater than zero, the inner loop is repeated. (The loop is executed 5 times.)
7. When the iteration count is zero, an exit is made from the inner loop.
8. At the bottom of the outer loop, the value of I is incremented, the iteration count for the loop is decremented, and a test is made for completion of the loop.
9. As long as the iteration count for the outer loop is greater than zero, the outer loop is repeated, which causes the inner loop to be entered again.

The process continues until an exit is made from the outer loop. The outer loop is repeated 10 times, and for each of these repetitions the inner loop is executed 5 times. Thus the statements READ (5,*)Y and X = X+Y are executed 50 times (10 X 5 = 50). In general, for structured programs, once a DO loop is entered, it is repeatedly executed until its iteration count has been decremented to zero.

The nesting of DO statements can lead to the execution of statements for a huge number of times. For the program fragment

```
        .
        .
        .
DO I = 1, 10, 2
      READ (5,*) U
      DO J = 1, 500
            READ (5,*) V
            DO K = 1, 100
                  READ (5,*) W
                  Z = U + V + W
            ENDDO
      ENDDO
ENDDO
        .
        .
        .
```

1. READ (5,*) U is executed 5 times, since I will have successive values of 1, 3, 5, 7, 9, and 11.
2. READ (5,*) V is executed 2500 times, since there are 500 repetitions of the loop for each execution of the outer loop (5 × 500 = 2500).
3. READ (5,*) W is executed 250,000 times, since there are 100 repetitions of the inner loop for each execution of the middle loop (5 × 500 × 100 = 250,000).

10.2.3 A Sample Program

The application of DO loops will now be illustrated by means of a programming example that appears in several textbooks either as a sample program or as a problem to be done by the students. Incidentally, this example has served me well in demonstrations of the computer's speed. Individuals can estimate the effort that would be required to solve the problem by hand, and they are generally amazed when the answers are printed in 1 second or less. The problem is:

Find all the numbers between 0 and 999 that satisfy the property that the sum of the cubes of the individual digits is equal to the number. For example, for the number 153,

$$1^3 + 5^3 + 3^3 = 1 + 125 + 27$$
$$= 153$$

The method for solving this problem is not obvious, especially for an individual who has little experience in writing computer programs. Typically, a student proposes as a first attempt a solution in which the numbers are generated sequentially, 1, 2, 3, . . . , 999. In this method, the difficult step is to find a technique for obtaining the individual digits of the number so that they can be cubed. A high-level solution of this type is

```
initialize
WHILE (number .LE. 999)
    get individual digits
    compute sum of cubes of digits
    IF (number .EQ. sum of cubes)
        write number
    ENDIF
    increase number
ENDWHILE
STOP
END
```

The problem can be solved using this method, although it is not obvious how to extract the individual digits from the number. We are going to try a different approach, but you may also want to try solving the problem by using the previous method.

Since the extraction of the individual digits appears difficult, let us consider the problem from the opposite point of view. If we knew the individual digits, can the original number be generated? Yes, it can. Let

$$HD \equiv \text{hundreds digit}$$

$$TD \equiv \text{tens digit}$$

$$UD \equiv \text{units digit}$$

Then the original number can be computed using

$$NUMBER = 100*HD + 10*TD + UD$$

Using this approach, the most difficult part of the problem is the generating of the individual digits in the proper sequence, but this can be accomplished by generating the hundreds digit, HD, in an outer loop, by generating the tens digit, TD, in an inner loop, and by generating the units digit, UD, in the innermost loop. Using WHILE loops, this gives

Note: The problem will be solved first with WHILE loops, then with DO loops, and finally the two techniques will be compared:

A. Level 1 Solution

generate hundreds digits, HD
generate tens digits, TD

```
          generate units digit, UD
                NUMBER = 100*HD + 10*TD + UD
                SUMCUB = HD**3 + TD**3 + UD**3
                IF (NUMBER .EQ. SUMCUB) THEN
                      write HD, TD, UD
                ENDIF
```

Replacing the "generate" statements by WHILE loops gives the final solution.

B. *Level 2 Solution*

```
              INTEGER HD, TD, UD, SUMCUB
         1000 FORMAT (3I2)
              HD = 0
              WHILE (HD .LE. 9)
                 TD = 0
                 WHILE (TD .LE. 9)
                    UD = 0
                    WHILE (UD .LE. 9)
                       NUMBER = 100*HD + 10*TD + UD
                       SUMCUB = HD**3 + TD**3 + UD**3
                       IF (NUMBER .EQ. SUMCUB) THEN
                          WRITE (6,1000) HD, TD, UD
                       ENDIF
                       UD = UD + 1
                    ENDWHILE
                    TD = TD + 1
                 ENDWHILE
                 HD = HD + 1
              ENDWHILE
              STOP
              END
```

Note: The use of the variables NUMBER and SUMCUB can be avoided by using a more complicated condition in the IF statement:

```
   IF (100*HD + 10*TD + UD .EQ. HD**3 + TD**3 + UD**3) THEN
       WRITE (6,1000) HD, TD, UD
   ENDIF
```

The initial solution using DO statements can be obtained by a simple translation of the WHILE statement solution. The resulting solution is quite elegant.

```
                    INTEGER HD, TD, UD, SUMCUB
              1000 FORMAT (3I2)
                    DO HD = 0, 9
                       DO TD = 0,9
                          DO UD = 0, 9
                             NUMBER = 100*HD + 10*TD + UD
                             SUMCUB = HD**3 + TD**3 + UD**3
                             IF (NUMBER .EQ. SUMCUB) THEN
                                WRITE (6,1000) HD, TD, UD
                             ENDIF
                          ENDDO
                       ENDDO
                    ENDDO
                    STOP
                    END
```

Figure 10.2 gives the computer printout for the WHILE and DO programs for the problem.

10.3 DO STATEMENT

The FORTRAN standard DO statement is quite similar to the DO. . .ENDDO statement. The ENDDO statement is replaced by a regular FORTRAN statement having an identifying statement number, and this statement number is inserted in the DO statement immediately following the word DO. A typical DO loop is

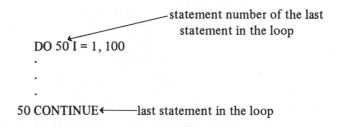

```
                                          ┌─statement number of the last
                                          │  statement in the loop
     DO 50 I = 1, 100
        .
        .
        .
     50 CONTINUE←──────last statement in the loop
```

Note: The CONTINUE statement is an executable FORTRAN statement having the meaning: continue program execution by going to the next sequential statement. It is used in programs to insert a statement number into the sequence of instructions without disrupting the logic of the program. Generally, FORTRAN compilers do not produce any machine-language instructions corresponding to the CONTINUE statement, although the statement number associated with the CONTINUE is saved for use in the compiling process. It is, therefore, ideal for use as the last statement in a DO loop.

```
1  C
2  C              SUM OF CUBE OF DIGITS
3  C              USE OF WHILE STATEMENT
4  C
5          INTEGER HD,TD,UD,SUMCUB
6  1000 FORMAT(3I2)
7          HD=0
8          WHILE( HD .LE. 9)
9             TD=0
10            WHILE( TD .LE. 9)
11               UD=0
12               WHILE(UD .LE. 9)
13                  NUMBER = 100*HD + 10*TD + UD
14                  SUMCUB = HD**3 + TD**3 + UD**3
15                  IF( NUMBER .EQ. SUMCUB)
16                     WRITE(6,1000)HD,TD,UD
17                  ENDIF
18                  UD = UD + 1
19               ENDWHILE
20               TD = TD + 1
21            ENDWHILE
22            HD = HD + 1
23         ENDWHILE
24         STOP
25         END

   0  0  0
   0  0  1
   1  5  3
   3  7  0
   3  7  1
   4  0  7

1  C
2  C              SUM OF CUBES OF DIGITS
3  C              USE OF DO STATEMENT
4  C
5          INTEGER HD,TD,UD,SUMCUB
6  1000 FORMAT(3I2)
7          DO HD=0,9
8             DO TD=0,9
9                DO UD=0,9
10                  NUMBER = 100*HD + 10*TD + UD
11                  SUMCUB = HD**3 + TD**3 + UD**3
12                  IF( NUMBER .EQ. SUMCUB) THEN
13                     WRITE(6,1000)HD,TD,UD
14                  ENDIF
15               ENDDO
16            ENDDO
17         ENDDO
18         STOP
19         END

   0  0  0
   0  0  1
   1  5  3
   3  7  0
   3  7  1
   4  0  7
```

FIGURE 10.2   *Three-digit numbers equal to the sum of the cubes of their digits*

The form of the DO statement is

$$DO \ n \ I1 = I2, I3, I4$$

where n is an integer constant corresponding to the statement number of the last
statement in the range of the DO statement
I1 is the Do-variable
I2 is the initial parameter of the Do-variable
I3 is the terminal parameter of the Do-variable
I4 is the incrementation parameter of the Do-variable
The syntax rules for I1, I2, I3, and I4 are the same as those given for the
DO. . .ENDDO statement.

FORTRAN prohibits certain types of statements from being the last statement
in a DO loop. The control statements

> arithmetic IF
> block IF
> STOP
> PAUSE
> GO TO
> computed GO TO
> DO

are not allowed to be the last statement in a DO loop. This limitation is apparently
the result of implementation difficulties in writing the FORTRAN compiler. If in a
particular problem one of these "forbidden" statements would be appropriate to end
a DO loop, a CONTINUE statement should be placed at the end of the loop. This is
by far the most common use for the CONTINUE statement. Since using the
CONTINUE statement does not take extra computer time or memory, and since
using CONTINUE helps clarify programs by making the end of a loop more obvious,
use CONTINUE to end a DO loop, whether or not it is required by the syntax. There
is no restriction, however, that prevents an arithmetic statement or input/output statement from ending a DO loop.

In using DO statements, care must be taken to ensure that the loops are properly
nested—loops are never allowed to cross each other. An example of properly nested
loops is

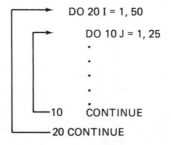

The following is an example of incorrectly nested loops:

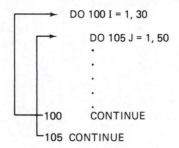

For this invalid example, the arrows, which have been inserted to help visualize the loop, are observed to cross each other.

Nesting of loops can take many different forms, provided that the loops do not cross. Some valid configurations are:

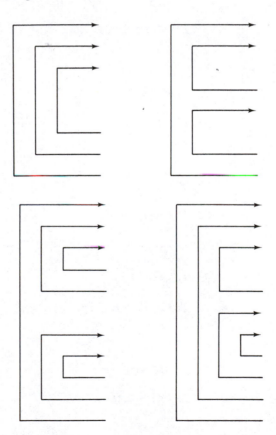

The possibility of improperly nesting loops arises because statement numbers are used to identify the last statement in the range of a loop. In addition, the reasonable habit of numbering statements consecutively can cause an error if you are not careful. The statements

$$DO\ 10\ I = 1,\ 100$$
$$DO\ 20\ J = 1,\ 100$$
$$.$$
$$.$$
$$.$$
$$.$$

$$10 \qquad CONTINUE$$
$$20\ CONTINUE$$

produce loops that cross. DO...ENDDO statements cannot be improperly nested since no statement numbers are used to identify the last statement in a loop.

Find the syntax error, if any, in each of the following:

1.　　DO 50 I = 1, 50
　　　.

　　　.

　　　.

　　50　CONTINUE

2. 30　DO 50 K = 1, 30
　　　.

　　　.

　　　.

　　50　X = X + Y

3. 40　DO 50 J = 1, 40
　　　.

　　　.

　　　.

　　50　GO TO 40

4.　　DO 25 IY = 75, 1, -1
　　　.

　　　.

　　　.

　　25　CONTINUE

5.　　DO KL = 2, 50, 2
　　　.

　　　.

　　　.

　　50　CONTINUE

6.   DO 45 X = 1, 100, 2
          .
          .
          .
  45   READ (5, 1000) Y

7.   DO 37 NEXT = 2, 50, 3
          .
          .
          .
  37 IF (Y .GT. 100.0) GO TO 50

8.   DO 37 KK = 1, 100
         DO 36 KK = 1,100
            .
            .
            .
  36   CONTINUE
  37 CONTINUE

9.   DO 65 KL = 1, 50
         DO 75 KM = 1, 25
            DO 100 KN = 1, 25
              .
              .
              .
 100   CONTINUE
  65   CONTINUE
  75 CONTINUE

10.   DO 10 KI = 1, 5
         DO 15 KJ = 1, 5
         DO 20 KL = 1, 10
           .
           .
           .
  20   CONTINUE
         DO 25 KM = 1, 15
           .
           .
           .
  15   CONTINUE
           .
           .
           .
  25   CONTINUE
  10 CONTINUE

Answers:

1. Valid
2. Valid   An arithmetic statement can be the last statement in a DO loop.
3. Invalid   A GO TO statement cannot be the last statement in a DO loop.
4. Valid
5. Invalid   The statement number is missing in the DO statement.
6. Valid
7. Valid
8. Invalid   The same index, KK, is used for both DO loops.
9. Invalid   The DO loops are not properly nested.
10. Invalid   The DO loops are not properly nested.

For FORTRAN DO statements that have valid syntax, the semantics are exactly like that described for the DO. . .ENDDO statement. There is automatic initialization of the Do-variable and the iteration count just before the beginning of the loop. A test is made at the beginning of the loop to determine if it should be executed. At the end of the loop, there is automatic incrementing of the Do-variable, automatic decrementing of the iteration count, and testing for completion of the loop. Thus the FORTRAN DO statement is used in exactly the same way as the DO. . .ENDDO statement.

REVIEW QUESTIONS

1. Why is an understanding of loops so important in computer programming?
2. Name the five components that are inherent in any loop.
3. What is a counter?
4. For WHILE loops, where is the test done for the completion of the loop? When is an exit made from a WHILE loop?
5. In a satisfactory WHILE loop, what logical requirement (not a syntactical requirement) exists for the loop-controlling variable?
6. What is the difference between the DO. . .ENDDO and the standard DO statement?
7. Give the syntax of the DO statement. What is meant by the terms Do-variable, initial parameter, terminal parameter, and incrementation parameter?
8. What is meant by the term "iteration count"?
9. When a DO loop is translated to machine language, where does the initialization occur? Where do incrementing and testing occur?
10. What happens if the incrementation parameter is omitted from a DO statement?
11. In a DO statement, the initialization parameter is greater than the terminal parameter, and all parameters are positive. How many times will the loop be executed? Why?
12. What is the purpose of the CONTINUE statement?
13. For nested standard DO statements, what restriction exists on the use of statement numbers?

REVIEW QUIZ

1. For the loop

```
N = 0
I = 2
J = 4
WHILE (I .LE. J)
    N = N+I*J
    WRITE (6,100) N
100 FORMAT ('b', I10)
    N = N+1
ENDWHILE
```

The missing essential loop component is (A) initialization, (B) modification, (C) branch to test, (D) body, (E) test.

2. Given:

```
DO IJ = 1,3
DO J = 1,8,2
    X = X-2.5
ENDDO
ENDDO
```

The number of times the statement $X = X-2.5$ is executed is (A) 9, (b) 11, (C) 12, (D) 24, (E) none of the previous answers.

3. For the statement DO NEXT = 1,1000,N...ENDDO, (A) the Do-variable has an invalid name; (B) the test for completion is made at the beginning of the loop; (C) the Do-variable increases N units for every pass through the loop; (D) the maximum value of the Do-variable is $1000 + N$; (E) the maximum number of statements within the body of the loop is 1000.

4. The statements

```
DO K = 10,N,2
    SUM = SUM+K
ENDDO
```

are equivalent to

(A)
```
    DO K = 1,10
    DO L = 2,N
        SUM = SUM+K+L
    ENDDO
    ENDDO
```

(B)
```
    K = 10
2 SUM = SUM+K
    K = K+2
    IF (K .EQ. N) GO TO 2
```

(C)
```
    K = 10
2 SUM = SUM+N
    K = K+2
    IF (SUM .LE. N) GO TO 2
```

(D)
```
    K = 10
2 SUM = SUM+K
    K = K+2
    IF (K .LE. N) GO TO 2
```

(E)
```
    K = 10
2 SUM = SUM+K
    K = K+N
    IF (K .GE. N) GO TO 2
```

5. The last statement in a standard DO loop may be (A) a CONTINUE statement, (B) an IF statement, (C) an assignment statement, (D) A and C, (E) B and C.

6. Given:

$$DO\ I = 1,100,10$$
.
.
.
$$ENDDO$$

What value will the Do-variable, I, have during the last execution of the loop? (A) 1, (B) 9, (C) 10, (D) 100, (E) none of these.

7. Given:

```
DO 1 I = 1,20,2
DO 2 J = 1,10
DO 3 K = 1,5
1 X = 2.*K+5
2 CONTINUE
3 CONTINUE
```

The number of times statement 1 will be executed is (A) none, because the statements shown contain an error; (B) 10; (C) 20; (D) 100; (E) 500.

8. Given:

```
DO 20 IX = 1,50
DO 10 IY = 1,25
5 X = 2.*A+B
.
.
.
10 CONTINUE
20 CONTINUE
```

The number of times statement 5 is executed is (A) 25, (B) 50, (C) 75, (D) 1250, (E) none of the previous answers.

9. A DO loop that will be executed exactly one time results from
   (A) DO 10 K = 1,10,2.5
   (B) DO 75 NN = 1,10
   (C) DO 150 I = 1,LIMIT+2
   (D) DO 35 LJ = 5,6,2
   (E) DO 100 KK = 50,1,-2

10. Given:

```
I = 10
M = 0
DO J = 1,5
   M = M+I*J
ENDDO
```

The value of M at the conclusion of the execution of the loop is (A) 0, (B) 15, (C) 50, (D) 150, (E) none of the previous answers.

EXERCISES

1. Give the value of the Do-variable upon exit from the loop for each of the following:
   a. DO 10 J = 1, 10
   b. DO 10 J = 1, 10, 2
   c. DO 10 J = 1, 10, 3
   d. DO 10 J = 10, 9
   e. DO J = 20, 30, 2
      .
      .
      .
      ENDDO
   f. DO J = 10, 1, -1
      .
      .
      .
      ENDDO
   g. DO J = 10, 1, 2
      .
      .
      .
      ENDDO
   h. DO J = 10, 3, -1
      .
      .
      .
      ENDDO
   i. I = 4
      J = 10
      DO K = I, J, 2
      .
      .
      .
      ENDDO
   j. I = 4
      J = 10
      K = 2
      DO LL = K, J, I
      .
      .
      .
      ENDDO

2. Give the value of N upon exit from the following:
   a. N = 0
      DO I = 1,10
          N = I
      ENDDO

   b. N = 0
      DO I = 1,10
          N = N + I
      ENDDO

   c. N = 0
      DO I = 1,2
          DO J = 1,5
              N = N+J
          ENDDO
      ENDDO

3. Write loops to solve the following problems:
   a. Find the sum of the first 50 integers.
   b. Find the sum of the first 50 odd integers.
   c. Find the sum of the odd integers less than 50.
   d. Find the number of consecutive integers starting with zero that must be added to give a sum of at least 2000.
   e. Write a DO loop that reads cards and exits from the loop as soon as a negative value is read.

PROGRAMMING EXERCISES

1. Modify the sum-of-cubes problem, Figure 10.2, to find all the four-digit numbers that are equal to the sum of the fourth power of their individual digits. That is, if the number is represented in symbols as $abcd$, then

$$abcd = a^4 + b^4 + c^4 + d^4$$

The leftmost digit should not equal zero.

2. Print all the four-digit permutations (1234, 1243, 1324, etc.) of the digits 1, 2, 3, and 4.

3. For a satellite moving in a circular orbit about a celestial body, the speed in miles per hour is given approximately by

$$s = \sqrt{C/r}$$

where s = speed of satellite, in miles per hour
C = a constant that depends upon the particular celestial body
r = distance from the center of the celestial body to the satellite, in miles

For the earth, moon, and Mars, the values of the constant, C, are 1.2×10^{12}, 1.5×10^{10}, and 1.3×10^{11}, respectively. For these bodies print a table of the speed of a satellite for orbits at distances from the center of the bodies of 4000 to 20,000 miles in steps of 1000 miles.

ORBITAL SPEEDS OF A SATELLITE			
DISTANCE FROM CENTER OF BODY	EARTH	CELESTIAL BODY MOON	MARS
4000	17320	1936	5700
5000	15490	1732	5099
.	.	.	.
.	.	.	.
.	.	.	.

4. The theory of biorhythm, which has not been proven, speculates that a person's performance is significantly affected by three cycles that begin at birth. The physical, intellectual, and emotional cycles each form a sine curve having periods of 23, 33, and 28 days, respectively. Each curve has amplitude 1. A person's biorhythm index on a given day is the sum of the values for the individual cycles.

For today's date, compute the biorhythm index for individuals having the following birth dates. (Include any other dates that interest you.)

Month	Day	Year
04	21	1931
02	12	1933
09	06	1945
06	18	1956
11	07	1958
08	30	1957
etc.		

5. Roots of numbers can be computed by making an initial guess, obtaining a better estimate by using the guess, and combining the last two guesses to make a new estimate. This processing is continued until sufficient accuracy is obtained. In the case of square roots, the procedure can be represented as

$$E_0 = \frac{X}{2}$$

$$E_n = \frac{E_{n-1} + X/E_{n-1}}{2}$$

where X = number whose square root is needed
E_0 = initial estimate
E_{n-1} = estimate after $n - 1$ attempts
E_n = estimate after n attempts

Use this method to compute the square of the integers from 2 to 25 to an accuracy of 0.0001 unit.

6. The cubes of the integers can be expressed as sums of adjacent odd integers. For example,

$$
\begin{aligned}
2^3 &= 8 &&= 3 + 5 \\
3^3 &= 27 &&= 7 + 9 + 11 \\
4^3 &= 64 &&= 13 + 15 + 17 + 19 \\
5^3 &= 125 &&= 21 + 23 + 25 + 27 + 29 \\
6^3 &= 216 &&= 31 + 33 + 35 + 37 + 39 + 41
\end{aligned}
$$

For the integers $n = 2$ through $n = 25$, write a program that finds the successive odd integers whose sum equals n^3.

7. The roots of a polynomial equation such as

$$f(x) = 4x^3 - 20x^2 + 27x - 9 = 0$$

are the values of x for which the left half of the equation equals zero. For example, when $x = 1.5$, the terms on the left combine to become zero. If the equation is evaluated for successive values of x, a change in the sign of the answer implies that a root occurs between these values. When $x = 1$, the value of the equation is 2, and when $x = 2$, the value of the equation is -3; consequently, a root must occur between 1 and 2. After an interval containing a root is found, a binary search technique can be used to estimate the value of the root to the desired accuracy. The midpoint of the interval is calculated, and the equation is evaluated for this x. A new interval is selected by using the midpoint and the previous value of x that gave the opposite sign for the value of the equation. The process is repeated for smaller intervals until the desired accuracy is obtained. The process is illustrated in the figure.

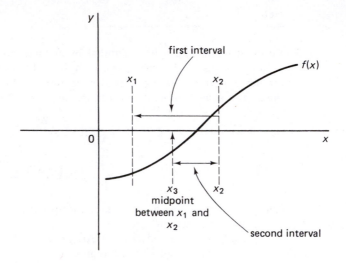

Use this method to find the real roots of

$$f(x) = x^3 - 9.6x^2 + 25.8375x - 19.25 = 0$$

8. The Pearson correlation coefficient, R, is a statistical quantity that estimates the interdependence of two variables, X and Y. For computing the value of R directly from raw experimental measurements using a desk calculator, the following rather formidable-appearing formula is recommended by some textbooks.

$$R = \frac{\dfrac{\Sigma XY}{N} - \overline{X}\,\overline{Y}}{\sqrt{\dfrac{\Sigma X^2}{N} - \overline{X}^2}\sqrt{\dfrac{\Sigma Y^2}{N} - \overline{Y}^2}}$$

where ΣXY = sum of the products of each X and its associated Y
$\overline{X}$ = average of the X's
$\overline{Y}$ = average of the Y's
N = number of pairs of X and Y's
ΣX^2 = sum of the squares of the individual X's
ΣY^2 = sum of the squares of the individual Y's

Write a program that computes R using the formula, and test the program using the following data:

X	Y
5.8	3.2
8.1	4.6
10.8	5.0
12.9	5.9
15.3	7.3
17.4	9.2
20.4	9.3
22.0	11.5
24.7	11.4
25.9	12.8

9. The number 55 has the interesting property that its square can be divided into two-digit integers whose sum is 55. That is,

$$55^2 = 3025$$

and

$$55 = 30 + 25$$

Find all the two-digit integers that have this property.

CHAPTER 11 ONE-DIMENSIONAL ARRAYS

At this point in our study of FORTRAN, we have considered arithmetic, input/output, and control statements in reasonable detail and have learned to use the language to write programs. In a sense, we have completed one level of our study of FORTRAN. Yet there are many problems that are inconvenient or even impossible to solve using the methods presented so far. This chapter introduces a new concept, arrays, which will greatly extend the range of problems that can be solved using FORTRAN.

The idea of an array is a familiar one, although you probably have not used this particular terminology before. An *array* is an ordered sequence of data items. A list of phone numbers, a shopping list, and a tax table are everyday examples of items that can be considered to be arrays. Vectors and matrices are examples of arrays in mathematics.

In this chapter, our task is to clarify this concept and to learn to use it. The fuzziness of our ordinary, everyday use of the concept must be replaced with precise terminology. Particular attention will be given to the following questions:

1. How is the compiler notified that a variable is to be treated as an array? As a specific example, suppose that we want the variable GRADES to refer to the set of all the grades made by a class and not to just a single value. A method is needed to signal this to the compiler.
2. How is the maximum number of elements associated with an array determined? For example, how can the compiler be informed that the maximum number of individual grades associated with GRADES will be 35?
3. How can individual elements of an array be accessed and used in a program? For example, how can the first and second members of GRADES be accessed and compared to determine which individual grade is larger?

You will find that understanding the answers to these and related questions is practically all that is necessary to allow you to use arrays. Mastery of the topic will greatly expand your ability to use the computer effectively. Many programming examples will be given in this and subsequent chapters—in fact, most of the remaining programs will use arrays.

Before proceeding with the specifics of arrays, let us consider them in broad perspective. An array is an example of a data structure, that is, a structure based on the logical relationships between the individual items of the information. Computer science and programming are quite concerned with the nature of data structures, and entire courses are devoted to the study of various structures. Often the key to finding a reasonable (or better) solution to a programming problem is the recognition of the

288

structure associated with the data of the problem. Arrays are simultaneously one of the simplest types of data structures and the most complex data structure that is built into FORTRAN. The lack of even more complex structures that can be manipulated directly in FORTRAN is one of the major weaknesses of the language. On the other hand, it should be noted that FORTRAN was invented before the importance of data structures was recognized, and in addition, FORTRAN satisfies quite well its design criterion of providing a high-level language for solving mathematical problems.

11.1 AN INTRODUCTORY EXAMPLE

To improve our intuitive grasp and understanding of arrays, let us consider a simple example before the subject is considered more formally. Suppose that we write a program for the following problem:

A class of 35 students has taken a quiz. Read all 35 grades from a set of cards (one grade per card), and store the grades in computer memory. Then calculate the average grade. Finally print all the grades, five per line, and print the class average on the last line.

The fact that all the grades are to be in computer memory before the calculation begins makes the program awkward to write using our current knowledge of FORTRAN. We could (1) invent a series of 35 names such as GRADE1, GRADE2, GRADE3, . . . , GRADE35; (2) write 35 READ statements using these names to get the grades into computer memory; (3) sum the values of the variables and compute the average; and (4) write a series of statements to print the grades and the average. Awkward as this procedure is, it is possible. But if the program were being written to calculate the average grade made by 1050 freshmen on a mathematics placement test, the method becomes completely impractical.

To solve the problem in a more general and satisfactory manner, we will set aside a large enough block of memory cells to hold the 35 grades and will give the name GRADES to this block of memory cells. The individual grades in the block can be identified by their position in the block by enclosing the position number in parentheses at the end of the name GRADES. Thus the individual grades (called "members" of GRADES or "elements" of GRADES) are the values of

GRADES(1)	1st member of the block
GRADES(2)	2nd member of the block
GRADES(3)	3rd member of the block
.	
.	
.	
GRADES(35)	35th member of the block

This procedure resembles the pencil-and-paper technique of writing the word GRADES at the top of a page, numbering 35 lines, and writing the values for the grades on these lines.

GRADES is an example of a name of an array, and the constants enclosed in parentheses at the right of the name are examples of subscripts. A name refers to an array if it is legitimate to attach subscripts to the name. This properly implies that an array may have more than one value. The subscript can be a variable, as in GRADES(I), with the value of I determining which element of GRADES is to be referenced. For example, if I = 4, then GRADES(I) refers to the 4th value in the block of grades.

One method of notifying the compiler that a variable refers to an array is to give the name of the variable in a declaration statement and enclosing the maximum number of values for the variable in parentheses at the end of the name. The statement

$$\text{REAL GRADES(35)}$$

would cause a block of memory cells sufficient in number to hold 35 values to be set aside and named GRADES. The statement

$$\text{REAL GRADES(1050)}$$

would cause enough memory cells to be set aside to hold up to 1050 values.

A program that solves the problem is

```
        REAL GRADES(35)
   1000 FORMAT ('1', T20, 'QUIZ GRADES')
   1010 FORMAT ('b', 5F10.0)
   1020 FORMAT ('0', 'THE AVERAGE GRADE IS', F10.0)
   1030 FORMAT (F10.0)
C           READ ALL VALUES
        I = 1
        WHILE (I .LE. 35)
            READ (5, 1030) GRADES(I)
            I = I + 1
        ENDWHILE
C           COMPUTE AVERAGE
        SUM = 0.0
        I = 1
        WHILE (I .LE. 35)
            SUM = SUM + GRADES(I)
            I = I + 1
        ENDWHILE
        AVG = SUM/35.
C           PRINT GRADES AND AVERAGE
        WRITE (6, 1000)
        I = 1
```

```
      WHILE (I .LE. 35)
            WRITE (6,1010) GRADES(I), GRADES(I+1), GRADES (I+2),
      1     GRADES(I+3), GRADES(I+4)
            I = I + 5
      ENDWHILE
      WRITE (6,1020) AVG
      STOP
      END
```

The program operates as follows:

1. The REAL statement causes the compiler to reserve memory cells for 35 values of GRADES.
2. The read loop is executed 35 times with successive values of I from 1 to 35. This causes GRADES(1), GRADES(2), . . . , GRADES(35) to be read in turn.
3. The summation loop is executed 35 times, causing GRADES(1) through GRADES(35) to be added.
4. The printing loop is executed seven times, with values for I of 1, 6, 11, 16, 21, 26, and 31. For each pass through the loop, five grades are printed. When I = 1, values are computed for the subscripts as

$$
\begin{aligned}
I &= 1 \\
I+1 &= 2 \\
I+2 &= 3 \\
I+3 &= 4 \\
I+4 &= 5
\end{aligned}
$$

Thus, the first five grades are printed during the first execution of the loop, grades 6 through 10 during the second execution, and so on.

The program can easily be changed to average 1050 freshmen placement test scores. The REAL statement should be changed to

REAL GRADES(1050)

Each of the WHILE statements should be changed to

WHILE (I .LE. 1050)

An even more general method would be to introduce a variable, N, whose value is the number of grades to be averaged. The value of N could be read from the first input card, or it could be initialized by an arithmetic statement at the beginning of the program. The WHILE statements could then be written

WHILE (I .LE. N)

The quiz-grade averaging program, as just considered, is artificial because there would almost never be a need to perform the computation in the manner required by the statement of the problem. Despite this artificiality, the problem allowed us to consider various features of arrays without distracting details. It is easy to change the problem into a realistic one that requires arrays: just include the restriction that the grades should be printed in sorted order with highest grades being printed first. This more realistic problem was not used as the introductory example because additional discussion would have been necessary to explain the method used to sort the values.

11.2   CHARACTERISTICS OF ARRAYS

An array is a name given to an ordered sequence of values. Any particular value in the set can be accessed by using an appropriate subscript. The form of an array is

name of variable (subscripts)

1. The regular FORTRAN rules for naming variables apply to arrays:
   a. The name consists of one to six characters.
   b. The first character must be alphabetic, and the remaining characters may be either alphabetic or numeric.
   c. The first character implies the mode of the variable:

I-N	implies integer mode
A-H, O-Z	implies real mode

2. The name of the array must be placed in a declaration statement with the name being followed by the maximum number of elements, enclosed in parentheses. If the statements REAL or INTEGER are used, the first character of the name no longer implies the mode of the variable. Other possible declaration statements will be discussed later.
3. Subscripts may be integer constants, integer variables, or integer-mode arithmetic expressions. Subscripts are restricted to integer values, since subscripts are used to designate particular members of a block of values. It makes sense to talk about the 1st value, 5th value, or 100th value, but it is meaningless to talk about values identified by real-mode subscripts, such as the 6.37th value.

The range of allowed values for a subscript can be stated explicitly when the variable is listed in a declaration statement, or it can be implied. For example, the statement

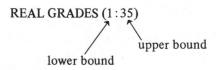

explicitly gives the subscript bounds for the variable GRADES. The bounds must be separated by a colon, and the lower bound must precede the upper bound. Moreover, the value of the upper bound must always be greater than or equal to the value of the lower bound. Negative or zero values are allowed for bounds on subscripts. Some valid examples are

REAL GRADES (-35:0)
REAL GRADES (-10:24)
REAL GRADES (0:34)

Note: Although the explicit designating of subscript bounds is a standard feature of FORTRAN, not all compilers include it.

The including of a lower bound for a subscript is optional. If it is omitted, the value of the lower bound is implied to be 1. Thus the following have the same meaning:

REAL GRADES (35)
REAL GRADES (1:35)

optional

During the execution of a program, if the subscript becomes less than the lower bound or greater than the upper bound, invalid results will be produced. Some compilers generate instructions to test for this error during program execution, and if the error occurs, the program is terminated with an error message such as "SUBSCRIPT OUT OF BOUNDS" being printed. Other compilers do not cause testing for this error during the execution of the program. In this case, the results can be very strange, and the program can be quite difficult to debug. You will do yourself a favor by checking programs for valid subscript ranges before you execute them.

An array can have more than one subscript, as in FREQ(I,J). I and J are both subscripts, and a value must be specified for each of them to select a particular element of FREQ. Nearly all FORTRAN compilers allow three subscripts to be used, most allow seven subscripts (the standard number), and a few have no limit to the number of subscripts.

The number of subscripts associated with an array is called its *dimension*. In the grade-averaging program, GRADES was a one-dimensional array because any element of GRADES could be selected using one subscript. One-dimensional arrays can be visualized as a linear sequence of values. Two-dimensional arrays represent tables (matrices) with the two subscripts giving the row and column in which the value is located. For example, TABLE (2,5) refers to the value found at the intersection of the 2nd row and 5th column of the two-dimensional array named TABLE. Three-dimensional arrays can be visualized as a set of pages of tables. VAR (2,5,3) refers to the value found on the 2nd page, at the intersection of the 5th row and 3rd column of the three-dimensional array called VAR. Arrays of dimension greater than three are difficult to visualize. In this chapter we emphasize one-dimensional arrays. More information about two- and three-dimensional arrays is given in Chapter 13.

Array names can be used in assignment statements in the same manner as ordinary variables. The only additional requirement is that a subscript be used with the variable—use of the name without a subscript is an error. Some sample assignment statements involving arrays are shown below. In these statements, the arrays VECTOR, TABLE, and BIGTBL are assumed to be one-, two-, and three-dimensional arrays, respectively.

$$X = VECTOR(1) + VECTOR(2)$$

$$SUM = SUM + VECTOR(K)$$

$$TOTAL = TOTAL + TABLE(I,J)$$

$$DIFF = TABLE(1,I) - TABLE(2,I)$$

$$RESULT = (BIGTBL(K,L,M) - TABLE(M,N)) * VECTOR(I+2)$$

$$CALC = SQRT (VECTOR(I)**2 + VECTOR(J)**2)$$

$$VECTOR(1) = 2.5*X/Y$$

$$VECTOR(L) = TABLE(K,5) - VECTOR(K-1)$$

$$TABLE(1,1) = TABLE(2,2) + 1$$

$$TABLE(I,J) = TABLE(I,K)*TABLE(K,J)$$

Notice that the subscript could be either a constant, a variable, or an expression, but regardless of the form of the subscripts, it had to be present.

11.3 THE DIMENSION STATEMENT

The DIMENSION statement is a declaration statement that can be used instead of INTEGER or REAL to inform the compiler that one or more variables are arrays and to indicate the maximum number of elements that can be associated with an array. For example, the statement

$$DIMENSION\ X(10),\ Y(200),\ Z(50)$$

indicates that X, Y, and Z are arrays having a maximum of 10, 200, and 50 elements, respectively. Because DIMENSION statements are declaration statements, they must be placed before the first executable statement in the program. Moreover, they are non-executable statements, since they give directions to the compiler and cause no actions during the execution of the program.

The following rules apply to DIMENSION statements:

1. A programmer can use as many DIMENSION statements in a program as he or she wishes. As noted previously, DIMENSION statements must be placed before the first executable statement in the program.

2. A single DIMENSION statement can be used to define any number of arrays. The statement

DIMENSION X(10), Y(50)

is equivalent to the following pair of statements:

DIMENSION X(10)
DIMENSION Y(50)

3. In a DIMENSION statement, the order of listing of variables is not important. The following statements are equivalent:

DIMENSION X(10), Y(50), Z(100)

DIMENSION Y(50), X(10), Z(100)

DIMENSION Y(50), Z(100), X(10)

4. Each variable declared in a DIMENSION statement must include an integer constant for each dimension which gives the maximum size for that dimension. As an option, the lower bound for each dimension may be included as an integer constant.

Find the syntax errors, if any, in each of the following statements:

1. DIMENSION X(50), GRADES, MASS(50), Z(100)
2. DIMENSION TAX (100,5), PAY(50)
3. DIMENSION A(10), B(10), C(20), X(15), A(15), Y(15)
4. DIMENSION SCORES(25), AVER(25.6)
5. DIMENSION FREQ(N)
6. DIMENSION X(10+5)
7. DIMENSION Y(I+1)

Answers:

1. Invalid   GRADES does not have the number of values indicated.
2. Valid
3. Invalid   The variable A appears twice.
4. Invalid   AVER uses a real-mode constant instead of an integer-mode constant to designate the number of values.
5. Invalid   FREQ cannot use a variable, N, within a DIMENSION statement to designate the number of values.
6. Invalid   The computation 10+5 (or any other computation) is not allowed.
7. Invalid   The expression I+1 (or any other expression) is not allowed.

Earlier in the chapter it was noted that the INTEGER or the REAL statement can be used as if it were a DIMENSION statement. For example, to reserve cells for

100 values of GRADES and make the variable be integer mode, you can use

INTEGER GRADES(100)

Incidentally, if you need to dimension an array in a program and accidentally fail to do so, a large number of errors will result. Every statement which uses an array that has not been declared will contain an error. The compiler will assume the undeclared arrays to be functions. Notice the similarity in form of SQRT(X) and GRADES(I). When the program is prepared for execution, the assumed functions will not be found and a list of errors will be printed. Many times I have seen the compiler print a list of errors as long as the program it was trying to translate, merely because the arrays had not been declared.

11.4   INPUT/OUTPUT OF ONE-DIMENSIONAL ARRAYS

A variety of methods exist for the reading and writing of the elements of one-dimensional arrays, and this section discusses several, giving emphasis to the subtle differences between them. A new method, the use of implied DO loops, will be introduced.

A standard technique for input or output of arrays is the use of a DO (or WHILE) loop. In such loops the index is used as a subscript. The statements

```
        .
        .
        .
     DO J = 1,100
            READ (5,1025) GRADES(J)
1025       FORMAT (F10.2)
     ENDDO
        .
        .
        .
```

will read 100 values, one value per card. Thus the loop reads 100 cards. How many cards would be read by the following sequence of statements?

```
        .
        .
        .
     DO J = 1,100
            READ (5,1030) GRADES(J)
1030       FORMAT (8F10.2)
     ENDDO
        .
        .
        .
```

If you guessed 13 cards, you were wrong. The read statement is executed 100 times. Each time it is executed, one value of GRADES is read from the first field in the card. The remaining fields on a card are ignored.

Implied DO loops in READ or WRITE statements have the form

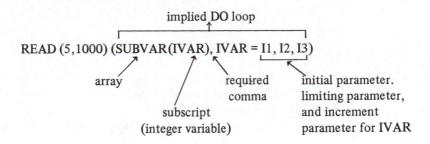

An implied DO loop behaves in practically the same way as an ordinary DO loop. For example, the statement

$$\text{READ } (5,1000) \text{ (GRADES(K), K = 1,100)}$$

will cause the reading of 100 values of GRADES, starting with GRADES(1), increasing the subscript by 1 (this is implied since no increment value is given), stopping after GRADES(100) has been read.

For the pair of statements

$$\text{READ } (5,1030) \text{ (GRADES(J), J = 1,100)}$$
$$1030 \text{ FORMAT } (8F10.2)$$

how many cards will be read to obtain 100 values for GRADES? The answer is 13 cards. Notice that this is quite different from the behavior just described for the DO loop, which used the same FORMAT statement. In the case of the implied DO loop, the READ statement is executed a single time to obtain all 100 values. Thus, all eight fields on a card are used in the reading process, with 12 cards being used for the first 96 values and the 13th card being used for the last four values. (*Note:* To avoid difficulties in future program writing, remember that DO loops and implied DO loops operate differently in reading and printing values.)

A technique that is frequently used in reading arrays is to read a card that contains the number of values to be input and then to use this value to control a DO loop or an implied DO loop. Let N be the number of values to be input for the arrays, X and Y. Then the statements

.
.
.

$$\text{READ } (5,1040) \text{ N}$$

```
          1040 FORMAT (I4)
             DO I = 1,N
                READ (5,1045) X(I), Y(I)
     1045        FORMAT (2F10.2)
             ENDDO
                .
                .
                .
```

perform the desired actions. Notice that N is used as the limiting parameter for the DO loop. The number of cards that are input because of the READ statement within the DO loop is determined by the value of N.

The DO loop in the previous example can be replaced by an implied DO loop.

```
                .
                .
                .
          READ (5,1040) N
     1040 FORMAT (I4)
          READ (5,1045) (X(I), Y(I), I = 1,N)
     1045 FORMAT (2F10.2)
```

A deck of input cards that could be used by these statements has the following appearance:

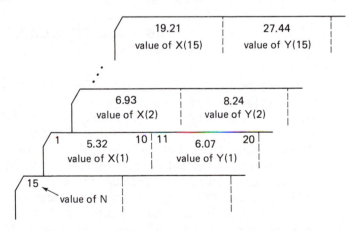

By changing the value in the first card (the value of N), we can cause different numbers of cards to be input. Techniques such as this are useful in generalizing a program so that it can be used for a variety of cases. Incidentally, you would not want to employ this particular technique if there were many values of X and Y. First, counting the cards (so the value of N can be punched into a card) would be time consuming, and second, the probability of making a counting error increases as the number of cards becomes larger.

In the statement

$$READ (5,1045) (X(I), Y(I), I = 1,N)$$

two variables X and Y appeared within the implied DO loop. Any number of variables can be used within the implied DO loop. For example, the following are valid statements:

$$READ (5,1050) (X(I), Y(I), Z(I), I = 1,N)$$

$$READ (5,1055) (A(J), B(J), C(J), D(J), J = 1, 100)$$

$$READ (5,1060) (IVAR(K), X(K), Y(K), K = 1,L)$$

If you use such statements, you must be careful about two things. Consider as an example the last statement for reading values of IVAR, X, and Y:

1. Before the statement is executed the value of L (the limiting value in the implied DO loop) must be known. The value of L can be assigned in an arithmetic statement, or it can be obtained as a result of executing a READ statement.
2. The specifications in the FORMAT statement 1060 must agree in number and mode with the variables as they appear in the READ statement. For example, the following is valid:

$$READ (5,1060) (IVAR(K), X(K), Y(K), K = 1,L)$$
$$1060 FORMAT (I5, 2F10.2)$$

The reading of the value of N and the values of X and Y in the statements

.

.

.

$$READ (5,1040) N$$
$$1040 FORMAT (I4)$$
$$READ (5,1045) (X(I), Y(I), I = 1,N)$$
$$1045 FORMAT (2F10.2)$$

.

.

.

.

can be compressed into a single READ statement:

$$READ (5, 1065) N, (X(I), Y(I), I = 1,N)$$
$$1065 FORMAT (I4/(2F10.2))$$

note the slash   note the extra parentheses

A slash used within a FORMAT statement means that a description of a card (or print-line) has been completed. Thus this particular FORMAT statement contains the specifications for two cards.

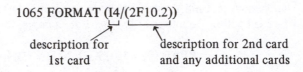

1065 FORMAT (I4/(2F10.2))

description for   description for 2nd card
1st card   and any additional cards

The pattern of parentheses at the end of the FORMAT statement

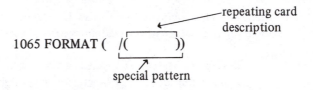

1065 FORMAT (/(   ))

repeating card description

special pattern

means that the specifications within the parentheses are to be used repeatedly as a description of a card (or printline) for reading all additional cards. You can think of this configuration of parentheses as a trap: once the trap is entered in the reading (or writing) process, the computer cannot get out until all the reading is complete.

FORTRAN allows the reading or writing of the values of an array without the explicit use of subscripts. For example, the statements

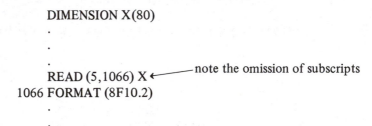

DIMENSION X(80)
.
.
.
READ (5,1066) X ←——— note the omission of subscripts
1066 FORMAT (8F10.2)
.
.
.

will cause all 80 values of X to be read from 10 cards, eight values per card. The omission of the subscript from the name of the array is always interpreted by the compiler to mean that the number of values given in the declaration statement is to be input or output.

The technique of omitting the subscript is not very useful. Ordinarily, a program is designed to handle a maximum number of values in an array, but typically in a given execution of the program less than the maximum number of values is used. This makes statements such as

READ (5,1045) (X(I), I = 1,N)

more practical. Special difficulties arise if subscripts are omitted from multidimensional arrays. These difficulties will be discussed in Section 13.2.

All that has been said about the input of values of arrays also applies to the output of values of arrays. It is necessary, however, to supply the carriage control character in the writing process. Both of the following are valid:

```
        DO J = 1,100
              WRITE (6,1070) GRADES(J)
1070          FORMAT ('b', 8F10.2)
        ENDDO

        WRITE (6,1075) (GRADES(J), J = 1, 100)
1075 FORMAT ('b', 8F10.2)
```

The DO loop will print one value per line despite the appearance of eight specifications in the FORMAT statement, but the implied DO loop will print eight values per line.

In writing FORMAT statements for output of data, the slash can often be used advantageously. The pair of statements

```
        WRITE (6,1075) N, (X(I), Y(I), I = 1,N)
1075 FORMAT ('1', I4/('b', 2F10.2))
```

will cause (1) a skip to the top of a page, (2) the printing of the value of N in the first four columns of the first line of the page, and (3) the printing of a value of X and a value of Y on a line, with the printing of this type of line being repeated N times.

The slash, which allowed us to describe more than one printline in a single FORMAT statement, is also commonly used to allow the description of several lines of page headings in one statement. The following statements will cause two heading lines to be printed.

```
        WRITE (6,1080)
1080 FORMAT('1', T19, 'SAMPLE REPORT'/'0', T10, 'ID NUM',
        1T20, 'RATE', T30, 'HOURS', T40, 'PAY')
```

The result is

```
                        SAMPLE REPORT

        ID NUM       RATE      HOURS      PAY
```

Notice that a carriage control character was included for each line.

Another common use for the slash is the printing of blank lines. For every slash appearing at the beginning or end of a FORMAT statement, exactly one blank line will be "printed." For adjacent slashes appearing within a FORMAT statement, the number of blank lines is one less than the number of slashes. For example, the statements

WRITE (6,1085)
1085 FORMAT ('1', T19, 'SAMPLE REPORT'//T10, 'ID NUM',
1T20, 'RATE', T30, 'HOURS', T40, 'PAY')

will cause one blank line to appear between the two heading lines because of the two slashes. The statements

WRITE (6,1090) P
1090 FORMAT (///'b', F10.2)

will cause three blank lines to be printed before the value of P is printed. This behavior can be understood by considering that each consecutive slash completes the description of a line. The interpretation of the FORMAT statement is:

1. The printer is positioned over the line printed by the previous WRITE statement. The new WRITE statement is executed, causing the FORMAT statement to be scanned, left to right, until the leftmost slash is encountered.

1090 FORMAT (/   /   /'b', F10.2)

scan to here

A line with nothing on it has been described. This infers a carriage control character of blank. The printer skips to the next line.

Line number	*Contents of line*
0	Line printed by previous WRITE statement
1	Skip to here (i.e., this is the new printer position)

2. FORMAT is scanned to the next slash.

1090 FORMAT (/   /   /'b', F10.2)

scan to here

A skip to the next line occurs.

Line number	Contents of line
0	Line printed by previous WRITE statement
1	Blank line
2	New printer position

3. FORMAT is scanned to the next slash, and a skip to the next line occurs.

1090 FORMAT (/   /   /'b', F10.2)

scan to here

Line number	Contents of line
0	Line printed by previous WRITE statement
1	Blank line
2	Blank line
3	New printer position

4. The value of the variable P is printed using the carriage control character in the last part of the FORMAT statement.

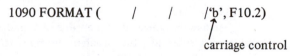

1090 FORMAT (/   /   /'b', F10.2)

carriage control

Line number	Contents of line
0	Line printed by previous WRITE statement
1	Blank line
2	Blank line
3	Blank line
4	Value of P

As a final example of the output of one-dimensional arrays, consider the introductory problem given at the beginning of the chapter. The problem contained the statements

    .

    .

    .

I = 1
WHILE (I .LE. 35)
     WRITE (6,1010) GRADES(I), GRADES(I+1), GRADES(I+2),

```
     1       GRADES(I+3), GRADES(I+4)
  1010       FORMAT ('b', 5F10.0)
             I = I + 5
          ENDWHILE
             .
             .
             .
```

for printing the 35 grades, 5 grades per line. This sequence could be replaced by

$$\text{WRITE } (6,1010) \text{ (GRADES(I), I = 1,35)}$$
$$\text{1010 FORMAT ('b', 5F10.0)}$$

11.5 PROGRAMMING EXAMPLES

11.5.1 Frequency Distribution

Suppose that a freshman placement test has just been given. The quiz has been graded by computer; various statistics, such as the average and standard deviation have been computed and printed. In addition, a count is needed of the number of times each grade was made (i.e., the frequency of occurrence of the grades is wanted). We are asked to write a program to obtain the frequency distribution assuming a maximum of 2000 grades. All grades are integers in the range 0 to 100. (*Note:* This is 101 possible grades.)

If one recognizes that the value of a grade (remember: it is an integer) can be the value of a subscript, the problem becomes relatively easy. Let FREQ be an integer array of 101 elements that is to contain the count for possible grades. Elements of FREQ and grades correspond according to the scheme

Element of FREQ	Corresponding grade
FREQ(0)	0
FREQ(1)	1
FREQ(2)	2
.	.
.	.
.	.
FREQ(98)	98
FREQ(99)	99
FREQ(100)	100

Notice that the subscript of FREQ is equal to the value of GRADE. If the available compiler does not allow zero as a subscript, the subscripts for FREQ would have ranged from 1 to 101. The appropriate subscript for FREQ would be GRADE+1. Thus assuming that zero is not allowed as a subscript, to count the occurrence of a particular grade we can use

$$FREQ(GRADE+1) = FREQ(GRADE+1) + 1$$

This statement says: take the value stored at location GRADE+1 in the array FREQ, add 1 to the value, and store this resulting value at location GRADE+1.

Before the counting process begins, all the elements in FREQ should be set to zero. This can be accomplished using a DO loop.

```
DO I = 1, 101
     FREQ(I) = 0     (FREQ will be defined as INTEGER)
ENDDO
```

Ignoring details of output, the program is

```
        INTEGER FREQ(101), GRADE
1000 FORMAT (I3)
        DO I = 1, 101
              FREQ(I) = 0
        ENDDO
        READ (5,1000) GRADE
        WHILE (GRADE .GE. 0)
              FREQ (GRADE+1) = FREQ(GRADE+1) + 1
              READ (5,1000) GRADE
        ENDWHILE
        .
        .
        .
```

The program is surprisingly short. Computer printout is given in Figure 11.1. A count of the number of grades, NUM, has been added to the program. The final program is not restricted to 2000 grades, but instead it will work for any number of grades up to 2000.

The previous program has the defect of giving more detail than is probably needed. Ordinarily, the grades would be grouped in intervals of approximately 10 points, instead of every grade constituting an interval. Suppose that the problem is changed to require a count of the number of grades in the following intervals:

0–9	1st interval
10–19	2nd interval
20–29	3rd interval
.	
.	
.	
80–89	9th interval
90–100	10th interval

How can the program be changed to consider just these 10 intervals?

```
 1  C
 2  C                 FREQUENCY DISTRIBUTION OF GRADES
 3  C
 4          INTEGER FREQ(101),GRADE
 5  1000    FORMAT(I3)
 6  1010    FORMAT('1',T10,'FREQUENCY DISTRIBUTION OF GRADES')
 7  1020    FORMAT('0',T12,'GRADE',T26,'COUNT')
 8  1030    FORMAT(T13,I3,T27,I4)
 9  1040    FORMAT('0',T10,'TOTAL NUMBER OF GRADES = ',I4)
10          DO I=1,101
11              FREQ(I)=0
12          ENDDO
13          NUM=0
14          READ(5,1000)GRADE
15          WHILE(GRADE .GE. 0)
16              FREQ(GRADE+1) = FREQ(GRADE+1) + 1
17              NUM=NUM+1
18              READ(5,1000)GRADE
19          ENDWHILE
20          WRITE(6,1010)
21          WRITE(6,1020)
22          DO I=1,101
23              K=I-1
24              WRITE(6,1030)K,FREQ(I)
25          ENDDO
26          WRITE(6,1040)NUM
27          STOP
28          END
```

FREQUENCY DISTRIBUTION OF GRADES

GRADE	COUNT
0	0
1	0
2	0
3	0
4	0
5	0
6	0
7	0
8	0
.	.
.	.
.	.
38	0
39	0
40	0
41	0
42	1
43	1
44	0
45	0
46	0
47	1

FIGURE 11.1   *Frequency distribution of grades*

```
              .                 .
              .                 .
              .                 .
             96                 1
             97                 1
             98                 2
             99                 2
            100                 1

    TOTAL NUMBER OF GRADES =    76
```

FIGURE 11.1 (*cont.*)

Again the problem is to find a method of using a grade to calculate the subscript for the appropriate interval. A first guess is to divide the grade by 10. This gives the following for some typical grades:

Grade	Grade/10	Desired interval
8	0	1
48	4	5
52	5	6
73	7	8
85	8	9
93	9	10

It appears that the subscript can be obtained by adding 1 to the quotient of the grade and 10; that is,

$$ISUB = GRADE/10 + 1$$

Before concluding that this answer is correct, the limiting grades of 0 and 100 should be checked to see if the rule works for them. The rule works for zero, but ISUB for 100 is 11—a value that is too large. Consequently, a grade of 100 must be treated as a special case or another rule must be found. Arbitrarily, we decide to treat 100 as a special case. A sequence of statements that will perform the required actions is

```
              .
              .
              .
    READ (5,1000) GRADE
    WHILE (GRADE .GE. 0)
        IF (GRADE .EQ. 100) THEN
            ISUB = 10
        ELSE
            ISUB = GRADE/10 + 1
```

```
                              ENDIF
                              FREQ(ISUB) = FREQ(ISUB) + 1
                              READ (5,1000) GRADE
                       ENDWHILE
                          .
                          .
                          .
```

The complete program is given in Figure 11.2.

There are techniques other than the ones given here that could be used to write a program for frequency distribution of grades. For example, a series of ELSEIF statements such as

```
                          .
                          .
                          .
         IF (GRADE .GE. 90) THEN
             ISUB = 10
         ELSEIF (GRADE .GE. 80) THEN
             ISUB = 9
         ELSEIF (GRADE .GE. 70) THEN
             .
             .
             .
         ELSEIF (GRADE .LT. 10) THEN
             ISUB = 1
         ENDIF
             .
             .
             .
```

would work satisfactorily. (Such a technique would be more trouble in the case of 101 intervals.) The sequence of IF statements takes more computer memory and much more computer time for execution than the subscript computation method illustrated in this section. The computation method, when it can be used, is generally the best approach.

11.5.2 Prime Numbers, Sieve of Eratosthenes

In Example 3 of Chapter 6, the prime numbers from 1 to 1000 were computed using a "division and testing for remainder" technique. Now the problem will be solved using an elegant algorithm known as the sieve of Eratosthenes, after the ancient Greek who discovered it. A description of the method follows:

List the integers from 1 to 1000 (or whatever upper value is of interest). Starting at 2, mark out every second value following 2. Then mark out

```
1  C
2  C                    FREQUENCY DISTRIBUTION OF GRADES
3  C                    10 POINT INTERVALS
4  C
5          INTEGER FREQ(10),GRADE
6  1000    FORMAT(I3)
7  1010    FORMAT('1',T7,'FREQUENCY DISTRIBUTION OF GRADES')
8  1020    FORMAT('0',T12,'GRADE',T26,'COUNT')
9  1030    FORMAT(T11,I2,'-',I3,T27,I4)
10 1040    FORMAT('0',T7,'TOTAL NUMBER OF GRADES = ',I4)
11         DO I=1,10
12            FREQ(I)=0
13         ENDDO
14         NUM=0
15         READ(5,1000)GRADE
16         WHILE(GRADE .GE. 0)
17            IF(GRADE .EQ. 100) THEN
18               ISUB=10
19            ELSE
20               ISUB=GRADE/10 + 1
21            ENDIF
22            FREQ(ISUB)=FREQ(ISUB)+1
23            NUM=NUM+1
24            READ(5,1000)GRADE
25         ENDWHILE
26         WRITE(6,1010)
27         WRITE(6,1020)
28         DO I=1,10
29            J=(I-1)*10
30            K=J+9
31            IF(K .EQ. 99) THEN
32               K=K+1
33            ENDIF
34            WRITE(6,1030)J,K,FREQ(I)
35         ENDDO
36         WRITE(6,1040)NUM
37         STOP
38         END
```

```
              FREQUENCY DISTRIBUTION OF GRADES

                  GRADE           COUNT
                  0-  9             0
                 10- 19             0
                 20- 29             0
                 30- 39             0
                 40- 49             4
                 50- 59             5
                 60- 69             6
                 70- 79            23
                 80- 89            25
                 90-100            13

              TOTAL NUMBER OF GRADES =    76
```

FIGURE 11.2   *Frequency distribution of grades: 10-point intervals*

every 3rd value after 3. Continue this process with subsequent integers. At the beginning of each marking process skip integers that have been marked out—for example, 4 will be marked out when it is reached, so do not mark out every 4th value (this was done when every 2nd value was marked out). The method is illustrated below for the first 18 integers.

1			1		1	
2	←— mark out		2		2	
3	every 2nd		3	←— mark out	3	
4̸	value		4̸	every 3rd	4̸	←— skip
5			5	value	5	←— mark out
6̸			6̸		6̸	every 5th
7			7		7	value
8̸			8̸		8̸	
9			9̸		9̸	
10̸			10̸		10̸	
11			11		11	
12̸			12̸		12̸	
13			13		13	
14̸			14̸		14̸	
15			15̸		15̸	
16̸			16̸		16̸	
17			17		17	
18̸			18̸		18̸	

The primes in the first 18 integers are 1, 2, 3, 5, 7, 11, 13, and 17. Notice that the marking process can be stopped after starting with the integer equal to the square root of N, where N is the largest integer in the set.

Implementing the algorithm in FORTRAN is easy after a satisfactory method is found for representing the marking-out process.

A. Level 1 Solution

The marking-out problem can be solved by using an array. The subscript of an element will correspond to the integer being considered. A value of 1 for an element will mean that it *has not* been marked out, and a value of 0 will mean that it *has* been marked out. Let PRIME be the name of this array (make an integer array), and I be the position being considered for starting a marking-out sequence. This leads to the following high-level solution for the problem:

```
initialize
WHILE (I .LE. SQRT of largest integer)
      IF (PRIME(I) .EQ. 1) THEN
            mark out every Ith element thereafter
      ENDIF
      I = I + 1
```

```
ENDWHILE
write prime numbers
STOP
END
```

B. Level 2 Solution

The initialization process requires that the elements of **PRIME** be set to one . Also, the upper limit for the **WHILE** loop should be computed. This gives

$$
\text{initialization} \rightarrow \left[
\begin{array}{l}
\text{INTEGER PRIME (1000)} \\
\text{I = 1} \\
\text{WHILE (I .LE. 1000)} \\
\quad\quad \text{PRIME (I) = 1} \\
\quad\quad \text{I = I + 1} \\
\text{ENDWHILE} \\
\text{LIMIT = SQRT (FLOAT(1000))}
\end{array}
\right.
$$

The marking out of every Ith element implies a loop for stepping through the array.

$$
\begin{array}{l}
\text{mark out every} \rightarrow \\
\text{Ith element}
\end{array}
\left[
\begin{array}{l}
\text{J = I+I} \\
\text{WHILE (J .LE. 1000)} \\
\quad\quad \text{PRIME (J) = 0} \\
\quad\quad \text{J = J+I} \\
\text{ENDWHILE}
\end{array}
\right.
$$

The writing of the prime numbers implies a loop for testing each element of **PRIME** and printing the subscript when **PRIME**(I) = 1 .

$$
\begin{array}{l}
\text{write prime} \rightarrow \\
\text{numbers}
\end{array}
\left[
\begin{array}{l}
\text{I = 1} \\
\text{WHILE (I .LE. 1000)} \\
\quad\quad \text{IF (PRIME(I) .EQ. 1) THEN} \\
\quad\quad\quad\quad \text{WRITE (5,1010) I} \\
\quad\quad \text{ENDIF} \\
\quad\quad \text{I = I+1} \\
\text{ENDWHILE}
\end{array}
\right.
$$

Incorporating these changes into the solution gives the final program. The result is shown in Figure 11.3.

The program could have been written using the **DO** statement instead of the **WHILE** statement. The loop for setting elements of **PRIME** to zero is particularly well suited for control by a **DO** loop. The sequence of statements can be translated to give

```
 1  C
 2  C                PRIME NUMBERS
 3  C                SIEVE OF ERATOSTHENES
 4  C
 5           INTEGER PRIME(1000)
 6  1000     FORMAT('1','THE PRIME NUMBERS LESS THAN 1000')
 7  1010     FORMAT(' ',T15,I3)
 8           I=1
 9           WHILE(I .LE. 1000)
10              PRIME(I)=1
11              I=I+1
12           ENDWHILE
13           LIMIT=31
14           WRITE(6,1010)LIMIT
15           I=2
16           WHILE(I .LE. LIMIT)
17              IF(PRIME(I) .EQ. 1) THEN
18                 J=I+I
19                 WHILE(J .LE. 1000)
20                    PRIME(J)=0
21                    J=J+I
22                 ENDWHILE
23              ENDIF
24              I=I+1
25           ENDWHILE
26           WRITE(6,1000)
27           I=1
28           WHILE(I .LE. 1000)
29              IF(PRIME(I) .EQ. 1) THEN
30                 WRITE(6,1010)I
31              ENDIF
32              I=I+1
33           ENDWHILE
34           STOP
35           END

        31
        THE PRIME NUMBERS LESS THAN 1000
                          1
                          2
                          3
                          5
                          7
                         11
                         13
                         17
                         19
                         23
                         29
                         31
                         37
                          .
                          .
                          .
                        967
                        971
                        977
                        983
                        991
                        997
```

FIGURE 11.3 *Prime numbers: sieve of Eratosthenes*

.
.
.

```
I = 2                          DO I = 2, LIMIT
WHILE (I .LE. LIMIT)              IF (PRIME(I) .EQ. 1) THEN
    IF (PRIME(I) .EQ. 1) THEN         K = I+I
        J = I+I                       DO J = K, 1000, I
        WHILE (J .LE. 1000)               PRIME(J) = 0
            PRIME(J) = 0              ENDDO
            J = J+I              ENDIF
        ENDWHILE             ENDDO
    ENDIF
    I = I+1
ENDWHILE
```

.
.
.

The sequence using DO statements is shorter and perhaps easier to understand in this particular problem. The statement

$$DO\ J = K, 1000, I$$

expresses the looping conditions quite concisely: (1) start looping with J = K, (2) increase J by the amount I for each pass through the loop, and (3) stop looping whenever J exceeds 1000. The complete program using DO loops is shown in Figure 11.4.

11.5.3 Standard Deviation

The standard deviation of a set of values is a statistical measure of the dispersion of the values, and it is frequently calculated for experiments in the sciences, psychology, sociology, and other areas. It assumes that the values follow a normal distribution, and if graphed, would give a normal curve (the same curve teachers sometimes use in assigning grades). Knowing the mean (also called average) and standard deviation of a set of values immediately gives us significant information about the values. For example, if for a quiz the mean is 85 with standard deviation 4.3, practically everyone made a grade between 72.1 and 97.9. For a mean of 70 with standard deviation 9.8, practically everyone made a grade between 40.6 and 99.4. These deductions are based upon the fact that the values are distributed about the mean to give

68.26% of values within ±1 S.D. of the mean

95.55% of values within ±2 S.D. of the mean

99.74% of values within ±3 S.D. of the mean

Thus the ranges cited for the examples should be accurate for 99.74% of the grades (±3 S.D. were used to estimate the range). Since our goal is to write a program to

```
 1 C
 2 C               PRIME NUMBERS
 3 C               SIEVE OF ERATOSTHENES
 4 C               USE OF DO STATEMENT
 5 C
 6               INTEGER PRIME(1000)
 7 1000    FORMAT('1','THE PRIME NUMBERS LESS THAN 1000')
 8 1010    FORMAT(' ',T15,I3)
 9               DO I=1,1000
10                  PRIME(I)=1
11               ENDDO
12               LIMIT=SQRT(FLOAT(1000))
13               DO I=2,LIMIT
14                  IF(PRIME(I) .EQ. 1) THEN
15                     K=I+I
16                     DO J=K,1000,I
17                        PRIME(J)=0
18                     ENDDO
19                  ENDIF
20               ENDDO
21               WRITE(6,1000)
22               DO I=1,1000
23                  IF(PRIME(I) .EQ. 1) THEN
24                     WRITE(6,1010)I
25                  ENDIF
26               ENDDO
27               STOP
28               END
```

FIGURE 11.4   *Prime numbers: sieve of Eratosthenes—use of DO statement*

compute the standard deviation and not to consider its theoretical basis or reasons for using it, additional examples will not be given.

The standard deviation can be calculated using the formula

$$\text{S.D.} = \sqrt{\frac{\sum_{i=1}^{N}(X_{\text{mean}} - X_i)^2}{N-1}}$$

where X_i is the ith value of X
X_{mean} is the mean value of the X's

$$X_{\text{mean}} = \frac{\sum_{i=1}^{N} X_i}{N} = \frac{X_1 + X_2 + X_3 + \cdots + X_N}{N}$$

$\sum_{i=1}^{N} X_i$ is an abbreviation for: compute the sum of the values of X_i, letting i vary from 1 to N in steps of 1.

This example was chosen not only because of its value in statistics but also because it is quite easy, despite the formidable appearance of the equation. The program is easy to write because we do not have to develop an algorithm—the formula itself describes the algorithm.

Consider the calculation of the mean using the equation

$$X_{\text{mean}} = \frac{\sum\limits_{i=1}^{N} X_i}{N}$$

The equation states:

1. An array X has N values, with the subscript ranging from 1 to N.
2. The N values of X are to be summed.
3. The mean is obtained by dividing the sum by N.

Using a DO loop to perform the summation allows us to make a direct translation of these statements into FORTRAN.

```
    .
    .
    .
SUM = 0.0
DO I = 1,N
    SUM = SUM + X(I)
ENDDO
XMEAN = SUM/FLOAT(N)
    .
    .
    .
```

Calculating the standard deviation is also straightforward, but we will consider a numerical example before writing a program. Suppose that the grades on a quiz are 100, 90, 80, 70, and 60 (selected to make the arithmetic easy). The mean, X_{mean}, is 80. Then in tabular form the computation is

X(I)	XMEAN − X(I)	(XMEAN − X(I))^2
100	−20	400
90	−10	100
80	0	0
70	10	100
60	20	400

sum this column:

$$\text{SUMSQ} = \sum_{i=1}^{N} (\text{XMEAN} - \text{X(I)})^2 = 1000$$

$$S.D. = \sqrt{\frac{1000}{5-1}} = \sqrt{250} = 15.8$$

A portion of a program for performing the calculations is

.

.

.

```
SUM = 0.0
DO I = 1,N
       SUM = SUM + X(I)
ENDDO
XMEAN = SUM/FLOAT(N)
SUMSQ = 0.0
```

```
1   C
2   C               STANDARD DEVIATION        METHOD 1
3   C
4           DIMENSION X(1000)
5   1000    FORMAT(I4/(F10.0))
6   1010    FORMAT('1','INPUT VALUES'/(' ',5F10.2))
7   1020    FORMAT(///' ','STANDARD DEVIATION = ',F10.2)
8           READ(5,1000)N,(X(I),I=1,N)
9           WRITE(6,1010)(X(I),I=1,N)
10          SUM = 0.0
11          DO I=1,N
12              SUM = SUM+X(I)
13          ENDDO
14          XMEAN=SUM/FLOAT(N)
15          SUMSQ=0.0
16          DO I=1,N
17              SUMSQ=SUMSQ+(XMEAN-X(I))**2
18          ENDDO
19          SD=SQRT(SUMSQ/FLOAT(N-1))
20          WRITE(6,1020)SD
21          STOP
22          END
```

```
INPUT VALUES
      83.00      87.00      77.00      94.00      68.00
      81.00      82.00      79.00      63.00      79.00
      80.00      75.00      78.00      82.00      85.00
      77.00      78.00      47.00      76.00      75.00
      60.00      65.00      88.00      79.00      81.00
      54.00      84.00      74.00      62.00      91.00
      73.00      78.00      69.00      78.00
```

```
STANDARD DEVIATION =        10.13
```

FIGURE 11.5 *Calculation of standard deviation—method 1*

```
        DO I = 1,N
                SUMSQ = SUMSQ + (XMEAN- X(I))**2
        ENDDO
        SD = SQRT (SUMSQ/FLOAT(N-1))
```
.
.
.

Computer printout for the program is given in Figure 11.5. It would be quite easy to change the program into one that uses a function.

In hand calculations of the standard deviation, the formula

$$S.D. = \sqrt{\frac{N \sum_{i=1}^{N} X_i^2 - \left(\sum_{i=1}^{N} X_i \right)^2}{N(N-1)}}$$

```
 1  C
 2  C              STANDARD DEVIATION       METHOD 2
 3  C
 4         DIMENSION X(1000)
 5  1000   FORMAT(I4/(F10.0))
 6  1010   FORMAT('1','INPUT VALUES'/(' ',5F10.2))
 7  1020   FORMAT(///' ','STANDARD DEVIATION = ',F10.2)
 8         READ(5,1000)N,(X(I),I=1,N)
 9         WRITE(6,1010)(X(I),I=1,N)
10         SUMX2=0.0
11         SUMX =0.0
12         DO I=1,N
13            SUMX2=SUMX2+X(I)**2
14            SUMX =SUMX +X(I)
15         ENDDO
16         XN=N
17         SD=SQRT((XN*SUMX2-SUMX**2)/(XN*(XN-1)))
18         WRITE(6,1020)SD
19         STOP
20         END
```

```
INPUT VALUES
      83.00     87.00     77.00     94.00     68.00
      81.00     82.00     79.00     63.00     79.00
      80.00     75.00     78.00     82.00     85.00
      77.00     78.00     47.00     76.00     75.00
      60.00     65.00     88.00     79.00     81.00
      54.00     84.00     74.00     62.00     91.00
      73.00     78.00     69.00     78.00
```

```
STANDARD DEVIATION =         10.13
```

FIGURE 11.6 *Calculation of standard deviation—method 2*

is normally used to avoid calculating the mean. It is also easy to write a program for this method. ΣX_i^2 implies that the X_i are to be squared and then added, and $(\Sigma X_i)^2$ implies that all the X_i's are added and then the result squared. A program using this technique is given in Figure 11.6.

REVIEW QUESTIONS

1. Give a definition for the term "array."
2. Give a definition for the term "subscript." Why are subscripts restricted to be integer values?
3. What is the purpose of the DIMENSION statement? Is the DIMENSION statement an executable statement?
4. How is the range of subscript values determined for a particular array?
5. How can an array be defined so that it will have a different mode from that implied by the first character of its name?
6. What is meant by the "dimension" of an array? If you were reading a program, how could you determine the dimension of the arrays in the program?
7. How many variables can be listed in a single DIMENSION statement?
8. Give the syntax of an implied DO loop.
9. How are implied DO loops used in READ and WRITE statements?
10. In a FORMAT statement, what is the purpose of a slash?
11. In a FORMAT statement, what is the purpose of an extra pair of parentheses enclosing input/output specifications at the end of the statement?
12. Suppose that in a READ or WRITE statement an array appears without an associated subscript. What will happen?
13. Suppose that in an arithmetic expression an array appears without an associated subscript. What will happen?
14. Suppose that an attempt is made to access an element of an array outside the subscript range declared for the array. What happens?
15. In FORMAT statements, what is the purpose of multiple consecutive slashes?
16. Describe the algorithm known as the sieve of Eratosthenes for finding prime numbers.

REVIEW QUIZ

1. An important characteristic of arrays is:
   (A) Their mode is always determined by their appearance in the DIMENSION statement.
   (B) A single name refers simultaneously to more than one value.
   (C) An array is a component of an element.
   (D) A DIMENSION statement can appear only one time in a program.
   (E) two of the previous answers.
2. The FORTRAN compiler can be notified that a variable refers to an array by using (A) a DIMENSION statement, (B) a WRITE statement, (C) subscripts, (D) implied DO loops, (E) two of the previous answers are valid.
3. In a program, the following statement occurs:

   DIMENSION X(50),NEXT(100),M(75)

The maximum number of values that can be stored for NEXT is (A) 50, (B) 100, (C) 150, (D) 200, (E) none of the previous answers.

4. An example of an *invalid* DIMENSION statement is:
    (A) DIMENSION X(100), Y(100)
    (B) DIMENSION X(1),Y(100)
    (C) DIMENSION X(5,20)
    (D) DIMENSION X(50), LIST(10)
    (E) none of the previous answers

5. An example of an *invalid* statement is:
    (A) X(I)=X(I)+I
    (B) LIST(JX=JX**2+2*(NEXT(I)/MISS(K))
    (C) X(I+1)=X(I)+I
    (D) X(I)=X(I-1)**2-10
    (E) LIST(2*J)=LIST(J)-2*J

6. Given:

$$\text{DIMENSION VALUE (100)}$$
$$L = 3$$

An example of an *invalid* array element is:
    (A) VALUE(L-1)
    (B) VALUE(3*L-10)
    (C) VALUE(L+15)
    (D) VALUE(3*L+20)
    (E) VALUE(L)

7. A format statement that is equivalent to

$$20 \text{ FORMAT (F10.2,I1, I1, I2, F6.2, F6.2, F6.2)}$$

is:
    (A) 20 FORMAT (F10.2, I2, I2, 3F6.2)
    (B) 20 FORMAT (F10.2, 2I1, I2, F6.2)
    (C) 20 FORMAT (F10.2, 2I1, I2, 3F6.2)
    (D) 20 FORMAT (F10.2, I1, I1, I2, 2F6.2)
    (E) two of the previous answers

8. An *invalid* READ statement is:
    (A) READ(5,10)N,(X(K),K=1,N)
    (B) READ(5,10)(X(J),J=1,100)
    (C) READ(5,10)N,(N(I),I=1,N)
    (D) READ(5,10)X(10-2)
    (E) READ(5,10)X

9. An example of a READ statement that contains a syntax error is:
    (A) READ(5,10)(X(I),I=1,10)
    (B) READ(5,10)(I(J),J-1,20)
    (C) READ(5,10)ANS(I)
    (D) READ(5,10)Y(10)
    (E) none of the answers contains a syntax error

10. Given:

WRITE(6,7)PRICE(I),NUMBER(I),AMOUNT(I)

A satisfactory FORMAT statement would be:
(A) 6 FORMAT (F10.2,I6,2F8.1)
(B) 7 FORMAT (F12.4,I10)
(C) 7 FORMAT (F6.2,I4,2I6,F10.1,I4)
(D) 6 FORMAT (2F12.1,I6)
(E) two of the previous answers

11. The number of nonblank lines produced by

WRITE (6,10)A,B,C,D
10 FORMAT ('1',F8.1///2F8.2//F6.2)

is (A) 1, (B) 2, (C) 3, (D) 4, (E) none of the previous answers.

12. The number of cards that will be read as a result of the statements

DIMENSION X(100)
XYZ = 12
READ (5,10)(X(I),I=1,25)
10 FORMAT(3F10.2)

is (A) 1, (B) 3, (C) 12, (D) 25, (E) none of the previous answers.

13. Given:

DO J = 1,10,2
READ(5,10)YX(2*J-1)
ENDDO

The last value of YX read by these statements will be (A) YX(18), (B) YX(10),
(C) YX(17), (D) YX(19), (E) none of the previous answers.

14. Given:

DIMENSION X(100)
DO 20 I = 2,10,2
20 READ(5,30)X(2*I),X(2*I+1)

(A) 10 values of X will be read; (B) the third value of X read will be assigned to
X(3); (C) the first value read will be assigned to X(2); (D) the last value of X read
will be assigned to X(21); (E) two of the previous answers.

15. The statements

DIMENSION Y(100)
READ (5,20)Y
20 FORMAT (8F10.0)

(A) will cause 10 cards to be read; (B) will cause 12 cards to be read; (C) will cause 100 cards to be read; (D) contain a syntax error; (E) none of the previous answers.

EXERCISES

1. Give an appropriate declaration statement for each of the following:
   a. An array X of 100 elements.
   b. An array TEMPS of 200 elements.
   c. An array NEXT of 200 elements starting with subscript 0.
   d. An array NEXT of 200 elements starting with subscript −99.
   e. A real array INTR of 1000 elements.
   f. Arrays A, B, C, D of 25, 50, 100, and 25 elements, respectively.

2. Give statements that assign to X the following:
   a. The sum of the Ith element of GRADE and 5.
   b. The I+1 element of GRADE.
   c. The difference in the Ith element of A and the Jth element of B.
   d. The difference in the Ith and I−1 elements of A.
   e. The product of the square of the Ith element of A and the I+1th element of B.

3. Give program segments to perform each of the following:
   a. Add the N elements of array X.
   b. Add the squares of the N elements of array X.
   c. Interchange the Ith element of array X and the Jth element of array Y.
   d. Calculate the individual differences DIFF(I) for the corresponding N elements of arrays X and Y.
   e. Reverse the order of the elements in array X.
   f. Find the largest value in array X.
   g. Print the elements in an array, five elements per line.
   h. Read the elements of an array from cards, eight elements per card.
   i. Print the elements of an array in reverse order (i.e., last element printed first and the first element printed last).
   j. Read the number of elements in an array from a card, then read that number of elements from cards containing five values per card.
   k. For arrays X, Y, and Z each containing 50 elements, print 50 lines each containing a value of X, Y, and Z. Use a regular DO loop.
   l. For arrays X, Y, and Z each containing 50 elements, print 50 lines each containing a value of X, Y, and Z. Use an implied DO loop.
   m. For a class of 30 students, read the values of arrays IDNUM and GRADES from cards. Each card contains an element of IDNUM and a corresponding value of GRADES. Use an implied DO loop.

4. Answer the following:
   a. How many lines are printed by

$$\text{WRITE } (6,6)(\text{FREQ}(N), N = 1, 20)$$
$$6 \text{ FORMAT } (5F15.2)$$

   b. How many blank lines are printed by

$$\text{WRITE } (6,100)(X(I), I = 1,4)$$
$$100 \text{ FORMAT } ('1', F8.1/2F8.2//5F8.2)$$

c. Given:

$$N = 5$$
$$DO\ I = 2,N$$
$$X(I) = 2*I$$
$$ENDDO$$

What value is assigned to X(3)?

PROGRAMMING EXERCISES

1. Write a program that reads the elements of a 25-element array and then prints the elements in the following different formats:
   a. 1 element per row in the order read
   b. 5 rows of 5 elements
   c. 3 rows of 7 elements
      1 row of 4 elements
   d. 1 element per row in reverse order (first element printed last, last element printed first)

2. A computer science professor needs a program to produce a frequency distribution of grades on a quiz using the following ranges:

Grade
Less than 50
50–59
60–69
70–85
86–100

Help him by writing an appropriate program. Use your own data to test the program.

3. A fairly common operation in working with arrays is the filling of an array with some particular value. For example, as a prelude to other processing, it may be necessary to set each element of an array to 0.0. Write a program which reads a value that is to be used to fill an array, and then fills the array with that value.

4. Another common operation with arrays is the moving of the contents of one array to a different array. Write a program to accomplish this operation.

5. Generalize the program of the preceding problem to allow the designating of a starting and stopping position in the source array and the starting position in the destination array. The program should, for example, allow:
   a. Moving elements 1 through 10 of array X to Y starting at element 20.
   b. Moving elements 5 through 20 of array X to Y starting at element 1.

6. The restriction on the size of integers in computers was discussed in Chapter 8. For example, in computers having a 16-bit memory cell, the allowed integers range from −32,768 to 32,767. Many real-life computations involve the manipulation of larger integers. One way of handling larger numbers with computers is to read them into arrays, one digit per array element, and to use special programs to

manipulate the array elements. For example, the addition of 1,079,345 and 936,204 can be visualized as:

| 0 | 0 | 0 | 0 | 0 | 0 | 1 | 0 | 7 | 9 | 3 | 4 | 5 | Array IX

| 0 | 0 | 0 | 0 | 0 | 0 | 0 | 9 | 3 | 6 | 2 | 0 | 4 | Array IY

| 0 | 0 | 0 | 0 | 0 | 0 | 2 | 0 | 1 | 5 | 5 | 4 | 9 | Array IZ

where IZ(1) = IX(1) + IY(1) = 5 + 4 = 9
        IZ(2) = IX(2) + IY(2) + CARRY FROM PREVIOUS ADDITION = 4 + 0 +
        0 = 4

Write a program that uses this technique to add two 50-digit integers.

7. Using the array technique of problem 6, write a program that will multiply large integers. Test your program by computing 20 factorial.

8. Two arrays each contain a set of numbers that have been sorted into ascending numerical sequence. Write a program that will read the arrays, print their contents, and then merge them into a single array having all the numbers in ascending sequence. Print the contents of the resulting array.

9. In Chapter 10, Programming Exercise 8, a method was presented for computing the Pearson correlation coefficient. An alternative method using arrays is based on the formula

$$R = \frac{N \sum X_i Y_i - \sum X_i \sum Y_i}{\sqrt{[N \sum X_i^2 - (\sum X_i)^2][N \sum Y_i^2 - (\sum Y_i)^2]}}$$

Write a program that uses this formula to compute the correlation coefficient. Test your program using the data for the programming exercise in Chapter 10.

10. The method of least squares can be used to determine the location of the "best straight line" through a set of experimental data. The slope and intercept of this statistically "best" line are given by

$$\text{slope} = \frac{\sum X_i \sum Y_i - N \sum X_i Y_i}{(\sum X_i)^2 - N \sum X_i^2}$$

$$\text{intercept} = \frac{\sum X_i \sum X_i Y_i - \sum Y_i \sum X_i^2}{(\sum X_i)^2 - N \sum X_i^2}$$

Write a program that makes this computation, and test the programs with the data from Programming Exercise 8, Chapter 10.

11. The overall grade average in a course is computed using the following scheme (see Programming Exercise 10, Chapter 9):

quizzes	50%
programs	30%
final examination	20%

For each class member, read four quiz grades, a numerical grade based on programs, and the final grade. The lowest quiz grade is not to be counted in computing the average. Design and print a report that includes for each student the input data and the overall grade average. The initial portion of the report should be printed in student ID number sequence. A second portion of the report should be printed in sequence of decreasing overall grade average.

12. The stock status report for the Acme Manufacturing Company (Chapter 9, Programming Exercise 11) assumed that all data for a given part number were punched in adjacent cards. This is most unrealistic since transactions would occur in random sequence for the parts. Revise the program so that data can be read in any sequence. The program should sort the data into part number sequence and then print the report.

13. Redo the "life event" problem of Chapter 9 using an array. The first element of the array would have the value 100 (for death of a spouse), the second element would have the value 73 (for divorce), and so on. The input indicator for the number of an event will allow an immediate determination of the associated value.

14. For the Acme Manufacturing Company, the commission paid to salespersons upon the amount of a sale is summarized in the following table:

Amount of sale	Commission (percent of sale)
$ 0.00–$10.00	0.5
10.01– 25.00	0.63
25.01– 50.00	0.70
50.01–100.00	0.80
100.01–200.00	1.00
200.01–500.00	1.25
500.01–750.00	1.50
750.01–1000.00	1.75
1000.01–2500.00	2.50
2500.01–5000.00	3.00
5000.01–10,000.00	4.00
10,000.01–50,000.00	5.00
50,000.01–100,000.00	7.00
More than $100,000.00	10.00

Store amount-of-sale information in an array, and store commission information in corresponding positions of a second array. Read sales data for salespersons and compute the commission for each sale. When a particular sales value is read, make a search through the amount of sale array to determine the relative size of the sale. Then use this value to find the percent to be used in computing the commission. Print the input data and commissions in a report suitable to give to a sales manager.

15. This is a more realistic (and more challenging) version of Programming Exercise 14. The sales manager of Acme Manufacturing Company is not satisfied with the sales commission report printed by the computer center. He wishes *all* sales printed in the report. This means that for a given salesperson multiple lines may be printed, one for each sale, as a series of consecutive lines. For each salesperson, subtotals for his commissions and sales are to be printed. Grand totals are to be printed at the end of the report. Unfortunately, the programmer cannot assume that all data for a salesperson are together. Output is to be printed in the sequence of increasing salesperson identification number.

CHAPTER 12 SUBROUTINES

The importance of dividing programs into meaningful modules was emphasized earlier. In writing programs to manipulate a turtle (Chapter 4), programs were developed in a top-down manner using procedures and subprocedures, and techniques for writing user-defined functions were presented in the discussion of arithmetic (Chapter 8). In this chapter, methods will be introduced for defining and using *subroutines*, the most general type of FORTRAN subprogram. By means of relatively minor changes, any program can be made into a subroutine. The discussion of subroutines has been delayed until now because most useful subroutines manipulate the contents of arrays, and we needed to study first the characteristics of arrays.

The importance of subprograms as intellectual tools can hardly be overemphasized. In using the SQRT function, you did not need to know the individual instructions that were required to define it or even the algorithm upon which it was based. This reduction in the detail that must be remembered improves our ability to write more complex and error-free programs. By defining subroutines and using them, you will be able to write programs that are easier to understand and to modify.

Subroutines are usually defined, compiled, and stored as separate entries in a subroutine library. Details of the storing process differ from one computer to another, but in any case, when your program references a subroutine, it will be found in the library and incorporated into your program before execution begins. If you reference a subroutine that is not in the library, an error message is printed, and your program is not allowed to execute.

12.1 DEFINING SUBROUTINES

The defining technique for a FORTRAN subroutine is remarkably similar to that which was used to define a procedure to draw a square:

```
TO    SQUARE     SIDE
10    FORWARD    SIDE
20    RIGHT      90
30    FORWARD    SIDE
40    RIGHT      90
50    FORWARD    SIDE
60    RIGHT      90
70    FORWARD    SIDE
80    RIGHT      90
90    RETURN
END
```

The word "TO" was the signal that the definition of a procedure was being given. The name of the procedure, SQUARE, and its argument were listed after TO. The word "END" was the signal that the definition had been completed. Thus the definition of a procedure was given by the form

> TO   name of procedure   list of dummy arguments
> .
> .
> .
>
> body
> .
> .
> .
>
> END

To define a subroutine subprogram in FORTRAN, we use the form

> SUBROUTINE   name of subroutine (list of dummy arguments)
> .
> .
> .
>
> body
> .
> .
> .
>
> END

In FORTRAN, the word "SUBROUTINE" is the signal that the definition for a subroutine follows, and "END" signals the completion of the definition. The rules for naming subroutines are the same as those for naming variables, but the first character of the name of the subroutine does not imply integer or real mode since there is no value associated with the name. The list of dummy arguments may contain any number of arguments (of any mode), and the arguments may appear in any sequence. The order of dummy arguments used in the definition will, however, determine the order in which the actual arguments must appear in using the subroutine.

All the types of FORTRAN statements we have studied can appear in the body of a SUBROUTINE. Input and output can be performed, calculations can be done, control statements can be used as in a main program,* and the STOP statement can even be used to stop execution of the program. A special statement, RETURN, must be inserted one or more times in the body of the subroutine. RETURN causes a branch from the subroutine back to the next executable statement in the routine that was using the subroutine.

*The term *main* or *mainline program* is used to indicate that a sequence of instructions is not a subprogram, but rather the kind of program we have been considering to this point.

To illustrate these rules, we define a subroutine to compute the mean value for a set of data. A program for computing the mean value of X is as follows:

```
        DIMENSION X(1000)
1000    FORMAT (F10.2)
1010    FORMAT ('1', 'THE INPUT VALUES ARE'/(10F10.2))
1020    FORMAT (//'b', 'THE MEAN IS', F10.2)
        I = 1
        READ (5,1000) X(I)
        WHILE (X(I) .NE. -9999.0)
            I = I+1
            READ (5,1000) X(I)
        ENDWHILE
        N = I-1
        SUM = 0.0
        DO I = 1,N
            SUM = SUM + X(I)
        ENDDO
        XMEAN = SUM/N
        WRITE (6,1010) (X(I), I = 1,N)
        WRITE (6,1020) XMEAN
        STOP
        END
```

We must decide how much of this program to include in the subroutine. All the statements could be included, but generality is normally favored by omitting the input/output statements except for error messages. Omission of the input/output statements leads to the following definition:

```
        SUBROUTINE MEAN (X, N, XMEAN)
        DIMENSION X(1)
        SUM = 0.0
        DO I = 1,N
            SUM = SUM + X(I)
        ENDDO
        XMEAN = SUM/N
        RETURN
        END
```

How to use a subroutine will be treated in detail shortly. For now, notice that the following program, which uses the subroutine, makes the same computation as the original program:

```
        DIMENSION X(1000)
1000    FORMAT (F10.2)
```

```
1010   FORMAT ('1', 'THE INPUT VALUES ARE'/(10F10.2))
1020   FORMAT (//'b', 'THE MEAN IS', F10.2)
       I = 1
       READ (5,1000) X(I)
       WHILE (X(I) .NE. -9999.0)
          I = I+1
          READ (5,1000) X(I)
       ENDWHILE
       N = I-1
       CALL MEAN (X, N, XMEAN)
       WRITE (6,1010) (X(I), I = 1,N)
       WRITE (6,1020) XMEAN
       STOP
       END
```

Let us examine the definition of MEAN, considering it as a model for defining other subroutines. The first line of the definition

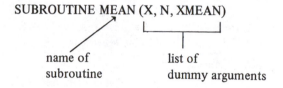

SUBROUTINE MEAN (X, N, XMEAN)

name of
subroutine

list of
dummy arguments

signals that a subroutine is being defined and gives the name and list of dummy arguments for the subroutine. Any name could have been used for the subroutine, although the name is normally selected so as to convey meaningful information about the purpose of the subroutine. Some other reasonable possibilities are

SUBROUTINE AMEAN (X, N, XMEAN)

SUBROUTINE MEANX (X, N, XMEAN)

SUBROUTINE AVERAG (X, N, XMEAN)

but the following is invalid because the name contains too many characters:

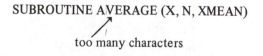

SUBROUTINE AVERAGE (X, N, XMEAN)

too many characters

The variables that appear in the list of dummy arguments could have been written in any order. For example, any of the following could have been used:

SUBROUTINE MEAN (X, N, XMEAN)

SUBROUTINE MEAN (X, XMEAN, N)

SUBROUTINE MEAN (N, X, XMEAN)

SUBROUTINE MEAN (N, XMEAN, X)

SUBROUTINE MEAN (XMEAN, X, N)

SUBROUTINE MEAN (XMEAN, N, X)

Once the sequence of dummy arguments is selected, the sequence must be remembered. The position selected for each dummy argument will determine the interpretation made of the actual arguments during the use of the subroutine.

The variables that appear in the list of dummy variables are useable outside the subroutine; that is, they are global variables. Any variable that appears in the body of the subroutine but not in the list of dummy arguments is a local variable; programs that use the subroutine will not know these variables exist. Moreover, the calling programs cannot affect these variables. In the subroutine MEAN, SUM and I are local variables. No difficulties would arise if variables having the same names, SUM and I, were used in the calling program. (*Note:* The term *calling program* means the program that uses the subprogram.)

The names of the variables upon which the subprogram will operate and the names of the answers must appear in the list of dummy arguments. Suppose that we had attempted to define MEAN as

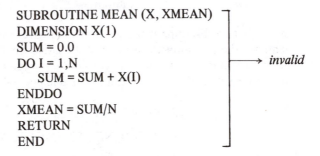

```
SUBROUTINE MEAN (X, XMEAN)
DIMENSION X(1)
SUM = 0.0
DO I = 1,N
    SUM = SUM + X(I)
ENDDO
XMEAN = SUM/N
RETURN
END
```
→ *invalid*

The compiler would print an error message indicating that N is an undefined variable. If XMEAN had been omitted, as in

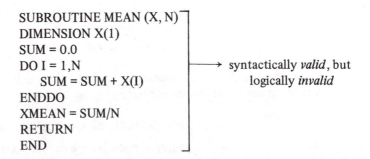

```
SUBROUTINE MEAN (X, N)
DIMENSION X(1)
SUM = 0.0
DO I = 1,N
    SUM = SUM + X(I)
ENDDO
XMEAN = SUM/N
RETURN
END
```
→ syntactically *valid*, but logically *invalid*

the compiler would successfully translate the subroutine; but when it is used, the computed value of XMEAN will not be available outside the subroutine. The subroutine would, therefore, be worthless.

Within the body of MEAN, notice the DIMENSION statement

$$\text{DIMENSION X(1)}$$

The term X(1) in the statement is interesting. It does not define an array X that is one element in length. The appearance of an argument in a DIMENSION statement is merely a signal to the compiler that the variable refers to an array. This causes the compiler to generate instructions for locating individual elements of the array based on the starting address of the array. For variables that are passed to subroutines as arguments, the memory cells associated with the variables are allocated in the calling program. The address of the variable is what is actually made available to the subprogram. To summarize: for one-dimensional arrays passed as arguments, the number of elements indicated within the DIMENSION statement of the subprogram is irrelevant (i.e., 1, 10, 5000 are equally satisfactory).

For higher-level arrays, only the rightmost dimension of a given array is a dummy value. The remaining dimensions should match those used in the calling program to provide essential information for computing the location of individual elements. For example, a legitimate pair of DIMENSION statements for a mainline and a subprogram is

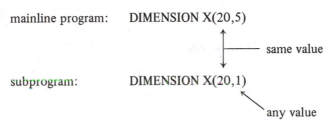

12.2 USING SUBROUTINES

Before a subroutine is used, it can be defined and stored in the computer's program library, or the cards for the subroutine can be appended to the cards for the mainline program. In either case, to use the subroutine in a mainline program (or another subroutine), a statement of the form

CALL name of subroutine (list of actual arguments)

is required. The word "CALL" is the signal to the compiler that a subroutine is to be used. The name of the subroutine must match exactly the name that was used to define the subroutine. The list of actual arguments gives the names of the actual arguments upon which the subroutine instructions will operate. The actual arguments must agree with the dummy arguments used in the definition process in order (position in the list of arguments), type (real, integer, logical, etc.), and number (number of arguments in the list of arguments). An example of valid use of the subroutine MEAN is

DIMENSION YVAR(500)

.

.

.

CALL MEAN (YVAR, NUM, YAVG)

A single copy of the instructions associated with a subroutine is sufficient to allow the subroutine to be used any number of times (with different arguments) in a program. As an example suppose that the subroutine MEAN is called three times in a program:

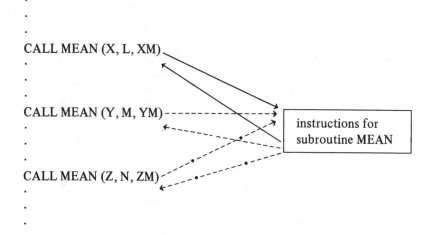

When the first CALL statement is encountered, a branch is made to MEAN and the computations are performed for array X. When the RETURN statement is executed within MEAN, a branch is made from MEAN to the statement immediately following the first CALL statement. Eventually, the second CALL statement is reached, which causes a branch to MEAN where computations are made for the array Y. Execution of RETURN causes a branch back to the statement immediately following the CALL statement. A similar process is performed when the third CALL statement is encountered.

Notice how the dummy arguments and actual arguments of a subroutine must match:

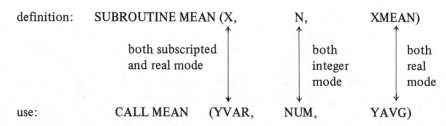

The need for this exact matching of dummy and actual arguments can be understood by considering the method of operation of the subroutine. A subroutine is designed to operate using different sets of actual arguments. When a subroutine is called, a series of initialization instructions generated by the compiler changes the addresses of the dummy arguments to the addresses of the actual arguments. The effect is to change the body of the subroutine to make it appear to be written for the actual arguments. It is not necessary for you to understand the details of how this changing of addresses is accomplished, but it is essential for you to understand the overall effect. Consider the effect of execution of the statement given below on the body of the subroutine MEAN:

CALL MEAN (GRADES, NUM, AVGGD)

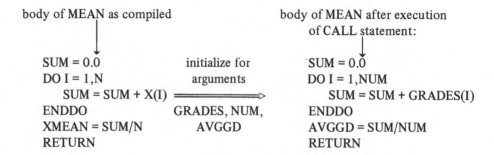

body of MEAN as compiled

body of MEAN after execution of CALL statement:

```
SUM = 0.0                 initialize for        SUM = 0.0
DO I = 1,N                  arguments           DO I = 1,NUM
    SUM = SUM + X(I)  ===========>                  SUM = SUM + GRADES(I)
ENDDO               GRADES, NUM,               ENDDO
XMEAN = SUM/N          AVGGD                   AVGGD = SUM/NUM
RETURN                                         RETURN
```

Notice within the body of MEAN: X has been changed into GRADES, N has been changed into NUM, and XMEAN has been changed into AVGGD.

The substitution of variables in the body of the subroutine is based solely upon the position of the arguments. If the arguments are in the wrong order, the substitutions are made incorrectly. For example, if the CALL statement is written incorrectly as

CALL MEAN (AVGGD, GRADES, NUM)

the initialization process will change the body of MEAN into

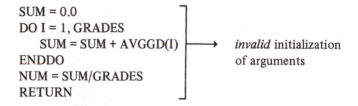

```
SUM = 0.0
DO I = 1, GRADES
    SUM = SUM + AVGGD(I)          invalid initialization
ENDDO                            of arguments
NUM = SUM/GRADES
RETURN
```

because the following associations are made:

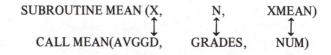

```
SUBROUTINE MEAN (X,        N,         XMEAN)
                  ↕         ↕           ↕
      CALL MEAN(AVGGD,   GRADES,      NUM)
```

Subroutine DESCST

PURPOSE

The purpose of DESCST is to compute descriptive statistics for an array of values. Quantities computed are

maximum
minimum
mean
median
standard deviation

USAGE

CALL DESCST (X, N, XMAX, XMIN, XMEAN, XMED, STDEV)

X	array containing data to be summarized
N	number of values in X
XMAX	maximum value of X
XMIN	minimum value of X
XMEAN	mean value of X
XMED	median value of X
STDEV	standard deviation of values of X

ERRORS DETECTED AND ERROR MESSAGES

None.

REMARKS

No input or output is done within the subroutine.

METHOD

Mean: $XMEAN = \left(\sum_i X_i \right) / N$

Median: X is sorted using the improved interchange method. If N is odd, the middle value is assigned to XMED. If N is even, the average of the values at N/2 and N/2+1 is assigned to XMED. For large numbers of values of X, the sorting will be slow.

Standard deviation:

$$STDEV = \sqrt{\frac{N \sum_i X_i^2 - \left(\sum_i X_i \right)^2}{N(N-1)}}$$

FIGURE 12.1   *Hypothetical description of a subroutine in a subroutine library*

12.3   SUBROUTINE LIBRARIES

Significant effort has been expended in developing large libraries of subprograms for special purposes. Computer centers generally have subprograms to perform many statistical and mathematical operations. Sets of subprograms have been developed to extend FORTRAN into application areas such as commercial applications and manipulation of strings of characters, for which the language was not designed. The existence of subroutine libraries makes it possible for you to reduce the effort that you must invest in writing a program by using the work of others. The extent of these libraries is difficult to appreciate until you have used them, but some feeling for their size can be obtained by considering the manuals that describe the libraries. Some examples are:

1. *IBM System/360 and System/370, IBM 1130 and IBM 1800, Subroutine Library-Mathematics, User's Guide (SH12-5300):* 728 pages of brief descriptions (2 to 3 pages per description) of subroutines to perform mathematical computations.

2. *THE IMSL Library*:* A continually expanding library of mathematical and statistical subroutines. Short descriptions of the routines fill two volumes of approximately 500 pages each.

3. *Statistical Pack for the Social Sciences (SPSS):* A set of programs and subroutines of interest to social scientists involved in statistical analysis of data. The package is available in many university computer centers. A book[†] describing the routines is 661 pages long.

Schucany and Minton[‡] describe 37 packages of routines related to statistics. Of course, subroutine packages exist for many areas other than mathematics and statistics. If you have a programming problem that you know will require considerable time and effort to complete, you should inquire at the computer center you are using about subroutines that might be useful to you.

Figure 12.1 shows the kind of information about a subroutine that you might find in a manual for a subroutine library. Notice that sufficient detail is given to allow you to use the subroutine, but details are omitted. The subroutine itself is not listed.

12.4   PROGRAMMING EXAMPLES

12.4.1   Sorting

Sorting of values into increasing or decreasing sequence is a common programming task, but a very important one. Complete books have been devoted to the topic of sorting, and students interested in more detail should consult the standard reference

---

[*]International Mathematical and Statistical Libraries, Inc. (IMSL), 7500 Bellaire Blvd, Houston, Tex.

[†]N. H. Nie, C. H. Hall, J. G. Jenkins, K. Steinbrenner, and D. H. Bent, *Statistical Package for the Social Sciences*, 2nd ed. (New York: McGraw-Hill Book Company, 1975).

[‡]W. R. Schucany and P. D. Minton, "A Survey of Statistical Packages," *Computing Surveys, 4* (June 1972), 65–79.

book written by Donald Knuth.* It has been estimated that 25% or more of the computer time used is devoted to sorting. If you can invent a better (i.e., faster) method of sorting large numbers of values, your fame is assured.

In this section, several procedures for sorting are illustrated. In every case, it will be assumed that the problem to be solved is the following one:

> Read the values of the elements of a one-dimensional array, X, sort the values into ascending order, and print the resulting sorted array. The actual number of values is not known, but the maximum number of values is 1000. Elements of X may have positive or negative values. A value of −9999.0 signals the end of the data deck.

We will represent each sorting technique we develop as a subroutine to emphasize its generality and ease of transferral to other programs. This implies that for each method a very high level solution is

<pre>
            initialize
            read values to be sorted
            CALL SORT (list of arguments)
            print the sorted values
            STOP
            END
</pre>

Our primary task is to develop the statements of the body of the subroutine.

Method 1: Extra Memory Cells Available

The first sorting method we shall consider is also the simplest method. It depends upon having at least as many extra memory cells available as the maximum size of the array to be sorted. Before attempting to write the SORT subroutine, let us become familiar with the method by performing the sorting for five values using pencil and paper. We will use two columns and the following procedure:

<pre>
        place the values in the left column
        WHILE (there are values to be transferred to the right column)
            find the smallest value that has not been transferred
            transfer the value to the next position in the right column
            mark out this value in the left column
        ENDWHILE
        write the values in the right-hand column
        STOP
        END
</pre>

Assume that the values to be used are 80.5, −11.7, 12.3, 19.6, and 43.2. Then the sorting will proceed through the following stages:

*Donald E. Knuth, *The Art of Computer Programming: Sorting and Searching*, vol. 3 (Reading, Mass.: Addison-Wesley Publishing Company, Inc., 1973).

Stage 1   Read the values into the left-hand column:

	left column		*right column*
1	80.5	1	
2	−11.7	2	
3	12.3	3	
4	19.6	4	
5	43.2	5	

Stage 2

1	80.5	1	−11.7
2	~~−11.7~~	2	
3	12.3	3	
4	19.6	4	
5	43.2	5	

Stage 3

1	80.5	1	−11.7
2	~~−11.7~~	2	12.3
3	~~12.3~~	3	
4	19.6	4	
5	43.2	5	

Stage 4

1	80.5	1	−11.7
2	~~−11.7~~	2	12.3
3	~~12.3~~	3	19.6
4	~~19.6~~	4	
5	43.2	5	

Stage 5

1	80.5	1	−11.7
2	~~−11.7~~	2	12.3
3	~~12.3~~	3	19.6
4	~~19.6~~	4	43.2
5	~~43.2~~	5	

Stage 6

1	~~80.5~~	1	−11.7
2	~~−11.7~~	2	12.3
3	~~12.3~~	3	19.6
4	~~19.6~~	4	43.2
5	~~43.2~~	5	80.5

Stage 7   Write the contents of the right-hand column.

It is probable that you would have used a method similar to this if you had been given a list of numbers to sort.

A. *Level 1 Solution*

To transform this technique to a subroutine, we can use the array X to represent the left-hand column, the array Y to represent the right-hand column, and COUNT to represent the actual number of values in X. The level 1 solution becomes

```
SUBROUTINE SORT(X,Y,COUNT)
DIMENSION X(1), Y(1)
WHILE (number of values transferred .LT. count of values)
    find the smallest value in X
    transfer the smallest value to Y
    mark out this value in X
ENDWHILE
RETURN
END
```

B. Level 2 Solution

Finding the smallest value of X for transferring to Y is tricky if you do not already know the technique. We will set up a loop that compares the first element of X, that is, X(1), with all the remaining values of X. If a smaller value is found than the value of X(1), this new, smaller value will be used in the remaining comparisons within the loop. For the comparison process to work in successive passes through the loop, we must remember to "mark out" values that have been transferred; but a line cannot be drawn through a value to indicate it has been transferred. Instead, we will store a very large number in the location. This number needs to be so large that it would not ordinarily be found as a member of X. Since the number is so large, there will be no danger of its being transferred to Y in some subsequent pass through the loop. These ideas give

```
SUBROUTINE SORT (X, Y, COUNT)
DIMENSION X(1), Y(1)
initialize
WHILE (number of values transferred .LT. count of values)
    initialize
    WHILE (I .LE. count of values)
        IF (X(I) .LT. smallest X value so far) THEN
            location of smallest X value = I
        ENDIF
        increase I
    ENDWHILE
    transfer smallest X(I) to Y
    set smallest X(I) to large value
    increase number of values transferred
ENDWHILE
RETURN
END
```

C. Level 3 Solution

At this stage we practically have the final solution. Our remaining problems are primarily in the category of using specific variables to replace the English language statements. Some required variables can be identified by scanning the preceding solution. Let

number of values transferred so far $\equiv$ NTRANS

count of number of values of X $\quad\equiv$ COUNT (make integer)

location of smallest value of X $\quad\equiv$ LOCX

location of next available place in Y $\equiv$ LOCY

Using the variables gives the following:

```
SUBROUTINE SORT(X,Y,N)
INTEGER COUNT
DIMENSION X(1), Y(1)
initialize
WHILE (NTRANS .LT. COUNT)
    initialize
    WHILE (I .LE. COUNT)
        IF (X(I) .LT. X(LOCX)) THEN
            LOCX = I
        ENDIF
        I = I+1
    ENDWHILE
    Y(LOCY) = X(LOCX)
    X(LOCX) = BIG
    NTRANS = NTRANS +1
    LOCY = LOCY + 1
ENDWHILE
RETURN
END
```

D. Level 4 Solution

To obtain the final subroutine we must perform the appropriate actions for the two initializations. What variables need to be initialized before the loop that begins WHILE (NTRANS .LT. COUNT)? The answer is NTRANS, LOCY, and BIG. Appropriate statements are

NTRANS = 0   no values have been transferred

LOCY = 1   the first value transferred to Y should
                go in location 1

$$BIG = 1.0E\ 20$$ the largest value that can be stored in the computer to be used would be an even better value

What variables need to be initialized outside the loop that begins WHILE (I. LE. COUNT)? The answer is I and LOCX. Each time this loop is executed we will assume that the smallest value within X is in location 1 and that comparisons should begin with element 2. This gives as initialization statements

$$LOCX = 1$$

$$I = 2$$

Incorporating these statements into the subroutine gives the final solution.

To obtain the mainline program that uses the SORT subroutine, statements must be written to read, count, and print the values. The reading and counting can be accomplished using a WHILE loop that will be terminated when a value of -9999.0 is read. It will be necessary within the loop to increase the value of the subscript so that the next element of X goes into the next position in the array. The number of values to be sorted will be one less than the number of cards read. The FORMAT, READ, and WHILE statements are easy so they will not be discussed further. Incorporating them gives the final solution. The computer printout is shown in Figure 12.2. (*Note:* An extra statement has been inserted to print the unsorted input values.) An alternative solution using DO statements is given in Figure 12.3.

```
 1   C
 2   C          SORTING    ADDITIONAL MEMORY METHOD
 3   C                     USE OF WHILE STATEMANT
 4   C
 5          INTEGER COUNT
 6          DIMENSION X(1000),Y(1000)
 7   1000 FORMAT(F10.3)
 8   1010 FORMAT('1','INPUT VALUES'/(' ',5F10.3))
 9   1020 FORMAT(///' ','SORTED VALUES'/(' ',5F10.3))
10          I=1
11          READ(5,1000)X(I)
12          WHILE( X(I) .NE. -9999.0)
13             I=I+1
14             READ(5,1000)X(I)
15          ENDWHILE
16          COUNT=I-1
17          WRITE(6,1010)( X(I),I=1,COUNT)
18          CALL SORTAM(X,Y,COUNT)
```

FIGURE 12.2 *Sorting using additional memory: WHILE statement method*

```
19          WRITE(6,1020)( Y(I),I=1,COUNT)
20          STOP
21          END
22  C
23  C
24  C
25          SUBROUTINE SORTAM(X,Y,COUNT)
26          INTEGER COUNT
27          DIMENSION X(1),Y(1)
28          NTRANS=0
29          LOCY=1
30          BIG=1.0E20
31          WHILE(NTRANS .LT. COUNT)
32             LOCX=1
33             I=2
34             WHILE(I .LE. COUNT)
35                IF( X(I) .LT. X(LOCX) ) THEN
36                   LOCX=I
37                ENDIF
38                I=I+1
39             ENDWHILE
40             Y(LOCY)=X(LOCX)
41             X(LOCX)=BIG
42             LOCY=LOCY+1
43             NTRANS=NTRANS+1
44          ENDWHILE
45          RETURN
46          END
```

INPUT VALUES

75.231	21.042	2.736	9.041	12.762
998.421	23.000	96.110	-12.630	407.000
98.170	9.041	-2.730	.012	443.000
33.700	11.040	-5.230	92.100	86.300
44.750	66.900	102.300	31.100	57.700
72.500	-12.700	15.300	42.230	145.310
76.200	85.300	4028.980	-103.820	55.570
22.370	-189.340	437.660	887.210	8431.801
.025	.754	4.870	52.770	

SORTED VALUES

-189.340	-103.820	-12.700	-12.630	-5.230
-2.730	.012	.025	.754	2.736
4.870	9.041	9.041	11.040	12.762
15.300	21.042	22.370	23.000	31.100
33.700	42.230	44.750	52.770	55.570
57.700	66.900	72.500	75.231	76.200
85.300	86.300	92.100	96.110	98.170
102.300	145.310	407.000	437.660	443.000
887.210	998.421	4028.980	8431.801	

FIGURE 12.2 *(cont.)*

```
 1  C
 2  C           SORTING    ADDITIONAL MEMORY METHOD
 3  C                      USE OF DO STATEMENT
 4  C
 5          INTEGER COUNT
 6          DIMENSION X(1000),Y(1000)
 7  1000 FORMAT(F10.3)
 8  1010 FORMAT('1','INPUT VALUES'/(' ',5F10.3))
 9  1020 FORMAT(///' ','SORTED VALUES'/(' ',5F10.3))
10          I=1
11          READ(5,1000)X(I)
12          WHILE( X(I) .NE. -9999.0 )
13             I=I+1
14             READ(5,1000)X(I)
15          ENDWHILE
16          COUNT=I-1
17          WRITE(6,1010)( X(I),I=1,COUNT)
18          CALL SORTAM(X,Y,COUNT)
19          WRITE(6,1020)(Y(I),I=1,COUNT)
20          STOP
21          END
22  C
23  C
24  C
25          SUBROUTINE SORTAM(X,Y,COUNT)
26          INTEGER COUNT
27          DIMENSION X(1),Y(1)
28          BIG=1.0E20
29          DO LOCY=1,COUNT
30             LOCX=1
31             DO I=2,COUNT
32                IF( X(I) .LT. X(LOCX) ) THEN
33                   LOCX=I
34                ENDIF
35             ENDDO
36             Y(LOCY)=X(LOCX)
37             X(LOCX)=BIG
38          ENDDO
39          RETURN
40          END
```

```
INPUT VALUES
        75.231      21.042       2.736       9.041      12.762
       998.421      23.000      96.110     -12.630     407.000
        98.170       9.041      -2.730        .012     443.000
        33.700      11.040      -5.230      92.100      86.300
        44.750      66.900     102.300      31.100      57.700
        72.500     -12.700      15.300      42.230     145.310
        76.200      85.300    4028.980    -103.820      55.570
        22.370    -189.340     437.660     887.210    8431.801
          .025        .754       4.870      52.770
```

FIGURE 12.3 *Sorting using additional memory: DO statement method*

342

SORTED VALUES

-189.340	-103.820	-12.700	-12.630	-5.230
-2.730	.012	.025	.754	2.736
4.870	9.041	9.041	11.040	12.762
15.300	21.042	22.370	23.000	31.100
33.700	42.230	44.750	52.770	55.570
57.700	66.900	72.500	75.231	76.200
85.300	86.300	92.100	96.110	98.170
102.300	145.310	407.000	437.660	443.000
887.210	998.421	4028.980	8431.801	

FIGURE 12.3 (*cont.*)

Method 2: Exchange Method

The exchange method for sorting is one of the simplest sorting techniques that does not use an additional array to store the sorted values. The sorting is done within the original array by exchanging values that are out of sequence. To find the smallest value that should go at the beginning of the array, the 1st element is compared to the 2nd element and interchanged if necessary. Then the 1st and 3rd elements are compared and interchanged if necessary. This process is repeated for the 1st and 4th, 1st and 5th, . . . , 1st and last positions. At each stage the 1st position contains the smallest value found so far, and when the process is completed, the 1st position will contain the smallest value in the list. As an illustration of the method, consider the values 80.5, 43.2, 12.3, −11.7, and 19.6. Then the process proceeds as follows (an arrow indicates elements being compared, and an "E" on the arrow means that the elements are to be exchanged):

(1)	(2)	(3)	(4)	array at end of processing for 1st element
80.5	43.2	12.3	−11.7	−11.7
43.2	80.5	80.5	80.5	80.5
12.3	12.3	43.2	43.2	43.2
−11.7	−11.7	−11.7	12.3	12.3
19.6	19.6	19.6	19.6	19.6

Now that the smallest element has been placed in the 1st position, that position need not be considered again. The entire process is now repeated to find the element that should be in the second position.

(1)	(2)	(3)	array at end of processing for 2nd element
−11.7	−11.7	−11.7	−11.7
80.5	43.2	12.3	12.3
43.2	80.5	80.5	80.5
12.3	12.3	43.2	43.2
19.6	19.6	19.6	19.6

Repeat the process to find the appropriate element for the 3rd position.

```
-11.7          -11.7          -11.7
 12.3           12.3           12.3
 80.5 ┐E        43.2 ┐         19.6
 43.2 ◄┘E       80.5 │E        80.5
 19.6           19.6 ◄┘        43.2

  (1)            (2)        array at end of processing
                            for 3rd element
```

Repeat the process to find the appropriate element for the 4th position.

```
-11.7          -11.7
 12.3           12.3
 19.6           19.6
 80.5 ┐E        43.2
 43.2 ◄┘E       80.5

  (1)        array at end of processing
```

Notice that processing for the next-to-last value also places the correct value in the last position.

A. Level 1 Solution

A subroutine corresponding to this technique will have two loops: (1) an outer loop, which gives the position (1st, 2nd, 3rd, etc.) of the element into which the smallest remaining value is to be placed; and (2) an inner loop, which compares the current value of the position of interest with the remaining values in the array. Within the inner loop, values are exchanged when a smaller value is encountered. This gives

```
SUBROUTINE SORT (X,COUNT)
DIMENSION X(1)
initialize
WHILE (there are unsorted elements in the array)
      initialize
      WHILE (elements remain for comparing with the element of
             interest)
            IF (element of interest .GT. current element) THEN
                exchange elements
            ENDIF
      ENDWHILE
ENDWHILE
RETURN
END
```

B. *Level 2 Solution*

The outer loop must consider, in turn, the 1st, 2nd, 3rd, . . . to next-to-last element. Thus, if I is the subscript for the position of interest within the array, I should go from 1 to COUNT-1. The inner loop should compare the Ith element with the I+1, I+2, I+3, and subsequent elements. Thus, if J is the subscript for the position being compared with the Ith position, J should go from I+1 to COUNT. These considerations give

```
SUBROUTINE SORT(X,COUNT)
INTEGER COUNT
DIMENSION X(1)
I = 1
WHILE (I .LE. COUNT-1)
    J = I+1
    WHILE (J .LE. COUNT)
        IF(X(I) .GT. X(J)) THEN
            exchange elements
        ENDIF
        J = J+1
    ENDWHILE
    I = I+1
ENDWHILE
RETURN
END
```

C. *Level 3 Solution*

To complete the subroutine, statements must be written to interchange the values. The interchange cannot be done directly using the statements

$$X(I) = X(J)$$

$$X(J) = X(I)$$

The bug is that statement $X(I) = X(J)$ causes the previous value of $X(I)$ to be erased and lost. For example, suppose that we have

| 80.5 | X(1) |

and

| 43.2 | X(2) |

which need to be interchanged. X(1) = X(2) gives

$$\boxed{43.2} \quad X(1)$$

and

$$\boxed{43.2} \quad X(2)$$

The original value of X(1) has been lost. To avoid this problem, the value of X(I) will be saved as the value of a temporary variable, TEMP, before the exchange begins. The sequence

$$TEMP = X(I)$$
$$X(I) = X(J)$$
$$X(J) = TEMP$$

will properly interchange the elements. Since the interchanging of elements is a common process in computer programming, you should remember this technique. Computer printouts for WHILE and DO versions of the program are shown in Figures 12.4 and 12.5, respectively.

```
1  C
2  C            EXCHANGE METHOD FOR SORTING
3  C            USE OF WHILE STATEMENT
4  C
5          INTEGER COUNT
6          DIMENSION X(1000)
7  1000 FORMAT(F10.3)
8  1010 FORMAT('1','INPUT VALUES'/(' ',5F10.3))
9  1020 FORMAT(///' ','SORTED VALUES'/(' ',5F10.3))
10         I=1
11         READ(5,1000)X(I)
12         WHILE( X(I) .NE. -9999.0)
13            I=I+1
14            READ(5,1000)X(I)
15         ENDWHILE
16         COUNT=I-1
17         WRITE(6,1010)(X(I),I=1,COUNT)
18         CALL SORTEX(X,COUNT)
19         WRITE(6,1020)(X(I),I=1,COUNT)
20         STOP
21         END
22  C
23  C
24  C
25         SUBROUTINE SORTEX(X,COUNT)
26         INTEGER COUNT
```

FIGURE 12.4 *Exchange method for sorting: WHILE statement method*

```
27         DIMENSION X(1)
28         I=1
29         WHILE( I .LE. COUNT-1)
30             J=I+1
31             WHILE(J .LE. COUNT)
32                 IF( X(I) .GT. X(J) ) THEN
33                     TEMP=X(I)
34                     X(I)=X(J)
35                     X(J)=TEMP
36                 ENDIF
37                 J=J+1
38             ENDWHILE
39             I=I+1
40         ENDWHILE
41         RETURN
42         END
```

```
INPUT VALUES
      75.231      21.042       2.736       9.041      12.762
     998.421      23.000      96.110     -12.630     407.000
      98.170       9.041      -2.730        .012     443.000
      33.700      11.040      -5.230      92.100      86.300
      44.750      66.900     102.300      31.100      57.700
      72.500     -12.700      15.300      42.230     145.310
      76.200      85.300    4028.980    -103.820      55.570
      22.370    -189.340     437.660     887.210    8431.801
        .025        .754       4.870      52.770
```

```
SORTED VALUES
    -189.340    -103.820     -12.700     -12.630      -5.230
      -2.730        .012        .025        .754       2.736
       4.870       9.041       9.041      11.040      12.762
      15.300      21.042      22.370      23.000      31.100
      33.700      42.230      44.750      52.770      55.570
      57.700      66.900      72.500      75.231      76.200
      85.300      86.300      92.100      96.110      98.170
     102.300     145.310     407.000     437.660     443.000
     887.210     998.421    4028.980    8431.801
```

FIGURE 12.4 (*cont.*)

```
1  C
2  C              EXCHANGE METHOD FOR SORTING
3  C              USE OF DO STATEMENT
4  C
5         INTEGER COUNT
6         DIMENSION X(1000)
7  1000 FORMAT(F10.3)
8  1010 FORMAT('1','INPUT VALUES'/(' ',5F10.3))
9  1020 FORMAT(///' ','SORTED VALUES'/(' ',5F10.3))
10        I=1
```

FIGURE 12.5 *Exchange method for sorting: DO statement method*

```
11          READ(5,1000)X(I)
12          WHILE( X(I) .NE. -9999.0)
13            I=I+1
14            READ(5,1000)X(I)
15          ENDWHILE
16          COUNT=I-1
17          WRITE(6,1010)(X(I),I=1,COUNT)
18          CALL SORTEX(X,COUNT)
19          WRITE(6,1020)(X(I),I=1,COUNT)
20          STOP
21          END
22 C
23 C
24 C
25          SUBROUTINE SORTEX(X,COUNT)
26          INTEGER COUNT
27          DIMENSION X(1)
28          LAST=COUNT-1
29          DO I=1,LAST
30            K=I+1
31            DO J=K,COUNT
32              IF( X(I) .GT. X(J)) THEN
33                TEMP=X(I)
34                X(I)=X(J)
35                X(J)=TEMP
36              ENDIF
37            ENDDO
38          ENDDO
39          RETURN
40          END
```

```
INPUT VALUES
    75.231      21.042       2.736       9.041      12.762
   998.421      23.000      96.110     -12.630     407.000
    98.170       9.041      -2.730        .012     443.000
    33.700      11.040      -5.230      92.100      86.300
    44.750      66.900     102.300      31.100      57.700
    72.500     -12.700      15.300      42.230     145.310
    76.200      85.300    4028.980    -103.820      55.570
    22.370    -189.340     437.660     887.210    8431.801
      .025        .754       4.870      52.770

SORTED VALUES
  -189.340    -103.820     -12.700     -12.630      -5.230
    -2.730        .012        .025        .754       2.736
     4.870       9.041       9.041      11.040      12.762
    15.300      21.042      22.370      23.000      31.100
    33.700      42.230      44.750      52.770      55.570
    57.700      66.900      72.500      75.231      76.200
    85.300      86.300      92.100      96.110      98.170
   102.300     145.310     407.000     437.660     443.000
   887.210     998.421    4028.980    8431.801
```

FIGURE 12.5 (*cont.*)

Method 3: Improved Exchange Sort

The exchange method, as just presented, does more exchanges than necessary. This deficiency can become quite serious in the case of sorting alphabetic data, a topic that will be presented later. In the sorting example with five numerical values, three exchanges were done during the process of finding the value that should be stored in the first position. A better technique would have been: save the position of the smallest value found so far; after all comparisons were completed, make a single exchange. For example, for the sequence

$$80.5 \longleftarrow X(I)$$
$$43.2$$
$$12.3$$
$$-11.7 \longleftarrow LOC = 4$$
$$19.6$$

we want (1) to discover that the location of the smallest value is 4, and (2) to interchange $X(I)$ and $X(LOC)$ using

$$TEMP = X(I)$$
$$X(I) = X(LOC)$$
$$X(LOC) = TEMP$$

This interchange needs to be done outside the inner loop. The comparison step should be changed to use the smallest value found so far, $X(LOC)$, instead of $X(I)$, and instead of interchanging the values, $LOC = J$ will save the location of the smallest value. A program that incorporates these changes is shown in Figure 12.6.

Although this program sorts values in less time than the simple exchange sort, it is not suitable for sorting large numbers of values. For example, the sorting of 10,000 values by a routine that uses a more complex algorithm may take less than 1/1000 of the time required by the improved interchange sort.

```
 1  C
 2  C           IMPROVED EXCHANGE METHOD FOR SORTING
 3  C
 4       INTEGER COUNT
 5       DIMENSION X(1000)
 6  1000 FORMAT(F10.3)
 7  1010 FORMAT('1','INPUT VALUES'/(' ',5F10.3))
 8  1020 FORMAT(///' ','SORTED VALUES'/(' ',5F10.3))
 9       I=1
10       READ(5,1000)X(I)
11       WHILE( X(I) .NE. -9999.0)
12          I=I+1
13          READ(5,1000)X(I)
14       ENDWHILE
```

FIGURE 12.6 *Improved exchange method of sorting*

```
15          COUNT=I-1
16          WRITE(6,1010)(X(I),I=1,COUNT)
17          CALL SORTEX(X,COUNT)
18          WRITE(6,1020)(X(I),I=1,COUNT)
19          STOP
20          END
21 C
22 C
23 C
24          SUBROUTINE SORTEX(X,COUNT)
25          INTEGER COUNT
26          DIMENSION X(1)
27          LAST=COUNT-1
28          DO I=1,LAST
29             LOC=I
30             K=I+1
31             DO J=K,COUNT
32                IF( X(LOC) .GT. X(J) ) THEN
33                   LOC=J
34                ENDIF
35             ENDDO
36             TEMP=X(I)
37             X(I)=X(LOC)
38             X(LOC)=TEMP
39          ENDDO
40          RETURN
41          END
```

```
INPUT VALUES
      75.231      21.042       2.736       9.041      12.762
     998.421      23.000      96.110     -12.630     407.000
      98.170       9.041      -2.730        .012     443.000
      33.700      11.040      -5.230      92.100      86.300
      44.750      66.900     102.300      31.100      57.700
      72.500     -12.700      15.300      42.230     145.310
      76.200      85.300    4028.980    -103.820      55.570
      22.370    -189.340     437.660     887.210    8431.801
        .025        .754       4.870      52.770

SORTED VALUES
    -189.340    -103.820     -12.700     -12.630      -5.230
      -2.730        .012        .025        .754       2.736
       4.870       9.041       9.041      11.040      12.762
      15.300      21.042      22.370      23.000      31.100
      33.700      42.230      44.750      52.770      55.570
      57.700      66.900      72.500      75.231      76.200
      85.300      86.300      92.100      96.110      98.170
     102.300     145.310     407.000     437.660     443.000
     887.210     998.421    4028.980    8431.801
```

FIGURE 12.6 *(cont.)*

350

12.4.2 Table Lookup: Payroll Calculation

In Section 7.4, a program was developed to print a payroll report. The program was extremely simple relative to a program that would be used in a real situation. One way in which the program was unrealistic was in the reading of all the data from cards. In a real situation, each employee's identification number, pay rate, hospitalization charges, cumulative data (total pay to date, state tax to date, federal tax to date), number of deductions for tax purposes, and other miscellaneous information would be stored as a group in magnetic form on a disk or tape. Keypunching of information for each employee for a given pay period would be reduced to a minimum of perhaps an identification number and the number of hours worked. The computer program would read this minimum information from cards and would "look up" the prestored information by matching the employee's identification number with the identification number stored on the disk.

In this section, the payroll report program will be made more realistic by looking up the employee's pay rate. Since we do not know how to read data from a disk or magnetic tape, this part of the program will be simulated by reading the data from cards into two arrays, IDNUM and RATE. For each employee a card is prepared of the form

```
1001      3.75

IDNUM (I)  RATE (I)
```

The resulting set of cards will be input at the beginning of the program using

```
          .
          .
          .
          DO I = 1, NUM
                READ (5,1000) IDNUM(I), RATE(I)
1000          FORMAT (I4, 1X, F5.2)
          ENDDO
          .
          .
          .
```

Such a deck would have to be prepared only one time per year, although the deck would have to be maintained in a current status by replacing a card whenever the pay rate changes for an employee. Businesses having very small computers often use such a deck, containing more information per employee, as a master payroll deck.

For a particular pay period, an employee's card will be keypunched with the employee identification number, hours worked, and deductions.

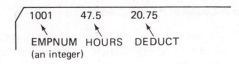

After one of these cards is read, the value of **EMPNUM** must be matched with a value in IDNUM. When a matching identification number is found at location **LOC**, the corresponding pay rate at location **LOC** can be looked up to be used in the payroll calculations. Several techniques for performing the search for a matching identification number will be described in this section.

A revised description that incorporates the changes just discussed will now be given for the payroll report problem.

> Write a program to print a payroll report: A master payroll deck containing the identification number and hourly pay rate of all employees is to be read into the computer memory. Then for each employee a data card will be read containing the employee's identification number, hours worked, and tax to be deducted. Look up the employee's hourly pay rate in the table already in memory. Print all the employee information, together with the gross pay before deductions, the net pay after deductions, and the gross pay from overtime work in excess of 40 hours per week. The overtime rate is 1.5 times the regular rate.

A payroll report program without table lookup, based on Figure 7.2, is listed below with needed modifications being noted.

```
      REAL NET
      INTEGER EMPNUM
1000 FORMAT ('1', T65, 'PAYROLL REPORT')
1010 FORMAT ('0', T23, 'EMPLOYEE', T86, 'GROSS', T103, 'NET,
     1       T113, 'OVERTIME')
1020 FORMAT ('b', T25, 'NUMBER', T41, 'HOURS', T57, 'RATE',
     1       T67, 'DEDUCTION', T88, 'PAY', T103, 'PAY', T118, 'PAY'/)
1030 FORMAT ('b', T26, I5, F15.1, 5F15.2)
1040 FORMAT (I10, 3F10.2)
      WRITE (6,1000)
      WRITE (6, 1010)
      WRITE (6,1020)

      ←——————— (1) insert reading of arrays IDNUM and RATES

      READ (5,1040) EMPNUM, HOURS, RATE, DEDUCT

                └——— (2) change READ statement to omit RATE

      WHILE (EMPNUM .GE. 0)

      ←——————— (3) look up hourly pay rate
```

```
        IF (HOURS .LE. 40.) THEN
            GROSS = HOURS * RATE
            NET = GROSS - DEDUCT
            WRITE (6,1030) EMPNUM,HOURS,RATE,DEDUCT,GROSS,NET
        ELSE
            OVPAY = 1.5*(HOURS - 40.) *RATE
            GROSS = 40.*RATE + OVPAY
            NET = GROSS - DEDUCT
            WRITE (6,1030) EMPNUM,HOURS,RATE,DEDUCT,GROSS,NET,
1                   OVPAY
        ENDIF
        READ (5,1040) EMPNUM, HOURS, RATE, DEDUCT
```

                    (4) change **READ** statement to omit **RATE**

```
    ENDWHILE
    STOP
    END
```

All of the changes except the lookup technique have been discussed in the introduction to the problem. The reading of arrays **IDNUM** and **RATES**, insert (1), will be done using

```
            .
            .

            DIMENSION IDNUM (500), RATES (500)
            .
            .

            READ (5,1050) NUM
1050 FORMAT (I3)
            DO I = 1, NUM
                READ (5,1060) IDNUM(I), RATES(I)
1060        FORMAT (I4, F5.2)
            ENDDO
            .
            .
```

The READ statements, changes (2) and (4), will become

```
        READ (5,1040) EMPNUM, HOURS, DEDUCT
```

with the value of RATE being obtained in the lookup process instead of being input here. For the lookup process, it will be assumed that due to keypunching errors there will not necessarily be an entry in IDNUM corresponding to EMPNUM. To accommodate this possibility, we will insert for modification (3)

.

.

.

look up EMPNUM in array IDNUM ←——————this step will be
IF (match found) THEN   considered in sub-
    RATE = RATES (location of match)   sequent discussions

    .

    .

    .

    make calculations as given in original program

    .

    .

    .

ELSE
    write error message
ENDIF

.

.

.

Now we direct our attention to methods of looking up EMPNUM in IDNUM. The final method, which we will use in a program, will be expressed as a subroutine.

A. Direct Table Lookup

Let us assume that the employee identification numbers as stored in the array IDNUM are in increasing sequence beginning with ID number 1001, that is,

$$IDNUM(1) = 1001$$
$$IDNUM(2) = 1002$$
$$IDNUM(3) = 1003$$
$$IDNUM(4) = 1004$$

    .   .

    .   .

    .   .

If there are no gaps in the sequence of ID numbers, the subscript of the appropriate element in IDNUM could be calculated directly from the value of EMPNUM:

$$LOC = EMPNUM - 1000$$

and

$$RATE = RATES (LOC)$$

Notice that for this fortunate situation, there would be no reason to have identification numbers stored in array IDNUM. Further, checking for a keypunch error in EMPNUM is easy: any value outside the range 1 through NUM is an error.

In realistic business situations, it is difficult to maintain the simple sequence of ID numbers that made the foregoing solution so easy. Resignation of employees, addition of new employees, and computing equipment limitations contribute to the difficulty of maintaining the required simple sequence. Circumstances having nothing to do with payroll computations might make social security numbers (or some other number) the best choice for employee identification numbers. Then gaps in the sequence will invalidate the method. A technique called *hashing* can be used in such cases to retain the direct lookup method provided that extra memory cells are available. In hashing, the programmer devises a function to map ID numbers onto locations in the array IDNUM. The ID numbers and the rates (as well as any other data) are stored beginning with the computed location. To find a value for RATE, the hashing process would use EMP-NUM to calculate the location at which the information was stored previously. The hashing method usually involves complications such as more than one ID number mapping into a given location. For a discussion of this problem and possible solutions, consult the book by Donald Knuth.

B. Linear Table Search

A simple lookup method that will always work is the testing of each element of array IDNUM for a possible match with EMPNUM until either a match is found or all elements of IDNUM have been tested. A suitable sequence of statements is

```
              .
              .
              .
          LOC = 0
          I = 1
          WHILE ((LOC .EQ. 0) .AND. (I .LE. NUM))
                IF (EMPNUM .EQ. IDNUM(I)) THEN
                    LOC = I
                ENDIF
                I = I+1
          ENDWHILE
          IF (LOC .NE. 0)
                RATE = RATES (LOC)
                  .
                  .
                  .
          ENDIF
              .
              .
              .
```

This method can require long search times if there are many employees. For a payroll for 8000 employees an average of 4000 tests would be required to look up the data. To save computer time, a faster method is needed when the number of employees is large.

C. Binary Search Method

The idea of a binary search involves asking questions designed to eliminate half the remaining possibilities. The method can be adapted to speed the search process in table-lookup problems. The values of IDNUM must be arranged in increasing sequence, but gaps in the sequence are allowed. Two integer pointers, which we shall call LOWER and UPPER, are used to mark the boundaries of the portion of the array that remains to be searched. Initially, LOWER will be set to 1, and UPPER will be set to the location of the last element in IDNUM. The location, LOC, of the element to be tested for a match is computed using

$$LOC = (LOWER + UPPER)/2$$

Thus LOC points to the middle of the array, effectively dividing the search space in half. If a match is not found, LOWER is moved to LOC + 1, or UPPER is moved to LOC − 1, depending upon which remaining portion of IDNUM might contain the matching ID number. Eventually, a match is found or LOWER becomes equal to or greater than UPPER. For 8000 employees a maximum of 13 comparisons (2^{13} = 8192) will be required to find the desired location instead of 4000 on the average for the linear search.

To illustrate the method, a binary search will be made to find EMPNUM = 1017 in array IDNUM. To save space in the discussion, IDNUM will be assumed to have only 10 elements. Initial values for the points will be

$$LOWER = 1, UPPER = 10, \text{ and } LOC = (1 + 10)/2 = 5$$

The contents of the array and the processing sequence are described next.

I	IDNUM (I)		
1	1003 ← LOWER = 1		
2	1007		
3	1008		
4	1015		
5	1016 ← LOC = 5		
6	1017	← LOWER = 6	← LOWER = 6, LOC = 6
7	1025		← UPPER = 7
8	1036	← LOC = 8	
9	1041		
10	1050 ← UPPER = 10	← UPPER = 10	

I	IDNUM (I)

1st comparison	2nd comparison	3rd comparison
1017 > 1016	1017 < 1036	1017 = 1017
∴ move LOWER to 6	∴ move UPPER to 7	∴ required LOC = 6

A sequence of statements that will perform the binary search is

```
SUBROUTINE BSRCH (IDNUM, EMPNUM, NUM, FOUND, LOC)
INTEGER UPPER, EMPNUM
LOGICAL FOUND
DIMENSION IDNUM(1)
LOWER = 1
UPPER = NUM
FOUND = .FALSE.
WHILE (.NOT.FOUND .AND. LOWER .LE. UPPER)
     LOC = (LOWER + UPPER)/2
     IF (EMPNUM .EQ. IDNUM(LOC)) THEN
          FOUND = .TRUE.
     ELSE
          IF (EMPNUM .GT. IDNUM(LOC)) THEN
               LOWER = LOC + 1
          ELSE
               UPPER = LOC - 1
          ENDIF
     ENDIF
ENDWHILE
RETURN
END
```

A program for the payroll report using the binary search method is given in Figure 12.7.

```
1  C
2  C          PAYROLL REPORT USING BINARY SEARCH
3  C
4          DIMENSION IDNUM(500),RATES(500)
5          REAL NET
6          INTEGER EMPNUM
7          LOGICAL FOUND
8  1000    FORMAT('1',T65,'PAYROLL REPORT')
9  1010    FORMAT('0',T23,'EMPLOYEE',T86,'GROSS',T103,'NET',T113,'OVERTIME')
10 1020    FORMAT(' ',T25,'NUMBER',T41,'HOURS',T57,'RATE',T67,'DEDUCTION',
11       *     T88,'PAY',T103,'PAY',T118,'PAY'/)
12 1030    FORMAT(' ',T26,I5,F15.1,5F15.2)
13 1040    FORMAT(I4,2F10.2)
```

FIGURE 12.7 *Payroll report program using binary search*

```
14 1050     FORMAT(I3)
15 1060     FORMAT(I4,F5.2)
16 1070     FORMAT(' ',T27,'EMPLOYEE NUMBER ',I4,' IS NOT VALID')
17          WRITE(6,1000)
18          WRITE(6,1010)
19          WRITE(6,1020)
20          READ(5,1050)NUM
21          DO I=1,NUM
22              READ(5,1060)IDNUM(I),RATES(I)
23          ENDDO
24          READ(5,1040)EMPNUM,HOURS,DEDUCT
25          WHILE(EMPNUM .GE. 0)
26              CALL BSRCH(IDNUM,EMPNUM,NUM,FOUND,LOC)
27              IF(FOUND) THEN
28                  RATE=RATES(LOC)
29                  IF(HOURS .LE. 40.) THEN
30                      GROSS=HOURS*RATE
31                      NET=GROSS-DEDUCT
32                      WRITE(6,1030)EMPNUM,HOURS,RATE,DEDUCT,GROSS,NET
33                  ELSE
34                      OVPAY=1.5*(HOURS-40.)*RATE
35                      GROSS=40.*RATE+OVPAY
36                      NET=GROSS-DEDUCT
37                      WRITE(6,1030)EMPNUM,HOURS,RATE,DEDUCT,GROSS,NET,OVPAY
38                  ENDIF
39              ELSE
40                  WRITE(6,1070)EMPNUM
41              ENDIF
42              READ(5,1040)EMPNUM,HOURS,DEDUCT
43          ENDWHILE
44          STOP
45          END
46 C
47 C
48 C
49          SUBROUTINE BSRCH(IDNUM,EMPNUM,NUM,FOUND,LOC)
50          INTEGER EMPNUM,UPPER
51          LOGICAL FOUND
52          DIMENSION IDNUM(1)
53          LOWER=1
54          UPPER=NUM
55          FOUND=.FALSE.
56          WHILE( .NOT. FOUND  .AND. LOWER .LE. UPPER)
57              LOC=(LOWER+UPPER)/2
58              IF(EMPNUM .EQ. IDNUM(LOC)) THEN
59                  FOUND=.TRUE.
60              ELSE
61                  IF(EMPNUM .GT. IDNUM(LOC)) THEN
62                      LOWER=LOC+1
63                  ELSE
64                      UPPER=LOC-1
65                  ENDIF
66              ENDIF
```

FIGURE 12.7   *(cont.)*

```
67        ENDWHILE
68        RETURN
69        END
```

PAYROLL REPORT

EMPLOYEE NUMBER	HOURS	RATE	DEDUCTION	GROSS PAY	NET PAY	OVERTIME PAY
1003	36.0	3.25	25.37	117.00	91.63	
1008	51.5	2.75	29.50	157.44	127.94	47.44
1005	46.5	3.35	31.70	166.66	134.96	32.66
1001	38.0	2.75	26.10	104.50	78.40	
1002	42.0	2.75	27.45	118.25	90.80	8.25
1006	43.0	3.20	29.60	142.40	112.80	14.40
1050	49.5	3.25	37.20	176.31	139.11	46.31
1025	37.0	3.67	30.25	135.79	105.54	
EMPLOYEE NUMBER 1022 IS NOT VALID						
1051	52.5	3.50	39.75	205.63	165.88	65.63
1013	20.0	3.08	15.60	61.60	46.00	
1009	40.0	3.65	25.36	146.00	120.64	

FIGURE 12.7 (*cont.*)

12.4.3 Descriptive Statistics

Suppose that we find ourselves in a situation which requires using the computer on a continual basis to make statistical calculations. A sensible approach to reducing the programming effort, and perhaps to reducing the number of programming errors, would be to develop a set of subroutines to compute the required statistical quantities. To demonstrate this approach, a subroutine, DESCST, will be developed to compute descriptive statistics consisting of the maximum, minimum, mean, median, and standard deviation. A high-level description of DESCST, which we will assume does no input or output, is the obvious sequence

SUBROUTINE DESCST (list of arguments)
    compute maximum
    compute minimum
    compute mean
    compute median
    compute standard deviation
    RETURN
END

This description can be changed easily into the final subroutine by using other subroutines to make the computations—a subroutine or function subprogram can use subroutines or functions! Applying this idea gives

```
            SUBROUTINE DESCST (X, N, XMAX, XMIN, XMEAN, XMED, STDEV)
C              SUBROUTINE TO COMPUTE DESCRIPTIVE STATISTICS
C              INTERPRETATION OF VARIABLES
C                  X          ARRAY CONTAINING DATA TO BE SUMMARIZED
C                  N          NUMBER OF VALUES
C                  XMAX       MAXIMUM VALUE OF X
C                  XMIN       MINIMUM VALUE OF X
C                  XMEAN      MEAN VALUE OF X
C                  XMED       MEDIAN VALUE OF X
C                  STDEV      STANDARD DEVIATION OF X
        DIMENSION X(1)
C           COMPUTE MAXIMUM
        CALL MAXIM (X, N, XMAX)
C           COMPUTE MINIMUM
        CALL MINIM (X, N, XMIN)
C           COMPUTE MEAN
        CALL MEAN (X, N, XMEAN)
C           COMPUTE MEDIAN
        CALL MEDIAN (X, N, XMED)
C           COMPUTE STANDARD DEVIATION
        CALL STDDEV (X, N, STDEV)
        RETURN
        END
```

The writing of subroutine DESCST has now been reduced to the development of five simpler subroutines. Notice that top-down design is being used. If the subroutines were very complex and time consuming to write, they could be assigned to several programmers. Each programmer could write, test, and debug the routines assigned to him. The debugged subprograms could then be used to produce the routine that was originally of interest. This technique can be extended to any depth.

The writing of subroutines for computing the maximum, minimum, and mean is straightforward. Suitable subroutines for **MAXIM** and **MINIM** are

```
            SUBROUTINE MAXIM (X, N, XMAX)
            DIMENSION X(1)
            XMAX = X(1)
            DO I = 2, N
                IF (X(I) .GT. XMAX) XMAX = X(I)
            ENDDO
            RETURN
            END
```

and

```
            SUBROUTINE MINIM (X, N, XMIN)
            DIMENSION X(1)
            XMIN = X(1)
```

```
          DO I = 2,N
               IF (X(I) .LT. XMIN) XMIN = X(I)
          ENDDO
          RETURN
          END
```

The subroutine for computing the mean is (this subroutine was used earlier to illustrate various concepts)

```
          SUBROUTINE MEAN (X, N, XMEAN)
          DIMENSION X(1)
          SUM = 0.0
          DO I = 1, N
               SUM = SUM + X(I)
          ENDDO
          XMEAN = SUM/N
          RETURN
          END
```

The writing of a subroutine to obtain the median of a set of values is more complex. (Recall that the median is the value found in the middle of an array of values after the values have been sorted.) The problem is that we have no knowledge of the circumstances in which the subroutine will be used; consequently, we do not know what sorting technique to incorporate into the subroutine. If the subroutine is to be executed frequently for large numbers of values, a fast sorting algorithm should be used to reduce computer costs; this will require more programming effort. There might even be circumstances in which a tabulation procedure would be better than sorting. Since we do not have additional information to guide us in our writing of the subroutine, we will use the interchange sorting technique to reduce programming effort. A subroutine based on this approach is

```
          SUBROUTINE MEDIAN (X, N, XMED)
          DIMENSION X(1)
C         SORT VALUES OF X
          LIMIT = N-1
          DO I = 1, LIMIT
               LOC = I
               K = I+1
               DO J = K, N
                    IF (X(J) .LT. X(LOC)) THEN
                         LOC = J
                    ENDIF
               ENDDO
               TEMP = X(I)
```

```
                X(I) = X(LOC)
                X(LOC) = TEMP
            ENDDO
C           IF N IS ODD, USE MIDDLE VALUE
            IF N IS EVEN, AVERAGE THE TWO MIDDLE VALUES
            MID = N/2
            IF (MOD(N,2) .EQ. 1) THEN
                XMED = X(MID)
            ELSE
                XMED = (X(MID) + X(MID+1))/2.0
            ENDIF
            RETURN
            END
```

Notice that after the subroutine MEDIAN has sorted the values of X, the values of the maximum and minimum could be obtained using

$$XMIN = X(1)$$

$$XMAX = X(N)$$

Does this mean that the subroutines MAXIN and MINIM are unnecessary? The answer is yes, for the narrow viewpoint of merely writing the subroutine DESCST. An alternative program for DESCST is

```
SUBROUTINE DESCST (X, N, XMAX, XMIN, XMEAN, XMED, STDEV)
DIMENSION X(1)
CALL MEDIAN (X, N, XMED)
XMIN = X(1)
XMAX = X(N)
CALL MEAN (X, N, XMEAN)
CALL STDDEV (X, N, STDEV)
RETURN
END
```

Despite the fact that the subroutines MAXIM and MINIM could be eliminated for the problem under discussion, there are good reasons for not doing so. First, to eliminate these routines, it was necessary to understand how MEDIAN worked internally, but we would like to be able to use subroutines without having to be concerned with how the results are computed within the subroutine—the fewer details we have to remember the better. Second, any future modifications to MEDIAN because of changes in the nature of the problem being solved could affect the method used to compute the maximum and minimum. Such a change in MEDIAN would, therefore, require changes in the calling program. We would like to restrict all changes to the program being modified. Finally, defining MAXIM and MINIM as independent subroutines makes it possible for us to use them in other subroutines in which **MEDIAN** is not present.

The subroutine **STDDEV** can be obtained by adapting the program given in Figure 11.6 for the standard deviation. The resulting subroutine is

```
SUBROUTINE STDDEV (X, N, STDEV)
DIMENSION X(1)
SUMX2 = 0.0
SUMX = 0.0
DO I = 1, N
    SUMX2 = SUMX2 + X(I)**2
    SUMX = SUMX + X(I)
ENDDO
XN = N
STDEV = SQRT ((XN*SUMX2 - SUMX**2)/(XN*(XN-1)))
RETURN
END
```

A program that uses DESCST is given in Figure 12.8. The program can be understood at several levels. At the highest level (least detailed level) is the program itself—the program somehow computes the descriptive statistics using DESCST. At the next level is DESCST, which can be examined to discover what it is doing. At the lowest level (most detailed level) are the subroutines that compute the individual statistical quantities. This hierarchical approach to thinking and problem solving has been one of the major themes of the book. The approach can be a major aid to thinking regardless of the subject involved.

```
 1  C
 2  C                  DESCRIPTIVE STATISTICS
 3  C
 4        DIMENSION GRADES(1000)
 5  1000  FORMAT(F10.0)
 6  1010  FORMAT('1','INPUT DATA'/(' ',5F10.0))
 7  1020  FORMAT(//' ','DESCRIPTIVE STATISTICS')
 8  1030  FORMAT('0',T6,'MAXIMUM',T28,F8.0)
 9  1040  FORMAT('0',T6,'MINIMUM',T28,F8.0)
10  1050  FORMAT('0',T6,'MEAN',T28,F8.1)
11  1060  FORMAT('0',T6,'MEDIAN',T28,F8.1)
12  1070  FORMAT('0',T6,'STANDARD DEVIATION',T28,F8.3)
13  C
14  C             READ ALL INPUT
15        I=1
16        READ(5,1000)GRADES(I)
17        WHILE(GRADES(I) .GE. 0)
18            I=I+1
19            READ(5,1000)GRADES(I)
```

FIGURE 12.8 *Descriptive statistics*

```
20          ENDWHILE
21          NUM=I-1
22          WRITE(6,1010)(GRADES(I),I=1,NUM)
23 C
24 C               COMPUTE DESCRIPTIVE STATISTICS
25 C
26          CALL DESCST(GRADES,NUM,GMAX,GMIN,GMEAN,GMED,SD)
27 C
28 C               PRINT THE RESULTS
29 C
30          WRITE(6,1020)
31          WRITE(6,1030)GMAX
32          WRITE(6,1040)GMIN
33          WRITE(6,1050)GMEAN
34          WRITE(6,1060)GMED
35          WRITE(6,1070)SD
36          STOP
37          END

38          SUBROUTINE DESCST(X,N,XMAX,XMIN,XMEAN,XMED,STDEV)
39 C
40 C               SUBROUTINE TO COMPUTE DESCRIPTIVE STATISTICS
41 C                 INTERPRETATION OF VARIABLES
42 C                 X         ARRAY CONTAINING DATA TO BE SUMMARIZED
43 C                 N         NUMBER OF VALUES
44 C                 XMAX      MAXIMUM VALUE OF X
45 C                 XMIN      MINIMUM VALUE OF X
46 C                 XMEAN     MEAN VALUE OF X
47 C                 XMED      MEDIAN VALUE OF X
48 C                 STDEV     STANDARD DEVIATION OF X
49 C
50          DIMENSION X(1)
51 C               COMPUTE MAXIMUM
52          CALL MAXIM(X,N,XMAX)
53 C
54 C               COMPUTE MINIMUM
55          CALL MINIM(X,N,XMIN)
56 C
57 C               COMPUTE MEAN
58          CALL MEAN(X,N,XMEAN)
59 C
60 C               COMPUTE MEDIAN
61          CALL MEDIAN(X,N,XMED)
62 C
63 C               COMPUTE STANDARD DEVIATION
64          CALL STDDEV(X,N,STDEV)
65 C
66          RETURN
67          END

68          SUBROUTINE MAXIM(X,N,XMAX)
```

FIGURE 12.8   *(cont.)*

```
69          DIMENSION X(1)
70          XMAX=X(1)
71          DO I=2,N
72             IF(X(I) .GT. XMAX) XMAX=X(I)
73          ENDDO
74          RETURN
75          END


76          SUBROUTINE MINIM(X,N,XMIN)
77          DIMENSION X(1)
78          XMIN=X(1)
79          DO I=2,N
80             IF(X(I) .LT. XMIN) XMIN=X(I)
81          ENDDO
82          RETURN
83          END


84          SUBROUTINE MEAN(X,N,XMEAN)
85          DIMENSION X(1)
86          SUM=0.0
87          DO I=1,N
88             SUM=SUM+X(I)
89          ENDDO
90          XMEAN=SUM/N
91          RETURN
92          END


93          SUBROUTINE MEDIAN(X,N,XMED)
94          DIMENSION X(1)
95  C                SORT VALUES OF X
96          LIMIT=N-1
97          DO I=1,LIMIT
98             LOC=I
99             K=I+1
100            DO J=K,N
101               IF(X(J) .LT. X(LOC)) THEN
102                  LOC=J
103               ENDIF
104            ENDDO
105            TEMP=X(I)
106            X(I)=X(LOC)
107            X(LOC)=TEMP
108         ENDDO
109 C
110 C                IF N IS ODD, USE MIDDLE VALUE
111 C                IF N IS EVEN, AVERAGE THE TWO MIDDLE VALUES
112 C
113         MID=N/2
114         IF(MOD(N,2) .EQ. 1) THEN
115            XMED=X(MID)
116         ELSE
```

FIGURE 12.8   *(cont.)*

```
117              XMED=(X(MID) + X(MID+1))/2.0
118         ENDIF
119         RETURN
120         END

121         SUBROUTINE STDDEV(X,N,STDEV)
122         DIMENSION X(1)
123         SUMX2=0.0
124         SUMX=0.0
125         DO I=1,N
126              SUMX2=SUMX2+X(I)**2
127              SUMX=SUMX+X(I)
128         ENDDO
129         XN=N
130         STDEV=SQRT( (XN*SUMX2 - SUMX**2)/(XN*(XN-1)) )
131         RETURN
132         END
```

INPUT DATA

83.	87.	77.	94.	68.
81.	82.	79.	63.	79.
80.	75.	78.	82.	85.
77.	78.	47.	76.	75.
60.	65.	88.	79.	81.
54.	84.	74.	62.	91.
73.	78.	69.	78.	

DESCRIPTIVE STATISTICS

MAXIMUM	94.
MINIMUM	47.
MEAN	75.9
MEDIAN	78.0
STANDARD DEVIATION	10.129

FIGURE 12.8 (*cont.*)

REVIEW QUESTIONS

1. What is a subroutine?
2. Why are subprograms such important intellectual tools for the programming process?
3. What is a subroutine library? What happens when a program references a subroutine?
4. Name four types of subprograms available in FORTRAN.
5. What statements are required in the defining of a subroutine? What are the rules for naming a subroutine?

6. What restrictions, if any, exist for placing different types of statements in the body of a subroutine?

7. What is a dummy argument? Where do dummy arguments appear?

8. In a subroutine, which variables are global and which are local?

9. What is the purpose of DIMENSION statements in subprograms? Can arguments be arrays?

10. In a program, what is the signal to the compiler that a subroutine is to be used?

11. In what ways must the actual arguments of a subroutine agree with the dummy arguments used during the definition of the subroutine?

12. How many different times with different arguments may a subroutine be used within a program?

13. Describe what happens during the execution of a program when a subroutine is encountered. How are dummy arguments handled?

14. How are the techniques of top-down programming and stepwise refinement related to the use of subroutines?

15. How do subroutines and functions differ in the number of answers they return? Why?

16. A program is to be changed into a subprogram. When should it be changed into a function instead of a subroutine?

17. What is the principle upon which direct table lookup is based?

18. Explain the binary search technique for looking up values in an array. In an array of 1050 values, how many elements must be examined using binary search to find a particular value?

19. Describe the algorithm for sorting using extra memory.

20. Describe the algorithm for the interchange sort.

REVIEW QUIZ

1. A type of subprogram whose definition always appears with the specification statements (INTEGER, REAL, DIMENSION, etc.) is: (A) intrinsic function, (B) statement function, (C) function, (D) subroutine, (E) none of the previous answers.

2. The arguments in the definition of a subprogram are called "dummy arguments" or "dummy variables" because (A) they indicate the number and mode of the actual arguments, (B) they do not give the actual storage size in the case of arrays, (C) in the definition, they do not cause any values to be transferred, (D) in using the subprogram, different variables can be used in the argument list, (E) all of the previous answers.

3. A valid statement is (A) a statement function may make calculations on entire arrays, (B) a FUNCTION is called by means of the CALL statement, (C) a statement function may return two or more values to the main program, (D) when a subroutine is used, the order of the arguments is important, (E) two of the previous answers are valid.

4. A problem that would be solved by writing and then using a subroutine subprogram is (A) calculating the average of a set of numbers, (B) determining the location of a particular value within an array, (C) determining the maximum grade in a set of grades, (D) reversing the order of the elements in a one-dimensional array, (E) all of the previous answers.

5. Given the statements:

> SUBROUTINE JCARD(X,Y,NUM)
> DIMENSION X(10), Y(20)
> .
> .
> .
> JCARD = X(1)/NUM
> .
> .
> .
> RETURN
> END

(A) The definition of the subroutine is invalid because of the appearance of JCARD in an arithmetic statement.
(B) X must contain exactly 10 values.
(C) The subprogram is integer mode.
(D) NUM is not allowed to change its value in the subprogram.
(E) None of the previous answers.

6. How many values can be returned to a calling program by a subroutine? (A) one, (B) any number, (C) one per dummy variable, (D) none.

7. Given:

> SUBROUTINE XYZ(A,B,C,D)
> A = B*C*D
> B = C*D
> C = D
> D = A*B*C*D
> RETURN
> END

A valid statement is:
(A) P = 2.0*XYZ(DAT1,DAT2,R,S)   (B) CALL XYZ(A-2.0,PQ**2,DOT)
(C) CALL XYZ(A,P,X,R)   (D) CALL XYZ(15,P,Q,R)
(E) CALL XYZ(X,Y,Z,V)**2

8. A *valid* statement is:
(A) A subroutine may have any number of arguments.
(B) The list of arguments serves exactly the same purpose in subroutines and functions.
(C) An array cannot be an argument in a subroutine.
(D) The STOP statement cannot appear within a subroutine.
(E) Two of the previous statements are valid.

EXERCISES

1. The following program finds the occurrence of a value in an array. Change it into:
   a. Subroutine
   b. Function
   Why can't it be changed into an arithmetic statement function?

```
         DIMENSION X(1000)
1000     FORMAT (I4, F10.0/(8F10.0))
1010     FORMAT (' ', 'THE LOCATION OF ', F10.0, ' IS ', I4)
         READ (5,1000) N, VALUE, (X(I), I = 1, N)
         LOC = 0
         I = 1
         WHILE (I. LE. N)
             IF (X(I) .EQ. VALUE) THEN
                 LOC = I
                 I = N
             ENDIF
             I = I + 1
         ENDWHILE
         WRITE (6,1010) VALUE, LOC
         STOP
         END
```

2. Each of the following contains an error. Correct the errors and indicate whether the error involves syntax or not.

   a.
```
SUBROUTINE EMPTY
X = 20.0*COS(X)
RETURN
END
```

   b.
```
SUBROUTINE SUMVAL(X,N)
DIMENSION X(1)
SUM = 0.0
DO I = 1,N
    SUM = SUM+X(I)
ENDDO
CALCX = SUM
END
```

   c.
```
SUBROUTINE AVG(A,B,AXY)
AXY = (A+B)/2.0
A = B
END
```

3. Given the following definition:

```
              SUBROUTINE CNTX (NUM,X,Y,L)
              DIMENSION X(1), Y(1)
              L = 0
              DO I = 1, NUM
                  IF (X(I) .GT. Y(I)) L = L+1
              ENDDO
              RETURN
              END
```

Which of the following is a valid use of the subroutine?
In the case of invalid usage, explain what is wrong.

   a. CALL CNTX(10,A,B,M)　　　　　　　　b. CALL CNTX (M,X,Y,Z)

c. CALL CNTX (L,X,Y,L)
d. CALL CNTX (100,X,A,10)
e. CALL CNTX (A,B,C,D)
f. CALL CNTX (H,X,Y,M)
g. CALL CNTX (L,MX,YZ,N)
h. CALL CNTX (20.0, R,Q,I)
i. CALL CNTX (N,AX,BX)
j. ANS = CNTX (NUM,X,Y,K)
k. IANS = CNTX (I,X,Y,J)

PROGRAMMING EXERCISES In each of the following exercises, you are asked to write one or more subroutines. To test a subroutine, you will need to write and execute a mainline program that uses it.

1. Revise one of the programs for scoring bowling so that a subroutine is used to compute the score for a frame.

2. Write a subroutine to move a group of consecutive values from one array to another. The call statement should have the form

(CALL MOVE (IARRAY, I, J, NARRAY, K)

where IARRAY = integer array containing the values to be moved
I = starting position in IARRAY for moving values
J = ending position in IARRAY for moving values
NARRAY = integer array to receive values being moved
K = starting position in NARRAY for receiving values

The MOVE subroutine should not modify the contents of IARRAY.

3. Write a subroutine FILL that will fill the indicated portion of an array with a specified value. The call statement has the form

CALL FILL (IARRAY, I, J, KAR)

where IARRAY = integer array in which values are to be inserted
I = starting position in IARRAY
J = ending position in IARRAY
KAR = variable whose value is the value to be used in filling IARRAY

4. Write a set of subroutines to perform arithmetic on 80-digit integers. See Programming Exercise 11.6 for a suggested method for performing the calculations.

5. Write a subroutine to compute the Pearson correlation coefficient. A formula for this statistical quantity is given in Programming Exercise 11.9.

6. Write a subroutine that computes the slope and intercept for the line produced by a least-squares analysis of a set of experimental data. Formulas are given in Programming Exercise 11.10.

7. Suppose that two sorted arrays must be combined into a single new sorted array. Write and test a subroutine for this purpose. The CALL statement should have the form

CALL MERGE2 (IARRAY,ITOT,INUM,JARRAY,JNUM,KARRAY)

where IARRAY = integer array of sorted values
ITOT = total number of elements declared for IARRAY
INUM = number of values in IARRAY
JARRAY = integer array of sorted values

JNUM   = number of values in JARRAY
KARRAY = integer array into which elements of IARRAY and JARRAY
         are to be placed

The subroutine MERGE should not do any sorting.

8. The previous programming exercise used an extra array for storing the merged
   values from two other arrays. Using an extra array is not feasible when the amount
   of computer memory is limited, and in that case it may be possible to merge the
   values in one array directly into the other array. Write and test a subroutine to
   perform the following actions:

   1. Check to see if array IARRAY has sufficient space to hold all its values
      and the values from array JARRAY.
   2. If adequate space is available, merge the elements of JARRAY into
      IARRAY; otherwise, set an error indicator and exit from the subroutine.

   Do not use an additional array in the subroutine. The call statement should have
   the form

   CALL MERGE2 (IARRAY,ITOT,INUM,JARRAY,JNUM)

   where IARRAY = integer array of sorted values
         ITOT   = total number of elements declared for IARRAY
         INUM   = number of elements in use in IARRAY
         JARRAY = integer array whose elements are to be merged into IARRAY
         JNUM   = number of elements of JARRAY to be merged

9. In Section 11.5.1, a frequency distribution was obtained for a set of grades. That
   problem occurs in many different forms for various types of data—not just grades.
   Consequently, it is sensible to write a subroutine that could be used in different
   programs. Write and test a subroutine for that purpose. Use a tabulation technique instead of sorting. The values whose frequency are to be determined are
   stored in array IARRAY. The call statement should have the form

   CALL FREQD (IARRAY,INUM,IMIN,IMAX,NUMINT,IFREQ)

   where IARRAY = integer array containing the values whose frequencies are to be
                    determined
         INUM   = number of values stored in IARRAY
         IMIN   = the minimum value which might be stored in IARRAY
         IMAX   = the maximum value which might be stored in IARRAY
         NUMINT = the number of intervals to be used
         IFREQ   = integer array containing the frequency counts

CHAPTER 13 TWO- AND THREE-DIMENSIONAL ARRAYS

This chapter is concerned primarily with demonstrating by programming examples how to use two- and three-dimensional arrays. The syntax of these arrays was presented in Chapter 11, but a brief review will be given together with additional techniques for input/output.

13.1 DESCRIPTIONS OF TWO- AND THREE-DIMENSIONAL ARRAYS

Two-dimensional arrays are normally used to refer to tables, and two subscripts are used to identify the location of a particular element in the table. By convention, the leftmost subscript designates a row of the table, and the rightmost subscript designates a column of the table; that is

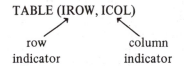

Suppose that a class of 27 students has taken five quizzes during a semester. The grades on the quizzes can be arranged into a table of 27 rows (one row for each student) and five columns (one column for each quiz). To cause the compiler to set aside memory cells for this array, we can use the statement

DIMENSION GRADES (27,5)

Notice that GRADES has a total of 135 elements (27 × 5). Let a portion of the table be

	Column				
Row	*1*	*2*	*3*	*4*	*5*
1	71	82	78	79	74
2	85	78	86	86	83

		Column			
Row	1	2	3	4	5
3	94	100	97	87	92
4	83	83	81	92	88
.					
.					
.					
27	87	51	75	83	86

Then by consulting the table, we find

Element	Row	Column	Value
GRADES (1,4)	1	4	79
GRADES (2,3)	2	3	86
GRADES (4,2)	4	2	83
GRADES (27,1)	27	1	87

It is meaningless to ask for the values of

GRADES (2,7)   (There is no 7th column.)

GRADES (31,3)   (There is no 31st row.)

GRADES (30,6)   (There is neither a row 30 nor a column 6.)

It is the responsibility of the programmer to prevent the subscripts from exceeding the maximum values given in the DIMENSION statement.

Two-dimensional arrays can be manipulated in much the same way as one-dimensional arrays, but the programmer must use two subscripts. For example, to add the five elements of a one-dimensional array, we can write

```
        .
        .
        .
SUM = 0.0
DO I = 1,5
    SUM = SUM + X(I)
ENDDO
        .
        .
        .
```

To add the five elements of the first row of grades, we can write

```
        .
        .
        .
    SUM = 0.0
    DO J = 1,5
        SUM = SUM + GRADES (1, J)
    ENDDO
        .
        .
        .
```

note use of constant

Or alternately, we can write

```
        .
        .
        .
    SUM = 0.0
    I = 1
    DO J = 1,5
        SUM = SUM + GRADES (I,J)
    ENDDO
        .
        .
        .
```

note that value does not change
within the loop

To add a column of GRADES, we can write either of the following:

```
        .
        .
        .
    SUM = 0.0
    DO I = 1,27
        SUM = SUM + GRADES (I,1)
    ENDDO
        .
        .
        .
```

note use of constant

or

```
        .
        .
        .
    SUM = 0.0
```

```
J = 1
DO I = 1,27
     SUM = SUM + GRADES (I,J)
ENDDO
     .
     .
     .
```

note that value does not change
within the loop

The sum of all the grades, five grades for 27 students, can be obtained by writing

```
     .
     .
     .

SUM = 0.0
DO I = 1,27
     DO J = 1,5
          SUM = SUM + GRADES (I, J)
     ENDDO
ENDDO
     .
     .
     .
```

In the programming examples, these ideas will be extended, but even now you should realize that the techniques used for one-dimensional arrays can be applied to two- and three-dimensional arrays.

In developing computer programs, it is important to be able to recognize the need for a two-, three-, or higher-dimensional array. Some other examples of information that can be represented by a two-dimensional array are: an inventory chart, a tax table, a chart of baseball statistics, a daily stock market report, a calendar, a seating chart for a class, a matrix in mathematics, and a chessboard.

Three-dimensional arrays can be visualized as a set of similar two-dimensional arrays. A typical example is

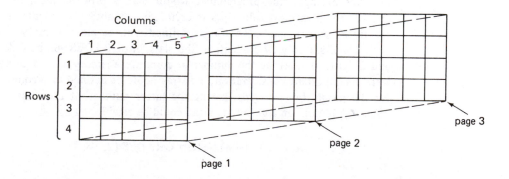

in which there are three pages of 4 by 5 two-dimensional arrays. Notice that the tables on the different pages must all have the same number of rows and columns. An equally satisfactory alternative description involves visualizing the three-dimensional array as a stack of two-dimensional arrays with the position of a given two-dimensional array being given by a level number.

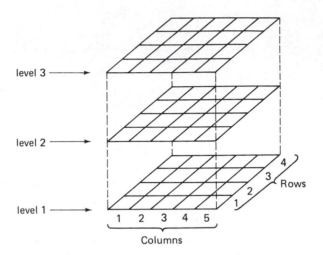

Regardless of the mental picture chosen, an appropriate DIMENSION statement is

DIMENSION EXAMPL (3, 4, 5)

Three-dimensional arrays arise in programming whenever the data are to be summarized on the basis of three variables. If the class grades considered earlier in this section also needed to be analyzed on the basis of the sex of the students, a suitable array could be set aside by

DIMENSION GRADES (2, 27, 5)

For this example, the programmer would plan a program assuming the leftmost, middle, and rightmost subscripts refer to sex, number of students, and quizzes, respectively. Notice that GRADES as defined will use more memory cells than necessary. There are only 27 students in the class, but GRADES will hold data for 27 boys and 27 girls. If reducing the number of computer memory cells required for the array were an important consideration, the array could be defined to accommodate the data for the group, boys or girls, having the larger number. If the class consisted of 16 boys and 11 girls, an appropriate array could be established by

DIMENSION GRADES (2, 16, 5)

The manipulation of three-dimensional arrays involves the same technique as for two-dimensional arrays with the introduction of an additional subscript. The sum of the grades for the third male student could be obtained using

```
        .
        .
        .
SUM = 0.0
DO K = 1,5
    SUM = SUM + GRADES (1, 3, K)
ENDDO
        .
        .
        .
```

or

```
        .
        .
        .
SUM = 0.0
I = 1
J = 3
DO K = 1,5
    SUM = SUM + GRADES (I,J,K)
ENDDO
        .
        .
        .
```

Further discussion of the manipulation of three-dimensional arrays will be delayed until specific programs are described.

13.2   INPUT/OUTPUT OF TWO- AND THREE-DIMENSIONAL ARRAYS

Methods for reading and writing of the elements of multidimensional arrays are an extension of the techniques used for one-dimensional arrays. Nested loops controlled by DO or WHILE statements, implied DO loops, and nested implied DO loops can be used for input/output.

If DO loops are used to control the input/output process, there will normally be one DO statement for each dimension of the array. Each DO statement will be used to generate values for one of the subscripts. Consider the following sequence of statements:

```
                    DIMENSION EXAMPL (10,5)
                        .
                        .
                        .

                    DO I = 1,10
                        DO J = 1,5
                            READ (5,1000) EXAMPL (I, J)
        1000            FORMAT (F10.2)
                        ENDDO
                    ENDDO
                        .
                        .
                        .
```

1. EXAMPL is a two-dimensional array consisting of 10 rows and 5 columns—50 elements in all.
2. The READ statement will be executed 50 times, 5 times for each of the 10 executions of the outer loop.
3. A total of 50 cards will be read since there is only one value requested in the READ statement.
4. The subscript J has successive values of 1, 2, 3, 4, and 5 for each value of I since J is generated by the inner DO loop. Thus the sequence of subscripts produced is

I	J
1	1
1	2
1	3
1	4
1	5
2	1
2	2
2	3
2	4
2	5
.	.
.	.
.	.
10	3
10	4
10	5

The subscripts have been generated in the order required for reading the elements of the first row, followed by the elements of the second row, and so on. The array is read by rows.

An understanding of whether the data are being read (or otherwise manipulated) by rows or by columns is critical for success in using two-dimensional arrays. Consequently, let us consider this example from another point of view. The subscripts for the array EXAMPL form the following pairs:

			Column		
Row	1	2	3	4	5
1	1,1	1,2	1,3	1,4	1,5
2	2,1	2,2	2,3	2,4	2,5
3	3,1	3,2	3,3	3,4	3,5
.					
.					
.					
10	10,1	10,2	10,3	10,4	10,5

Notice that as we read across a row the right-hand subscript changes more rapidly, and as we read down a column the left-hand subscript changes more rapidly.

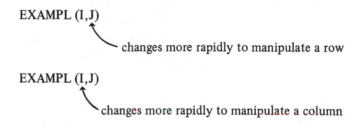

EXAMPL (I,J)

    changes more rapidly to manipulate a row

EXAMPL (I,J)

    changes more rapidly to manipulate a column

It is the position (right- or left-hand) of the subscript that is important, not the name of the subscript, since any valid name could be used. To read the values by columns, use

```
                    .
                    .
                    .
            DO J = 1,5
                DO I = 1,10
                    READ (5,1000) EXAMPL (I,J)
1000                FORMAT (F10.2)
                ENDDO
            ENDDO
                    .
                    .
                    .
```

Suppose that the values of the elements of EXAMPL have been punched into cards, one row per card:

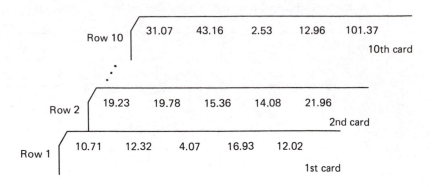

An implied DO loop can be used to simplify the reading.

```
        .
        .
        .
      DO I = 1,10
           READ (5,1010) (EXAMPL (I,J), J = 1,5)
1010       FORMAT (5F10.2)
      ENDDO
        .
        .
        .
```

Each execution of the READ statement will cause one row (five values) to be input. Incidentally, the following statements could not be used to read these cards. Why?

```
        .
        .
        .
      DO I = 1, 10
         DO J = 1,5
            READ (5,1020) EXAMPL (I,J)
1000        FORMAT (5F10.2)
         ENDDO
      ENDDO
        .
        .
        .
```

Although the FORMAT statement allows five values to be punched into a card, execution of the READ statement will input only the leftmost value on a card. The other values on the card would be ignored, and an attempt would be made to read 50 cards.

Nested implied DO loops, that is, implied DO loops within implied DO loops, can be used in READ and WRITE statements. The entire 10 by 5 array named EXAMPL could be read by a single execution of

READ (5,1030) ((EXAMPL (I,J), J = 1,5), I = 1,10)

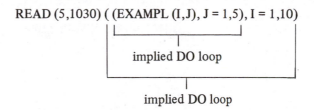

A nested implied DO loop is executed repeatedly for all allowed values of its index for each value of the index of the loop in which it is nested. J goes from 1 to 5 for each value of I. This behavior is identical with the behavior of ordinary nested DO loops.

The statement

READ (5,1030) ((EXAMPL (I,J), J = 1,5), I = 1,10)

changes rapidly

reads values punched in order by rows. The following statement will read values punched in column order:

READ (5,1040) ((EXAMPL (I,J), I = 1,10), J = 1,5)

changes rapidly

Implied DO loops can be extended to three-dimensional arrays. The following statement reads a page (or level) of the array by rows, then reads the next page by rows, and continues in this manner until four pages have been read.

READ (5,1050 (((EXPL (I,J,K), K = 1,5), J = 1,10), I = 1,4)

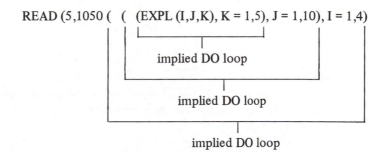

As the designer of a program, you can choose to input the values of an array in whatever manner you wish. Since in our society we have learned to read from left to right (instead of top to bottom), you will probably make fewer errors in punching data if the values are punched by rows instead of columns.

The techniques just described can be applied, with proper inclusion of carriage control, directly to the output of multidimensional arrays. The two-dimensional array EXAMPL can be printed by rows using either of the following:

```
           DIMENSION EXAMPL (10,5)
             .
             .
             .
           DO I = 1,10
                WRITE (6, 1060) (EXAMPL (I,J), J = 1,5)
    1060        FORMAT ('b', 5F10.2)
           ENDDO
```

or

```
           WRITE (6,1060) ((EXAMPL(I,J), J = 1,5), I = 1,10)
    1060 FORMAT ('b', 5F10.2)
```

A more challenging problem is to print the levels of a three-dimensional array, placing each level on a different page. One method is

```
           DIMENSION EXPL (4,10,5)
             .
             .
             .
           DO I = 1,4
                WRITE (6,1070)
    1070        FORMAT ('1')
                WRITE (6,1080) ((EXPL (I,J,K), K = 1,5), J = 1,10)
    1080        FORMAT ('b', 5F10.2)
           ENDDO
             .
             .
             .
```

What other methods would work?

Multidimensional arrays can be read or written by merely using the name of the array (without subscripts) in an appropriate READ or WRITE statement. All of the following are valid statements:

DIMENSION EXAMPL (10,5), EXPL (4,10,5)

.

.

.

READ (5,1090) EXAMPL
READ (5,1090) EXPL
WRITE (6,1090) EXAMPL
WRITE (6,1090) EXPL

.

.

.

Each statement implies that all values associated with the array should be read or written. So far there is nothing new about this technique; the same technique was allowed for one-dimensional arrays. But in the case of multidimensional arrays, the designers of the FORTRAN compiler had to make an arbitrary decision about the sequence of subscripts to be used. They decided to vary the leftmost subscript most rapidly and to vary the rightmost subscript least rapidly. This decision means that the statement

WRITE (6,1090) EXPL

will write all 200 values with the subscripts varying as

EXPL (I, J, K)

             vary least rapidly
          vary next most rapidly
      vary most rapidly

Thus the statement is equivalent to

WRITE (6,1090) (((EXPL (I,J,K), I = 1,4), J = 1,10), K = 1,5)

It will be quite difficult to recognize the values printed as corresponding to the original array. To illustrate the difficulty, let INT be a 2 by 3 array with values punched into cards as

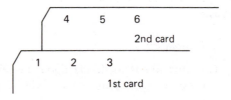

to represent the two rows of the array. Then execution of the statements

$$\text{DIMENSION INT (2,3)}$$

.

.

.

$$\text{READ (5,1100) ((INT (I,J), J = 1,3), I = 1,2)}$$
$$\text{1100 FORMAT (3I5)}$$
$$\text{WRITE (6,1100) INT}$$

.

.

.

will print the two rows

1	4	2
5	3	6

This appears to be a different array.

13.3   PROGRAMMING EXAMPLES

13.3.1   Student and Class Averages

In the beginning of the chapter, various concepts associated with two-dimensional arrays were illustrated with an array of grades for five quizzes and 27 students. In this section, we show the power of this data representation for making arithmetic computations. We want to write a program to do the following:

1. Read an array of grades made by students during a semester.
2. All grades are integers in the range 0 to 100. Compute:
    a. Each student's average.
    b. The class average for each quiz.
    c. The average of the individual student averages.
3. No printing is to be done until all computations are complete. The program should work for 100 or fewer students and 10 or fewer quizzes.

To simplify the problem, we will assume that every student takes all the quizzes during a semester.

A. Level 1 Solution

Our first job is to decide upon the representation of the data and the various averages. Three arrays will be used, and they can be visualized using the accompanying figure. The grades are stored in array GRADES, with each row giving the quiz grades for one student and with each column giving the grades of all students for one quiz. The average grade for each student will be stored in the array STUAVG (for student average) at the position that corresponds to the row in which his grades are found. The

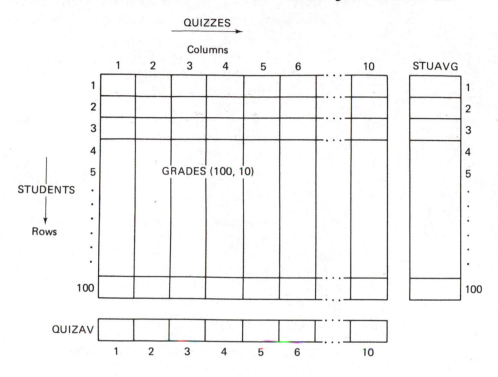

average grades for quizzes will be stored in the array QUIZAV (for quiz average). A high-level solution using these arrays is

    read values for the number of quizzes and number of students
    read into GRADES the grades for the appropriate number of
        students and number of quizzes
    compute the average for each row and store in STUAVG
    compute the average for each column and store in QUIZAV
    compute the average of STUAVG
    print the rows of GRADES with corresponding element of STUAVG
        on the same line
    print the quiz averages, QUIZAV, at the bottom of each column
    print the average of the student averages
    STOP
    END

B. Level 2 Solution

Expansion of the individual steps of the level 1 solution would be easy if you had some previous practice with two-dimensional arrays. We will proceed by expanding each step in sequence to obtain the final solution. Let NSTU be the number of students and NQUIZ be the number of quizzes. Then the procedure through the reading of the data is

```
      INTEGER GRADES (100,10)
      DIMENSION STUAVG (100), QUIZAV (10)
      READ (5,1000) NQUIZ, NSTU
1000 FORMAT (2I5)
      DO I = 1, NSTU
          READ (5,1010) (GRADES (I,J), J = 1, NQUIZ)
1010      FORMAT (10I5)
      ENDDO
        .
        .
        .
```

The technique selected for the reading of the grades allows us to punch the quizzes for a given student on a card. If there were four quizzes, four values will be punched per card. If there were seven quizzes, seven values will be punched per card. Any unused fields on a card will be ignored since no request is made to read values from these fields. Using a statement such as

READ (5,1010) ((GRADES(I,J), J = 1,NQUIZ), I = 1, NSTU)

is valid, but it would require that a value be punched into all 10 fields on a card (except possibly for the last card).

Computing the average for each row involves two loops: an outer loop for considering each row in turn, and an inner loop to add the quiz scores in a given row. This gives

```
          .
          .
          .
      DO I = 1, NSTU
          SUM = 0.0
          DO J = 1, NQUIZ
              SUM = SUM + GRADES (I,J)
          ENDDO
          STUAVG(I) = SUM/NQUIZ
      ENDDO
          .
          .
          .
```

Computation of the quiz averages is quite similar to the computation just completed. Two loops are needed, but in this case the subscript for the row should change more rapidly. A suitable method of writing the statements is

```
            .
            .
            .
        DO J = 1, NQUIZ
            SUM = 0.0
            DO I = 1, NSTU
                SUM = SUM + GRADES(I,J)
            ENDDO
            QUIZAV(J) = SUM/NSTU
        ENDDO
```

Calculating the average of the student averages involves summing the contents of a one-dimensional array—a process that has been used in previous problems. (You should strive to remember programming techniques as they tend to recur in other problems. By remembering them you can save considerable time in writing programs.) Applying the technique for summing one-dimensional arrays gives

```
            .
            .
            .
        SUM = 0.0
        DO I = 1,NSTU
            SUM = SUM + STUAVG(I)
        ENDDO
        AVG = SUM/NSTU
```

No directions were given in the problem for writing the report title and column headings. Consequently, we can print any headings we want. One possibility is

```
     WRITE (6,1020)
1020  FORMAT ('1', T25, 'REPORT OF STUDENT AND QUIZ '
    1 'AVERAGES'//'b', 'STUDENT', T35, 'QUIZ GRADES', T74,
    2 'AVERAGES'/)
```

This WRITE statement causes two lines to be printed—a title line and a line of column headings.

The next output problem—the printing of rows of grades with the corresponding element of STUAVG on the same line—requires special care.

As a first guess a statement such as the following could be tried for writing one line.

> WRITE (6,1030) (GRADES(I,J), J = 1, NQUIZ), STUAVG(I)
> 1030 FORMAT ('b', T11, 10I6, F10.1)

The idea is to print the row of quiz grades in the fields specified by 10I6 and then to print the student's average in the F10.1 field. Unfortunately, the technique fails if fewer than 10 grades are printed. In that case, the next available specification will be one of the remaining I6 fields, and a real-mode value for STUAVG(I) cannot be printed in the field. A solution to the problem is to use two WRITE statements, with the second having a carriage control for printing on the line just printed.

> WRITE (6,1030) (GRADES(I,J), J = 1, NQUIZ)
> 1030 FORMAT ('b', T11, 10I6)
> WRITE (6,1040) STUAVG(I)
> 1040 FORMAT ('+', T71, F10.1)

In the FORMAT statement for the second WRITE statement, it was necessary to skip beyond the previous printing using T71 to avoid overprinting. These statements can be embedded in a loop to cause the printing of one line for each student. We will also print the subscript for the row on each line, although this is not required. Thus the final result is

> .
> .
> .

> DO I = 1, NSTU
>   WRITE (6,1030) I, (GRADES(I,J), J = 1, NQUIZ)
> 1030   FORMAT ('b', I5, T11, 10I6)
>   WRITE (6,1040) STUAVG(I)
> 1040   FORMAT ('+', T71, F10.1)
> ENDDO

Printing the quiz averages and overall student average is straightforward.

> .
> .
> .

> WRITE (6,1050)
> 1050 FORMAT ('0', T2, 'QUIZ')
> WRITE (6,1060) (QUIZAV(I), I = 1, NQUIZ)
> 1060 FORMAT ('b', T2, 'AVERAGES', T11, 10F6.1)
> WRITE (6,1070) AVG
> 1070 FORMAT (//'b', 'THE AVERAGE OF THE STUDENT AVERAGES
>   IS', F6.1)

The computer printout for the program is shown in Figure 13.1.

This program illustrates several techniques for manipulating two-dimensional arrays. The use of nested loops for performing arithmetic is a standard technique. Comparisons and related activities could be performed in the same manner by substituting the appropriate statements for the arithmetic statements. Rows or columns

```
 1  C
 2  C              STUDENT AND CLASS AVERAGES
 3  C
 4          INTEGER GRADES(100,10)
 5          DIMENSION STUAVG(100),QUIZAV(10)
 6  1000    FORMAT(2I5)
 7  1010    FORMAT(10I5)
 8  1020    FORMAT('1',T25,'REPORT OF STUDENT AND QUIZ AVERAGES'//' ',
 9        * 'STUDENT',T35,'QUIZ GRADES',T74,'AVERAGES'/)
10  1030    FORMAT(' ',I5,T11,10I6)
11  1040    FORMAT('+',T71,F10.1)
12  1050    FORMAT('0',T2,'QUIZ')
13  1060    FORMAT(' ',T2,'AVERAGES',T11,10F6.1)
14  1070    FORMAT(//' ','THE AVERAGE OF THE STUDENT AVERAGES IS ',F6.1)
15          READ(5,1000)NQUIZ,NSTU
16          DO I=1,NSTU
17             READ(5,1010)(GRADES(I,J),J=1,NQUIZ)
18          ENDDO
19          DO I=1,NSTU
20             SUM=0.0
21             DO J=1,NQUIZ
22                SUM=SUM+GRADES(I,J)
23             ENDDO
24             STUAVG(I)=SUM/NQUIZ
25          ENDDO
26          DO J=1,NQUIZ
27             SUM=0.0
28             DO I=1,NSTU
29                SUM=SUM+GRADES(I,J)
30             ENDDO
31             QUIZAV(J)=SUM/NSTU
32          ENDDO
33          SUM=0.0
34          DO I=1,NSTU
35             SUM=SUM+STUAVG(I)
36          ENDDO
37          AVG=SUM/NSTU
38          WRITE(6,1020)
39          DO I=1,NSTU
40             WRITE(6,1030)I,(GRADES(I,J),J=1,NQUIZ)
41             WRITE(6,1040)STUAVG(I)
42          ENDDO
43          WRITE(6,1050)
44          WRITE(6,1060)(QUIZAV(I),I=1,NQUIZ)
45          WRITE(6,1070)AVG
46          STOP
47          END
```

FIGURE 13.1   *Student and class averages*

REPORT OF STUDENT AND QUIZ AVERAGES

STUDENT	QUIZ GRADES								AVERAGES
1	90	91	89	98	94	75	79	80	87.0
2	88	67	89	79	89	86	78	84	82.5
3	65	72	71	67	74	72	69	73	70.4
4	78	70	79	75	82	90	81	72	78.4
5	83	91	95	93	92	89	94	90	90.9
6	86	88	88	88	86	86	87	87	87.0
7	92	95	93	87	89	92	89	91	91.0
8	55	59	81	65	52	47	50	46	56.9
9	31	49	53	51	59	56	62	58	52.4
10	92	88	95	100	98	99	97	96	95.6
11	63	74	73	79	69	80	77	75	73.8
12	78	78	76	76	78	76	78	76	77.0
13	81	79	82	66	85	79	78	82	79.0
14	45	55	65	67	69	75	80	80	67.0
15	80	80	80	80	88	86	89	88	83.9

| QUIZ AVERAGES | 73.8 | 75.7 | 80.6 | 78.1 | 80.3 | 79.2 | 79.2 | 78.5 | |

THE AVERAGE OF THE STUDENT AVERAGES IS   78.2

FIGURE 13.1 (*cont.*)

could be manipulated with equal ease by merely changing the order of generating the subscripts. The methods can be extended to three-dimensional arrays by performing arithmetic (or whatever else is of interest) inside three loops that vary the three subscripts in an appropriate fashion.

13.3.2 Frequency Distributions

In Chapter 11, a frequency distribution was produced for a set of quiz grades. The problem involved finding the subscript that corresponded to the grade interval in which the grade should be counted and then increasing the count for that interval. The one-dimensional array FREQ was used for accumulating the counts. In this section, the problem is expanded to two and three dimensions. The methods used to solve the problem for one dimension are expected to be useful in the new problem.

Suppose we suspect that the grades on a quiz depend upon the classification of students as freshmen, sophomores, juniors, and seniors. As a first step in testing this hypothesis, we want to generate a table of grade intervals versus classification, with the entries in the table being the frequency with which grades occur. That is, a table of the following type is needed.

DISTRIBUTION OF GRADES

GRADES	FRESHMAN	SOPHOMORE	JUNIOR	SENIOR
0–9	0	0	0	0
10–19	0	0	0	0

DISTRIBUTION OF GRADES (*cont.*)

GRADES	FRESHMAN	SOPHOMORE	JUNIOR	SENIOR
20–29	0	0	0	0
30–39	0	0	0	0
40–49	1	2	0	1
50–59	2	0	3	0
60–69	2	2	1	1
70–79	7	5	6	5
80–89	4	6	8	7
90–100	3	2	4	4

The program that generates the table should work for any number of students, but we will assume that the maximum count entered in the table is 999.

In the one-dimensional frequency distribution problem, it was possible to calculate the subscript from the value of the grade, and a similar procedure can be used in this problem for determining the row corresponding to the grade. A method must be found for determining the appropriate column. This can be done by encoding the classification as

Classification	*Code*
Freshman	1
Sophomore	2
Junior	3
Senior	4

Then each card will contain a grade and the code for the classification of the student who made the grade.

On the basis of the one-dimensional problem, we know that the program has the form

```
initialize the frequency table
read a card—contains grade and classification code
WHILE (GRADE .GE. 0)
    compute the subscripts
    increase entry in frequency table
    read a card
ENDWHILE
print title and column headings
print frequency table
STOP
END
```

Thus the program (omitting FORMAT statements) is

```
INTEGER FREQ (10,4), GRADE, CLASS
DO I = 1,10
    DO J = 1,4
        FREQ (I,J) = 0
    ENDDO
ENDDO
READ (5,1000) GRADE, CLASS
WHILE (GRADE .GE. 0)
    IF (GRADE .EQ. 100) THEN
        I = 10
    ELSE
        I = GRADE/10 + 1
    ENDIF
    FREQ (I,CLASS) = FREQ (I,CLASS) + 1
    READ (5,1000) GRADE, CLASS
ENDWHILE
print title
print column headings
print FREQ
STOP
END
```

Let us make the printout of the frequency table even more useful by adding a column that contains the sum of all entries in each row and by adding a row that contains the sum of all entries in each column. (This is practically identical to the problem in Section 13.3.1.) To sum the rows, we will insert after the WHILE loop the statements

```
        .
        .
        .
DO = I = 1,10
    ISUM = 0
    DO J = 1,4
        ISUM = ISUM + FREQ(I,J)
    ENDDO
    SUMROW(I) = ISUM
ENDDO
```

The new array SUMROW will be placed in the INTEGER statement. The integer array SUMCOL will be used for storing the sum of the columns, and the following statements will be inserted to perform the summing:

```
          .
          .
          .
        DO J = 1,4
            ISUM = 0
            DO I = 1,10
                ISUM = ISUM + FREQ(I,J)
            ENDDO
            SUMCOL(J) = ISUM
        ENDDO
```

The final program is shown in Figure 13.2.

The program for a one-dimensional distribution of grades has been extended by relatively simple modifications to give a two-dimensional distribution of grades versus classification. This latter program can be extended using the same types of modifications to produce three-dimensional (or higher-dimensional) distributions. To illustrate this point, suppose that the table of grades versus classification is to be printed for men and for women. The problem now involves three variables—grades, classification, and sex—so a three-dimensional array should be used in writing the program. In general, the number of related variables will determine the dimension of the array used.

To expand the program to give a breakdown of grades by sex, the array INTEGER FREQ (2,10,4) will be used. The sex of a student will be encoded as

Sex of student	Code
Male	1
Female	2

```
 1  C
 2  C               DISTRIBUTION OF GRADES BY STUDENT CLASSIFICATION
 3  C
 4          INTEGER FREQ(10,4),GRADE,CLASS,SUMROW(10),SUMCOL(4)
 5  1000    FORMAT(I3,I2)
 6  1010    FORMAT('1',T23,'DISTRIBUTION OF GRADES')
 7  1020    FORMAT('0',' GRADE',T14,'FRESHMAN',T26,'SOPHOMORE',T39,
 8       *  'JUNIOR',T51,'SENIOR',T63,'TOTALS'/)
 9  1030    FORMAT(' ',I2,'-',I3,T16,I3,T29,I3,T40,I3,T52,I3,T64,I3)
10  1040    FORMAT('0','TOTALS',T16,I3,T29,I3,T40,I3,T52,I3)
11          DO I=1,10
12             DO J=1,4
13                FREQ(I,J)=0
14             ENDDO
15          ENDDO
16          READ(5,1000)GRADE,CLASS
17          WHILE(GRADE .GE. 0)
```

FIGURE 13.2 *Distribution of grades by student classification*

```
18          IF(GRADE .EQ. 100) THEN
19              I = 10
20          ELSE
21              I=GRADE/10+1
22          ENDIF
23          FREQ(I,CLASS)=FREQ(I,CLASS)+1
24          READ(5,1000)GRADE,CLASS
25       ENDWHILE
26       DO I=1,10
27          ISUM=0
28          DO J=1,4
29              ISUM=ISUM+FREQ(I,J)
30          ENDDO
31          SUMROW(I)=ISUM
32       ENDDO
33       DO J=1,4
34          ISUM=0
35          DO I=1,10
36              ISUM=ISUM+FREQ(I,J)
37          ENDDO
38          SUMCOL(J)=ISUM
39       ENDDO
40       WRITE(6,1010)
41       WRITE(6,1020)
42       DO I=1,10
43          L=(I-1)*10
44          M=L+9
45          IF(M .EQ. 99) THEN
46              M=M+1
47          ENDIF
48          WRITE(6,1030)L,M,(FREQ(I,J),J=1,4),SUMROW(I)
49       ENDDO
50       WRITE(6,1040)(SUMCOL(I),I=1,4)
51       STOP
52       END
```

DISTRIBUTION OF GRADES

GRADE	FRESHMAN	SOPHOMORE	JUNIOR	SENIOR	TOTALS
0- 9	0	0	0	0	0
10- 19	0	0	0	0	0
20- 29	0	0	0	0	0
30- 39	0	0	0	0	0
40- 49	1	2	0	1	4
50- 59	2	0	3	0	5
60- 69	2	2	1	1	6
70- 79	7	5	6	5	23
80- 89	4	6	8	7	25
90-100	3	2	4	4	13
TOTALS	19	17	22	18	

FIGURE 13.2   *(cont.)*

The code for the sex of a student will be punched into a card together with the student's grade and classification. Most modifications to convert the two-dimensional program to the three-dimensional case consist of using an additional subscript and embedding existing loops within another loop to manipulate the additional subscript. No changes are necessary in our basic approach to writing the program. A program for the expanded problem is given in Figure 13.3.

```
1  C
2  C           DISTRIBUTION OF GRADES BY STUDENT CLASSIFICATION AND SEX
3  C
4        INTEGER FREQ(2,10,4),GRADE,CLASS,SUMROW(2,10),SUMCOL(2,4),SEX
5  1000  FORMAT(I3,I2,I2)
6  1010  FORMAT('1',T24,'DISTRIBUTION OF GRADES')
7  1020  FORMAT('0','MALES ONLY')
8  1030  FORMAT('0','FEMALES ONLY')
9  1040  FORMAT('0',' GRADE',T14,'FRESHMAN',T26,'SOPHOMORE',T39,
10       *   'JUNIOR',T51,'SENIOR',T63,'TOTALS')
11 1050  FORMAT(' ',I2,'-',I3,T16,I3,T29,I3,T40,I3,T52,I3,T64,I3)
12 1060  FORMAT('0','TOTALS',T16,I3,T29,I3,T40,I3,T52,I3)
13       DO I=1,2
14          DO J=1,10
15             DO K=1,4
16                FREQ(I,J,K)=0
17             ENDDO
18          ENDDO
19       ENDDO
20       READ(5,1000)GRADE,CLASS,SEX
21       WHILE(GRADE .GE. 0)
22          IF(GRADE .EQ. 100) THEN
23             I =10
24          ELSE
25             I=GRADE/10+1
26          ENDIF
27          FREQ(SEX,I,CLASS)=FREQ(SEX,I,CLASS)+1
28          READ(5,1000)GRADE,CLASS,SEX
29       ENDWHILE
30       DO I=1,2
31          DO J=1,10
32             ISUM=0
33             DO K=1,4
34                ISUM=ISUM+FREQ(I,J,K)
35             ENDDO
36             SUMROW(I,J)=ISUM
37          ENDDO
38       ENDDO
39       DO I=1,2
40          DO K=1,4
41             ISUM=0
42             DO J=1,10
43                ISUM=ISUM+FREQ(I,J,K)
44             ENDDO
45             SUMCOL(I,K)=ISUM
```

FIGURE 13.3 *Distribution of grades by student classification and sex*

```
46              ENDDO
47           ENDDO
48           WRITE(6,1010)
49           DO I=1,2
50              IF(I .EQ. 1) THEN
51                 WRITE(6,1020)
52              ELSE
53                 WRITE(6,1030)
54              ENDIF
55              WRITE(6,1040)
56              DO J=1,10
57                 L=(J-1)*10
58                 M=L+9
59                 IF(M .EQ. 99) THEN
60                    M=M+1
61                 ENDIF
62                 WRITE(6,1050)L,M,(FREQ(I,J,K),K=1,4),SUMROW(I,J)
63              ENDDO
64              WRITE(6,1060)(SUMCOL(I,J),J=1,4)
65           ENDDO
66           STOP
67           END
```

DISTRIBUTION OF GRADES

MALES ONLY

GRADE	FRESHMAN	SOPHOMORE	JUNIOR	SENIOR	TOTALS
0- 9	0	0	0	0	0
10- 19	0	0	0	0	0
20- 29	0	0	0	0	0
30- 39	0	0	0	0	0
40- 49	1	2	0	1	4
50- 59	2	0	3	0	5
60- 69	0	0	0	0	0
70- 79	0	3	6	4	13
80- 89	0	0	3	7	10
90-100	3	0	0	0	3
TOTALS	6	5	12	12	

FEMALES ONLY

GRADE	FRESHMAN	SOPHOMORE	JUNIOR	SENIOR	TOTALS
0- 9	0	0	0	0	0
10- 19	0	0	0	0	0
20- 29	0	0	0	0	0
30- 39	0	0	0	0	0
40- 49	0	0	0	0	0
50- 59	0	0	0	0	0
60- 69	2	2	1	1	6
70- 79	7	2	0	1	10
80- 89	4	6	5	0	15
90-100	0	2	4	4	10
TOTALS	13	12	10	6	

FIGURE 13.3 *(cont.)*

396

OPINION ON EQUAL RIGHTS AMENDMENT

Your sex:

☐ Male   ☐ Female
1   2

Your age:

☐ 18-24   ☐ 25-30   ☐ 31-40   ☐ over 40
1   2   3   4

Your opinion:

The Equal Rights Amendment should become law.

☐ Yes   ☐ No   ☐ Undecided
1   2   3

FIGURE 13.4   *Sample questionnaire*

13.3.3   Questionnaires

Questionnaires are often used to test public opinion in such diverse areas as consumer market surveys and political candidate analysis. Designing a questionnaire so that the format does not bias the answers requires care, especially for longer questionnaires on controversial topics. Further, selecting a population of subjects to answer a questionnaire can be a complex scientific problem. Fortunately, using a computer to summarize the answers is relatively easy if the questionnaire has been designed to allow encoding the answers as integers. In that case the same techniques can be used to produce the analysis of the questionnaire as were used to produce the frequency distribution report. To illustrate the similarity of the programming techniques, a program will be written to summarize the results for the questionnaire shown in Fig. 13.4. The output desired for the program consists of the following:

1. Total responses without regard to sex:

ALL RESPONSES
XXX YES   XXX NO   XXX UNDECIDED

where the XXX represents the number of answers of that type.

2. Total responses for each sex:

ANSWERS BY MALES
XXX YES   XXX NO   XXX UNDECIDED

ANSWERS BY FEMALES
XXX YES   XXX NO   XXX UNDECIDED

3. Table of responses by age for males and females:

AGE	YES	NO	UNDECIDED
MALES			
18–24	XXX	XXX	XXX
25–30	XXX	XXX	XXX
31–40	XXX	XXX	XXX
Over 40	XXX	XXX	XXX
FEMALES			
18–24	XXX	XXX	XXX
25–30	XXX	XXX	XXX
31–40	XXX	XXX	XXX
Over 40	XXX	XXX	XXX

Below each answer in the questionnaire is a number to be used as a code for that answer—note that each code is an integer so it can be used as a subscript. The answers for a given questionnaire will be punched into the first three columns of a card. A typical card is

The value read from a card will be assigned to the variables, SEX, AGE, and OPIN, which will be explicitly declared to be integer variables. The last card in the data deck will be indicated by a code of 9 for sex and a code of 9 for age.

Within the computer program, the responses will be saved in a three-dimensional integer array SUMMRY, which is set up as

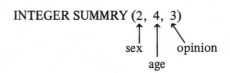

Initially, each element in SUMMRY will be given a value of zero. Then as each card is read, the values of SEX, AGE, and OPIN will be used as subscripts for SUMMRY in a

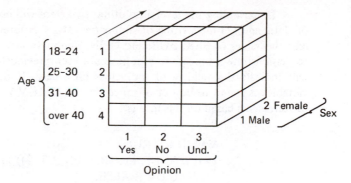

counting process, given by the statement

SUMMRY (SEX, AGE, OPIN) = SUMMRY (SEX, AGE, OPIN) +1

Thus each card will cause the value of an element in SUMMRY to increase by one. At the end of the processing of data cards, for example, a count of 504 in SUMMRY (2, 3, 1) will mean that 504 women of age 31–40 had the opinion that the equal rights amendment should become law.

During the processing of cards, the values of SEX, AGE, and OPIN should be tested to assure that each value is a legitimate value—that is, the input should be edited. Because of the design of the questionnaire, the only legitimate values are

SEX   1 and 2
AGE   1, 2, 3, and 4
OPIN   1, 2, and 3

Any other value, such as AGE = 5, is an error. As each card is read, its contents should be printed, and an additional error message should be printed on the same line if the data are incorrect.

By analogy with the frequency distribution programs, a level 1 solution for the questionnaire program is

```
initialize
read a card
WHILE (not last card)
     edit for valid data
     IF (valid) THEN
          write input data
          increase proper element in SUMMRY
     ELSE
          write input data and error message
     ENDIF
     read a card
ENDWHILE
write summaries
STOP
END
```

In expanding the level 1 solution, two steps will be troublesome: (1) the editing of data, and (2) the writing of summaries. Many different methods could be used to edit the values of SEX, AGE, and OPIN. The method actually employed was selected to demonstrate a procedure you have not seen previously. A logical variable, VALID, will indicate the validity of the values on a card. If the value of any of the three variables is found to be out of range (i.e., invalid), VALID will be set to false. A set of statements based on this idea is

```
VALID = .TRUE.
IF ((SEX .LT. 1) .OR. (SEX .GT. 2)) THEN
    VALID = .FALSE.
ELSEIF ((AGE .LT. 1) .OR. (AGE .GT. 4)) THEN
    VALID = .FALSE.
ELSEIF ((OPIN .LT. 1) .OR. (OPIN .GT. 3)) THEN
    VALID = .FALSE.
ENDIF
```

Then the subsequent IF statement and its associated statements can be written as

```
        IF (VALID) THEN
            WRITE (6, 1010) SEX, AGE, OPIN
1010        FORMAT ('b', 3I2)
            SUMMRY (SEX, AGE, OPIN) = SUMMRY (SEX, AGE, OPIN) + 1
        ELSE
            WRITE (6, 1020) SEX, AGE, OPIN
1020        FORMAT ('b', 3I2, 'bbINVALID DATA. CARD IGNORED. ')
        ENDIF
```

Writing the summaries of the data is actually a multistep process that can be done using a variety of approaches. One of the most straightforward methods is

```
compute the opinions expressed by everyone without regard to sex or age
    write the summary of all opinions
compute the opinions expressed by males without regard to age
    write the summary of opinions of males
compute the opinions expressed by females without regard to age
    write the summary of opinions of females
write the table of ages versus opinions for males
write the table of ages versus opinions for females
```

To compute the opinions expressed by everyone without regard to sex or age, we want to add all the elements corresponding to a slice of the array SUMMRY along the "opinion" axis and to store the answers in a one-dimensional array TOTALS. This can

be visualized as

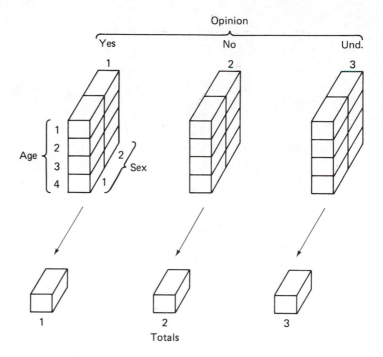

A set of DO loops that makes these computations is

```
        .
        .
        .
DO OPIN = 1,3
     ISUM = 0
     DO SEX = 1,2
          DO AGE = 1,4
               ISUM = ISUM + SUMMARY (SEX, AGE, OPIN)
          ENDDO
     ENDDO
     TOTALS (OPIN) = ISUM
ENDDO
```

Note: TOTALS will be defined as integer mode.

Computing the opinions expressed by males without regard to age is quite similar to the last calculation. We can write

```
        .
        .
        .
SEX = 1
DO OPIN = 1,3
      ISUM = 0
      DO AGE = 1,4
            ISUM = ISUM + SUMMRY (SEX, AGE, OPIN)
      ENDDO
      TOTALS (OPIN) = ISUM
ENDDO
        .
        .
        .
```

The statements for women will be like these except SEX = 2 should be used. This similarity suggests that the two calculations should be combined in a DO loop:

```
              .
              .
              .
DO SEX = 1,2
              .
              .
              .
ENDDO
              .
              .
              .
```

This revision will change the steps

```
      compute the opinions expressed by males without regard to age
            write the summary of opinions of males
      compute the opinions expressed by females without regard to age
            write the summary of opinions of females
```

to

```
DO for each sex
      compute the opinions expressed by this sex without regard to age
      write the summary of opinions for this sex
ENDDO
```

The final version is

```
DO SEX = 1,2
    DO OPIN = 1,3
        ISUM = 0
        DO AGE = 1,4
            ISUM = ISUM + SUMMRY (SEX, AGE, OPIN)
        ENDDO
        TOTALS (OPIN) = ISUM
    ENDDO
    IF (SEX .EQ. 1) THEN
        WRITE (6,1050)
1050    FORMAT ('0', 'ANSWERS BY MALES')
    ELSE
        WRITE (6,1060)
1060    FORMAT ('0', 'ANSWERS BY FEMALES')
    ENDIF
    WRITE (6,1040) (TOTALS (I), I = 1,3)
1040    FORMAT ('b', T6, I3, 1X, 'YES', 5X, I3, 1X, 'NO', 5X,
    1        I3, 1X, 'UNDECIDED')
ENDDO
    .
    .
    .
```

Notice how the nesting of DO loops determines the quantity computed.

The writing of tables of age versus opinion does not require any computation, since the tables already exist as the slices of SUMMRY having SEX = 1 and SEX = 2. A problem arises, however, in printing the lines of the tables. We were told to print in the leftmost column the identifying information

AGE

18–24
25–30
31–40
Over 40

There is no simple relationship between the ages on the different lines, so a different WRITE statement will have to be used for each line. This allows us to use a different FORMAT statement number with each WRITE statement.

The program corresponding to this discussion is given in Figure 13.5. Notice that a substantial portion of the program is devoted to input/output requirements, such as editing data, FORMAT statements, READ and WRITE statements, and IF

```
 1  C
 2  C             QUESTIONAIRE SUMMARY
 3  C
 4          INTEGER SUMMRY(2,4,3)
 5          INTEGER SEX,AGE,OPIN
 6          INTEGER TOTALS(3)
 7          LOGICAL VALID
 8  1000    FORMAT(3I1)
 9  1010    FORMAT(' ',3I2)
10  1020    FORMAT(' ',3I2,' INVALID DATA.  CARD IGNORED.')
11  1030    FORMAT('1',' SUMMARY OF EQUAL RIGHTS SURVEY'//' ',
12      *     'ALL RESPONSES')
13  1040    FORMAT(' ',T6,I3,1X,'YES',5X,I3,1X,'NO',5X,I3,1X,'UNDECIDED')
14  1050    FORMAT('0',' ANSWERS BY MALES')
15  1060    FORMAT('0',' ANSWERS BY FEMALES')
16  1070    FORMAT(///' ',' MALES'/)
17  1080    FORMAT('0',T4,'AGE',T17,'YES',T27,'NO',T32,'UNDECIDED'/)
18  1081    FORMAT(' ','  18-24',T17,I3,T26,I3,T35,I3)
19  1082    FORMAT(' ','  25-30',T17,I3,T26,I3,T35,I3)
20  1083    FORMAT(' ','  31-40',T17,I3,T26,I3,T35,I3)
21  1084    FORMAT(' ','OVER 40',T17,I3,T26,I3,T35,I3)
22  1090    FORMAT(///' ',' FEMALES'/)
23          DO I=1,2
24            DO J=1,4
25              DO K=1,3
26                SUMMRY(I,J,K)=0
27              ENDDO
28            ENDDO
29          ENDDO
30          READ(5,1000)SEX,AGE,OPIN
31          WHILE( SEX .NE. 9   .AND.   AGE .NE. 9)
32            VALID=.TRUE.
33            IF( (SEX .LT. 1) .OR. (SEX .GT. 2) ) THEN
34              VALID=.FALSE.
35            ELSEIF( (AGE .LT. 1) .OR. (AGE .GT. 4) ) THEN
36              VALID=.FALSE.
37            ELSEIF( (OPIN .LT. 1) .OR. (OPIN .GT. 3) ) THEN
38              VALID=.FALSE.
39            ENDIF
40            IF(VALID) THEN
41              WRITE(6,1010)SEX,AGE,OPIN
42              SUMMRY(SEX,AGE,OPIN)=SUMMRY(SEX,AGE,OPIN) + 1
43            ELSE
44              WRITE(6,1020)SEX,AGE,OPIN
45            ENDIF
46            READ(5,1000)SEX,AGE,OPIN
47          ENDWHILE
48  C         ALL RESPONSES
49          DO OPIN=1,3
50            ISUM=0
51            DO SEX=1,2
52              DO AGE=1,4
53                ISUM=ISUM+SUMMRY(SEX,AGE,OPIN)
54              ENDDO
55            ENDDO
56            TOTALS(OPIN)=ISUM
57          ENDDO
```

FIGURE 13.5 *Questionnaire summary*

404

```
58          WRITE(6,1030)
59          WRITE(6,1040)(TOTALS(I),I=1,3)
60 C            OPINIONS EXPRESSED BY EACH SEX
61          DO SEX=1,2
62             DO OPIN=1,3
63                ISUM=0
64                DO AGE=1,4
65                   ISUM=ISUM+SUMMRY(SEX,AGE,OPIN)
66                ENDDO
67                TOTALS(OPIN)=ISUM
68             ENDDO
69             IF(SEX .EQ. 1) THEN
70                WRITE(6,1050)
71             ELSE
72                WRITE(6,1060)
73             ENDIF
74             WRITE(6,1040)(TOTALS(I),I=1,3)
75          ENDDO
76 C            AGE VERSUS OPINION FOR EACH SEX
77          DO SEX=1,2
78             IF(SEX .EQ. 1) THEN
79                WRITE(6,1070)
80             ELSE
81                WRITE(6,1090)
82             ENDIF
83             WRITE(6,1080)
84             WRITE(6,1081)(SUMMRY(SEX,1,I),I=1,3)
85             WRITE(6,1082)(SUMMRY(SEX,2,I),I=1,3)
86             WRITE(6,1083)(SUMMRY(SEX,3,I),I=1,3)
87             WRITE(6,1084)(SUMMRY(SEX,4,I),I=1,3)
88          ENDDO
89          STOP
90          END
```

part of input data

```
1 1 1 ◄
1 1 1
1 1 1
1 1 1
1 1 2
1 1 2
1 1 5  INVALID DATA.  CARD IGNORED.
1 1 3
1 2 1
1 2 1
1 2 1
1 2 1
1 2 1
1 2 1
      .
      .
      .
1 4 2
1 4 2
```

FIGURE 13.5 *(cont.)*

```
1  4  2
1  4  3
3  4  3  INVALID DATA.  CARD IGNORED.
2  1  1
2  1  1
2  1  1
2  1  1
        .
        .
        .
2  2  2
2  2  2
2  2  2
2  2  3
2  2  3
2  3  1
2  0  1  INVALID DATA.  CARD IGNORED.
2  3  1
2  3  1
2  3  1
2  3  1
2  3  1
```

SUMMARY OF EQUAL RIGHTS SURVEY

ALL RESPONSES
      68 YES   53 NO   21 UNDECIDED

ANSWERS BY MALES
      31 YES   27 NO   11 UNDECIDED

ANSWERS BY FEMALES
      37 YES   26 NO   10 UNDECIDED

MALES

AGE	YES	NO	UNDECIDED
18-24	4	2	1
25-30	12	10	4
31-40	9	5	5
OVER 40	6	10	1

FEMALES

AGE	YES	NO	UNDECIDED
18-24	14	2	0
25-30	9	6	2
31-40	12	7	2
OVER 40	2	11	6

FIGURE 13.5   *(cont.)*

statements related to printing different headings. Many questionnaire programs share this characteristic.

13.3.4 Eight Queens Problem

In this section we consider the eight queens problem, which has attained a classic status as a problem for illustrating the need for the development of programs using stepwise refinement. It has been discussed in detail by Niklaus Wirth* and by Edsger Dijkstra,[†] and you are urged to read their outstanding presentations. A special effort is made here to follow the spirit of the solution given by Wirth, so you will find his paper of particular interest. The problem is as follows:

> Find all possible configurations of eight hostile chess queens on an 8 X 8 chessboard, such that no queen can be taken by another queen. A queen can be taken if it is on the same row, column, or diagonal as any other queen.

Another statement of the problem is:

> Find all possible configurations of eight hostile chess queens on an 8 X 8 chessboard, such that no queen is in the same row, column, or diagonal as any other queen.

There are 92 different solutions, ignoring symmetry, and we want to find them all. For illustration purposes, one solution is given below.

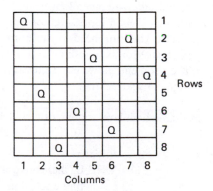

There are a variety of reasons for us to study this problem:

1. It will provide further practice in using arrays.

*Niklaus Wirth, "Program Development by Stepwise Refinement," *Communications of the ACM, 14* (April 1971), 221–227.
[†]O. J. Dahl, E. W. Dijkstra, and C. A. R. Hoare, *Structured Programming* (New York: Academic Press, Inc., 1972), pp. 72–82.

2. The problem is nonnumeric and of a type normally associated with human puzzle solving. It is important to recognize that the computer is not limited to numerical computations but can be applied to any problem that we know how to solve.

3. A brute-force attempt to solve the problem is too time consuming even for computers. Wirth has estimated that the approach of generating all possible configurations at the rate of one configuration every 100 microseconds would require 7 hours for finding a single solution. (If you could perform the same process by hand at the rate of one configuration per second, you would need 70,000 hours—approximately 8 years—to find a solution.) One of our design goals will be to find a method that is relatively fast.

4. Writing a satisfactory program for this problem is challenging. Normally, many hours (days?) are required to find a good solution and debug it. Moreover, there are many different, interesting approaches that can be discovered to solve the problem. I have been amazed by the number of different approaches my students have found.

5. This problem clearly illustrates that program length and programming difficulty are quite different. The program contains approximately the same number of statements as the longer programs we have written, but writing this program is by far the most difficult project we have undertaken to this point.

6. There is a clear distinction between what the program does and how the program works. If I were to give you the program immediately, you would have no difficulty understanding the individual statements. Thus you could decide rather quickly what the program does. Discovering why the program works would take you much longer.

7. Finding a good representation for data is often a central issue in writing programs, and this need is quite apparent in solving this problem. It will be necessary for us to refine the program and the data specifications in parallel.

8. The problem allows us to illustrate an important general programming technique—backtracking.

A suitable high-level statement of the desired program is

```
initialize
WHILE (there are possibly solutions to be found)
        find a solution
        write a solution
ENDWHILE
STOP
END
```

It is not at all clear how to express the condition for completion of the program or how to find a solution, but it seems likely that the two will be related. (In the condition it would not be fair to use the fact that there are 92 solutions—suppose that you are the first person to solve this problem and you do not know how many solutions there are!) For now we concentrate our effort on discovering a method for finding a solution.

If the program is to find solutions in a reasonable time, we must take advantage of our knowledge that the queens must be in different rows, columns, and diagonals. The approach we will adopt is to place each queen in a different column. The problem then becomes one of finding a configuration with the queens in different rows and diagonals. Wirth has estimated that this restriction alone would reduce the time to find a solution from 7 hours to 100 seconds, assuming that a configuration can be generated in 100 microseconds.

Now we must consider the problem of finding a method for placing the queens on the board. The method must satisfy the condition of allowing efficient testing for conflicts along rows and diagonals. Consider the example solution that was given at the beginning of the section. Suppose that the queen has not yet been placed in column 8, so we have

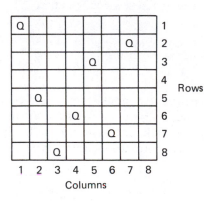

⟵— If we place the queen in column 8, we quickly find conflicts with rows 1 through 3. On placing the queen in row 4, we discover that a solution has been generated.

If the configuration had been ⟶ the solution could have been generated by adding queens to columns 7 and 8. A solution can be generated only if the configuration so far is correct. Thus we will use the approach of adding queens in sequence starting with column 1 to generate partial solutions.

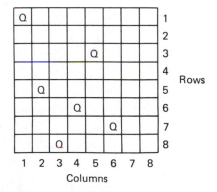

What should be done in the adding of queens if a conflict occurs? First, an attempt will be made to find another row in the same column for the queen. If no row can be found, the configuration of queens in previous columns cannot lead to a solution. So we back up to the previous column and try to find a new position for that queen. This finding of partial solutions and backing up in case of failure is much more efficient than trying to find a solution with all eight queens on the board at one time. Applying this approach gives

```
initialize for first column
WHILE (there are possibly solutions to be found)
    try a column
    IF (safe) THEN
        place queen on column
        consider next column
        IF (last column done) THEN
            write solution
            backtrack to begin hunt for a new solution
        ENDIF
    ELSE
        backtrack to hunt a new configuration
    ENDIF
ENDWHILE
STOP
END
```

Before proceeding, let us try to express the more complex, self-contained operations as subroutines. Ultimately, this should allow us to focus our attention on small parts of the program and to simplify the work. Let us rather arbitrarily assume that the following subroutines can be used to perform the indicated operation:

Subroutine	Operation
INIT	Initialize for first column
TRYCOL	Try a column
PQUEEN	Place queen on column
BTRACK	Backtrack to begin hunt for a new solution, or backtrack to hunt a new configuration

At this stage we do not know what steps should be included in any subroutine or what arguments to associate with them. These details will have to be supplied after we gain some insight into the problem. The solution can now be expressed as

```
CALL INIT
WHILE (there are possibly solutions to be found)
    CALL TRYCOL
    IF (safe) THEN
        CALL PQUEEN
        consider next column
```

```
            IF (last column done) THEN
                write solution
                CALL BTRACK
            ENDIF
        ELSE
            CALL BTRACK
        ENDIF
    ENDWHILE
    STOP
    END
```

Now let us consider lines in our current version of the program. The process of "trying a column," CALL TRYCOL, involves starting with the present square in the column and attempting to find a row that is safe. If such a row is found, the variable SAFE should be set to TRUE. "Placing a queen on a column," CALL PQUEEN, requires that the queen be assigned to a safe row. The line "consider next column" requires only that the pointer for the column be increased. A value greater than 8 for the column will mean that the last column has been done successfully and that the solution should be printed.

Three major problems remain in expanding the solution: (1) the condition for termination must be discovered, (2) a method must be found for testing a square for being safe, and (3) the backtracking method must be elucidated. In generating possible solutions, the queen is placed on column 1 in row 1. The backtracking technique will eventually march the queen down column 1 to row 8. When all appropriate configurations starting with the queen in column 1 and row 8 have been considered, the backtracking technique will decrease the column indicator from 1 to 0. This is the signal for stopping the program. In the backtracking process, it may be necessary to backtrack two columns if the first backtracking step refers to a queen that is already in row 8. This implies as a first approximation, that backtracking should be defined by

```
    SUBROUTINE BTRACK
    consider previous column (i.e., decrease column indicator)
    IF (column still on board) THEN
        reset row indicator
        remove queen
        IF (queen was in row 8) THEN
            consider previous column
            IF (column still on board) THEN
                reset row indicator
                remove queen
            ENDIF
        ENDIF
    ENDIF
    RETURN
    END
```

We cannot be more specific with the backtracking process until we decide how to represent the locations of the queens. The representation of locations will affect the procedure used for testing for a safe square.

An obvious method for representing the locations is to use an 8 by 8 array to represent the board and let a value of 0 represent an empty square and a 1, an occupied square. This representation requires unnecessary searching within a column to find an occupied square. This problem can be eliminated by using a one-dimensional array with the subscripts representing columns and the values representing rows occupied. For the sample solution, this representation can be visualized as

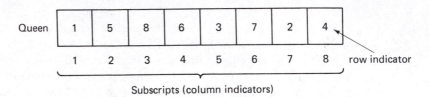

This representation can be used directly to test for conflicts along rows by means of a loop. Successive elements of QUEEN could be compared with the proposed row of the queen being added. For example, if six queens had been correctly positioned for our sample solution, an attempt to place the 7th queen in row 1 would be discovered as an error [QUEEN(1) = 1]. If row is increased to 2 for the 7th queen, comparison with QUEEN(1) through QUEEN(6) would tell us that no conflict exists. It is desirable, however, to reduce the number of comparisons, so an alternative representation will be used. Let A be a LOGICAL array of eight elements, such that

$$A(K) = .TRUE. \quad \text{implies that row K is available for placement of a queen (or a queen is not already positioned in row K)}$$

For our sample solution after the adding of six queens, elements of A are

$$A(1) = .FALSE.$$
$$A(2) = .TRUE.$$
$$A(3) = .FALSE.$$
$$A(4) = .TRUE.$$
$$A(5) = .FALSE.$$
$$A(6) = .FALSE.$$
$$A(7) = .FALSE.$$
$$A(8) = .FALSE.$$

To determine whether row 2 can be used for the 7th queen, check A(2). It is true that the row is available, so that it is a possible location for the 7th queen.

There are 15 upward-sloping diagonals. Along any of these diagonals the value of ROW + COLUMN is a constant. (This is not obvious.) The sums range from 2 through 16. There are 15 downward-sloping diagonals, and along any of them the value of ROW – COLUMN is a constant. These differences range from –7 through +7. Let us define two LOGICAL arrays, B and C, such that

> B(K) = .TRUE.   implies that the upward-sloping diagonal K is available (or a queen is not already positioned in the upward-sloping diagonal K)

and

> C(K) = .TRUE.   implies that the downward-sloping diagonal K is available (or a queen is not already positioned in the downward diagonal K)

Then the test for a safe square is

$$\text{SAFE} = \text{A(ROW) .AND. B(ROW + COLUMN) .AND. C(ROW – COLUMN)}$$

It will be necessary, of course, to initialize these arrays and modify their contents when a queen is placed on the board or removed. This statement for SAFE can be used without modification by indicating the bounds for the arrays B and C as

$$\text{DIMENSION B}(2:16), \text{C}(-7:7)$$

Assuming that the available compiler does not allow bounds specification for subscripts, SAFE can be written as

$$\text{SAFE} = \text{A(ROW) + B(ROW + COLUMN – 1) + C(ROW – COLUMN + 8)}$$

Note: ROW + COLUMN – 1   (range: 1 through 15)
            ROW – COLUMN + 8   (range: 1 through 15)

(All variables in the program will be defined as integer mode.) Using these ideas, the definitions for "try a column" and "backtrack" can be expressed precisely as

```
C    TRY A COLUMN
     SUBROUTINE TRYCOL(ROW,COLUMN,A,B,C,SAFE)
     INTEGER ROW,COLUMN
     LOGICAL A(8),B(15),C(15),SAFE
     SAFE = .FALSE.
```

```
                  WHILE (.NOT. SAFE .AND. ROW .LT. 8)
                     ROW = ROW + 1
                     SAFE = A(ROW) .AND. B(ROW+COLUMN-1) .AND.
                                                    C(ROW-COLUMN+8)
                  ENDWHILE
                  RETURN
                  END


C     BACKTRACK
                  SUBROUTINE BTRACK (ROW,COLUMN,A,B,C,QUEEN)
                  INTEGER ROW,COLUMN,QUEEN(8)
                  LOGICAL A(8), B(15), C(15)
                  COLUMN = COLUMN - 1
                  IF (COLUMN .GE. 1) THEN
C                    REMOVE QUEEN
                     ROW = QUEEN (COLUMN)
                     A(ROW) = .TRUE.
                     B(ROW+COLUMN-1) = .TRUE.
                     C(ROW-COLUMN+8) = .TRUE.
C                       IS MORE BACKTRACKING NECESSARY
                     IF (ROW .EQ. 8) THEN
C                       MORE BACKTRACKING
                        COLUMN = COLUMN - 1
                        IF (COLUMN .GE. 1) THEN
C                          REMOVE QUEEN
                           ROW = QUEEN (COLUMN)
                           A(ROW) = .TRUE.
                           B(ROW+COLUMN-1) = .TRUE.
                           C(ROW-COLUMN+8) = .TRUE.
                        ENDIF
                     ENDIF
                  ENDIF
                  RETURN
                  END
```

The final solution for the eight queens problem is given in Figure 13.6. (*Note:* The IMPLICIT statement, which is used instead of INTEGER, is discussed in Section 14.5.5.) Another solution is given in Figure 13.7. This solution was produced by a student several years ago using a FORTRAN compiler that allowed only arithmetic IF statements and did not allow LOGICAL variables. The program satisfied very well its design goal of rapid execution, and I was pleased when it was submitted to me. Now I think that it is an excellent example of a program that is very difficult to understand. Study the program to see if you can understand it.

```
 1  C
 2  C              EIGHT QUEENS
 3  C
 4         IMPLICIT INTEGER(A-Z)
 5         DIMENSION QUEEN(8)
 6         LOGICAL A(8),B(15),C(15),SAFE
 7  1000   FORMAT('0',8I4)
 8  C              INITIALIZE
 9         CALL INIT(ROW,COLUMN,A,B,C)
10         WHILE(COLUMN .GE. 1)
11  C            TRY COLUMN
12            CALL TRYCOL(ROW,COLUMN,A,B,C,SAFE)
13            IF(SAFE) THEN
14  C            PLACE QUEEN
15              CALL PQUEEN(ROW,COLUMN,A,B,C,QUEEN)
16  C                CONSIDER NEXT COLUMN
17                COLUMN=COLUMN+1
18                ROW=0
19  C                IS THIS A SOLUTION
20                IF(COLUMN .GT. 8) THEN
21  C                   A SOLUTION HAS BEEN FOUND
22                    WRITE(6,1000)QUEEN
23  C                   BACKTRACK
24                    CALL BTRACK(ROW,COLUMN,A,B,C,QUEEN)
25                ENDIF
26            ELSE
27  C            NO SAFE ROW COULD BE FOUND, SO BACKTRACK
28                CALL BTRACK(ROW,COLUMN,A,B,C,QUEEN)
29            ENDIF
30         ENDWHILE
31         STOP
32         END

33         SUBROUTINE INIT(ROW,COLUMN,A,B,C)
34         IMPLICIT INTEGER(A-Z)
35         LOGICAL A(8),B(15),C(15)
36         DO I=1,8
37            A(I)=.TRUE.
38         ENDDO
39         DO I=1,15
40            B(I)=.TRUE.
41            C(I)=.TRUE.
42         ENDDO
43         COLUMN=1
44         ROW=0
45         RETURN
46         END

47         SUBROUTINE TRYCOL(ROW,COLUMN,A,B,C,SAFE)
48         IMPLICIT INTEGER(A-Z)
49         LOGICAL A(8),B(15),C(15),SAFE
50         SAFE=.FALSE.
51         WHILE( .NOT.SAFE .AND. ROW .LT. 8)
52            ROW=ROW+1
53            SAFE=A(ROW).AND.B(ROW+COLUMN-1).AND.C(ROW-COLUMN+8)
```

FIGURE 13.6 *Eight queens problem*

```
54          ENDWHILE
55          RETURN
56          END

57          SUBROUTINE PQUEEN(ROW,COLUMN,A,B,C,QUEEN)
58          IMPLICIT INTEGER(A-Z)
59          DIMENSION QUEEN(8)
60          LOGICAL A(8),B(15),C(15)
61          A(ROW)=.FALSE.
62          B(ROW+COLUMN-1)=.FALSE.
63          C(ROW-COLUMN+8)=.FALSE.
64          QUEEN(COLUMN)=ROW
65          RETURN
66          END
67          SUBROUTINE BTRACK(ROW,COLUMN,A,B,C,QUEEN)
68          IMPLICIT INTEGER(A-Z)
69          DIMENSION QUEEN(8)
70          LOGICAL A(8),B(15),C(15)
71          COLUMN=COLUMN-1
72          IF(COLUMN .GE. 1)THEN
73 C                          REMOVE QUEEN
74            ROW=QUEEN(COLUMN)
75            A(ROW)=.TRUE.
76            B(ROW+COLUMN-1)=.TRUE.
77            C(ROW-COLUMN+8)=.TRUE.
78 C                          IS MORE BACKTRACKING NECESSARY
79            IF(ROW .EQ. 8)THEN
80 C                          MORE BACKTRACKING
81                COLUMN=COLUMN-1
82                IF(COLUMN .GE. 1)THEN
83 C                              REMOVE QUEEN
84                  ROW=QUEEN(COLUMN)
85                  A(ROW)=.TRUE.
86                  B(ROW+COLUMN-1)=.TRUE.
87                  C(ROW-COLUMN+8)=.TRUE.
88                ENDIF
89            ENDIF
90          ENDIF
91          RETURN
92          END
```

1	5	8	6	3	7	2	4
1	6	8	3	7	4	2	5
1	7	4	6	8	2	5	3
1	7	5	8	2	4	6	3
2	4	6	8	3	1	7	5
2	5	7	1	3	8	6	4
2	5	7	4	1	8	6	3
2	6	1	7	4	8	3	5

FIGURE 13.6 *(cont.)*

```
2   6   8   3   1   4   7   5

2   7   3   6   8   5   1   4

2   7   5   8   1   4   6   3

2   8   6   1   3   5   7   4

3   1   7   5   8   2   4   6

3   5   2   8   1   7   4   6

3   5   2   8   6   4   7   1
.                           .
.                           .
.                           .
7   4   2   8   6   1   3   5

7   5   3   1   6   8   2   4

8   2   4   1   7   5   3   6

8   2   5   3   1   7   4   6

8   3   1   6   2   5   7   4

8   4   1   3   6   2   7   5
```

FIGURE 13.6   (*cont.*)

```
 1  C
 2  C              EIGHT QUEENS
 3  C
 4         INTEGER Q(8)
 5  20     FORMAT('0',8I3)
 6         DO 18 L=1,8
 7         S=0
 8         Q(1)=L
 9         DO 9 I=2,8
10  1      N=I-1
11         DO 81 M=1,9
12         Q(I)=M
13  11     IF(Q(I)-9)2,15,15
14  2      DO 3 J=1,N
15         IF(Q(I)-Q(J))3,8,3
16  3      CONTINUE
17         DO 7 K=1,N
18         IF(Q(I)+I-Q(K)-K)5,8,5
19  5      IF(Q(I)-I-Q(K)+K)7,8,7
20  7      CONTINUE
21         GO TO 9
22  8      IF(S-1)81,31,81
23  31     Q(I)=Q(I)+1
24         GO TO 11
```

FIGURE 13.7   *Eight queens problem: Alternative solution*

```
25 81      CONTINUE
26         IF(S-1)9,21,9
27 21      I=I+1
28         GO TO 1
29 9       CONTINUE
30         WRITE(6,20)Q
31 15      Q(I-1)=Q(I-1)+1
32         IF(Q(2)-8)16,17,17
33 16      I=I-1
34         IF(I-1)18,18,161
35 161     N=I-1
36         S=1
37         GO TO 11
38 17      IF(Q(3)-6)16,171,16
39 171     IF(Q(4)-2)16,18,16
40 18      CONTINUE
41         STOP
42         END
```

```
1  5  8  6  3  7  2  4

1  6  8  3  7  4  2  5

1  7  4  6  8  2  5  3

1  7  5  8  2  4  6  3

2  4  6  8  3  1  7  5
.                    .
.                    .
.                    .
7  4  2  8  6  1  3  5

7  5  3  1  6  8  2  4

8  2  4  1  7  5  3  6

8  2  5  3  1  7  4  6

8  3  1  6  2  5  7  4

8  4  1  3  6  2  7  5
```

FIGURE 13.7 (*cont.*)

REVIEW QUESTIONS

1. What is a multidimensional array? What are some convenient ways of visualizing two- and three-dimensional arrays?

2. What is the significance of the order of subscripts in referencing an array?

3. How does a programmer declare an array to be multidimensional?

4. What are nested implied DO loops? How are they used for the input and output of multidimensional arrays?

5. Give the syntax of nested implied DO statements.

6. In nested implied DO loops, which subscripts change most rapidly?

7. Explain the technique of backtracking.

1. Given:

DIMENSION X(100),LIST(150),GROUP(50,10),GRADES(150)

   (A) The statement will be rejected by the compiler.
   (B) The variable having the smallest number of values is GRADES.
   (C) The variable having the largest number of values is GROUP.
   (D) The variables LIST and GRADES will ordinarily use the same number of memory cells.
   (E) The order in which the variables appear in DIMENSION is important.

2. Which of the following DIMENSION statements will reserve exactly 200 integer storage locations? (A) DIMENSION IRAY(100,100); (B) DIMENSION ARAY (10,20); (C) DIMENSION IRAY(100,2); (D) DIMENSION ARRAY(100,100); (E) both (B) and (C).

3. The listed array that could store the largest number of values is (A) X(500), (B) MASS(200,50), (C) Y(5,200), (D) X(50,50), (E) Z(10,10,10).

4. The following table represents the two-dimensional array named IJK, which is dimensioned 4 by 3:

$$
\begin{array}{ccc}
1 & 2 & 3 \\
4 & 5 & 6 \\
7 & 8 & 9 \\
10 & 11 & 12
\end{array}
$$

   The element denoted by IJK(3,2) is (A), 2 (B) 6, (C) 8, (D) 11, (E) none of the previous answers.

5. An example of a statement containing a syntax error is:
   (A) READ(5,5)X(10,2)
   (B) READ(5,5) (X(K,L),L=1,10)
   (C) READ(5,5) (X(I,J),I=1,5)
   (D) READ(5,5) ((X(II,I)H=1,5),I=1,10)
   (E) two of the previous answers

6. Given:

DO I = 1,50
   READ(5,20)X(I),Y(I)
ENDDO

   A statement that will produce the same result is: (A) READ(5,20) (X(J),Y(J), J=1,50); (B) READ(5,20)(X)(I),I=1,50),(Y(I),I=1,50); (C) READ(5,20) (X(I), Y(I),I=1,100); (D) READ(5,20) (X(J),J=1,50) and READ(5,20) (Y(J),J=1,50); (E) READ(5,20)X(1),Y(1),X(50),Y(50).

7. The number of times the statement READ(5,6) ((VAR(L,M),L=1,5),M=1,10) is executed in order to read 50 values is: (A) none, it contains an error; (B) 1; (C) 10; (D) 50; (E) undetermined because of the lack of knowledge of the FORMAT statement.

8. An example of reading data by *rows* is:
   (A) READ(5,5) ((X(J,I), I=1,10),J=1,10)   (B) READ(5,5) (X(J,I),J=1,15)

(C) DIMENSION Y(10,5)
    READ (5,10)Y
(E) Two of the previous answers

(D) DO I=1,15
    READ(5,5)X(I,J)
ENDDO

9. An example of a valid statement that would cause an array, DIMENSION X(5,10) to be printed in *column* order is
(A) WRITE (6,5)X(I,J)
(B) WRITE (6,5) ((X(I,J),J=1,5),I=1,10)
(C) WRITE (6,5) ((X(J,I),J=1,10),I=1,5)
(D) WRITE (6,5) ((X(I,J),I=1,5),J=1,10)
(E) WRITE (6,5) ((X(I,J),J=1,10),I=1,5)

10. Given:

$$
\begin{array}{l}
\text{DO I = 1,5} \\
\quad \text{DO J = 1,5} \\
\quad\quad \text{READ(5,10)A(I,J)} \\
10 \quad\quad \text{FORMAT(5F10.0)} \\
\quad \text{ENDDO} \\
\text{ENDDO}
\end{array}
$$

The number of values that is read is (A) 5, (B) 10, (C) 25, (D) 50, (E) 75.

11. The statements:

$$
\begin{array}{l}
\text{DIMENSION X(10,10)} \\
\text{AVGX = 0.0} \\
\text{J = 2} \\
\text{DO I=1,10} \\
\quad \text{AVGX = AVGX + X(I,J)} \\
\text{ENDDO}
\end{array}
$$

(A) will take the sum of the second row; (B) illustrate an invalid DO loop; (C) are invalid once J must be allowed to vary; (D) will take the sum of the second column; (E) will result in 20 elements being added.

12. The statement ANS(I)=X(I,J)*Y(J,I) (A) is valid; (B) requires only two arrays to be dimensioned; (C) is invalid due to confusion in the use of the subscripts; (D) is invalid because two-dimensional arrays cannot be used in assignment statements; (E) none of the previous answers.

13. A three-dimensional array, X, having 60 elements has three rows and five columns. In a DIMENSION statement X will appear as (A) X(4,3,5), (B) X(60), (C) X(5,4,5), (D) X(3,5,60), (E) X(3,5,3).

14. The statements

$$
\begin{array}{l}
\text{DIMENSION NCELL(3,5)} \\
\quad . \\
\quad . \\
\quad . \\
\text{WRITE (6,15) ((NCELL(I,J),J=1,5),I=1,3)} \\
15 \text{ FORMAT (' ', 5I7)}
\end{array}
$$

(A) will write a table of three rows and five columns; (B) will write a table with the rows written vertically on the page; (C) will write a table of five rows and three columns; (D) will cause a printing error; (E) have invalid syntax.

15. Given:

```
N=5
DO I=2,N
    WHAT(I)=5*I
ENDDO
```

The value assigned to WHAT(4) is (A) 5, (B) 10, (C) 15, (D) 20, (E) 25.

16. Given:

```
DIMENSION NUMBER(4,5)
K=1
DO N=1,4
   DO J=1,5
       NUMBER(N,J)=K
       K=K+2
   ENDDO
ENDDO
```

The value assigned to NUMBER(2,3) is (A) 1, (B) 5, (C) 15, (D) 21, (E) 23.

EXERCISES

1. Give an appropriate declaration statement for each of the following:
   a. A 10 by 10 array called NEXT.
   b. A real array to hold grades for 50 students for 3 quizzes.
   c. An array MATRIX having 10 rows and 200 elements.
   d. A square array having 121 elements.
   e. An integer array IARRAY having 4 pages, 12 rows, and 10 columns.
   f. A real array JARRAY having 5 pages, 4 rows, and 8 columns.
   g. A two-dimensional integer array suitable for recording moves in a game of tic-tac-toe.

2. Give statements to assign to X the following:
   a. The sum of 5 and the element of Y in row 3, column 6.
   b. The element of GRADE in row 4, column I.
   c. The sum of GRADES(3,2) and the element of GRADE in row I, column J+1.
   d. The difference in the element of TABLE in row I, column J and the element of TABLE in the same row and next column.
   e. The element of TABLE that is on the diagonal in row 3.

3. Give program segments to perform the following:
   a. Read all the elements of TABLE, a 5 X 10 array.
   b. Print all the elements of the 10 X 6 array X by rows.
   c. Print all the elements of the 10 X 6 array X by columns.
   d. Print the N elements of the Mth row of array X.
   e. Find the largest element in the 5 X 5 X 5 array TOTAL.
   f. Find the largest element in the L X M X N array GROUP.
   g. Add the elements of the 3rd row of array Y.

h. Add the elements of the 3rd column of array Y.
i. Add the elements of the downward-sloping diagonal of the 8×8 array CALC.
j. Add the elements of the upward-sloping diagonal of the 8×8 array CALC.
k. Add all the elements of the 8×8 array CALC.
l. Replace the elements in the 3rd row of the 10×10 array CALC by the square of the corresponding element.
m. Replace the elements of row 1 of the 8×9 array SCORE by the product of an element and the corresponding element of row 6.

4. Answer the following:

a. How many lines are printed by

```
          DO I = 1,10
              DO J = 1,5
                  WRITE (6,10) X(I,J)
       10         FORMAT (' ', 5F10.1)
              ENDDO
          ENDDO
```

b. How many lines are printed by

```
          DO I = 1,10
              WRITE (6,10) (X(I,J), J = 1,5)
       10     FORMAT (' ', 5F10.1)
          ENDDO
```

c. How many lines are printed by

```
          WRITE (6,10) ((X(I,J), J= 1,5), I = 1,10)
       10 FORMAT (' ', 10F10.1)
```

d. After the execution of the following, what value is stored in X(2,7)?

```
          DO I = 1,10
              DO J = 1,10
                  X(I,J) = I+J
              ENDDO
          ENDDO
```

e. In part (d), how many times is the statement X(I,J) = I+J executed?
f. After execution of the following, what values are stored in X(4,4) and X(4,5)?

```
          DO I = 1,5
              DO J = 1,10
                  X(I,J) = 0.0
              ENDDO
```

```
ENDDO
DO I = 1,5
    X(I,I+1) = I**2
ENDDO
```

PROGRAMMING EXERCISES

1. A group of 15 students take eight quizzes during an academic term. Read the grades into a two-dimensional array, GRADES. Then for each quiz, determine the maximum and minimum grades, saving them in arrays GMAX and GMIN, respectively. Print the grades in the form of a table with each row corresponding to a student's grades and each column corresponding to a quiz. At the bottom of the table, print the maximum grades under the corresponding columns. Finally, print the minimum grades under the corresponding columns. Use the data printed in Section 13.1 for input.

2. For the student quiz data of Figure 13.1, write a program that prints the ID number of the student who made the highest grade on each of the quizzes. Use a two-dimensional array for the input data.

3. Write a program that prints a multiplication table. Print suitable row and column identifications to make it easy for children to use the table.

4. Modify the multiplication table program developed for problem 3 so that it will print either a multiplication or addition table upon request. Make it possible for the program to print different-size tables.

5. Multiplication of matrix A by matrix B to give matrix C is defined by the statement

$$C_{IJ} = \sum_{K=1}^{L} A_{IK} B_{KJ}$$

Write a program that multiplies two matrices.

6. The trace of a matrix is the sum of the elements along the diagonal.

$$trace(A) = \sum_{I=1}^{N} A_{II}$$

Write a program which demonstrates that

$$trace(A)*trace(B) = trace(B)*trace(A)$$

7. Write a program that tests an array for symmetry about the diagonal.

8. Flunkout University has the reputation of being one of the most academically demanding institutions in the country. In fact, rumor has it that only geniuses can graduate. To test this statement, use the computer to prepare and print a distribution table of the following type.

FLUNKOUT UNIVERSITY
DISTRIBUTION TABLE FOR IQ AND GPA

IQ	GRADE–POINT AVERAGE						
	LESS THAN 1.00	1.00–1.49	1.50–1.99	2.00–2.49	2.50–2.99	3.00–3.49	3.50–4.00
GREATER THAN 159.							
150.–159.							
140.–149.							
130.–139.							
120.–129.							
110.–119.							
100.–109.							
90.–99.							
LESS THAN 90.							

Use the following data to test your program, or if you don't care too much for statistical rigor, make up your own data.

IQ	GPA	IQ	GPA	IQ	GPA
104	1.99	126	2.21	115	1.95
110	2.07	121	2.07	160	2.50
173	3.97	132	3.06	101	2.11
162	2.13	127	2.51	125	3.06
97	3.98	123	2.11	111	2.98
135	2.61	145	3.01	99	2.01
140	3.00	109	1.98	142	3.41
101	0.97	112	2.06	118	3.11
144	0.88	124	2.31	108	2.25
184	2.66	130	1.92	136	1.52
181	3.76	117	2.63	177	3.02

9. Read the IQ and GPA data of Programming Exercise 8 into a two-dimensional array. Sort the GPA data into descending sequence and print these values each with its corresponding IQ value.

10. A magic square is a square array in which the sums of the elements in any given row, the elements in any given column, and the elements in a diagonal are all equal. For example, the following is a magic square:

Sum of rows

									Sum of rows
5	46	15	56	25	66	35	76	45	369
54	14	55	24	65	34	75	44	4	369
13	63	23	64	33	74	43	3	53	369
62	22	72	32	73	42	2	52	12	369
21	71	31	81	41	1	51	11	61	369
70	30	80	40	9	50	10	60	20	369
29	79	39	8	49	18	59	19	69	369
78	38	7	48	17	58	27	68	28	369
37	6	47	16	57	26	67	36	77	369

369 369 369 369 369 369 369 369 369

Sum of Columns

Diagonal 369   Diagonal 369

Write a program that tests a square array for being a magic square. Be sure to use test data for both valid and invalid magic squares.

11. Write a program that generates magic squares. If you cannot develop your own algorithm, or if the topic particularly interests you, consult *Game Playing with Computers*, by D. D. Spencer, in which a variety of methods are presented.

12. The results of the democratic primary race for city manager are reported by precinct, with one input card per precinct. Typical data are:

	Candidate			
Precinct	*1*	*2*	*3*	*4*
1	209	51	395	28
2	127	96	401	42
3	194	98	117	41
4	119	18	303	26
5	245	21	204	25

Using subscripted variables, write a program to do the following:

a. Read the cards and print out the table with appropriate headings for the rows and columns.

b. Compute and print the total number of votes received by each candidate and the percentage of the total votes cast.

c. If any one candidate received over 50% of the votes, the program should print a message declaring that candidate the winner.

d. If no candidate received over 50% of the votes, the program should print a message declaring a runoff between the two candidates receiving the largest number of votes; the two candidates should be identified by their number.

The card format is:

Column 1	Precinct number
Columns 3–5	Candidate 1's votes
Columns 7–9	Candidate 2's votes
Columns 11–13	Candidate 3's votes
Columns 15–17	Candidate 4's votes

The number of precincts is always exactly five. Assume for simplicity that there are four candidates.

13. The output of the eight queens program, Figure 13.6, is not satisfactory for visualizing the solutions. Modify the program so that instead of printing solutions in the form

$$1 \quad 5 \quad 8 \quad 6 \quad 3 \quad 7 \quad 2 \quad 4$$

a two-dimensional array is printed with 1's in the position of the queens. The solution above would become

$$
\begin{array}{cccccccc}
1 & 0 & 0 & 0 & 0 & 0 & 0 & 0 \\
0 & 0 & 0 & 0 & 0 & 0 & 1 & 0 \\
0 & 0 & 0 & 0 & 1 & 0 & 0 & 0 \\
0 & 0 & 0 & 0 & 0 & 0 & 0 & 1 \\
0 & 1 & 0 & 0 & 0 & 0 & 0 & 0 \\
0 & 0 & 0 & 1 & 0 & 0 & 0 & 0 \\
0 & 0 & 0 & 0 & 0 & 1 & 0 & 0 \\
0 & 0 & 1 & 0 & 0 & 0 & 0 & 0 \\
\end{array}
$$

14. To save paper and make the solution to the eight queens problem even more readable (to some people), revise the program of Programming Exercise 13 to print several solutions across a page. Get as many solutions as possible on a page without losing readability.

CHAPTER 14

CHARACTER MANIPULATION

FORTRAN was designed to solve mathematical problems, and the features available within the language meet the design goal very well. Features are also available for manipulating alphabetic characters, but the features are not as convenient to use as those in languages that were designed for manipulating characters. FORTRAN requires us to think about the character-manipulation process in greater detail than we ordinarily use in our everyday lives. The situation is somewhat analogous to that of doing arithmetic in an assembly language instead of FORTRAN. Performing the calculation

$$X = (2.5*A+B**2-C)/D$$

is much easier in FORTRAN than in assembly language because it is not necessary to think about the details of the calculation.

It may help you in understanding the material presented in this chapter to recognize now that all information is stored within the computer in an encoded form. We have already seen that 1 is stored differently depending upon whether it is an integer-mode value or a real-mode value. Computers use a third type of code for information that is to be stored as characters. Typically, this code uses 8 bits to represent a character, so that the code allows 256 different characters to be encoded ($2^8 = 256$). Specific members of this set of codes have been assigned to members of the alphabet (A, B, . . . , Z), the digits (0, 1, . . . , 9), and various special characters such as comma, period, plus, dollar sign, and blank. All these characters are collectively called *alphabetic* (or alphanumeric, or alphameric) *characters*.

14.1 DECLARATION OF CHARACTER VARIABLES

The CHARACTER statement is a declaration statement, and as such, it must appear before any executable statement in the program. Any variable named in a CHARACTER statement will be considered to have a value consisting of a string of characters. The form of the statement is

CHARACTER*n list of variables

where n is the number of characters associated with each variable named in the list of variables

The statement

$$CHARACTER*10 \ IX, IY, IZ$$

declares IX, IY, and IZ to each consist of 10 characters. Other valid examples are

CHARACTER*4 X

CHARACTER*80 INFIX, POLISH

CHARACTER*20 LIST

CHARACTER*132 LINE, BUFFER

CHARACTER*6 A,B,C

Arrays can also be declared to be **CHARACTER** variables. For example, the statement

$$CHARACTER*5 \ MORSE(26)$$

declares an array, MORSE, of 26 elements with each element consisting of five characters. The statement

$$CHARACTER*20 \ ITEMP, NAMES(300)$$

declares two variables: ITEMP, which consists of 20 characters; and NAMES, which consists of 300 values of 20 characters each.

14.2   INPUT/OUTPUT OF CHARACTER VARIABLES

The rules for the input/output for character variables are almost identical to those for integers—the primary difference is the specification used in the FORMAT statement. The form of the specification is

character specification: A

where the number of characters to be input or output; that is, the field width, is determined by the number of characters declared in the CHARACTER statement;
a repetition parameter can precede the specification
Consider the following examples:

1.   CHARACTER*1 NEXT
      .
      .
      .
      READ (5,1000) NEXT
1000 FORMAT(A)

Reads 1 character as the value of NEXT.

2.   CHARACTER*25 X

            .

            .

            .

       READ (5,1010) X
1010 FORMAT(A)

Reads 25 consecutive characters as the value of X.

3.   CHARACTER*20 KARD

            .

            .

            .

       WRITE (6,1020) KARD
1020 FORMAT('1',A)

Prints the 20 characters associated with KARD (the value of KARD) at the top of a new page.

4.   CHARACTER*3 IX,IY

            .

            .

            .

       WRITE (6,1030), IX,IY
1030 FORMAT ('b',A,2X,A)

Prints the 3 characters associated with IX at the left side of a line, skips two spaces, and then prints the 3 characters associated with IY.

5.   CHARACTER*80 CARD

            .

            .

            .

       READ (5,1040) CARD
1040 FORMAT(A)

Reads all 80 columns of a card as the value of CARD.

The input/output of character variable arrays is also similar to that of integer arrays, and implied DO-loops can be used.

6.   CHARACTER*1 CARD(80)

            .

            .

            .

       READ (5,1050) CARD
1050 FORMAT(80A)

Reads 80 characters. Each character read is assigned as the value of an element of CARD. Notice the use of the 80A specification.

7.   CHARACTER∗1 CARD(80)

       .
       .
       .

       READ (5,1060) (CARD(I), I = 1,80)
1060 FORMAT(80A)

Reads 80 characters and has the same effect as the statements in example 6.

8.   CHARACTER∗20 NAMES(300)

       .
       .
       .

       READ (5,1070) (NAMES(I), I = 1,N)
1070 FORMAT(A)
       WRITE (6,1080)(NAMES(I), I = 1,N)
1080 FORMAT('b',A)

Reads N names, each consisting of 20 characters, one name per card. After the N names have been read, they are all printed.

14.3   ASSIGNMENT STATEMENTS INVOLVING CHARACTER VARIABLES

The manipulation of character variables in FORTRAN resembles in many ways the manipulation of integers. Suppose that we wish to assign the character A to the character variable IALPH. The obvious (and natural) method is to enclose the character in apostrophes and place it on the right of an equals sign in an assignment statement as

$$IALPH = \text{'A'}$$

In this legitimate statement the 'A' is called a *character constant*.

Consider the declaration statements

CHARACTER∗1 IP, IM

CHARACTER∗7 WORD

Then the following are legitimate assignment statements:

IP = '+'

IM = '−'   A character constant must be enclosed in apostrophes.

WORD = 'EXAMPLE'

Within a program an assignment statement can be used to fill the output line with blanks:

CHARACTER*1 LINE(132)

.

.

.

DO I = 1,132
    LINE(I) = 'b'
ENDDO

.

.

.

A character variable may be used on the right of an equals sign in an assignment statement. Given

CHARACTER*1 JX,JY

the following are valid:

IX = 'A'

IY = IX

IY is assigned the value of IX, that is, "A."
    If the declaration statement is

CHARACTER*20 ITEMP, NAMES(300)

the statement

ITEMP = NAMES(I)

assigns the 20 characters of the Ith element of NAMES to ITEMP, and

NAMES(I) = NAMES(LOC)

assigns the 20 characters of the LOCth position of NAMES to the Ith position of NAMES.
    If an assignment is made involving character variables of different lengths, the assigned string of characters is either truncated on the right or padded on the right with blanks, as appropriate. For

CHARACTER*4 SHORT

CHARACTER*7 WORD

the statements

$$WORD = \text{'EXAMPLE'}$$

$$SHORT = WORD$$

give the value of 'EXAM' for SHORT—extra characters are eliminated on the right. The statements

$$SHORT = \text{'EXAM'}$$

$$WORD = SHORT$$

will give a value of 'EXAMbbb' for WORD—extra blanks are added on the right.

14.4 COMPARISON OF CHARACTER VARIABLES

The codes for alphanumeric characters have been designed to have numerical values that correspond with our normal ideas of alphabetic order. The character "A" appears before other alphabetic characters, and thus the code for "A" is numerically smaller than the codes for the characters "B" through "Z." For example, if the following assignments are made

$$MP = \text{'A'}$$

$$MQ = \text{'C'}$$

$$MR = \text{'X'}$$

$$MS = \text{'C'}$$

$$MT = \text{'V'}$$

the following logical expressions will evaluate as indicated:

(MP .LT. 'C')	TRUE	since "A" < "C"
(MP .LT. 'X')	TRUE	since "A" < "X"
(MP .LT. 'V')	TRUE	since "A" < "V"
(MP .EQ. 'C')	FALSE	since "A" ≠ "C"
(MS .GT. MP)	TRUE	since "C" > "A"
(MS .GT. MT)	FALSE	since "C" < "V"
(MQ .GE. MS)	TRUE	since "C" = "C"
(MQ .EQ. MS)	TRUE	since "C" = "C"

Any of these logical expressions, or any other logical expression in which the variables refer to character codes, can be used as a condition in an IF statement or WHILE statement.

Consider the following program for locating the first blank in a string of characters:

```
      CHARACTER*1 CARD(80)
1000  FORMAT (80A)
1010  FORMAT (' ', 'IN THE STRING ', 80A/' ', 'THE FIRST BLANK IS '
     1       'FOUND IN POSITION', I3)
      READ (5,1000) CARD
      LOC = 0
      I = 1
      WHILE (LOC .EQ. 0 .AND. I .LE. 80)
          IF (CARD(I) .EQ. ' ') THEN
              LOC = I
          ELSE
              I = I+1
          ENDIF
      ENDWHILE
      WRITE (6,1010) CARD,LOC
      STOP
      END
```

Within the WHILE loop, the individual characters of the array CARD are compared with the value of a blank in the IF statement

```
      IF (CARD(I) .EQ. ' ') THEN
          .
          .
          .
      ENDIF
```

The condition will be TRUE only when CARD(I) contains the code for a blank. If the input card is

```
TO BE OR NOT TO BE
```

the condition is TRUE when CARD(3) is tested. Notice how similar the program is to one that would be used to scan an array for the occurrence of a particular numerical value.

A program to locate the last nonblank character in the string can be obtained by making simple changes to the previous program. Instead of scanning the string from left to right, the scan will go from right to left and will stop as soon as a non-blank character is encountered. The program is

```
        CHARACTER*1 CARD(80)
1000    FORMAT (80A)
1010    FORMAT (' ', 'IN THE STRING ', 80A/' ', 'THE LAST NON-BLANK',
   1         ' IS FOUND IN POSITION', I3)
        READ (5,1000) CARD
        LOC = 0
        I = 80
        WHILE (LOC .EQ. 0 .AND. I .GE. 1)
            IF (CARD(I) .EQ. ' ') THEN
                I = I-1
            ELSE
                LOC = I
            ENDIF
        ENDWHILE
        WRITE (6,1010) CARD, LOC
        STOP
        END
```

In both these programs, the IF statement is used in a manner that is analogous to its use in earlier programs. In general, the rules and techniques presented in previous chapters are valid for the manipulating of characters.

The ability to compare the values of character variables is a more powerful tool than these examples indicate. If the variables INPUT and LIST are defined to be character variables

```
        CHARACTER*80 INPUT, LIST
```

then the statement

```
        IF (INPUT .EQ. LIST) THEN
            .
            .
            .
        ENDIF
```

will automatically cause all 80 individual characters of the two variables to be compared. The condition will be true only if all characters associated with the two variables match. The condition in the statement

```
        IF (INPUT .LT. LIST) THEN
            .
            .
            .
        ENDIF
```

will be TRUE if the value of INPUT appears earlier in alphabetical order than the value of LIST.

14.5   PROGRAMMING EXAMPLES

14.5.1   Palindromes

A palindrome is a word, phrase, or sentence that reads the same from left to right and right to left. Two simple examples are the words *PEEP* and *RADAR*. A more famous example is *MADAM I'M ADAM*. (Ignore the apostrophe and blanks.) We want to write a program that will test a string of characters for being a palindrome. To simplify the problem, we will assume that all blanks and special characters have been deleted from the string. To make the problem more challenging, we will assume that the string does not have to begin in column 1 of the input card and that the program should work for any number of test cases.

One reasonable high-level solution is

```
read card contents
WHILE (not last card indicator)
        find string in input array
        test for being a palindrome
        IF (a palindrome) THEN
                write "is a palindrome"
        ELSE
                write "is not a palindrome"
        ENDIF
        read card contents
ENDWHILE
STOP
END
```

The difficult part of this problem is finding a satisfactory method to test a string for being a palindrome. Let us examine some examples and attempt to discover the mental technique we use in deciding whether the phrase is a palindrome. Consider the word *PEEP*; we compare the characters at the left and right ends of the word:

where LEND ≡ left end of phrase
       REND ≡ right end of phrase

If the characters are the same, that is,

IF (PHRASE(LEND) .EQ. PHRASE(REND))

where **PHRASE** is a character array containing the phrase under investigation

then the word is possibly a palindrome. To test further, increase the left-end pointer

$$LEND = LEND + 1$$

and decrease the right-end pointer

$$REND = REND - 1$$

Then compare the indicated characters

$$P \quad E \quad E \quad P$$
$$\uparrow \quad \uparrow$$
$$LEND \quad REND$$

The IF statement given above would still be suitable for this comparison. When do we stop the comparison process? If two characters do not match, the phrase is not a palindrome and the process should be stopped. If the pointer to the left end becomes larger than the pointer to the right end, that is,

$$P \quad E \quad E \quad P$$
$$\uparrow \quad \uparrow$$
REND LEND ←——— notice that the pointers have become interchanged

a palindrome has been discovered and the process should be stopped. Let **PAL** be an integer variable having the interpretation

PAL = 0   means that the phrase is not a palindrome

PAL = 1   means that the phrase may be a palindrome

Then the steps outlined above can be expressed as

```
          .
          .
          .
     WHILE ((LEND .LT. REND) .AND. (PAL .EQ. 1))
         IF (PHRASE(LEND) .EQ. PHRASE(REND)) THEN
             LEND = LEND + 1
             REND = REND - 1
         ELSE
             PAL = 0
         ENDIF
     ENDWHILE
```

To check these steps, we will play computer with the characters of the word *RADAR* being the first five elements of PHRASE. Then

Step	LEND	REND	PHRASE(LEND)	PHRASE(REND)	PHRASE(LEND) .EQ. PHRASE(REND)
1	1	5	R	R	TRUE
2	2	4	A	A	TRUE
3	3	3	leave WHILE loop since LEND .LT. REND is FALSE		

Initially, we assumed that the phrase was a palindrome by assigning the value 1 to the variable PAL. At the time the exit is made from the WHILE loop, PAL still has the value 1 indicating the phrase is a palindrome. RADAR is indeed a palindrome, so the method has worked satisfactorily.

To decide which message to print, we can test the value of PAL. The value will be 1 if the phrase was a palindrome. At this stage of our knowledge, the program is

```
      CHARACTER*1 PHRASE(80)
      INTEGER PAL, REND, LEND
1000 FORMAT (80A)
1010 FORMAT ('0', 'IS A PALDINDROME ', 80A)
1020 FORMAT ('0', 'IS NOT A PALINDROME ', 80A)
      READ (5,1000) PHRASE
      WHILE (not last case indicator)
          find string in PHRASE
          PAL = 1
          WHILE ((LEND .LT. REND) .AND. (PAL .EQ. 1))
              IF (PHRASE(LEND) .EQ. PHRASE(REND)) THEN
                  LEND = LEND + 1
                  REND = REND - 1
              ELSE
                  PAL = 0
              ENDIF
          ENDWHILE
          IF (PAL .EQ. 1) THEN
              WRITE (6,1010) PHRASE
          ELSE
              WRITE (6,1020) PHRASE
          ENDIF
          READ (5,1000) PHRASE
      ENDWHILE
      STOP
      END
```

To obtain a final solution, we must decide on a last card indicator and a method for locating the string in PHRASE. Arbitrarily, we will adopt the following convention

```
1   C
2   C            PALINDROMES
3   C
4            INTEGER PAL,REND,LEND
5            CHARACTER*1 PHRASE(80)
6   1000     FORMAT(80A)
7   1010     FORMAT('0','IS A PALINDROME ',80A)
8   1020     FORMAT('0','IS NOT A PALINDROME ',80A)
9            READ(5,1000)(PHRASE(I),I=1,80)
10           WHILE(PHRASE(1).NE.'/' .OR. PHRASE(2).NE.'*')
11              LEND=1
12              WHILE(PHRASE(LEND).EQ.' ')
13                 LEND=LEND+1
14              ENDWHILE
15              REND=80
16              WHILE(PHRASE(REND).EQ.' ')
17                 REND=REND-1
18              ENDWHILE
19              PAL=1
20              WHILE( LEND .LT. REND  .AND. PAL .EQ. 1)
21                 IF(PHRASE(LEND) .EQ. PHRASE(REND)) THEN
22                    LEND=LEND+1
23                    REND=REND-1
24                 ELSE
25                    PAL=0
26                 ENDIF
27              ENDWHILE
28              IF( PAL .EQ. 1) THEN
29                 WRITE(6,1010)(PHRASE(I),I=1,40)
30              ELSE
31                 WRITE(6,1020)(PHRASE(I),I=1,40)
32              ENDIF
33              READ(5,1000)(PHRASE(I),I=1,80)
34           ENDWHILE
35           STOP
36           END
```

        IS NOT A PALINDROME   AH

        IS A PALINDROME EE

        IS A PALINDROME   PEP

        IS A PALINDROME   PEEP

        IS NOT A PALINDROME   POUT

        IS A PALINDROME RADAR

        IS A PALINDROME   MADAMIMADAM

        IS A PALINDROME   ABLEWASIEREISAWELBA

FIGURE 14.1 *Palindromes*

438

for the last card indicator: a slash followed by an asterisk, /*, in columns 1 and 2 of a card designates the last card. The test for the last card is

.
.
.

```
READ (5,1000) PHRASE
WHILE ((PHRASE(1) .NE. '/') .OR. (PHRASE(2) .NE. '*'))
  .
  .
  .
ENDWHILE
```

.
.
.

Locating the string within PHRASE is equivalent to finding the leftmost and rightmost nonblank characters.

.
.
.

```
LEND = 1
WHILE (PHRASE(LEND) .EQ. ' ')
    LEND = LEND + 1
ENDWHILE
REND = 80
WHILE (PHRASE(REND) .EQ. ' ')
    REND = REND - 1
ENDWHILE
```

.
.
.

All the individual steps of the program have been deduced. The final program is shown in Figure 14.1.

14.5.2 Sorting Alphabetic Data

The need to sort data alphabetically arises frequently in applications of the computer. Payroll reports, class rolls, inventory summaries, and many other types of reports are normally printed in alphabetical order. We need to extend the previous sorting techniques to handle alphabetic data. This extension is easy to make if the number of items to be sorted is relatively small, so that all the data can be simultaneously in computer memory and if fast sorting is not critical.

Consider the exchange method for sorting as given in Figure 12.6. The logic of the program does not have to be changed for sorting character variables. The major difficulty is that the characters in two different names must be compared character by character. Suppose that the set of names to be alphabetized have been stored in a character array, NAMES, which has been declared as

CHARACTER*20 NAMES(300)

Each element of NAMES will contain one of the names to be alphabetized with a maximum of 300 names being possible for this array. Then the characters of one name must be compared with the characters of another name.

NAMES (LOC)   D O E   J O H N   ⎤ compare
              ↕ ↕ ↕ ↕ ↕ ↕ ↕ ↕ ↕ · · · · ⎬ elements
NAMES (J)   D O E   J A M E S   ⎦ of names

The comparison is performed automatically by the statements

```
          .
          .
          .

     IF (NAMES(LOC) .GT. NAMES(J)) THEN
          LOC = J
     ENDIF
          .
          .
          .
```

The final program is shown in Figure 14.2.

The postponing of the interchanging of names until the "smallest" name remaining has been found makes this program much faster than it would be if the more obvious method were used: that of interchanging names whenever they are found to be out of sequence. But even the program given as the solution is far too slow for sorting many names. If, for example, there are 30,000 names instead of 300, the sorting technique just described is impractically slow, and in addition, it is unlikely that all the names could be placed simultaneously in computer memory. An improved sorting algorithm must be discovered to handle the larger amount of data. Merely increasing the amount of data can have a profound effect on how we solve a problem. Edsger W. Dijkstra* has described this phenomenon elegantly: "One of my central themes will be that any two things that differ in some respect by a factor of a hundred or more, are utterly incomparable." As the amount of data to be manipulated increases, programs generally become much more complex.

*O. J. Dahl, E. W. Dijkstra, and C. A. R. Hoare, *Structured Programming* (New York: Academic Press, Inc., 1972), p. 2.

14.5.3 Translating Morse Code

Let us write a program that will translate messages in Morse code into standard English. Input to the program will be a deck of cards each of which contains a message in Morse code, such as

```
 1  C
 2  C              ALPHABETIC SORTING USING CHARACTER VARIABLES
 3  C
 4         INTEGER COUNT
 5         CHARACTER*20 NAMES(300),LAST
 6  C
 7  1000   FORMAT(A)
 8  1010   FORMAT('1','INPUT VALUES'/(' ',A))
 9  1020   FORMAT(///' ','SORTED VALUES'/(' ',A))
10         LAST='/*                           '
11         I=1
12         READ(5,1000)NAMES(I)
13         WHILE( NAMES(I) .NE. LAST)
14            I=I+1
15            READ(5,1000)NAMES(I)
16         ENDWHILE
17         COUNT=I-1
18         WRITE(6,1010)(NAMES(I),I=1,COUNT)
19         CALL ASORT(NAMES,COUNT)
20         WRITE(6,1020)(NAMES(I),I=1,COUNT)
21         STOP
22         END

23         SUBROUTINE ASORT(NAMES,COUNT)
24         INTEGER COUNT
25         CHARACTER*20 NAMES(300),ITEMP
26         LST=COUNT-1
27         DO I=1,LST
28            LOC=I
29            K=I+1
30            DO J=K,COUNT
31               IF(NAMES(LOC) .GT. NAMES(J)) THEN
32                  LOC=J
33               ENDIF
34            ENDDO
35            ITEMP=NAMES(I)
36            NAMES(I)=NAMES(LOC)
37            NAMES(LOC)=ITEMP
38         ENDDO
39         RETURN
40         END
```

FIGURE 14.2 *Alphabetic sorting: character variable method*

```
INPUT VALUES                              SORTED VALUES
ZERO                                      ALBERT
THOMAS                                    ARRINGTON
CAPTAIN                                   BART
SMOKE                                     BISH
WEEK                          Page 1      BLAKE                        Page 2
MARTIN                                    BRASINGTON
COOLEY                                    BROWN CG
ALBERT                                    BROWN RA
BART                                      BYARS
CATO                                      CAPTAIN
CATOE                                     CATO
WEATHER                                   CATOE
WEATHERLY                                 CHAPMAN MS
MCMILLIN                                  CHRISTOPH
ARRINGTON                                 CLOER
NORTON                                    COBB
OCONNOR                                   COLEMAN
RAGSDALE                                  COOLEY
MEDEW                                     EARLES
REN                                       FISHER
BYARS                                     FREDERICKSON
BLAKE                                     GADDY
BRASINGTON                                GADIENT
ROACH                                     GILREATH
SMITH PL                                  HEFNER
RICHMOND                                  HENSON
CHAPMAN MS                                HODGES
LESLEY                                    KELLY
MCELARTH                                  LABBAN
BROWN CG                                  LESLEY
BROWN RA                                  MARTIN
CLOER                                     MCELARTH
RODGERS                                   MCMILLIN
RYBURN                                    MEDEW
GADDY                                     NORTON
GADIENT                                   OCONNOR
COBB                                      PAUL
PAUL                                      PEEPLES
PEEPLES                                   PURIFOY
GILREATH                                  RACKLEY
HEFNER                                    RADULOCIC
SAMPSON                                   RAGSDALE
COLEMAN                                   REN
EARLES                                    RICHMOND
SANDLIN                                   ROACH
SMITH EE                                  RODGERS
YANDLE                                    RYBURN
SAVAGE                                    SAMPSON
PURIFOY                                   SANDLIN
RACKLEY                                   SAVAGE
RADULOCIC                                 SMITH EE
FISHER                                    SMITH PL
FREDERICKSON                              SMOKE
HENSON                                    THOMAS
HODGES                                    VANN
KELLY                                     WARREN
BISH                                      WEATHER
VANN                                      WEATHERLY
WARREN                                    WEEK
LABBAN                                    WILSON
CHRISTOPH                                 YANDLE
WILSON                                    ZERO
```

FIGURE 14.2   *(cont.)*

For each input card the program is to print the translated message, which for our present sample is

TO BE OR NOT TO BE

The last card in the deck contains /* in columns 1 and 2.

To reduce the difficulty of the problem, we should make simplifying assumptions wherever we can. To simplify and systematize the input data, we require all messages to begin in column 1. Individual characters will be separated by a blank, and two consecutive blanks will signal the end of a word.

The Morse alphabet can be stored in a table, then a table-lookup procedure can be used to match characters from the input card with rows of the table. When it is discovered, for example, that ·--- matches exactly with row 16, we know that the code for the 16th English character, P, was punched in the card. A problem arises, however, because the codes contain different numbers of dots and dashes. To illustrate the problem, suppose that the code for N (-·) had been punched in the card. If we merely compare these two characters with the entries of the table, a match is found with the code for B (-···) and several other entries in the table. We do not want any match to succeed until the correct entry, the row for N, is examined. A simple method of ensuring unique matching is to attach a blank to the end of each code and to attach a blank to the end of each character read from a card. Thus ·-- becomes ·--b, and this latter sequence matches only with the Morse code for W. We will adopt this convention. There are, of course, many other methods that could be used; you may wish to adopt some procedure that appeals to you and write your own program to solve the problem.

The decision to include a trailing blank with each Morse character implies that a 26 by 5 array will be needed for storing the Morse alphabet. Another array will be used to hold the corresponding alphabetic characters. These arrays can be visualized as

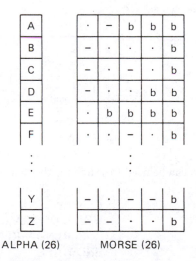

ALPHA (26)   MORSE (26)

Based on these conventions for the data, a high-level solution to the problem is

```
initialize
read message
WHILE (not last card)
     write message
     initialize
     WHILE (there are characters to be translated)
          locate character in message
          match character with row of MORSE
          transfer appropriate code from ALPHA to output line
     ENDWHILE
     write output line
     read message
ENDWHILE
STOP
END
```

The difficult part of the program is the inner loop:

```
WHILE (there are characters to be translated)
     locate character in message
     match character with row of MORSE
     transfer appropriate code from ALPHA to output line
ENDWHILE
```

To locate a character in the message (array MESSA), we will scan the message, left to right, to find the two ends. A blank will always appear at the right end. Let LEND point to the left end of a Morse character and REND point to the right end. This can be visualized as

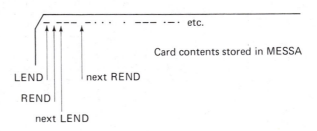

A loop can be used to search for the right end.

```
REND = LEND + 1
WHILE (MESSA(REND) .NE. BLANK)
     REND = REND + 1
ENDWHILE
```

The table-lookup procedure for matching the character with a row of MORSE will be a linear scan through MORSE until a match is found. It will be convenient to include the transferring of the character from ALPHA to the output line as the last major step in the lookup process. This gives

```
set row indicator to 1
WHILE (there are unexamined rows in MORSE and no match has been found)
      initialize
      WHILE (right end of character has not been examined and dots and
                                                    dashes match so far)
            compare element of character and element of row of MORSE
      ENDWHILE
      IF (match found) THEN
            transfer character from ALPHA to output
            set indicator for match
      ENDIF
      increase row indicator
ENDWHILE
```

Let

I	$\equiv$ row indicator
MATCH	$\equiv$ match indicator
	0 match not found yet
	1 character matches this row of MORSE
M	$\equiv$ pointer to dot or dash of MESSAG being compared with MORSE
K	$\equiv$ column indicator for MORSE
OUTPUT	$\equiv$ array containing translated characters for output
PTOUT	$\equiv$ pointer to position in OUTPUT for storing next character

then the lookup procedure given above becomes

```
MATCH = 0
I = 1
WHILE (I .LE. 26 .AND. MATCH .EQ. 0)
      M = LEND
      K = 1
      WHILE (M .LE. REND .AND. K .LE. 5)
            IF (MESSA(M) .EQ. MORSE (I,K)THEN
                  M = M+1
                  K = K+1
            ELSE
                  K = 10
```

```
                    ENDIF
                ENDWHILE
                IF (K .NE. 10)THEN
                    OUTPUT(PTOUT) = ALPHA(I)
                    PTOUT = PTOUT + 1
                    MATCH = 1
                ENDIF
                I = I+1
            ENDWHILE
```

In the comparison process, a failure for elements of **MESSA** and **MORSE** to match causes the column indicator to be set to 10. If the comparison loop is completed with K not equal to 10, the comparison succeeded and a character should be transferred to the output line.

The program is getting complicated, so we will expand the initial high-level solution by inserting the detailed statements. The resulting statement of the program will be examined to decide what part to expand next.

```
        initialize
        read MESSA
        WHILE (not last card)
            write MESSA
            initialize
            WHILE (there are characters to be translated)
                REND = LEND + 1
                WHILE (MESSA(REND) .NE. BLANK)
                    REND = REND + 1
                ENDWHILE
                MATCH = 0
                I = 1
                WHILE (I .LE. 26 .AND. MATCH .EQ. 0)
                    M = LEND
                    K = 1
                    WHILE (M .LE. REND .AND. K .LE. 5)
                        IF (MESSA(M) .EQ. MORSE(I,K)) THEN
                            M = M+1
                            K = K+1
                        ELSE
                            K = 10
                        ENDIF
                    ENDWHILE
                    IF (K .NE. 10) THEN
                        OUTPUT(PTOUT) = ALPHA(I)
                        PTOUT = PTOUT + 1
                        MATCH = 1
```

```
            ENDIF
            I = I+1
        ENDWHILE
        IF (end of a word) THEN
            increase PTOUT
            increase REND
        ENDIF
        set LEND to point to beginning of next character
    ENDWHILE
    write OUTPUT
    read MESSA
ENDWHILE
STOP
END
```

We will start with the first unexpanded statement in this solution and work our way to the end of the program. The first statement,

initialize

involves

read ALPHA and MORSE

or

```
        DO I = 1,26
            READ (5,1000) ALPHA(I), (MORSE(I,K), K = 1,5)
1000        FORMAT (A, 1X,5A)
        ENDDO
```

The statement

read MESSA

becomes

```
        READ (5,1010) MESSA
1010 FORMAT (80A)
```

with MESSA being declared for 80 characters.

Since the problem statement indicates the last card contains /* in columns 1 and 2, the statement

WHILE (not last card)

becomes

$$\text{WHILE (MESSA(1) .NE. '/' .OR. MESSA(2) .NE. '*')}$$

The writing of MESSA is given by

$$\text{WRITE (6,1020) MESSA}$$
$$\text{1020 FORMAT ('0', 80A)}$$

For the statement

$$\text{WHILE (there are characters to be translated)}$$

there will be characters to be translated while there are still dots and dashes to be considered. Let LIMIT point to the rightmost nonblank character. Then the condition for more translating becomes

$$\text{WHILE (REND .LE. LIMIT+1)}$$

The initialization preceding this statement must fill the output array, OUTPUT, with blanks to prevent printing portions of previous messages and must set the values of LEND, PTOUT, and LIMIT.

```
DO I = 1,80
    OUTPUT(I) = ' '
ENDDO
LEND = 1
PTOUT = 1
I = 80
WHILE (MESSA(I) .EQ. ' ')
    I = I-1
ENDWHILE
LIMIT = I
```

The condition for the end of a word that is required in

$$\text{IF (end of word) THEN}$$

is that the character following the right end of a Morse character be a blank. The IF statement becomes

```
IF (MESSA(REND + 1) .EQ. ' ') THEN
    PTOUT = PTOUT + 1
    REND = REND + 1
ENDIF
```

The left end of the next Morse character is the position immediately following the right end of the previous Morse character.

$$LEND = REND + 1$$

The writing of OUTPUT is given by

$$WRITE\ (6,1030)\ OUTPUT$$
$$1030\ FORMAT\ ('\ ',80A)$$

Inserting all these statements into the previous partial solution produces the final program, which is shown in Figure 14.3.

```
 1  C
 2  C            TRANSLATION OF MORSE CODE
 3  C
 4           CHARACTER*1 ALPHA(26),MESSA(80),OUTPUT(80)
 5           CHARACTER*1 MORSE(26,5)
 6           INTEGER PTOUT,REND
 7  1000     FORMAT(A,1X,5A)
 8  1010     FORMAT(80A)
 9  1020     FORMAT('0',80A)
10  1030     FORMAT(' ',80A)
11  C            INPUT ALL ALPHABETIC CHARACTERS AND CORRESPONDING
12  C            MORSE CODES
13           DO I=1,26
14              READ(5,1000)ALPHA(I),(MORSE(I,J),J=1,5)
15           ENDDO
16           READ(5,1010)MESSA
17  C            MAIN LOOP FOR PROCESSING MESSAGES
18           WHILE(MESSA(1).NE.'/' .OR. MESSA(2).NE.'*')
19              WRITE(6,1020)MESSA
20  C            INITIALIZE FOR THIS MESSAGE
21  C                FILL OUTPUT WITH BLANKS
22              DO I=1,80
23                 OUTPUT(I)=' '
24              ENDDO
25  C            ASSUME FIRST CHARACTER BEGINS IN COLUMN 1
26              LEND=1
27  C            SET POINTER TO NEXT AVAILABLE LOCATION IN OUTPUT LINE
28              PTOUT=1
29  C            PROCESS CHARACTERS IN MESSAGE
30              I=80
31              WHILE(MESSA(I) .EQ. ' ')
32                 I=I-1
33              ENDWHILE
34              LIMIT=I
35              WHILE(LEND .LE. LIMIT+1)
36  C                FIND RIGHT END OF CHARACTER
```

FIGURE 14.3 *Translation of Morse Code*

```
37              REND=LEND+1
38              WHILE(MESSA(REND) .NE. ' ')
39                  REND=REND+1
40              ENDWHILE
41   C             FIND CORRESPONDING MORSE CHARACTER
42              MATCH=0
43              I=1
44              WHILE(I .LE. 26  .AND.   MATCH .EQ. 0)
45                M=LEND
46                K=1
47                WHILE( M .LE. REND .AND. K .LE.5)
48                    IF(MESSA(M) .EQ. MORSE(I,K)) THEN
49                        K=K+1
50                        M=M+1
51                    ELSE
52                        K=10
53                    ENDIF
54                ENDWHILE
55   C            WAS A MATCHING CHARACTER FOUND
56                IF(K .NE. 10) THEN
57   C            MATCH FOUND
58                    OUTPUT(PTOUT)=ALPHA(I)
59                    PTOUT=PTOUT+1
60                    MATCH=1
61                ENDIF
62                I=I+1
63              ENDWHILE
64   C             IS THIS THE END OF A WORD.  IF YES, SKIP EXTRA SPACE.
65              IF(MESSA(REND+1) .EQ. ' ') THEN
66                PTOUT=PTOUT+1
67                REND=REND+1
68              ENDIF
69              PTOUT=PTOUT+1
70   C             MOVE LEFT END TO POINT AT NEXT CHARACTER
71              LEND=REND+1
72            ENDWHILE
73            WRITE(6,1030)OUTPUT
74            READ(5,1010)MESSA
75          ENDWHILE
76          STOP
77          END
```

... ...-. --- - .-. ..- -.
S E E   S P O T   R U N

-.-. --- -- .--. ..- - . .-. ... -.-. .. . -. -.-. . .. ... --. .-. . .- -
C O M P U T E R   S C I E N C E   I S   G R E A T

FIGURE 14.3   *(cont.)*

14.5.4   Polish Notation

In Chapter 8, a procedure based on the hierarchy of operations was described for determining the sequence of execution of operations in an arithmetic expression. Although that procedure would always allow you to calculate the answer produced by the expression, it does not necessarily give the actual order in which the arithmetic operations are performed. To illustrate this point:

1. The hierarchy rules predict

$$\underset{\underset{\text{2nd}}{\uparrow}}{A} - \underset{\underset{\text{3rd}}{\uparrow}}{B} + \underset{\underset{\text{1st}}{\uparrow}}{C} * D$$

2. But the actual order of evaluation normally is

$$\underset{\underset{\text{1st}}{\uparrow}}{A} - \underset{\underset{\text{3rd}}{\uparrow}}{B} + \underset{\underset{\text{2nd}}{\uparrow}}{C} * D$$

The difference arises because many compilers convert these infix forms to a postfix form called *Polish notation* in honor of the Polish logician J. Lukasiewicz, who invented it. (His name is not used to identify the notation, as it has various spellings in English.)

In the postfix form of Polish notation, an arithmetic operator *follows* the variables to which it applies:

AB+	means	A + B
AB-	means	A - B
BA-	means	B - A
AB*	means	A * B
AB/	means	A / B
AB**	means	A**B

The expression AB+C* is interpreted as:

1. Add A and B.
2. Multiply the previous result by C.

In these steps, the operands to which an operator applies can be identified by underlining them. Thus

$$\underline{A\,B} + C *$$

refers to the value produced by adding A and B

means that + is applied to A and B to give a single answer, which has been underlined. Moving to the right, * is encountered, and it must be applied to the two operands that immediately precede it, the answer for AB+ and C. This can be indicated by underlining:

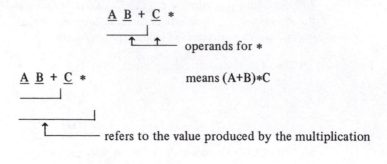

Consider the more complicated expression

$$AB - CD - *$$

Its structure is given by the underlining

$$\underline{A}\ \underline{B}\ -\ \underline{C}\ \underline{D}\ -\ *$$

Thus it can be seen that

$$AB - CD-* \quad \text{means} \quad (A-B)*(C-D)$$

Now consider the example that was used at the beginning of this section to demonstrate that the hierarchy rules do not always predict the order of evaluation of operations:

$$A - B + C * D$$

is converted into the Polish expression

$$AB - CD * +$$

which has the evaluation structure

$$\underline{A}\ \underline{B}\ -\ \underline{C}\ \underline{D}\ *\ +$$

Polish notation is used by compilers for the following reasons:

1. An algorithm exists for converting an infix expression into Polish notation.
2. A simple algorithm exists for testing the validity of a Polish expression. This allows easy detection of syntax errors.
3. Parentheses are eliminated in the conversion from infix to Polish notation.
4. Evaluation of a Polish expression is particularly convenient since the value of any subexpression will have been calculated before it is needed in further evaluations. This property allows the compiler to convert the expression to machine instructions with relative ease.

The algorithm for the transformation from infix to postfix Polish notation is known as the shunting-yard algorithm because of the power of this analogy in helping one visualize the operation of the procedure. In the analogy, each incoming element of the infix expression is considered to be the contents of a train car. At a junction, a car (i.e., element of the infix expression) goes on through or is temporarily shunted onto a siding, depending on the contents of the car. The situation is as follows:

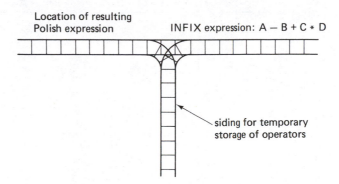

The shunting-yard algorithm is:

1. Incoming operands pass straight through the junction.
2. For incoming operations:
   a. Pause at the junction.
   b. Place the operation on the siding if it is a left parenthesis.
   c. Compare with the operation at the top of the siding (end of the siding nearest the junction).
      (1) If the incoming operation is of higher priority than the operation at the top of the siding, the incoming operation is placed on the siding.
      (2) If the incoming operation is of equal or lower priority than the operation at the top of the siding, operations are removed from the siding, moving them to the left, until the incoming operation has higher priority or the siding is empty. Then the incoming operation is added

to the siding. (On the siding, an operation cannot be placed on top of a higher-priority operation.)

(3) If the incoming operation is a right parenthesis, the siding is emptied, by moving operations to the left, until a left parenthesis is found. Then both parentheses are discarded.

The priorities for operations on the siding are as follows:

**	highest priority
* /	
+ −	
(	lowest priority

Notice that the left parenthesis is always placed on the siding, but once there, anything except a right parenthesis can be placed on it. The following sequence demonstrates the application of the algorithm:

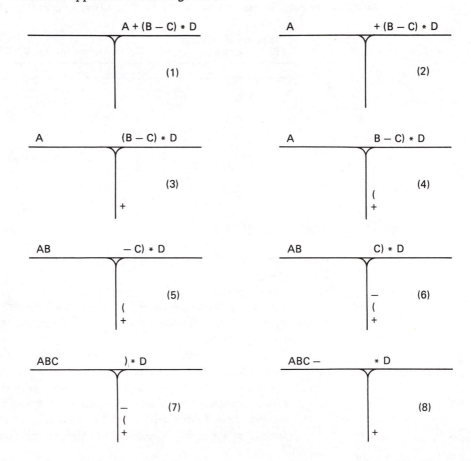

We want to implement the shunting-yard algorithm for the following specific situation:

Write a program that transforms infix arithmetic expressions to postfix Polish form. Input is a deck of cards, with each card containing an expression to be transformed. The last card contains /* in columns 1 and 2. Operands consist of single alphabetic characters. Allowed operations are +, -, *, /, and **. Unary minus is not allowed. Subexpressions may be enclosed in parentheses. Blanks may be inserted into the expression in an arbitrary manner. All input expressions are assumed to be error-free. Each expression is delimited by a dollar sign, $ (i.e., the first character and last character on each card is a $ sign and these signs are not part of the expression to be transformed).

This statement of the problem makes it more complex than necessary, but much less complicated than is required to handle all legitimate FORTRAN arithmetic expressions. The restriction of operands to a single alphabetic character and the elimination of unary minus as an operation simplify the problem, but the allowing of embedded blanks and the fact that the exponentiation operator is two characters complicate it.

The statement of the algorithm as given previously constitutes a high-level solution to the problem. The algorithm is not stated in a form that is convenient for computer implementation, and it is not specialized for the specific situation. In the following high-level solution, INFIX contains the incoming infix arithmetic expression, STACK contains the operations that are shunted to the siding, and POLISH contains the final postfix Polish string. The name STACK has been chosen for the siding because it behaves like a general data structure called a stack. An important property of a stack is that usually only the element at the top of the stack can be examined and manipulated.

```
initialize
read INFIX
WHILE (not last card)
    initialize
    find initial delimiter and place in STACK
    WHILE (final delimiter not processed)
        find next character
        determine type of character (operand, +, -, *, etc.)
            set indicator for type
```

```
                    IF (operand) THEN
                        move to POLISH
                    ELSEIF (final $) THEN
                        empty STACK
                    ELSEIF (left parenthesis) THEN
                        place on STACK
                    ELSEIF (operation) THEN
                        empty STACK until top operation has lower priority
                                    than incoming operator
                        place incoming operation on top of STACK
                    ELSEIF (right parenthesis) THEN
                        empty STACK through first left parenthesis
                    ENDIF
                ENDWHILE
                write INFIX
                write POLISH
                read INFIX
            ENDWHILE
            STOP
            END
```

To determine the type of incoming character, an IF. . .ELSEIF. . .ENDIF statement will be used—one condition for each possible type of character. The type of character will be saved as the value of INPTY (for input priority). The following code values will be used for INPTY so that the code will correspond to the priorities for stacking of characters.

Type character	Value of INPTY
operand	0
delimiter, $	1
(	2
+ –	3
* /	4
**	5
)	6

The variable STACK representing the siding will be defined as a two-column table. Column 1 will contain the actual operation, and column 2 will contain the value of INPTY. This arrangement will avoid having to identify the operation a second time during the processing of subsequent operations.

A program based on these decisions is given in Figure 14.4.

```
 1 C
 2 C                  CONVERSION FROM INFIX TO POSTFIX POLISH NOTATION
 3 C
 4 C                  OPERANDS ARE RESTRICTED TO ONE CHARACTER
 5 C
 6 C                  MEANING OF VARIABLES
 7 C                      INFIX      ARRAY CONTAINING ORIGINAL INFIX EXPRESSION
 8 C                      POLISH     ARRAY CONTAINING POSTFIX POLISH EXPRESSION
 9 C                      STACK      ARRAY CONTAINING OPERATIONS
10 C                                 COLUMN 1  OPERATION
11 C                                 COLUMN 2  PRIORITY OF OPERATION
12 C                      LOCI       POINTER TO LOCATION IN INFIX
13 C                      LOCP       POINTER TO LOICATION IN POLISH
14 C                      LOCS       POINTER TO ROW OF STACK
15 C                      INPTY      PRIOTITY OF INCOMING OPERATION
16 C                  EMBEDDED BLANKS ALLOWED
17 C
18 C                  OPERATIONS ALLOWED ARE
19 C                      **         EXPONENTIATION
20 C                      *   /      MULTIPLICATION, DIVISION
21 C                      +   -      ADDITION, SUBTRACTION
22 C                      $          STRING DELIMITER
23 C                      (   )      LEFT AND RIGHT PARENTHESES
24 C
25 C
26        CHARACTER*1 INFIX(80),POLISH(80),STACK(40,2),INPTY
27        CHARACTER*1 LPAR,RPAR
28        LOGICAL DLIMIT
29 1000   FORMAT(80A)
30 1010   FORMAT('0','INFIX FORM',2X,80A)
31 1020   FORMAT(' ','POLISH FORM',1X,80A)
32        LPAR='('
33        RPAR=')'
34        READ(5,1000)INFIX
35        WHILE(INFIX(1).NE. '/' .OR. INFIX(2).NE. '*' )
36            DO I=1,80
37                POLISH(I)=' '
38            ENDDO
39            DO I=1,40
40                STACK(I,1)=' '
41                STACK(I,2)=' '
42            ENDDO
43            LOCI=1
44            LOCP=1
45            LOCS=1
46            DLIMIT=.FALSE.
47 C
48 C                FIND DELIMITER AT BEGINNING OF INFIX
49 C
50            WHILE(INFIX(LOCI) .EQ. ' ' )
```

FIGURE 14.4 *Conversion from infix to postfix Polish notation*

```
51              LOCI=LOCI+1
52          ENDWHILE
53          STACK(LOCS,1)=INFIX(LOCI)
54          STACK(LOCS,2)='1'
55          LOCI=LOCI+1
56          LOCS=LOCS+1
57 C
58 C           PROCESS INFIX UNTIL FINAL DELIMITER FOUND
59 C
60          WHILE(.NOT. DLIMIT)
61 C
62 C           FIND NEXT CHARACTER IN INFIX
63 C
64              WHILE(INFIX(LOCI) .EQ. ' ' )
65                  LOCI=LOCI+1
66              ENDWHILE
67 C
68 C               DETERMINE TYPE OF SYMBOL
69 C
70              INPTY='0'
71              IF(INFIX(LOCI) .EQ. '$' ) THEN
72                  INPTY='1'
73              ELSEIF(INFIX(LOCI) .EQ. LPAR ) THEN
74                  INPTY='2'
75              ELSEIF(INFIX(LOCI) .EQ. '+' .OR. INFIX(LOCI) .EQ. '-' ) TH
76      *EN
77                  INPTY='3'
78              ELSEIF(INFIX(LOCI) .EQ. '/' ) THEN
79                  INPTY='4'
80              ELSEIF(INFIX(LOCI) .EQ. '*' ) THEN
81                  NEXT=LOCI+1
82                  WHILE(INFIX(NEXT) .EQ. ' ' )
83                      NEXT=NEXT+1
84                  ENDWHILE
85                  IF(INFIX(NEXT) .NE. '*' ) THEN
86                      INPTY='4'
87                  ELSE
88                      INPTY='5'
89                  ENDIF
90              ELSEIF(INFIX(LOCI) .EQ. RPAR ) THEN
91                  INPTY='6'
92              ENDIF
93 C
94 C           PROCESS INFIX CHARACTER BASED ON ITS TYPE, I.E., INPTY
95 C
96 C               OPERAND
97              IF(INPTY .EQ. '0' ) THEN
98                  POLISH(LOCP)=INFIX(LOCI)
99                  LOCP=LOCP+1
100                 LOCI=LOCI+1
101 C
```

FIGURE 14.4   *(cont.)*

458

```
102 C                    END OF INFIX STRING
103              ELSEIF(INPTY .EQ. '1' ) THEN
104 C                    EMPTY THE STACK
105                WHILE(STACK(LOCS-1,2) .GT. '1' )
106                    POLISH(LOCP)=STACK(LOCS-1,1)
107                    IF(STACK(LOCS-1,1) .EQ. '*' .AND. STACK(LOCS-1,2) .EQ.
108        * '5') THEN
109                        LOCP=LOCP+1
110                        POLISH(LOCP)='*'
111                    ENDIF
112                    LOCP=LOCP+1
113                    LOCS=LOCS-1
114                ENDWHILE
115                DLIMIT=.TRUE.
116 C
117 C                LEFT PARENTHESIS
118              ELSEIF(INPTY .EQ. '2') THEN
119                STACK(LOCS,1)=INFIX(LOCI)
120                STACK(LOCS,2)=INPTY
121                LOCS=LOCS+1
122                LOCI=LOCI+1
123 C
124 C                PLUS, MINUS,ASTR,SLASH,RIGHT PARENTHESIS,EXPONENTIATION
125              ELSEIF(INPTY .GE. '3'  .AND.  INPTY .LE. '5') THEN
126                WHILE(INPTY .LE. STACK(LOCS-1,2))
127                    POLISH(LOCP)=STACK(LOCS-1,1)
128                    IF(STACK(LOCS,2) .EQ. '5') THEN
129                        LOCP=LOCP+1
130                        POLISH(LOCP)='*'
131                    ENDIF
132                    LOCP=LOCP+1
133                    LOCS=LOCS-1
134                ENDWHILE
135 C
136 C                PLACE OPERATION ON STACK
137                STACK(LOCS,1)=INFIX(LOCI)
138                STACK(LOCS,2)=INPTY
139                LOCS=LOCS+1
140                IF(INPTY .EQ. '5') THEN
141                    LOCI=NEXT+1
142                ELSE
143                    LOCI=LOCI+1
144                ENDIF
145 C
146 C                    RIGHT PARENTHESIS, EMPTY STACK THROUGH LEFT
147 C                    PARENTHESIS
148              ELSEIF(INPTY .EQ. '6') THEN
149                WHILE(STACK(LOCS-1,2) .GT. '2')
150                    POLISH(LOCP)=STACK(LOCS-1,1)
151                    IF(STACK(LOCS-1,2) .EQ. '5') THEN
152                        LOCP=LOCP+1
```

FIGURE 14.4   *(cont.)*

```
153                          POLISH(LOCP)='*'
154                ENDIF
155                LOCP=LOCP+1
156                LOCS=LOCS-1
157             ENDWHILE
158             LOCS=LOCS-1
159             LOCI=LOCI+1
160           ENDIF
161         ENDWHILE
162         WRITE(6,1010)INFIX
163         WRITE(6,1020)POLISH
164         READ(5,1000)INFIX
165       ENDWHILE
166       STOP
167       END
```

```
INFIX FORM   $A + B$
POLISH FORM  AB+

INFIX FORM   $A - B$
POLISH FORM  AB-

INFIX FORM                $A * B$
POLISH FORM  AB*

INFIX FORM          $ A / B $
POLISH FORM  AB/

INFIX FORM   $A ** C$
POLISH FORM  AC**

INFIX FORM   $A + B * C$
POLISH FORM  ABC*+

INFIX FORM   $(A + B) * C$
POLISH FORM  AB+C*

INFIX FORM   $(A - B) / (C - D) *E$
POLISH FORM  AB-CD-/E*

INFIX FORM   $((A+B)(C-D))/(E*F)**G$
POLISH FORM  AB+CD-EF*G**/
```

FIGURE 14.4   *(cont.)*

14.5.5   Manipulation of Strings

Additional character and string-manipulating capabilities can be added to FORTRAN by defining appropriate functions and subroutines. This technique will be demonstrated in this section by writing subroutines to assist in counting the frequency of occurrence of words in an essay or other textual material. The method can be extended to make easier the solving of other problems such as translating languages (both human and computer languages), preparing Key Word in Context (KWIC) lists, developing concordances, making authorship studies, editing textual material, and setting type for newspapers.

Specifically, we want to write a program to perform the following actions:

Using character variables, read and store a paragraph (or other textual information). This information (call it TEXT) is to be analyzed for the occurrence of particular words. After a word is read and printed, its locations (if any) in TEXT are determined and printed. At the end of the searching process, the count of occurrences of the word should be printed. This process should be repeated for other words. A word consisting of all blank characters indicates that the program should be terminated. A high-level solution is

```
read TEXT
write TEXT
read WORD
WHILE (WORD contains some characters)
    initialize
    WHILE (there are unexamined characters in TEXT)
        search for an occurrence of WORD in TEXT
        write location
        increase count
    ENDWHILE
    write count
    read WORD
ENDWHILE
STOP
END
```

Before the solution is expanded, we must decide how we will represent the strings in computer memory. The obvious solution is to define an array, TEXT, which is large enough to store the longest string of information of interest. Adjacent characters in the string would be stored in adjacent elements of TEXT. A similar storage technique could be used for the words of interest. An array, WORD, will be defined that is large enough to hold the longest word. The count of the actual number of characters in each string must be known, so we will use two variables LTEXT (for length of text) and LWORD (for length of word) for this purpose.

Next we must decide how to indicate the beginning and ending of characters of a string. The beginning is easy to handle—arbitrarily require a string to begin in column 1 of the card in which it is punched. A special symbol (@) not ordinarily found in a string will be used arbitrarily to signal the end of a string. (The delimiter, @, is not part of the string.)

Care must be taken in submitting words to be counted. Suppose that we want to know the locations and count of occurrences of the word "THE." If the card

THE@

is read, the contents of the word will be

A search for occurrences of this string will find *all* sequences of "THE." In the following TEXT four occurrences (underlined) are found.

THE CLASS THOUGHT THE PROFESSOR DID A PATHETIC JOB OF EXPLAINING HIS THESIS.

If the string is submitted with a blank on both sides, as in

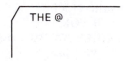

no match will occur with the "THE" in PATHETIC and THESIS. No match will be found for the initial "THE" in TEXT unless TEXT begins with a blank!

The initial high-level solution for the problem can be made more explicit by defining subprograms to perform the indicated steps. Subroutines RDSTR (for READ STRING) and OUTSTR (for OUTPUT STRING) will be used for input and output of strings. A function, LOCSUB (for LOCATE SUBSTRING), will be used to search for the starting location of a substring in a string. The form of the calling statement is

LOCSUB (TEXT, START, STOP, WORD, FINAL)

where TEXT   is the string to be searched
       START   is the location in TEXT at which the search is to start
       STOP   is the location in TEXT at which the search is to stop
       WORD   is the substring which is to be found in TEXT
       FINAL   is the location in WORD of the final character of the substring
      LOCSUB = $\begin{cases} \text{is 0 if no match is found} \\ \text{is the location of the beginning of the substring if a match is found} \end{cases}$

Thus the high-level solution becomes

```
CALL RDSTR (TEXT,LTEXT)
CALL OUTSTR (TEXT,LTEXT)
CALL RDSTR (WORD,LWORD)
WHILE (WORD contains some characters)
    initialize
    WHILE (there are unexamined characters in TEXT)
        LOC = LOCSUB (TEXT, START, STOP, WORD, FINAL)
```

```
          IF (substring found) THEN
              write LOC
              COUNT = COUNT +1
              set START to new location to continue search
          ELSE
              set indicator to get out of loop
          ENDIF
      ENDWHILE
      write COUNT
      CALL RDSTR (WORD,LWORD)
  ENDWHILE
  STOP
  END
```

The high-level solution will be completed before any of the subprograms are written. For the statement

> WHILE (WORD contains some non-blank characters)

a precise statement is required for the condition. If a string is empty, the LWORD will be zero. The statement becomes

> WHILE (LWORD .NE. 0)

Examination of the remaining part of the program reveals that the initialization step must assign values to COUNT, START, STOP, and FINAL. This is also a good place to print the contents of WORD. Initialization becomes

> COUNT = 0
> START = 1
> STOP = LTEXT
> FINAL = LWORD
> write WORD

Each time an occurrence of the substring is found, the value of START should be increased to begin subsequent searching at the next position after LOC. Eventually, START will become equal to or greater than STOP. This means that the statement

> WHILE (there are unexamined characters in TEXT)

can be replaced by

> WHILE (START .LE. STOP)

The new value of START after a successful match should be

$$START = LOC + 1$$

The final high-level solution is

```
      IMPLICIT INTEGER (A-Z)
      CHARACTER*1 TEXT(5000), WORD(80)
1000  FORMAT ('1', 'THE INPUT TEXT IS '/)
1010  FORMAT ('0', 'FOR THE WORD ' 80A)
1015  FORMAT ('b', 'THE LOCATIONS ARE ')
1020  FORMAT ('b', T6, I4)
1030  FORMAT ('b', T6, 'THE NUMBER OF OCCURRENCES IS ', I5)
      CALL RDSTR (TEXT,LTEXT)
      WRITE (6,1000)
      CALL OUTSTR (TEXT,LTEXT)
      CALL RDSTR (WORD,LWORD)
      WHILE (LWORD .NE. 0)
         COUNT = 0
         START = 1
         STOP = LTEXT
         FINAL = LWORD
         WRITE (6,1010) (WORD(I), I = 1,FINAL)
         WRITE (6,1015)
         WHILE (START .LE. STOP)
            LOC = LOCSUB (TEXT, START, STOP, WORD, FINAL)
            IF (LOC .NE. 0) THEN
               WRITE (6,1020) LOC
               COUNT = COUNT + 1
               START = LOC + 1
            ELSE
               START = STOP + 1
            ENDIF
         ENDWHILE
         WRITE (6,1030) COUNT
         CALL RDSTR (WORD,LWORD)
      ENDWHILE
      STOP
      END
```

The first statement in the program, the IMPLICIT statement, is used to describe to the compiler any deviations we wish to make in the mode implied by the first character of the name of a variable. The statement

IMPLICIT INTEGER (A–Z)

indicates that any name beginning with characters A through Z are to be assumed to be INTEGER mode. The statement

IMPLICIT INTEGER (A–K), REAL (L–Z)

implies that names beginning with A through K are INTEGER mode, and names beginning with L through Z are REAL mode. For the problem being solved in this section, all variables should have the same mode to reduce the probability of introducing a bug. A convenient way to accomplish this is by using the IMPLICIT statement.

The next stage in our top-down development of the program is the writing of routines for the subprograms that appeared in the mainline program. The first of these, subroutine RDSTR, must be capable of reading a string so long (i.e., contains so many characters) that many cards are required. The end of the string is signaled by the symbol @. A high-level solution for RDSTR is

```
initialize
WHILE (not end of string)
    read card
    find rightmost nonblank character in card
    IF (rightmost nonblank character .EQ. @) THEN
        set end of string indicator
        save location of end of string
    ELSE
        increase pointers for storing next card in string
    ENDIF
ENDWHILE
RETURN
END
```

Successive cards read within RDSTR must be stored in successive locations in the array, STRING, used to store the string. The contents of the first card must be placed in locations 1 through 80, the second card in locations 81 through 160, and so on. The variables M and N will be assigned the starting and ending positions, respectively, of a card within STRING.

The rightmost nonblank character in a card can be found by using a WHILE loop that processes the characters from right to left. A suitable set of steps is

```
I = N
WHILE (STRING(I) .EQ. ' ' .AND. I .GE. M)
    I = I - 1
ENDWHILE
```

The variable ENDSTR will be used as an indicator of whether or not the end of the string has been found. These ideas result in the following routine for RDSTR:

```
          SUBROUTINE RDSTR (STRING,LSTR)
          IMPLICIT INTEGER (A-Z)
          CHARACTER*1 STRING(1)
     1000 FORMAT (80A)
          M = 1
          N = 80
          ENDSTR = 0
          WHILE (ENDSTR .EQ. 0)
             READ (5,1000) (STRING(I), I = M,N)
             I = N
             WHILE (STRING(I) .EQ. ' ' .AND. I .GE. M)
                I = I - 1
             ENDWHILE
             IF (STRING(I) .EQ. '@') THEN
                ENDSTR = 1
                LSTR = I - 1
             ELSE
                M = M + 80
                N = N + 80
             ENDIF
          ENDWHILE
          RETURN
          END
```

The subroutine OUTSTR that prints a string is much easier to write than the routine for reading a string. The location of the last character in the string is obtained from the first element in STRING, and then the string is printed through this location. Thus the subroutine is

```
          SUBROUTINE OUTSTR(STRING,LSTR)
          IMPLICIT INTEGER (A-Z)
     1000 FORMAT (' ', 80A)
          WRITE (6,1000) (STRING(I), I = 1,LSTR)
          RETURN
          END
```

The heart of the program is the function LOCSUB, which finds a substring in another string. To obtain insight into how the function should operate, consider how we would find the substring ABLE in the string

MOST PEOPLE ARE CAPABLE OF DOING GOOD WORK.

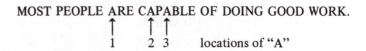

    1   2 3   locations of "A"

Since the first character of the substring is "A," we would search the string for an "A." When the first "A" is found, the subsequent characters of the substring and string would be compared to determine whether or not they are equal.

In this case, the matching process does not succeed, so we scan forward in the text looking for another "A." When the first "A" in "CAPABLE" is found, the comparison process is repeated, and it fails. Forward scanning is repeated until the second "A" in "CAPABLE" is found. This time the comparison is successful, and LOCSUB returns this location to the calling program. Thus a high-level description of LOCSUB is

```
FUNCTION LOCSUB (STRING, START, STOP, SUBSTR, FINAL)
initialize
WHILE (substring not found and there are unexamined characters in the string)
    try to find an occurrence of the first character of the substring in the string
    IF (first character found) THEN
        IF (subsequent characters in the substring and string match) THEN
            set LOCSUB to the location at which the substring is found
        ELSE
            set pointer to starting location of the next scan
        ENDIF
    ELSE
        string cannot contain the substring, so set indicator that
                all characters have been examined
    ENDIF
ENDWHILE
RETURN
END
```

In this high-level solution, it is not obvious how to "try to find an occurrence of the first character of the substring" and how to determine if "subsequent characters in the substring and string match." So to avoid getting lost in details now, we will define additional functions to perform these operations and write the functions later. Let LOCCH be a function that searches a string for the occurrence of a particular character, and let the calling statement have the form

LOCCH (STRING, START, STOP, CH)

where STRING   is the string to be searched
       START   is the location in STRING at which the search is to start
       STOP   is the location in STRING at which the search is to stop
       CH   is the character for which the search is made
       LOCCH = $\begin{cases} 0 \text{ if the character is not found} \\ \text{location of the character if it is found} \end{cases}$

Let ICMSTR be a function that compares successive characters in two strings, and let the calling statement have the form

ICMSTR (SUBSTR, START, STOP, STRING, BEGIN)

where SUBSTR   is the substring to be compared
       START   is the location in SUBSTR at which the comparison is to start
       STOP   is the location in SUBSTR at which the comparison is to stop
       STRING   is the string which is to be compared with the substring
       BEGIN   is the location in STRING at which the comparison is to start
       ICMSTR = $\begin{cases} 0 \text{ if the comparison fails} \\ 1 \text{ if the comparison succeeds} \end{cases}$

Incorporating these functions into the high-level solution for LOCSUB gives

```
FUNCTION LOCSUB (STRING, START, STOP, SUBSTR, FINAL)
initialize
WHILE (substring not found and there are unexamined characters
        in the string)
   LOC = LOCCH (STRING, I, UPPER, CH)
   IF (LOC .NE. 0) THEN
       IF (ICMSTR (SUBSTR,1,FINAL,STRING,LOC) .EQ. 1) THEN
           LOCSUB = LOC
       ELSE
           I = LOC + 1
       ENDIF
   ELSE
       I = position of final character to be examined + 1
   ENDIF
ENDWHILE
RETURN
END
```

In this partial solution, the arguments for LOCSUB, LOCCH, and ICMSTR had to be carefully considered. The definition of each function includes START and STOP as dummy arguments, but these arguments have a different meaning in each function. Also, in LOCCH and ICMSTR actual arguments are needed, not dummy arguments. Thus, in using LOCCH:

     I   is the location in STRING at which the search is to start;

     UPPER   is the location in STRING at which the search is to stop.

In using ICMSTR, the substring always begins in location 1, so the constant 1 is used as the starting position for the comparison. FINAL is the location of the last character used in the comparison.

The condition of the WHILE loop has two components—an indicator that the substring has not been found and a test for unexamined characters in the string. For the first component, we can use the fact that LOCSUB should be zero if the substring cannot be found

$$LOCSUB .EQ. 0$$

Since the variable I indicates the location for starting the search for an occurrence of the first character of the substring, the second component can be expressed as

$$I .LE. UPPER$$

where UPPER is the highest location from which the search for the substring can begin. It is pointless to examine the string for an occurrence of the substring unless the string contains at least as many unexamined characters as there are in the substring, so UPPER is given by

$$UPPER = \text{location of last character in STRING} - \text{number of characters}$$
$$\text{in SUBSTR} + 1$$
$$= STOP - (FINAL-1) + 1$$
$$= STOP - FINAL + 2$$

The final version of LOCSUB is

```
FUNCTION LOCSUB (STRING, START, STOP, SUBSTR, FINAL)
IMPLICIT INTEGER (A-Z)
CHARACTER*1 STRING(1), SUBSTR(1)
LOCSUB = 0
CH = SUBSTR(1)
UPPER = STOP - FINAL +2
I = START
WHILE (LOCSUB .EQ. 0 .AND. I .LE. UPPER)
   LOC = LOCCH (STRING, I, UPPER, CH)
   IF (LOC .NE. 0) THEN
      IF (ICMSTR (SUBSTR, 1, FINAL, STRING, LOC) .EQ. 1) THEN
         LOCSUB = LOC
      ELSE
         I = LOC + 1
      ENDIF
   ELSE
      I = UPPER + 1
   ENDIF
ENDWHILE
RETURN
END
```

At the next level of development of the program, we must write the instructions for the functions LOCCH and ICMSTR which appeared in LOCSUB. The routine LOCCH that searches for a character has the form

```
FUNCTION LOCCH(STRING, START, STOP, CH)
initialize
WHILE (character not found and there are unexamined characters
        in STRING)
    IF (this element of STRING is the character) THEN
        set indicator for character found
    ENDIF
    increase pointer to next location in STRING
ENDWHILE
RETURN
END
```

which can be translated into

```
FUNCTION LOCCH (STRING, START, STOP, CH)
IMPLICIT INTEGER (A-Z)
CHARACTER*1 STRING(1),CH
LOCCH = 0
I = START
WHILE (LOCCH .EQ. 0 .AND. I .LE. STOP)
    IF (STRING(I) .EQ. CH) THEN
        LOCCH = I
    ENDIF
    I = I + 1
ENDWHILE
RETURN
END
```

For the function ICMSTR, the heart of the routine is a loop that compares characters in the string and the substring. A high-level solution is

```
initialize
WHILE (there are characters to be compared and match has not failed)
    IF (characters in STRING and SUBSTR match) THEN
        increase pointers to indicate next characters
    ELSE
        set indicator for failure
    ENDIF
ENDWHILE
IF (not failure) THEN
    set ICMSTR
```

```
        ENDIF
        RETURN
        END
```

The final routine is shown below. Computer output for the program is given in Figure 14.5.

In solving this problem, two subroutines (RDSTR and OUTSTR) and three functions (LOCCH, ICMSTR, and LOCSUB) have been written. These routines can be used to solve other problems involving strings. By developing additional subprograms for manipulating strings, FORTRAN can be used effectively for many types of problems involving strings.

```
        FUNCTION ICMSTR (SUBSTR, START, STOP, STRING, BEGIN)
        IMPLICIT INTEGER (A-Z)
        CHARACTER*1 SUBSTR(1), STRING(1)
        ICMSTR = 0
        FAIL = 0
        I = START
        J = BEGIN
        WHILE (I .LE. STOP .AND. FAIL .EQ. 0)
            IF (SUBSTR(I) .EQ. STRING(J)) THEN
                I = I + 1
                J = J + 1
            ELSE
                FAIL = 1
            ENDIF
        ENDWHILE
        IF (FAIL .EQ. 0) THEN
            ICMSTR = 1
        ENDIF
        RETURN
        END
```

14.5.6   Finding Substrings—INDEX Function

To assist in the manipulation of strings defined as CHARACTER variables, FORTRAN has the intrinsic function INDEX. This function has the form

$$INDEX\ (s_1, s_2)$$

where s_1 and s_2 are CHARACTER variables. The string s_1 is searched for an occurrence of substring s_2. If s_2 is located in s_1, INDEX returns the position in s_1 at which the first character of s_2 occurs. If s_2 does not occur in s_1, INDEX returns the value zero.

```
 1  C
 2  C                   MANIPULATION OF STRINGS
 3  C
 4           IMPLICIT INTEGER(A-Z)
 5           CHARACTER*1 TEXT(5000),WORD(81)
 6           INTEGER LTEXT,LWORD
 7  1000     FORMAT('1','THE INPUT TEXT IS'/)
 8  1010     FORMAT('0','FOR THE WORD        '80A)
 9  1015     FORMAT(' ','   THE LOCATIONS ARE')
10  1020     FORMAT(' ',T6,I4)
11  1030     FORMAT(' ',T6,'THE NUMBER OF OCCURRENCES IS ',I5)
12           CALL RDSTR(TEXT,LTEXT)
13           WRITE(6,1000)
14           CALL OUTSTR(TEXT,LTEXT)
15           CALL RDSTR(WORD,LWORD)
16           WHILE(LWORD .NE. 0)
17              COUNT=0
18              START=1
19              STOP=LTEXT
20              FINAL=LWORD
21              WRITE(6,1010)(WORD(I),I=1,FINAL)
22              WRITE(6,1015)
23              WHILE( START .LE. STOP)
24                 LOC=LOCSUB(TEXT,START,STOP,WORD,FINAL)
25                 IF(LOC .NE. 0) THEN
26                    WRITE(6,1020)LOC
27                    COUNT=COUNT+1
28                    START=LOC+1
29                 ELSE
30                    START=STOP+1
31                 ENDIF
32              ENDWHILE
33              WRITE(6,1030)COUNT
34              CALL RDSTR(WORD,LWORD)
35           ENDWHILE
36           STOP
37           END

38           SUBROUTINE RDSTR(STRING,LSTR)
39           IMPLICIT INTEGER(A-Z)
40           CHARACTER*1 STRING(1)
41           INTEGER LSTR
42  1000     FORMAT(80A)
43           M=1
44           N=80
45           ENDSTR=0
46           WHILE(ENDSTR .EQ. 0)
47              READ(5,1000)(STRING(I),I=M,N)
48              I=N
49              WHILE(STRING(I) .EQ. ' '  .AND.  I .GE. M)
50                 I=I-1
51              ENDWHILE
52              IF(STRING(I) .EQ. '@' ) THEN
53                 ENDSTR=1
54                 LSTR=I-1
55              ELSE
56                 M=M+80
```

FIGURE 14.5 *Manipulation of strings using subprograms*

472

```
57              N=N+80
58          ENDIF
59      ENDWHILE
60      RETURN
61      END

62      SUBROUTINE OUTSTR(STRING,LSTR)
63      IMPLICIT INTEGER(A-Z)
64      CHARACTER*1 STRING(1)
65      INTEGER LSTR
66 1000 FORMAT(' ',80A)
67      LAST=LSTR
68      WRITE(6,1000)(STRING(I),I=1,LAST)
69      RETURN
70      END

71      FUNCTION LOCSUB(STRING,START,STOP,SUBSTR,FINAL)
72      IMPLICIT INTEGER(A-Z)
73      CHARACTER*1 STRING(1),SUBSTR(1),CH
74      LOCSUB=0
75      CH=SUBSTR(1)
76      UPPER=STOP-FINAL+2
77      I=START
78      WHILE( LOCSUB .EQ. 0 .AND. I .LE. UPPER )
79          LOC=LOCCH(STRING,I,UPPER,CH)
80          IF( LOC .NE. 0) THEN
81              IF(ICMSTR(SUBSTR,1,FINAL,STRING,LOC) .EQ. 1) THEN
82                  LOCSUB=LOC
83              ELSE
84                  I=LOC+1
85              ENDIF
86          ELSE
87              I=UPPER+1
88          ENDIF
89      ENDWHILE
90      RETURN
91      END

92      FUNCTION LOCCH(STRING,START,STOP,CH)
93      IMPLICIT INTEGER(A-Z)
94      CHARACTER*1 STRING(1),CH
95      LOCCH=0
96      I=START
97      WHILE( LOCCH .EQ. 0 .AND. I .LE. STOP )
98          IF(STRING(I) .EQ. CH) THEN
99              LOCCH=I
100         ENDIF
101         I=I+1
102     ENDWHILE
103     RETURN
104     END

105     FUNCTION ICMSTR(SUBSTR,START,STOP,STRING,BEGIN)
106     IMPLICIT INTEGER(A-Z)
107     CHARACTER*1 SUBSTR(1),STRING(1)
108     ICMSTR=0
109     FAIL=0
```

FIGURE 14.5 *(cont.)*

473

```
110        I=START
111        J=BEGIN
112        WHILE(I.LE.STOP .AND. FAIL.EQ.0)
113            IF(SUBSTR(I) .EQ. STRING(J)) THEN
114                I=I+1
115                J=J+1
116            ELSE
117                FAIL=1
118            ENDIF
119        ENDWHILE
120        IF(FAIL .EQ. 0) THEN
121            ICMSTR=1
122        ENDIF
123        RETURN
124        END
```

First execution of the program

```
THE INPUT TEXT IS

THE CLASS THOUGHT THE PROFESSOR DID A PATHETIC JOB OF EXPLAINING HIS THESIS.

FOR THE WORD        THE
   THE LOCATIONS ARE
         1
        19
        41
        70
      THE NUMBER OF OCCURRENCES IS        4

FOR THE WORD          THE
   THE LOCATIONS ARE
        18
      THE NUMBER OF OCCURRENCES IS        1
```

Second execution of the program

```
THE INPUT TEXT IS

THE IMPORTANCE OF SUBPROGRAMS AS INTELLECTUAL TOOLS CAN HARDLY BE
OVEREMPHASIZED.  IN USING THE SQRT FUNCTION YOU DID NOT NEED TO
KNOW EITHER THE INDIVIDUAL INSTRUCTIONS WHICH WERE REQUIRED TO
DEFINE IT OR EVEN TO KNOW THE ALGORITHM UPON WHICH IT WAS BASED.

FOR THE WORD        THE
   THE LOCATIONS ARE
         1
       107
       168
       173
       267
      THE NUMBER OF OCCURRENCES IS        5

FOR THE WORD          THE
   THE LOCATIONS ARE
       106
       172
       266
      THE NUMBER OF OCCURRENCES IS        3
```

FIGURE 14.5   *(cont.)*

The program of Figure 14.6 applies INDEX to find the locations of the substring "THE" in the variable TEXT. The processing is performed by the statements

```
CPTEXT = TEXT
LOC = 1
WHILE (LOC .NE. 0)
    LOC = INDEX (CPTEXT, WORD)
    IF (LOC .NE. 0) THEN
        WRITE (6,1050) LOC
        CPTEXT [LOC : 1] = '*'
    ENDIF
ENDWHILE
```

```
1         CHARACTER*80 TEXT,CPTEXT
2         CHARACTER*3 WORD
3    1000 FORMAT(A)
4    1010 FORMAT('1','THE INPUT TEXT IS:')
5    1020 FORMAT(' ',A)
6    1030 FORMAT('0','FOR THE WORD:    ',A)
7    1040 FORMAT(' ','   THE LOCATIONS ARE')
8    1050 FORMAT(' ',T6,I4)
9         READ(5,1000)TEXT
10        READ(5,1000)WORD
11        WRITE(6,1010)
12        WRITE(6,1020)TEXT
13        WRITE(6,1030)WORD
14        WRITE(6,1040)
15        CPTEXT=TEXT
16        LOC=1
17        WHILE( LOC.NE.0 )
18           LOC=INDEX( CPTEXT, WORD)
19           IF( LOC .NE. 0)THEN
20              WRITE(6,1050)LOC
21              CPTEXT[LOC:1]="*"
22           ENDIF
23        ENDWHILE
24        STOP
25        END
```

```
THE INPUT TEXT IS:
THE CLASS THOUGHT THE PROFESSOR DID A PATHETIC JOB OF EXPLAINING
                                                   HIS THESIS.

FOR THE WORD:    THE
   THE LOCATIONS ARE
       1
      19
      41
      70
```

FIGURE 14.6   *Use of INDEX function*

The substring "THE" has been assigned previously as the value of WORD. For each execution of the WHILE loop, the copy of TEXT, CPTEXT, is searched from the beginning of the string for an occurrence of WORD. If WORD is found by INDEX, its location is assigned to LOC, and this value is printed. The statement

$$\text{CPTEXT [LOC:1]} = \text{`*'}$$

means: replace the character at position LOC in CPTEXT with "*". This causes "THE" in CPTEXT to become "*HE," so that particular occurrence will not be found again in the next search by INDEX. When the substring can no longer be found, INDEX returns zero, and the loop is terminated.

REVIEW QUESTIONS

1. What is a CHARACTER variable? How do they differ from other types of FORTRAN variables?
2. What is a CHARACTER constant? Describe the use of a CHARACTER constant for assigning a value to a CHARACTER variable.
3. What is the difference in treating 2 as an integer and as a character?
4. Suppose that characters have been assigned to two variables. Describe a technique for determining which variable occurs earlier in the alphabet.
5. In the sorting of alphabetic data, what steps are necessary to interchange two names?
6. What is Polish notation for arithmetic expressions?
7. Why do compilers tend to use Polish notation?
8. List the steps in the shunting-yard algorithm.
9. What is the purpose of the intrinsic function INDEX?

REVIEW QUIZ

1. An example of a variable that could be used to store character data is (A) MER, (B) TWIST, (C) ABLE(10), (D) NEXT(I), (E) all the previous answers.
2. Given CHARACTER*80 TEXT, an appropriate specification for reading the value of TEXT is (A) 80A, (B) A, (C) 80I1, (D) I80, (E) two of the previous answers.
3. Given:

$$\text{CHARACTER*1 LPAR(100)}$$
$$\text{DO 10 I = 1,100}$$
$$\text{10 READ (5,15) LPAR(I)}$$
$$\text{15 FORMAT (80A)}$$

The number of cards that will be read is (A) 1, (B) 2, (C) 80, (D) 100, (E) none of the previous answers.

4. Given:

$$\text{CHARACTER*1 KARD(80)}$$
$$\text{READ (5,5) KARD}$$
$$\text{5 FORMAT (80A)}$$
$$\text{WRITE (6,5) KARD}$$

(A) Exactly 80 cards will be read.

(B) The read statement will be executed 80 times.

(C) The first character stored in KARD will not be printed by the WRITE statement.

(D) Exactly 80 lines will be printed.

(E) Two of the previous answers are valid.

5. A CHARACTER variable is (A) real-mode, (B) integer-mode, (C) declared in a DIMENSION statement, (D) a string of characters, (E) two of the previous answers are valid.

6. A CHARACTER constant (A) must be declared in a DIMENSION statement; (B) can appear on the left-hand side of an assignment statement; (C) is enclosed in apostrophes; (D) is restricted to four or fewer consecutive characters; (E) can be used in an arithmetic expression.

7. An example of an *invalid* statement is:

(A) X = 'TEXTBOOK'

(B) CHARACTER*2 X

(C) CHARACTER*20 NAMES(100)

(D) IF (X .EQ. 'THE') THEN
.
.
.
ENDIF

(E) NAMES ('I') = 'JOHN DOE'

8. The postfix Polish form of (A+B)/C*D is (A) A+BCD*/, (B) AB+C/D*, (C) AB+CD*/, (D) ABC/+D*, (E) ABC+/D*.

EXERCISES

1. Write statements to accomplish the following:

   a. Read 40 characters into CHARACTER variable KARD.

   b. Read 40 characters into array KARD, which is defined by CHARACTER*2 KARD(40).

   c. Read 40 characters into array KARD, which is defined by CHARACTER*4 KARD(40).

   d. Read 5 fields of 4 characters each into array PERSON.

   e. Read 80 characters into an array, then print the 20th through the 60th characters.

   f. Declare a character variable X to consist of 4 characters.

   g. Declare a character variable NAME of 20 characters.

2. Given:

```
CHARACTER*1 A,B,C(10),D
CHARACTER*2 X,Y
CHARACTER*4 R,S
A = 'A'
B = 'B'
D = 'C'
C(1)  = 'A'
C(2)  = 'B'
```

$$C(3) = \text{'C'}$$
$$C(4) = \text{'D'}$$
$$C(5) = \text{'E'}$$
$$C(6) = \text{'F'}$$
$$C(7) = \text{'G'}$$
$$C(8) = \text{'H'}$$
$$C(9) = \text{'I'}$$
$$C(10) = \text{'J'}$$
$$X = \text{'AB'}$$
$$R = \text{'TEST'}$$
$$S = \text{'NEXT'}$$

a. What is the outcome of the following comparisons:
   (1) IF (A .LT. B)
   (2) IF (C(2) .EQ. B)
   (3) IF (C(4) .LT. C(5))
   (4) IF (C(5) .GT. C(8))
   (5) IF (R .EQ. S)
   (6) IF (R .LT. S)

b. Write statements to accomplish the following:
   (1) Assign the value of X to Y.
   (2) Interchange the values of A and B.
   (3) Interchange the values of R and S.
   (4) Find the element of C which equals the value of D.
   (5) Assign the string "LAST" to R.
   (6) Determine which has the larger value, X or Y.
   (7) Print the value of A and B.
   (8) Print the contents of array C on a single line with no spaces between the elements.
   (9) Print the contents of array C on a single line with a single blank character between each element.
   (10) Print the elements of C as a vertical column.

3. Write program segments to perform the following:
   a. Read 20 names of 24 characters each into an array.
   b. Find the location of the name that is alphabetically the first in an array of 1000 names of 20 characters each.
   c. Find the location of the first "A" in TEXT.
   d. Find the location of the first occurrence of the word "THE" in the array TEXT.
   e. Count the number of occurrences of blanks in TEXT.
   f. Count the number of occurrences of "E" in TEXT.
   g. Count the number of nonblank characters in TEXT.

PROGRAMMING EXERCISES

1. Write a program that lists the contents of a deck of cards.
2. Expand the card listing program so that it:
   a. Lists exactly 55 lines per page.
   b. Prints the heading, "LISTING OF CARD DECK," at the top of each page.
   c. Prints in the upper right-hand corner of each page the word PAGE followed by the appropriate page number.

3. Read a message contained in any number of cards and print it with all blanks deleted. For example, HELP ME SOLVE THIS PROBLEM becomes HELPMESOLVETHISPROBLEM.

4. Write a program that reads a message and prints it with all blanks and all vowels deleted. For example, WHO CAN SOLVE THE PROBLEM EASIER. becomes WHCNSLVTHPRBLMSR.

5. Write a program that prints an exact copy of itself, that is, is a self-reproducing program. To make the program more interesting, no input statements are allowed.

6. In various computer applications, it is very helpful to be able to convert an integer into the corresponding sequence of characters. For example, the integer 1759 would be converted to '1', '7', '5', '9'. Write a program that makes conversions of this type.

7. This program is the reverse of the one in Programming Exercise 6. Read a set of characters, each representing a digit, and convert them into integers.

8. Some numbers are palindromes. For example, 1221, 373, and 9078709 are all palindromes. It has been speculated that any number can be made into a palindrome by the process of reversing the digits of the number and adding the results to the original number. If the sum is not a palindrome, the process is repeated until one is produced. Converting 84 to a palindrome involves the steps

$$
\begin{array}{r}
84 \\
\underline{48} \\
132 \\
\underline{231} \\
363
\end{array}
$$

Write a program that converts integers into palindromes. Be careful: numbers can grow to be thousands of digits long without a palindrome being produced.

9. Write a program that reads a message and prints the characters in reverse order. For example, HELP ME SOLVE THIS PROBLEM, would become MELBORP SIHT EVLOS EM PLEH.

10. Write a program that reads a message and prints the characters of each word in reverse order. For example, HELP ME SOLVE THIS PROBLEM would become PLEH EM EVLOS SIHT MELBORP.

11. Suppose that it becomes necessary to change in a computer program all the statements that contain a particular variable, say XCALC. In a long computer program it may be difficult to find all the statements. Write a program that helps solve this problem by:
   a. Reading the name of the variable of interest.
   b. Reading the card deck containing the program.
   c. Printing the contents of the card and the number of the card (count cards as they are read) containing the statement whenever a card contains the variable.

12. Write a program that prints address labels. Input is a deck of cards each containing a name and address. Output is the address labels in the form:

   Mr. John Doe, Jr.
   101 West Hamilton Road
   Rome, GA 30161

13. The printing of one address label at a time wastes printing time. Write a program that prints 3 address labels simultaneously. The output would have the appearance

Mr. John Doe, Jr.	Ms. Sue Helper	Dr. Sam Smith
101 West Hamilton Road	10 Maple Street	75 Highland Blvd.
Rome, GA 30161	Paris, IL 61944	Athens, ME 04912

14. The computer is an ideal tool for encoding and decoding messages. In its simplest form, encoding uses two arrays. A character to be encoded in the message is also found in the first array. The position at which it is found is noted, and the character in the corresponding position of the second array is used for encoding. Suppose that the arrays are:

ARRAY1   A B C D E F G H I J K L M N O P Q R S T U V W X Y Z
ARRAY2   D H A B C Q W X E O S Z L F M I G U Y J N R T P V K

Then the message   HELP   IS   ON   THE   WAY
becomes   XCZI   EY   MF   JXC   TDV

Write a program to encode a message. You may use the approach described above or a more complex method of your own design.

15. Hangman is a well-known computer game involving the guessing of words. The computer picks a word and tells you how many characters are in it. You guess a character, and if you are right the computer tells you the position of the character in the word. If the word is LUCK, and your first successful guess is U, the computer prints XUXX. If your next successful guess is L, the computer prints LUXX. Whenever you make a wrong guess, the computer adds the next part to a drawing of a hanging man. (Parts are head, body, left hand, right hand, left arm, right arm, left leg, and right leg.) If you guess the word before the drawing is complete, you win. Otherwise, you have been hanged, and you lose. A simple form of the drawing is

Write a program to implement the game. Help the player by printing all the letters he uses, even when they are wrong guesses. The program should make a clever comment after each guess and at the end of the game. If you wish, you can make the drawing fancier.

16. An important reason that compilers tend to translate arithmetic expressions into Polish notation before evaluating them is that an algorithm exists for checking Polish strings for proper formation. (Legitimate expressions are called well-formed formulas, or, wff.) This means that there is a straightforward method for a compiler to test an arithmetic expression for valid syntax. The method is

a. Assign ranks to components of the statement as follows:

Component	Rank
variable	+1
+, -, *, /	-1
**	-1
unary-	0

b. Begin at the left-hand end of a postfix Polish string and compute the sum of the ranks proceeding from left to right.

c. Examine the running sum at each step. If it ever becomes less than +1, the string is not a wff. At the right end of the string, the value of the sum must be exactly +1; otherwise, the string is not a wff.

Consider the Polish string AB-CD-* in which each uppercase letter represents a variable. Then the algorithm gives

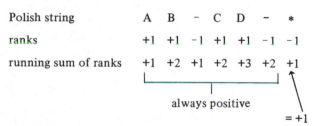

The string is a wff.

Write a program to implement this algorithm.

17. Write a program that will find a valid interpretation of the following in terms of numbers:

$$\begin{array}{r} \$ \quad SEND \\ MORE \\ \hline MONEY \end{array}$$

The problem has more than one solution. Can you modify your program to find all the solutions?

18. Computers can be used to provide drill and practice in arithmetic. You are to implement the initial stage of such a program. The program should read an arithmetic exercise and determine whether the answer given is correct or not. Each exercise has the syntax

$$\text{number operation number} = \text{answer}$$

For example,

$$192 + 31 = 222$$

or

$$19 - 35 = -16$$

Blanks are to be ignored, so the components of an exercise may appear anywhere in the input array. All numbers will be unsigned integers. For each exercise, print one line of output. It should contain the exercise, the notation "correct" or "incorrect," and in the case of an incorrect answer, the correct answer. For example:

$$192 + 31 = 222 \quad \text{INCORRECT } 223$$
$$19 - 35 = -16 \quad \text{CORRECT}$$

19. Write a program that counts the number of occurrences of four-letter words in array TEXT.

20. A popular type of puzzle involves finding words that are hidden horizontally, vertically, or diagonally in a two-dimensional array of letters. For example, the following 8 × 10 array contains the names of the states Alabama, Idaho, Indiana, Iowa, Kansas, Maine, New York, Ohio, Oregon, Texas, Vermont, Virginia.

```
T I N D I A N A
C E A M A I N E
V N X R S O E I
I E N A G P S D
R W R E S A A A
G Y R M S W Y H
I O O N O H I O
N R A I N N O P
I K I N K S T E
A L A B A M A I
```

Write a program that will find the hidden words in such puzzles.

21. Write a program that will generate hidden word puzzles.

CHAPTER 15
SOME THINGS COMPUTERS CAN DO

Newspapers, magazines, and books abound with comments about the benefits of using computers, the threat to society posed by computers, and the ultimate capabilities of computers. There is no doubt that computers have both expanded significantly the power of the human intellect and created frightening problems. As educated, knowledgeable individuals, you should be able to evaluate statements made about computers. How do you feel about the following:*

> A species is a distinctive form of life. There is no question that computers are distinctive, but most people would insist that it is ridiculous to compare a machine to a living being. I would like to argue that the traditional distinction between living and inanimate matter may be important to a biologist but is unimportant and possibly dangerously misleading for philosophical considerations.

The discussion concludes:

> Modern computers demonstrate the ability to think, to remember, and to communicate with the outside world. In these capabilities they are sufficiently like species of living beings to justify considering a possible symbiotic relationship between man and the computer.

Is this science fiction? The author, John G. Kemeny, an eminent mathematician and educator, would not be expected to make unfounded and rash statements.

In this chapter, the subject of what computers can do is considered from several points of view. The topics include:

1. Some theoretical results that will give you some understanding of the possible limits of computation.
2. Some problems that have been solved with programs which display "intelligent" behavior. (These programs are very different from those we have written in FORTRAN, and knowing about them will expand your understanding of what computers can do.)

*John G. Kemeny, *Man and the Computer* (New York: Charles Scribner's Sons, 1974), pp. 10 and 13.

3. The question of whether or not a computer can think.
4. The potential impact of computing on education.
5. The simulation of complex processes.

All these topics have positive and negative aspects associated with them, but emphasis will be placed on the potential benefits. In Chapter 16, some important social issues related to computing will be examined. As future leaders, you have a responsibility to understand these problems and to work for their satisfactory resolution.

15.1 SOME THEORETICAL RESULTS

15.1.1 Turing Machines

In 1936, long before the invention of modern computers, the British mathematician Alan M. Turing published a famous paper in which he discussed the theoretical limits of what could be computed if practical constraints such as the time required and the amount of memory necessary could be ignored. His arguments were presented in terms of a hypothetical machine which is called a Turing machine (abbreviated TM) in his honor. A TM has three components: (1) a control unit, (2) a magnetic tape of *infinite* length from which symbols can be read or on which symbols can be written, and (3) a read/write head (see Figure 15.1).

A Turing machine has associated with it a set of *states*. The number of states depends upon the problem being solved with the TM. As each step in the problem-solving process is executed, the TM changes state:

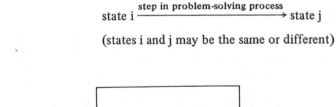

(states i and j may be the same or different)

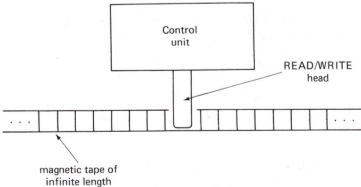

FIGURE 15.1 *Diagram of a Turing machine*

The operation of the machine proceeds as follows:

1. The symbol under the read/write head is read.
2. Depending upon the symbol read and the state of the machine, the same symbol or a different symbol is written on the tape.
3. The read/write head is moved one position to the left (L), one position to the right (R), or not moved (N).
4. The machine changes from state i to state j.

These steps are repeated until the problem has been solved. The purpose of the control unit of the TM is to store the state of the machine and the rules for changing states. The number of rules is assumed to be finite (although there may be a very large number of rules), but the infinite length of the tape allows the TM to escape the limitations of finite memory.

To solve a problem using a Turing machine, a program must be written. The process resembles writing a program for a modern computer, but the operations with the tape (L, R, N) are so simple that writing a program for a TM is more difficult. A programmer must decide upon the states he will use in solving the problem, and the number of states will depend upon the procedure (or algorithm) he selects. He must also develop appropriate rules for transitions between the states. In general, we are not interested in writing programs for TMs, but we will consider one example just to help clarify the ideas involved. Consider the following problem:

A tape contains a binary number delimited by asterisks. Other cells in the tape are blank. Write a program that reads the contents of the tape and prints to the right of the rightmost asterisk a 0 if the number of 1's is even and a 1 if the number is odd. For example, if the tape contains:

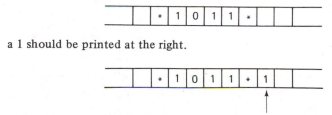

a 1 should be printed at the right.

Solving even this simple problem can be troublesome unless one has experience writing TM programs. After some trial and error, the following program involving four states (q is the standard symbol for state) was written:

q_{start} starting state

q_{even} the number of 1's is even so far

q_{odd} the number of 1's is odd so far

q_{stop} final state (the machine halts if it reads a blank while in the final state)

The idea of the program is to scan the tape, left to right, and to alternate between states q_{even} and q_{odd} as 1's are encountered. For the sample tape, the sequence will be

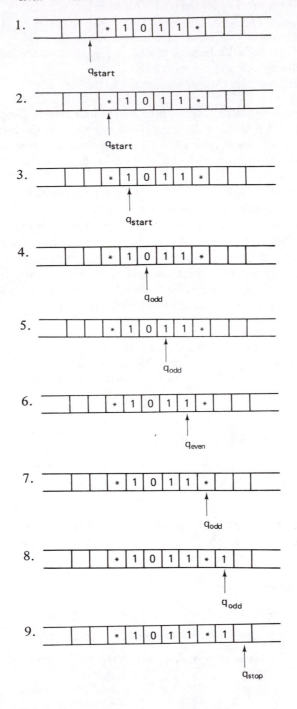

For each step:

1. Read the symbol.
2. Write the symbol.
3. Move the read/write head.
4. Change the state.

The state written below a tape cell is the state before the cell is read. For each step we must specify (1) the initial state, (2) the symbol read, (3) the next state, (4) the symbol written, and (5) the tape motion. For step 3, the sequence is q_{start}, 1, q_{odd}, 1, R. (*Note:* Moving the tape to the left is equivalent to moving the read/write head to the right. Here we assume that the read/write head moves.) The program for the TM is shown in tabular form below:

Input symbol	Current state			
	q_{start}	q_{even}	q_{odd}	q_{stop}
b	$bq_{start}R$	$0q_{stop}R$	$1q_{stop}R$	$bq_{stop}N$
*	$*q_{start}R$	$*q_{even}R$	$*q_{odd}R$	
0	$0q_{even}R$	$0q_{even}R$	$0q_{odd}R$	
1	$1q_{odd}R$	$1q_{odd}R$	$1q_{even}R$	

An entry in the table (e.g., $bq_{start}R$) gives the symbol to be written on the tape, the next state, and the movement of the read/write head. The table is used as a program by finding the column that corresponds to the current state and the row that corresponds to the symbol currently under the read/write head. The element at the intersection of the row and column describes the action the TM should take. For example, if the TM is in state q_{even} with a 1 under the read/write head, the element $1q_{odd}R$ indicates that the TM should write a 1 on the tape, change to state q_{odd}, and move the read/write head one position to the right. The table is stored in the control unit of the TM.

The extreme simplicity of the Turing machine makes program writing difficult, but this simplicity makes it ideal for a theoretical investigation of what a machine can do. Any limitations in what a TM can do defines the limits of what a modern computer can do—a computer is less powerful for problem solving than a TM—but the computer can be made to approximate a TM by adding more memory and magnetic tape, as needed, to the computer.

In his investigation of TMs, Turing found it convenient to assume that a separate TM existed for each possible program that could be stored in the control unit. He was then able to prove mathematically that there is one TM, called the Universal Turing Machine, which is capable of simulating the behavior of any TM. This is equivalent to stating that a sufficiently powerful computer (a computer having enough memory and magnetic tape) can be used to simulate the behavior of any other computer. It is common practice for computer companies to simulate a proposed, more powerful computer on existing, less powerful computers before actually manufacturing the proposed computer.

Turing was also able to demonstrate mathematically that TMs could always be developed to solve problems for certain types of effective procedures. (Earlier, an effective procedure was defined as a procedure that terminates if a solution can be found; otherwise, it may not terminate.) This result led him to speculate that a TM can solve any problem that can be expressed as an effective procedure. This corresponds to the programmer's intuition that he can solve any problem that he can express in a programming language.

Turing's approach to studying what can be computed is but one of several possible approaches. Alonzo Church investigated the properties of lambda calculus, Emil Post studied formal languages, and A. Markov studied the properties of strings. The results of these investigations have been shown to be mathematically equivalent, and they have led to general acceptance of the following hypothesis:

> *Thesis of Turing and Church:*
> A Turing machine can be constructed to realize any process that can be described by an effective procedure.

This hypothesis belongs to metamathematics and cannot be proven, but the fact that so many researchers starting from different viewpoints have reached the same conclusion gives strong support to the hypothesis.

Can any process be expressed as an effective procedure? No. There are some problems for which no effective procedure is possible. The most famous of these problems is called the "halting problem." The idea is to construct a procedure that will examine the steps in another procedure and determine whether or not the procedure will halt. This is similar to attempting to write a computer program that can examine any other computer program and decide whether the program will stop. The problem can be solved for specific programs, but not for all cases. Thus there is a theoretical limit to what computers (and human beings) can do.

There are practical limitations to what a computer can do. A problem may be expressible as an effective procedure, but in actually attempting to solve the problem, too much computer time may be required. (Remember, the theoretical studies ignored the time required for a computation.) Also, an effective procedure is not required to have a halting rule if the problem does not have a solution. If a program executes for a very long time, do we conclude that more time is required or that the problem has no solution?

What a TM or computer can do depends upon finding effective procedures, which in turn require precise use of the programming language of the machine. It therefore appears that there is a close relationship between machines and languages, and this has been found to be true. It has been discovered that two apparently unrelated research fields, formal language theory and automata theory, are mathematically equivalent. Formal language theory is concerned with discovering the properties of language based on features of their syntax. Automata theory studies the capabilities of Turing-like machines which have been constrained in some aspects of their operations. A given machine is able to understand and use languages of a particular complexity or lower complexity. Theorems proven for a given theory, formal language or automata, are transferable to the other theory. Our emphasis throughout the text on the precise use of language in computing even has some theoretical basis.

Are there problems that we can solve that cannot be solved (at least theoretically) by computers? Joseph Weizenbaum phrases the question in the form: "Are all the decisionmaking processes that humans employ reducible to effective procedures and hence to machine computation?"* He argues that people know more than they can tell and that the emphasis on "meaning" (instead of syntax) in natural language makes us different. He states: "We are at *least* universal Turing machines" (p. 71), and implies that we are more. There are, however, many computer scientists who disagree with him, and the issue of the relative capabilities of people and computers is not settled. What we can make a computer do depends upon what we can get it to know, and as yet we do not know this limit.

Weizenbaum is also quite concerned with what computers *ought* to do. In the preface of his book, he states:

> The rest of the book contains the major arguments, which are in essence, first, that there is a difference between man and machine, and, second, that there are certain tasks which computers *ought* not to be made to do, independent of whether computers *can* be made to do them.

Some of these tasks will be examined in Chapter 16 when we consider social issues.

15.1.2 Self-reproduction of Computers

In the introduction to this chapter, it was noted that John Kemeny believes computers to be species of living beings. This naturally raises the question: Might computers be considered now (or at a later date) to be living beings? This question is virtually impossible to answer because the term "living" is not well defined. Attempts to define "living" by enumerating properties of living beings has not been successful because counterexamples can always be found for a given property. Consider the following brief list of some "properties of living beings":

1. A living being metabolizes.
   Spores do not metabolize, but are considered living.
2. A living being is not man-made.
   Man has made new species of bacteria by DNA modifications.
3. A living being is made of protoplasm.
   Should a virus be considered made of protoplasm?
   A frankfurter is made of protoplasm but is not living.
4. A living being can reproduce itself.
   A virus can reproduce itself—is it living?
   A mule cannot reproduce itself.

*Joseph Weizenbaum, *Computer Power and Human Reason* (San Francisco: W. H. Freeman and Company, Publishers, 1976), p. 67. Reproduced by permission of W. H. Freeman and Company.

Instead of considering this question further, we will ask if computers can reproduce themselves. Most of us would agree that computers should have that property if they are to be considered a species.

An obvious property of machines is that they generally produce other machines that are less complicated—the machinery for making an automobile is more complicated than the automobile. There is a degradation in complexity when machines make other machines. Animals, however, produce offspring that appear to be at least as complicated as the parents. Is this a fundamental difference in machines and animals? Could a machine be constructed that could reproduce itself starting with parts so simple that the reproduction process is not trivial?

In 1951, these questions interested John von Neumann, who began a mathematical study of the project. He died in 1957 without having published the results of his investigation, but in 1966 Arthur W. Burks edited, completed, and published the work as the *Theory of Self-Reproducing Automata*. With a mathematical proof nearly 200 pages long, he demonstrated that a properly constructed Turing-like machine could reproduce itself. Other researchers have discovered alternative proofs that are much shorter. Michael Arbib needed only eight pages for his proof. Thus there is no theoretical obstacle to constructing a machine that can reproduce itself.

15.2 "INTELLIGENT" PROGRAMS

Can a computer program exhibit intelligent behavior in solving a problem? My answer would be yes, but not everyone would agree, since intelligence is difficult (perhaps impossible) to define. In this section, we discuss several programs that perform tasks which would be considered to involve intelligence if a person were performing them. The programs are very complex, and many are written in LISP or some extension of that language, so no attempt will be made to discuss the details of the programs. The programs presented represent only a fraction of those that display intelligent behavior.

How "intelligent" computers and their programs can become is, of course, a matter of speculation. If we admit that some capacity for learning exists, the following comment by Marvin Minsky in 1966 becomes quite interesting:

> Once we have devised programs with a genuine capacity for self-improvement a rapid evolutionary process will begin. As the machine improves both itself and its model of itself, we shall begin to see all the phenomena associated with the terms "consciousness," "intuition" and "intelligence" itself. It is hard to say how close we are to this threshold, but once it is crossed the world will not be the same.*

15.2.1 Checkers

It is generally conceded that playing a good game of checkers requires intelligence. There is no known algorithm for winning the game. The strategy of examining

*Marvin Minsky; originally published in *Scientific American*, September 1966, p. 260. From *Information* (San Francisco: W. H. Freeman and Company, Publishers, 1966), p. 210. Copyright © by Scientific American, Inc. All rights reserved.

the result of particular moves by looking ahead would guarantee a win if the looka-head could be extended to the end of the game for each possible move. This is impos-sible for both people and computers. The number of possible moves in a game of checkers has been estimated to be 10^{40}. If a computer could generate one move in 1 nanosecond (an impossibility), approximately 10^{21} centuries would be required to produce all possible moves for a game.

In the 1950s, A. L. Samuel, then a scientist at IBM, wondered if he could make the computer play a reasonable game of checkers. He wrote a program for that pur-pose and tested it in the evenings when the computer was not being used. The original program has been modified many times to incorporate new ideas. The program, which contains procedures for learning and improving its play, was soon beating Samuel. Transcripts of games played by masters were submitted to the program to aid it in its evaluation of what constituted good play. The program even played itself. By the mid-1960s, only checker champions of national stature had a reasonable probability of beating the program.

The major concepts built into the checker-playing program are a board evalua-tion function and a lookahead technique. The evaluation function examines a con-figuration of checkers for factors such as relative number of pieces, number of kings, control of the center of the board, and other factors believed to be of strategic signif-icance. Then it assigns a numerical value to the board configuration to indicate its relative desirability. The program changes the importance of the factors used in the evaluation depending upon the outcome of the game. This leads to improved strategy in the play of the program.

The lookahead procedure starts with a given board configuration and considers the possible moves that could be made from the configuration. Each of the resulting board configurations is then evaluated. Possible responses by the opponent are eval-uated, and it is assumed that the opponent will always make the move that is most advantageous to him. The lookahead is expanded through several future moves, with the actual number depending upon the situation. The technique is very clever and expands promising moves through more future moves than is done for less promising moves.

15.2.2 Chess

In 1950, Claude E. Shannon, famous for his development of information theory, proposed that a computer be programmed to play chess. He noted:

> The problem is sharply defined, both in the allowed operations (the moves of chess) and in the ultimate goal (checkmate). It is neither so simple as to be trivial nor too difficult for satisfactory solution. And such a machine could be pitted against a human opponent, giving a clear measure of the machine's ability in this type of reasoning.*

*Claude E. Shannon; originally published in *Scientific American*, February 1950, p. 48. From *Computers and Computation* (San Francisco: W. H. Freeman and Com-pany, Publishers, 1971), pp. 104–107. Copyright © by Scientific American, Inc. All rights reserved.

Shannon suggested that a chess-playing program should contain the following basic components:

1. An encoding procedure.

    Chess positions must be converted into a convenient internal representation within the computer.
2. A move evaluation procedure.

    This section must

    a. analyze positions and select moves to be examined.

    b. evaluate the moves selected.
3. A final choice procedure.

    A technique is needed to select the final move based upon the previous analysis and evaluation.

Implementing these procedures at a level of competence for playing a good game of chess has been quite difficult. There are many aspects of human chess playing that are not understood.

By 1957, a number of chess-playing programs had been written. Notable individuals in this activity were Bastian, Bernstein, Gillogly, McCarthy, and Newell. Some of these programs played a passable amateur game of chess. It was believed that the advent of faster computers would result in significantly improved play. Several noted scientists confidently predicted that a computer would beat the world champion in a game within 10 years (by 1967). This has not happened. The problem is much more difficult than was realized at the time.

In April 1967, the Greenblatt Chess Program won the Massachusetts Class D trophy—the first tournament chess won by a computer. The rating of the program was approximately 1400 points (the mean rating for all chess players is approximately 900, the mean for all tournament players is approximately 1800, and the rating of Bobby Fisher is 2785). For a number of years, this program was considered to be the best of the chess programs.

A national computer chess tournament was established in 1970. At the seventh tournament, in October 1976, eleven programs competed. The champion, CHESS 4.5 on a CDC Cyber 176 computer (written by David Slate and Larry Atkin), is the current version of an illustrious line of chess-playing programs. In July 1976, CHESS 4.5 was entered in the B-section (rating 1600 to 1799) of the Paul Masson Chess Classic in Saratoga, California. It surprised everyone, including the authors of the program, by scoring 5 wins and 0 losses against opponents having an average rating of 1735. One of the opponents complained that the program "was obviously too strong for the B-section." The performance rating for CHESS 4.5 for the tournament was 2136.

CHESS 4.5 was then entered in February 1977 in the 84th Minnesota Open tournament against Class A and expert players. It won the tournament! The score was 5 wins and 1 loss against players having rankings of 1969, 2019, 1965, 2175, 1947, and 1954. The performance rating for CHESS 4.5 was 2271.

In 1968, David Levy, an international master (rating 2325), made a wager of £1000 with several computer scientists that he would not be beaten by a computer in regular match play by August 31, 1976. In the final match before he collected the bet, Levy defeated the program CHESS 4.6 by a score of 3.5 to 1.5. (In five games the computer won one game and had a draw in another.) Earlier in 1977, Levy played a challenge game against the program CHESS 4.5. After 43 moves, CHESS 4.5 resigned. Hans Berliner, international master and former world correspondence champion, reported an impression of grandmaster-level play by CHESS 4.5 in sharp tactical situations. Immediately after the challenge game, a blitz game was played in which CHESS 4.5 beat Levy. In previous practice blitz games, CHESS 4.5 and Levy each won 4 games. The excitement generated by Levy's bet has prompted other wagers. Volmac, a Dutch software company, has offered a prize of $50,000 to anyone writing a chess program that beats former world champion Max Euwe by January 1, 1984.

There is no longer any doubt that a computer can be programmed to play a very good game of chess. If a person were playing as well, most of us would consider him to be quite intelligent. Is the computer displaying intelligent behavior?

15.2.3   Geometric Analogy Problems

The solving of geometric analogy problems is a standard part of human intelligence tests and is the kind of problem that most of us would not expect a computer to be able to solve. However, in 1968, Thomas G. Evans published a Ph.D. thesis which described a computer program that solves such problems. Typically, problems are stated in the form: Figure A is to figure B as figure C is to which of the following five figures? An example is*

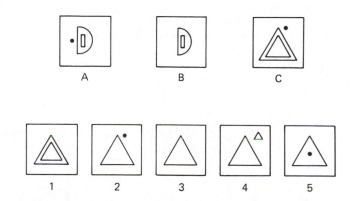

Other examples are given in Figure 15.2.† Descriptions of the figures are given to the program, which then deduces the answer. The problems are taken from standard IQ tests of the American Council on Education. The computer performed as well as an average tenth-grade student.

---

*Patrick H. Winston, *Artificial Intelligence* (Reading, Mass.: Addison-Wesley Publishing Company, Inc., 1977), p. 16. Reprinted with permission.
†Ibid., p. 27.

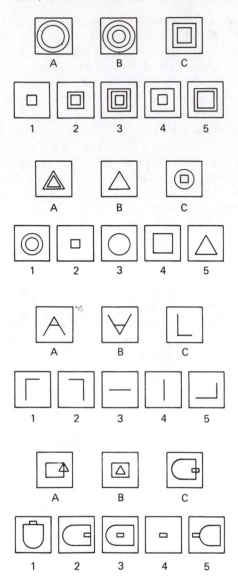

FIGURE 15.2 *Typical problems solved by geometric analogy programs*

The program operates by constructing a description of how figure A can be transformed into figure B, constructing descriptions of how figure C can be transformed into the other five figures, and matching the transformation rules for A into B with the transformations of C into other figures. The process usually does not result in an exact matching of the rules, so procedures are built into the program for estimating the closeness of the matching and determining the relative importance of the rules. This program has been important in computer science because it demonstrates clearly the value of good descriptions in solving problems.

15.2.4   Learning a Concept

Patrick H. Winston, director of the Artificial Intelligence Laboratory at MIT, demonstrated in 1970 in his Ph.D. thesis that a computer could learn the concept of an arch.* The program learns the concept by creating an appropriate description of an example that is given to it. Then additional examples, differing in some simple aspect, are submitted. Each example is used to generalize the previous description. *Near-miss* examples, which fail for some simple reason to illustrate the concept, must also be submitted. Comparison of the description of the concept and of the object that just missed allows the program to clarify and strengthen the description of the concept.

The description of the concept needs to be created using a technique that organizes the relationships in order of their importance; that is, the description needs to be hierarchical. For this purpose, Winston used a network with objects and properties being represented by circles and relationships between these represented by connecting arrows. If the program is given the following arch as an example,

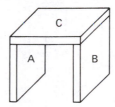

a network of the following type is constructed as a description of the arch.

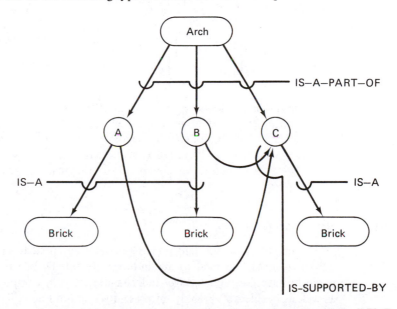

*Patrick H. Winston, "Learning Structural Descriptions from Examples," Ph.D. thesis, in *The Psychology of Computer Vision*, edited by Patrick H. Winston (New York: McGraw-Hill Book Company, 1975), pp. 185–209.

This example is followed by the presentation of a near-miss to the program:

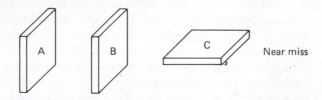

The program constructs a network for the near-miss and compares it with the current description of the arch. It deduces that the relationship C IS-SUPPORTED-BY A AND B should be replaced by C MUST-BE-SUPPORTED-BY A AND B. Additional examples further clarify the description:

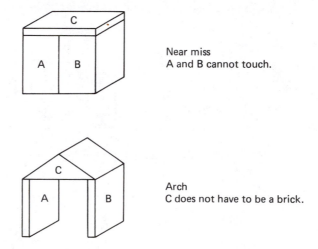

Near miss
A and B cannot touch.

Arch
C does not have to be a brick.

The description developed by the program is shown in Figure 15.3.

    This program has been very useful in drawing our attention to (1) the central role played by descriptions in the learning process, (2) the need for hierarchical descriptions, and (3) the importance of presenting near-misses in the teaching process. It is also a very instructive metaphor for the teaching–learning process in human beings.

15.2.5 Natural Language

    Our ability to use language is generally accepted to be a major component of our intelligence. We tend to attribute greater intelligence to those animals that apparently have greater language understanding. Can a computer understand language as well as people do? Frankly, at present we do not know. Early attempts to translate language using a computer were failures, but some progress has been made in this area. When the domain of discourse is limited, the computer does quite well. This

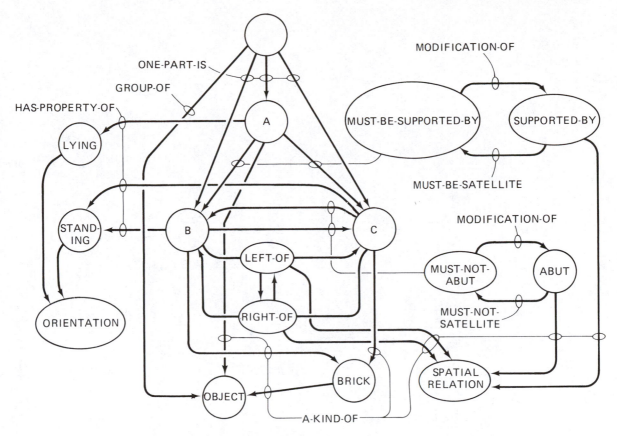

FIGURE 15.3 *Description of an arch*

limitation is necessary, in part, because the ability to use language effectively is intimately associated with other real-world knowledge, and at this stage our ability to supply this knowledge is limited.

An outstanding example of a program that understands natural language in a limited domain was written by Terry Winograd for his 1971 Ph.D. thesis. The program operates in the domain of the "blocks world," which consists of a collection of blocks and pyramids of different sizes and colors, an open box, and a robot hand to manipulate the objects. Commands can be given in English to the robot. A scene in the blocks world is given in Figure 15.4.*

It is important to realize that Winograd's program is an embodiment of a theory of natural language. It contains procedures intended to understand any reasonable question about the blocks world. It does *not* contain a set of sentences that are examined for a possible match with an input sentence. Instead, the system attempts to

*Terry Winograd, *Understanding Natural Language* (New York: Academic Press, Inc., 1972), p. 159. Reproduced by permission of Academic Press.

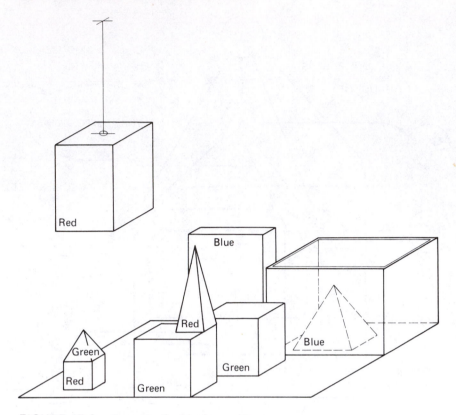

FIGURE 15.4   *Scene in the blocks world*

understand in a way believed to be similar to the way people understand, according to one theory of language. The system has built-in knowledge about how to move blocks, the need to clear a space before moving a block, and the fact that no block can rest on the tip of a pyramid.

An abbreviated version of an actual conversation* with the system is given in Figure 15.5. Most people, especially those who have some knowledge of the difficulties of understanding natural language, are astounded by the conversation.

The natural language understanding program of Winograd contained built-in knowledge of how to manipulate the objects of the blocks world. If the program could understand a sentence, the built-in procedures allowed it to perform the required actions. For example, for blocks A, B, and C,

A   B   C

*Ibid., pp. 8–15.

Pick up a big red block.
OK

Grasp the pyramid.
I DON'T UNDERSTAND WHICH PYRAMID YOU MEAN.
    (There are three pyramids in the scene, so the program does nothing.)

What does the box contain?
THE BLUE PYRAMID AND THE BLUE BOX.

What is the pyramid supported by?
THE BOX
    (The program assumes that we mean the pyramid just mentioned.)

Can a pyramid be supported by a block?
YES

Will you please stack up both of the red blocks and either a green cube or a
    pyramid?
OK
    (Some problem solving was necessary.)

Does the shortest thing the tallest pyramid's support supports support anything
    green?
YES, THE GREEN PYRAMID.
    (Some people have trouble with this one.)

Had you touched any pyramid before you put the green one on the little cube?
YES, THE GREEN ONE.
    (The system remembers. Note the need for analysis of verbs.)

When did you pick it up?
WHILE I WAS STACKING UP THE RED CUBE, A LARGE RED BLOCK,
    AND A LARGE GREEN CUBE.

Why?
TO GET RID OF IT.

Why did you do that?
TO CLEAN OFF THE RED CUBE.

Why did you do that?
BECAUSE YOU ASKED ME TO.

Thank you.
YOU'RE WELCOME!

FIGURE 15.5 *Abbreviated conversation in the blocks world (computer replies are in
CAPS)*

and the sentence

Place A on B, and place B on C.

as soon as the meaning of the sentence was understood, the robot would construct the stack

After Winograd's work, Gerald Sussman decided to reverse this problem. He wanted to know whether or not a program could of itself acquire the real-world skill to manipulate the blocks. Sussman's work was presented in his Ph.D. dissertation in 1973.*

15.3 THINKING

Can a machine think? This question is extremely difficult to answer, because we have no adequate definitions for the words "machine" and "think." In addition, it is difficult to consider the question in an objective and unemotional manner. In this section, we examine the proposal of Alan M. Turing† for answering the question and study a specific attempt to use his proposal.

15.3.1 The Imitation Game

The imitation game is played with three people, a man (A), a woman (B), and an interrogator (C), who may be of either sex. The object of the game is for the interrogator to identify the woman by asking questions. The individuals are in separate rooms, and the interrogator is in a third room. Communication is done with typewriter-like terminals to prevent the voices from providing clues (see Figure 15.6). The woman tries to fool the interrogator and cause him to make the wrong identification, and the man answers to help the interrogator. Any kind of question may be asked.

Person X, describe the most profound Shakespearean play.

Person Y, what kind of dresses do you like best?

Person X, why is football interesting?

---

*Gerald Jay Sussman, "A Computational Model of Skill Acquisition," Ph.D. dissertation (August 1973), AI-TR-297, MIT-AI-Laboratory, Cambridge, Mass.

†A. M. Turing, "Can a Machine Think?" from *Computing Machinery and Intelligence* in *Mind*, *59* (October 1950), 433–460. Reproduced by permission of Basil Blackwell, Publishers, Ltd.

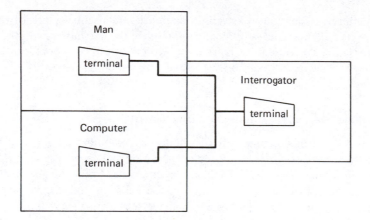

FIGURE 15.6 *Arrangement for the imitation game*

> Person Y, why is the queen so powerful in chess?
>
> Person X, please tell me how an automobile works.
>
> Person Y, how do you like men to behave during a date?

At the end of the game, the interrogator must identify X or Y as the woman.

Turing then raises the question as to how a computer would do if it took the place of A in the imitation game. Will the interrogator perform significantly better in the identification process when the computer plays the game? If the interrogator guesses wrong 50% of the time, Turing suggests that we should accept the proposition that the computer is thinking. The original question, "Can a machine think?" has thus been changed to "Can a digital computer do well in the imitation game?" The latter question can be investigated experimentally.

The validity of the imitation game as a test for thinking was discussed in detail by Turing in his paper. He apparently believed that digital computers would be able to pass the test.

> It may also be said that this identification of machines with digital computers, like our criterion for "thinking," will only be unsatisfactory if (contrary to my belief), it turns out that digital computers are unable to give a good showing in the game.*
>
> I believe that at the end of the century the use of words and general educated opinion will have altered so much that one will be able to speak of machines thinking without expecting to be contradicted.†

After stating these opinions, Turing considered various opinions opposed to his. He discussed (and many people believe he demolished) objections based on theology,

*Ibid., p. 437.
†Ibid., p. 442.

mathematics, consciousness, various disabilities of machines, lack of the ability for a machine to "originate" anything, continuity in the nervous system, the informality of behavior, and extrasensory perception. His entire article is nontechnical and is fascinating reading regardless of one's personal opinion on the subject.

15.3.2 An Experiment with an Imitation Game: PARRY

A somewhat limited test of whether a computer could satisfactorily play the imitation game was made by Kenneth M. Colby and his associates at Stanford University during the early 1970s.* It must be emphasized that the goal of the work was to investigate a theoretical model of neurotic behavior and *not* to play the imitation game. The model that interested Colby, a psychiatrist, was the conflict theory of neurosis, which hypothesizes that an individual faced with a severe conflict between two or more beliefs such as

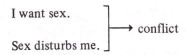

will attempt to reduce the conflict by transforming one or more of the beliefs. If the belief

I hate my father.

were in conflict with other beliefs, it might be transformed into

I hate my brother.

or

My father hates me.

This model of neurotic behavior proved to be too difficult to simulate, as there is no agreement on what constitutes a normal set of beliefs. Consequently, it was decided to simulate a more limited belief system, paranoid processes, about which psychiatrists were in general agreement. A set of beliefs were to be developed for a paranoid individual, and this belief system was to be incorporated into a computer program. The resulting program, PARRY, was used in conducting interviews by means of a teletype with a psychiatrist. In half the interviews, an actual paranoid patient was used.

*Kenneth M. Colby, "Simulations of Belief Systems," *Computer Models of Thought and Language*, edited by R. C. Schank and K. M. Colby (San Francisco: W. H. Freeman and Company, Publishers, 1973), pp. 251–286. Reprinted by permission of W. H. Freeman and Company.

Eight psychiatrists each conducted two interviews, one with the model (i.e., PARRY) and one with a paranoid patient. These interview judges were not told that a computer was involved. Transcripts of interviews with the paranoid model, a paranoid patient, and a nonparanoid patient were sent to 105 randomly selected psychiatrists, and 33 responded. None was told that a computer was involved. They were asked to rate the interviews on the degree of paranoia the patient was judged to have. The nonparanoid interview was successfully identified, and other judgments agreed with the anticipated results. The model was a successful simulation of paranoia.

The invented patient whose paranoia was simulated in PARRY is briefly described as:

> He is a 28 year old single man who works in the stockroom at Sears. He lives alone, has no siblings, and seldom sees his parents. He is sensitive

---

How did you come to be in the hospital?
I AM UPSET.

How long have you been in the hospital?
ABOUT A WEEK.

In what way are you upset?
PEOPLE MAKE ME NERVOUS.

In what way do they make you nervous?
PEOPLE GIVE ME A FUNNY LOOK SOMETIMES.

Is there anything about people in particular?
CERTAIN PERSONS.

Who are the certain persons and what is it that they do?
DO YOU KNOW HOW THE UNDERWORLD OPERATES?

Why did you ask about the underworld?
WHAT INFORMATION DO YOU HAVE ON THE UNDERWORLD?

I don't know about the underworld but when you mentioned the underworld I thought you must have some contact with it and that's what I would like to know more about.
I TRY TO AVOID THE UNDERWORLD.

Have you been actively trying to avoid the underworld?
NO ONE HAS ANY POWER OVER GANGSTERS.

Who brought you into the hospital?
THE POLICE.

Why did they bring you in?
COPS DON'T DO THEIR JOB.

Well I hope you didn't just lie down and let them drag you in.
COPS ARREST THE WRONG PEOPLE.

FIGURE 15.7 *Partial interview with PARRY (computer replies are in CAPS)*

TABLE 15.1   *Summary of imitation game results for PARRY*

Group	Number selected	Number of replies	Correct I.D.	Incorrect I.D.	Statistical conclusion
Psychiatrists	100	41	21 (51%)	20 (49%)	Chance guessing
Computer scientists	100	67	32 (48%)	35 (52%)	Chance guessing

about his lack of education, his religion, and the topic of sex. His hobby is gambling on horseraces both at the track and through bookies. A few months ago he quarrelled with a bookie, claiming the bookie did not pay off a bet correctly. After the quarrel it occurred to him that he so angered the bookie that the latter might have the underworld figures injure or kill him. He developed malevolence delusions about the underworld which became so frightening that he sought medical help and then accepted a recommendation of psychiatric hospitalization.*

A portion of an interview with PARRY is given in Figure 15.7.

It was decided to determine whether individuals could distinguish between an interview with PARRY and an interview with a real paranoid patient when the judges knew that one interview involved a computer program. A group of 100 randomly selected psychiatrists and a group of 100 randomly selected computer scientists were sent two interviews and asked to identify the computer program. The results are shown in Table 15.1.

PARRY succeeded in this limited form of the imitation game. Perhaps the result would have been different if those making the judgment also performed the interviewing. Certainly, the result would have been different if questions on any subject had been allowed. Nevertheless, the result is impressive.

15.4   EDUCATION

The use of computers to improve the educational process is less dramatic than applications discussed earlier in the chapter, but in the long run, this use may have profound effects upon society. Three quite different approaches to using the computer in education will be discussed briefly here. The first approach, the PLATO project, allows teachers to develop computer-assisted instruction (CAI) courses to supplement and improve existing educational materials. The other two approaches visualize a total revision in the educational process based on computer technology rather than the technology of pencil, paper, and books, but the emphasis is different in the projects. The LOGO project focuses upon constructing an environment based on computers in which children will discover principles for themselves instead of learning by

*Ibid., p. 269.

memorizing. The Personal Dynamic Media Project emphasizes the use of a very small computer, the dynabook, as an aid to creative thought.

15.4.1 The PLATO System

In the 1950s, it was apparent that computers had the potential for improving education through CAI by relegating the teaching of rote memory tasks to the computer, making these tasks more interesting, and individualizing the instruction to fit the needs of each student. An obvious problem was the cost of providing the necessary computer hardware. Donald L. Bitzer, University of Illinois at Urbana, believed that CAI could be made economically feasible by using a very large computer in a time-sharing mode to serve the needs of thousands of students simultaneously. Such a system would also be appropriate for testing the effectiveness of CAI concepts.

Supported by public funds, Bitzer proceeded in the 1960s with the development of the PLATO (*Programmed Logic for Automated Teaching Operation*) system. Initially, it was projected that by using a very large computer manufactured by Control Data Corporation, as many as 4000 terminals could be used simultaneously at a cost of approximately 50¢ per terminal hour. (Present costs are much higher.) Each terminal consisted of a special plasma screen display, microfiche projector, and keyboard. Other features, such as an audio disk, a touch panel for locating where the screen has been touched, and a general input/output jack for devices such as piano keyboards can be included if a particular course needs them. A special language, TUTOR, was implemented to make it easy for teachers to write CAI programs.

By 1975, the PLATO system had over 500 terminals attached, and enough additional terminals had been ordered by schools to bring the total to more than 1000. The system is very responsive, and users' communication with the computer involves delays of less than 1 second. Users of the system are very enthusiastic about it.

After the technical feasibility of PLATO was demonstrated, public funding was eliminated and rights to the system were obtained by Control Data Corporation.

15.4.2 The LOGO Project

The LOGO project was started by Seymour Papert at MIT in approximately 1969. A fundamental precept of the project is that the cognitive development of children can be accelerated by exposing them to appropriate learning environments. Such environments must be fun and exciting for the children so that the learning experience holds their attention in the same way that play does. The major task of the project is the development of these environments. This research was influenced significantly by Piaget's theory of cognitive development.

An approach used by LOGO is the teaching of concepts and ideas that allow children to articulate their thinking processes and to "think about thinking." The concepts of planning, procedure, subprocedure, naming, state, local, global, recursion, and extensibility are examples of powerful ideas that allow a person to organize the problem-solving process in a different way.

The LOGO and PLATO projects are totally different in their approach to education. The LOGO project concentrates on the intellectual aspects of the teaching-learning process, and it visualizes a total restructuring of what and how children learn. The PLATO project assists in the learning of present curricula. Both projects use the computer, but again the approach is different. PLATO uses a very large computer to reduce the cost per student. LOGO is betting (and at present it appears to be a good bet) that improved technology will reduce the cost of computers to a sufficiently low value that their cost will not be a major consideration.

15.4.3 The Personal Dynamic Media Project

The Personal Dynamic Media project, under the direction of Alan Kay of Xerox, concentrated on developing the dynabook. which is ultimately expected to be a notebook-sized computer of tremendous power. Present versions of the dynabook are about the size of a small desk. Members of this project believe that technology will soon reduce computers to the required size for the dynabook, with the cost being low enough to be affordable by practically everyone.

The dynabook will be highly portable because of its size. The user will be able to store within it the equivalent of thousands of pages of material: data, mathematical facts, novels, poetry, drawings, financial information, music, recipes, and so on. Since the dynabook is a portable library with the facilities of a computer, the world could become an interactive learning center. It should be able to handle the complete information needs of a user, whether the user is a child or a medical doctor concerned with patient records. Anything the user would like to remember could be entered in the dynabook.

A powerful computer language, SMALLTALK, has been developed for use with the dynabook. Emphasis is given to communication processes and to facilitating creative thought. With the interim dynabook, children have sketched, drawn, and "painted" animated cartoons, created movies, manipulated LOGO-like turtles, composed music, and done other interesting things. Adults have used it to simulate real-life situations, for example, the operation of a hospital.

15.5 WORLD DYNAMICS

The computer can be used in the construction and investigation of complex models. The term *model* refers to a set of assumptions and interrelationships that attempts to capture the important elements of some aspect of the real world. Engineers, when faced with a complex problem such as the construction of a dam or the development of a new type of aircraft, will normally construct a physical model that can be studied and tested. For some systems, physical models cannot be constructed. No physical model exists for the social interaction between human beings, so we employ mental models for helping us deal with the people and situations that we encounter. The assumptions implicit in an individual's mental model make him, for example, a leader, a political activist, or a criminal. In science, models can sometimes be expressed as systems of mathematical equations. Solving these equations may be impossible without the aid of computers. In the case of weather predictions, the mathematical model appears to be excellent, but improving the forecasts would require larger and faster computers—a completely accurate "forecast" is worthless if the computing is not finished before the time period being considered.

We now examine some features of a complex and important model, an analysis of the long-term prospects for mankind. Two small books, *The Limits to Growth** and *Mankind at the Turning Point*,† describe the results of the initial model and a subsequent revision to it. The work is very controversial. Anthony Lewis, in the *New York Times* Book Review, called *The Limits to Growth*, "one of the most important documents of our times." Economists Mark Roberts, Peter Passell, and Leonard Ross called it "an empty work . . . a rediscovery of the oldest maxim of computer science: garbage in, garbage out." Jan Tinberger, Nobel laureate in economics, in referring to *Mankind at the Turning Point*, called the work "an enormous step forward in our understanding of the essence of the worst bottlenecks our world is facing." Both books were published as reports to the Club of Rome in conjunction with its Project on the Predicament of Mankind.

The goal of the work was to investigate the following five trends, which are of global concern:

1. Accelerating industralization.
2. Rapid population growth.
3. Widespread malnutrition.
4. Depletion of nonrenewable resources.
5. Deteriorating environment.

An understanding of the causes of these trends, their interrelationships, and their implications for the future were sought.

The computer model for the initial study grew out of the work of Jay W. Forrester and his Systems Dynamics Group at MIT. This group took ideas and tools normally used to study the physical world and applied them to the social world. By 1971, a formal model of the world that gave attention to the effects of population growth had been developed. This is the prototype model for the study led by Dennis L. Meadows (MIT) of the limits to growth. The authors describe their model as "imperfect, oversimplified, and unfinished." They also note:

> Since ours is a formal, or mathematical, model it also has two important advantages over mental models. First, every assumption we make is written

---

*D. H. Meadows, D. L. Meadows, J. Randers, and W. H. Behrens III, *The Limits to Growth: A Report for The Club of Rome's Project on the Predicament of Mankind.* A Potomac Associates book published by Universe Books, New York, 1972, 1974. Graphics by Potomac Associates.

†M. Mesarovic and E. Pestel, *Mankind at the Turning Point* (New York: E. P. Dutton, 1974). Reproduced by permission of E. P. Dutton.

in a precise form so that it is open to inspection and criticism by all. Second, after the assumptions have been scrutinized, discussed, and revised to agree with our best current knowledge, their implications for the future of the world system can be traced without error by a computer, no matter how complicated they become.*

The world model used for the simulation assumes a complex interrelationship among many factors, with special attention given to feedback loops. For example, the total population depends upon the number of births and deaths per year. The number of births per year has a positive influence on the population in that it adds members to the population. But the number of births depends upon the population and the fertility of the population. This can be diagrammed as:

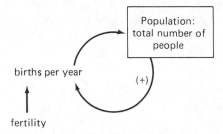

In a similar way, the number of deaths per year exerts a negative influence on the population, while it, in turn, is influenced by the population and the mortality of the population. This can be combined with the previous diagram as follows:

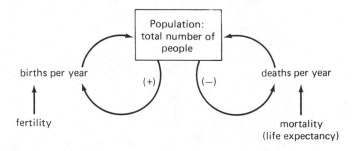

As more factors are considered, the feedback diagrams rapidly become more complicated. Figure 15.8 shows feedback loops for population, capital, agriculture, and pollution.† This diagram is only a tiny fraction of the model. The interrelationships are finally quantified into mathematical equations.

In the improved model, which was developed by Mihajlo Mesarovic and Eduard Pestel, whose results are reported in *Mankind at the Turning Point*, the system can be studied in blocks of countries or even individual countries. It thus has the potential of

*Meadows et al., *The Limits to Growth*, p. 27.
†Ibid., p. 106.

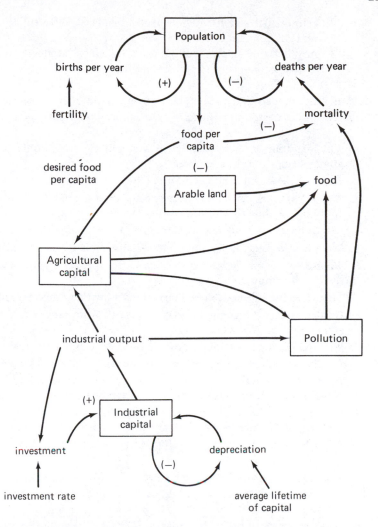

FIGURE 15.8 *Feedback loops of population, capital, agriculture, and pollution*

being useful to individual countries in formulating their policies. In the analyses made by the model, the world is viewed as a series of interacting regions in which the individual differences in culture, economic development, and tradition play an important role. Some feeling for the complexity involved can be obtained by realizing that about 100,000 relationships are incorporated into the model. It is impossible to manipulate a model of this complexity without a computer.

Both models predict:

1. A collapse of the world system by the middle of the next century if present trends continue. (The second model predicts that regional collapses will occur earlier.)

2. Only global action to implement a balanced, differentiated growth can prevent the collapse.

3. Any delay in implementing corrective global strategies results in disastrous human, economic, and political losses.

Whether the models and their predictions are valid or not, they clearly demonstrate the value of the computer in the process of understanding complex situations.

REVIEW QUESTIONS

1. Why did John Kemeny claim that a symbiotic relationship is possible between human beings and the computer?

2. What are the components of a Turing machine?

3. Why is a Turing machine more powerful than a computer? How can a computer approximate the behavior of a Turing machine?

4. Why is the study of Turing machines important to computer science?

5. State the thesis of Turing and Church and explain its significance.

6. What does Joseph Weizenbaum claim is the appropriate human attitude regarding the use of computers?

7. Theoretically, is it possible to create a machine that could reproduce itself?

8. How well can the computer play checkers? Who wrote the checker-playing program described in the text?

9. Why did Claude Shannon propose that a chess-playing program be developed?

10. Briefly summarize the history of development of chess-playing programs.

11. In a match between a human chess player of average ability and the best chess-playing computer program, what is the expected result?

12. Give an example of the kind of problem that is solved by the geometric analogy program of Thomas Evans. How well does it perform?

13. Describe the technique used by the program of Patrick Winston to learn the concept of "arch."

14. What is the "blocks world"? Why was it developed?

15. Describe the imitation game. Why is it so important? What was Turing's opinion regarding the eventual outcome of the game?

16. What is the purpose of the program PARRY? Describe the test of the imitation game that was made with PARRY.

17. Describe the PLATO, LOGO, and dynabook projects.

18. What is the world dynamics project? To what important class of computations does the project belong? Could the computations be made without a computer? What are the conclusions reached by it?

CHAPTER 16 SOCIAL ISSUES AND COMPUTING

One has only to read the newspaper to realize how significantly the computer affects our lives, both favorably and unfavorably. This Jekyll–Hyde behavior is characteristic of most great inventions—the automobile allows us to move about freely, but it also produces many tragic accidents and threatens our health through pollution. The potential of the computer for good appears to be matched by its potential for harm. The need to manipulate large quantities of information, the wish to improve corporate profits, and even the wish to improve public services by making them more efficient and economical provided the motivation for many computer applications. Only in retrospect were various harmful aspects of the applications recognized.

When social issues are considered, the complexity of the problems often makes impossible an unequivocal solution to a problem. Rather, the typical situation is for reasonable people to differ strongly on the appropriate action. In this chapter, we briefly consider possible trade-offs for a few particular situations, but in general no course of action will be recommended. Richard Hamming has proposed the following criterion for evaluating computer applications:

> The evil or good does not rest in the computer; it rests with the user. And if people demand that computers be used in ways to make life more pleasant than it is at present, then computers will be so used—but not unless people demand it. . . . There is a simple and natural test to apply to any new application of computers which interacts with humans and that is this: does the human have more options (freedom) now than he had before the use of the computer?*

Hamming's eloquent statement is reasonable and persuasive, but it is not the only plausible criterion that could be used in evaluating computer usage. If, for example, one believes that society as a whole is more important than the good of a particular individual, then a different evaluation criterion would be used. In reaching conclusions about the topics discussed in this chapter, you should try to determine what your own evaluation criteria are.

16.1 EDUCATION

Three projects that have the possibility of revolutionizing education were discussed in Chapter 15. Yet it is not obvious that these projects would have an overall

*Richard W. Hamming, *Computers and Society* (New York: McGraw-Hill Book Company, 1972), p. 17. Reproduced by permission of McGraw-Hill Book Company.

beneficial effect, especially in the case of computer-assisted instruction (CAI). In this section, we consider some of the possible negative aspects of using computers in education. The statement of potential negative features should not, however, be interpreted to mean that I believe they will actually occur, but we do need to consider all aspects. A fundamental problem is how to determine the relative importance of the potential positive and negative features. How can we find the answers to the questions raised in the following paragraphs?

The computer is not a warm, loving teacher, but a fundamentally cold, logical machine. How can such a machine cope with the human needs of children? If there were a family argument before the child came to school, would the computer be able to react in an appropriate manner? It can be argued that the computer can be programmed to behave in any manner desired. Is this, in fact, true? If it is true, can society afford the cost of the necessary computer programming to make the computer behave in a friendly, encouraging manner?

In any case, the computer will perform as it is programmed. It will be able to do only those things for which it was programmed. How do we program the computer to handle the vast range of behavior that a student might exhibit during a learning session? What will be the effect of errors in the teaching programs?

At a more general level, how can we be sure that the use of computers will improve the quality of education? Might computers actually be used to perpetuate and extend the poorer aspects of existing courses and further entrench the educational bureaucracy? It has been argued that computers will result in greater attention being given to the individual student, but might not inadequate computer programs and disinterested teachers cause the reverse effect? Remember the effect of the "new math" in our school systems.

What will be the effect of computers on teachers? Will their role change to that of educational computer programmer? Would teachers be able to adjust to changes induced by computers? What happens to teachers who cannot adjust to the new situation? Will society need more or fewer teachers?

Will the use of computers cause a dispersal of the educational process? Will students, for example, spend more of their time at home learning by means of a terminal connected to a central school computer? If this should occur, what would be the effect on the adult members of the family? Moreover, how would a child learn the social and other noncurricular aspects of life that are now learned in the school environment?

The widespread introduction of LOGO systems and the dynabook would have tremendous impact on education. At first, however, the equipment will cost so much that not everyone will be able to afford it. Will this create social problems by increasing the difference between the haves and the have-nots?

16.2 LIMITS TO GROWTH

The studies summarized in the books *Limits to Growth* and *Mankind at the Turning Point* have staggering implications for the future of mankind. If the studies are reasonably accurate, the implication is that we must change our life-style immediately. But the changes involve sacrifice for many citizens of the United States. How do we determine the validity of the model on which the studies were based? One answer is to wait and see if its predictions are valid. The waiting process is, however, costly if the model is valid. Greater sacrifices will be necessary in 25 years than are required if we start now to solve world problems. For example, the study predicts that the economic gap between the developed and underdeveloped nations can be reduced to a 5:1 ratio by investing $7200 billion in underdeveloped nations during the period 1975–2025. If action is delayed until the year 2000, then $10,700 billion must be invested in the period 2000–2025 to produce the 5:1 ratio. In the years of delay, great suffering can be expected in the underdeveloped nations.

Individual citizens in this country would be appreciably affected by the diversion of our capital funds to help underdeveloped nations. Assuming that we begin immediately, so as to decrease total costs, the per capita annual income in the year 2025 for the citizens of a developed nation will be $3000 less than if the aid had not been given. How can politicians in the developed countries justify this foreign aid to the economically depressed citizens of their own countries? What is necessary to convince politicians, in the first place, that action is needed?

The studies make clear that not everything can be maximized for everyone. We can have (1) more people or more wealth, (2) more wilderness or more automobiles, (3) more food for the poor or more services and materials for the rich, (4) more food for underdeveloped countries or more pleasure driving. Ten gallons of gasoline are sufficient to make fertilizer to produce the food necessary for one adult. What is important?

The problems go even deeper. We cannot have maximum good for each generation. If we maximize our own comforts, our children and their children must suffer. And individual action will not work—global action is required. What do we do if our neighbors (or other developed countries) disagree with the studies? How much of the belief or disbelief in the model can be attributed to the fact that a computer was involved?

16.3   PRIVACY

The conflict between the use of computer-based information systems and the individual's right to privacy is a highly emotional issue that has been discussed at length in Congress and in the news media. Opponents of the use of computers to maintain extensive data banks about individuals argue that we have a right to keep private a part of our lives and that any violation of this right reduces our freedom. They admit that information about individuals has always been available, but they claim that the greatly reduced cost of manipulating the information that the computer makes possible will lead to gross abuse of the individual's rights, and perhaps even to political repression.

Proponents of the use of computer data banks argue that the feared abuses of individual rights have not occurred, and they note that perfect freedom is an ideal that cannot be realized in society. Individuals give up part of their privacy to obtain other benefits, such as personal loans and efficient government, which they value more highly. It is claimed that computer data banks are not designed to hurt people but to provide a needed service at an affordable price.

A matter of great public concern has been the possible conversion of dossiers maintained by the federal government using manual methods into computerized dossiers. The amount of information is indeed astounding. A 1968 study by a senatorial subcommittee headed by Senator Edward V. Long discovered 27.27 billion data items. In addition to commonplace information such as name, address, and age, the data included items such as physical characteristics, credit rating, grade average, police record, psychiatric history, and personality inventory. The information was scattered through many government agencies, which made it extremely time consuming and expensive to consolidate all the information on any particular individual.

In the mid-1960s, a Bureau of the Budget task force recommended the establishment of a National Data Center to consolidate the dossiers maintained by various federal government agencies. Eventually FBI, criminal, Justice Department, armed forces, welfare, social security, medical, insurance, credit, loan, tax, and other records might have been combined within the data center. It would then be fast and inexpensive to obtain information on a particular individual. Such uses were not, however, to be allowed, and the data bank was to be used for statistical studies. The designers of the system unfortunately failed to include procedures to ensure the right to privacy and prevent the misuse of files. The result was an emotional public outcry against the system, which was described as a significant step in establishing the government as "Big Brother" and hastening the arrival of George Orwell's *1984*. The proposal was not approved, and the National Data Center did not come into existence.

Was the failure to establish a National Data Center good or bad? Could adequate safeguards have been designed to protect the rights of individuals? If such safeguards were available, would the center have been desirable? Could the center have resulted in a more efficient, less expensive federal government? Could the additional available information have been used to produce a more humane and effective welfare program? What, in fact, were the potential benefits of the system, and how do these compare with the dangers? What is the appropriate balance between the needs of the people as a whole—which the data center possibly emphasized—and the needs of individuals? There are no answers to these questions.

In 1973, the Department of Health, Education, and Welfare issued a report, *Records, Computers, and the Rights of Citizens*, which proposed a Code of Fair Information Practice. On December 31, 1974, the Federal Privacy Act, which reflected the viewpoint of the HEW report, was passed. This law required federal agencies to:

1. Permit an individual to determine what records pertaining to him are collected, maintained, used, or disseminated by such agencies.
2. Permit an individual to prevent records pertaining to him obtained by such agencies for a particular purpose from being used or made available for another purpose without his consent.

3. Permit an individual to gain access to information pertaining to him in Federal agency records, to have a copy made of all or any portion thereof, and to correct or amend such records.

4. Collect, maintain, use, or disseminate any record of identifiable personal information in a manner that assures that such action is for a necessary and lawful purpose, that the information is current and accurate for its intended use, and that adequate safeguards are provided to prevent misuse of such information.

5. Permit exemptions from the requirements with respect to records provided in this Act only in those cases where there is an important public policy need for such exemptions as has been determined by specific statutory authority.

6. Be subject to civil suit for any damages which occur as a result of willful or intentional action which violates any individual's rights under this Act.

Difficult problems not resolved by the Act were passed to a commission created by the Act for further study.

In the private business sector, threats to privacy exist. For example, the ease with which credit can be obtained is the result of the ready availability from computer files of information about individuals who are applying for credit. The gathering, storing, and selling of personal information is big business itself. Two of the larger consumer-reporting companies, TRW Credit Data and Equifax Inc., maintain computer files on approximately 55 million and 60 million people, respectively. The gross income of Equifax exceeded $300 million in 1978. These firms charged approximately $15 to gather the information to establish a new file. A copy of a preexisting file could be obtained for as little as $1.50.

Undoubtedly, the consumer reporting firms provide an invaluable service for business by making information so easily available at such a reasonable cost, and indirectly they also perform a valuable service for consumers by reducing the time required to obtain credit. Unfortunately, there is associated with the system an almost unlimited potential for abuse and unnecessary harm to individual reputations. In addition to the normally expected data items, information is routinely collected on shopping habits, debts, drinking habits, sexual behavior, and morals. Critics of the system have claimed that much of the information is irrelevant and is cut-rate gossip. How do we evaluate this threat to our privacy? What controls, if any, should be placed on the system?

Two laws regarding consumer-information-reporting procedures already exist which protect your rights. The Fair Credit Act of 1970 permits you to obtain a statement of the "nature and substance" of any file maintained about you by a reporting agency. The burden is on you to make the request, and the agencies are not required to explain the contents of the file.

The Fair Credit Billing Act of 1975 allows a consumer to complain in writing to a creditor about a possibly incorrect bill. The creditor must acknowledge the inquiry within 30 days, and it must resolve the dispute within 90 days, supplying written supporting evidence. During the investigation the creditor cannot report the debtor to a consumer reporting agency as a delinquent account. Again the burden of taking action rests on the consumer. If an account is incorrectly flagged as being delinquent in a consumer reporting agency file, the reporting agency is required to correct its records, but the agency does not have to track down previously issued flawed copies of your file. This serious weakness in the system allows unjustified damage to be done to individuals. Proposed legislation may shift the burden of protecting the consumer to the reporting agencies. This change would increase the operating costs of the consumer-reporting agencies, which in turn would increase the cost of obtaining credit.

16.4   THE CASHLESS SOCIETY

In the late 1960s it was asserted that the banking business had become so complex that without computers all the employable women in the country would be needed as clerks to do the required paperwork. Whether or not this claim is true, it is certainly the case that the amount of record keeping is immense in financial institutions. The increasing power of computers and their decreasing cost now make it possible to eliminate the use of money from most financial transactions, resulting in a cashless society. The transformation of society to this new form would occur over a period of many years and would perhaps never be completed. Movement of society in the direction of reducing our use of money appears to be inevitable, but we must ask to what extent the change is desirable.

In a thoughtful analysis* of the issues involved in electronic funds transfer (EFT) systems, Rob Kling has identified five value orientations upon which the system design could be based. These are:

1. Maximize the profitability of the firms using the system.
2. Improve the strength and efficiency of government.
3. Maximize the civil liberties of individuals.
4. Give social institutions the opportunity to serve the common man.
5. Make EFT well-organized, efficient, reliable, and esthetically pleasing.

A major problem is that these goals conflict for particular circumstances, and it is not obvious which goal should be given greatest emphasis in the system design. The goals actually emphasized will depend upon the values held by the developing institutions. The complexity of the issues can be glimpsed by considering a few of the potential effects of EFT.

Some presumably beneficial effects of EFT are the reduction of paperwork at banks, increased opportunity for earning interest because of the speed of transfer of funds, improved customer convenience, enhanced point-of-sale transactions, and the

---

*Rob Kling, "Value Conflicts and Social Choice in Electronic Funds Transfer System Developments," *Communications of the ACM* (August 1978), 642. Reproduced by permission of the Association for Computing Machinery, Inc.

reduction of some government paperwork. In the area of customer services, some conveniences are

1. Authorizing by telephone the direct payment of bills.
2. Eliminating of checks to write or mail.
3. Depositing of salaries directly into employee bank accounts without the writing of salary checks.
4. Depositing of government payments directly into the accounts of those receiving the payments.
5. Making banking services available on a 24-hour basis by means of automated teller machines.

Businesses using point-of-sale techniques will benefit from immediate transfer of funds and will be protected from loss due to bad checks. The reduction of government paperwork and the resulting cost reduction could be quite significant. The writing of social security benefit checks for 32 million people could be eliminated by automating the process. The Federal Reserve Board, which processes approximately 14 billion checks per year without any charge for its member banks, could realize substantial savings.

To obtain the benefits of EFT, individuals must accept certain risks. Each user of the system would be issued a machine-readable identification card and a "secret" personal identification number (PIN), which when used in conjunction with the card would give the individual access to the services of the system. In most states the banks determine the extent of their liability in the event the card and PIN are lost or stolen. An automated teller machine may malfunction and short-change the customer, or in an automated cash deposit an error may occur. This could cause individuals to lose substantial sums through no fault of their own. (There is presently no way to determine the actual amount of money deposited.) If these malfunctions occur, the actions taken depend upon the bank and its system. A customer's account may be inaccessible for days while these problems are resolved. Thus the customer may experience considerable inconvenience even though he has done nothing wrong. A more serious danger is the accidental loss of the magnetic tape that contains the current status of many accounts. In designing and implementing EFT systems, the compromises that will be made between achieving maximum benefits and reducing risks will depend upon the values of those who control the design.

For EFT systems, some applications may be considered either highly beneficial or harmful, depending upon your values. Point-of-sale data will allow the assembling of lists of persons who purchase various items. This information will be of great interest to advertisers and to companies that sell related items. Suppose that you purchase a stereo component, then receive a large volume of mail advertisements urging you to purchase related components. Is this good or bad? Since the nature of items purchased, cost, time of purchase, location of the store where the purchase is made, and other information will be recorded, surveillance for political purposes will be possible. This could be viewed as an advantage by those who value a strong central government and as a disadvantage by those who value civil liberties. The widespread use of EFT systems may force poorer people to start using bank accounts (approximately 20% of American households do not have bank accounts), which conflicts with the goal of serving the common man. To produce highly reliable and secure EFT systems (which many view as a worthy goal) will probably require more complex procedures, but this conflicts with serving the common man. The larger, more affluent banks may gain a competitive edge over less well financed banks—is this an advantage or disadvantage of EFT systems?

There are some obvious and serious dangers associated with EFT systems. Large-scale theft is possible. In manual banking systems the maximum money which can be stolen is limited to that which is physically available at the location of a robbery. In the EFT system all the funds in the particular banking system are available for robbery attempts. Data loss could be catastrophic. Access to the system could be curtailed for a variety of reasons, such as human error or a bug in the computer program, causing credit brownouts or blackouts. A snowstorm in Boston during the winter of 1978 caused the closing of banks for several days, and the lack of access to funds caused significant hardships for many citizens. With EFT systems, the credit blackout could affect a much greater geographic area.

What combination of procedures, hardware, and regulations is required to make EFT systems best serve American society? At this time, no one knows, since the issues are very complex and the answers depend upon the goals to be maximized. We can be certain that special-interest groups will press to make their values prevail.

16.5 SOME OTHER SOCIAL ISSUES

There are a significant number of social issues related to computing; the issues are quite complex, and many books, popular articles, and scholarly studies have been published discussing them. It has been estimated that these publications would fill a small library. To conclude our brief introduction to this subject, a few issues will be listed. Each deserves your careful consideration.

Elections

Computers are used in election campaigns, for example, to generate lists of voters, print special letters, analyze voting districts, analyze polls, and maintain records. What advantage does this give candidates who can afford these services? Should all candidates have equal access to computing facilities?

During elections, computers are used to count votes. How reliable are the equipment and the programs? Is there some way that computers can be used to improve voter participation in elections?

Computers are used to predict the outcome of national elections. What effect does this prediction process have on the outcome of a close election, and could it have the effect of disenfranchising voters in western states? Eliminating this election-night reporting, however, may be a violation of the rights of the press.

Employment

Computers have created many jobs, particularly in the areas of computer manufacturing, sales, software production, and business data processing. Many jobs have been lost as a result of computer-controlled manufacturing processes. It is claimed that the computer, by increasing productivity, lowers the cost of goods and thus is beneficial to society. But the associated jobs may be boring and dehumanizing. What should be done for those who lose their jobs as a result of automation?

Foreign Sales of Computers

Should computers be sold to foreign governments and businesses? Corporate executives certainly work hard to make foreign sales, and many stockholders benefit from these sales. Yet in 1977 the U.S government blocked the sale of a $13 million Control Data computer to the USSR on the grounds that it could be used for weapons research and other military applications. The company complained, to no avail, that safeguards had been incorporated into the system to prevent such use. What was the right decision?

In the case of underdeveloped nations, will purchasing computers help or hinder the progress of their technology? How are these countries to obtain personnel to operate the equipment? What effect will computing have upon local customs and traditions in the underdeveloped countries?

Health Care

Computer-controlled equipment is used to monitor vital life functions in hospital intensive-care units. In medical diagnostic laboratories, the instruments are almost completely automated. New instruments, such as computer tomography units, give the medical profession better diagnostic capabilities. Increased speed, greater accuracy, and improved care are claimed to result. Critics say that excessive reliance upon technology has dehumanized doctors and reduced their empathy for patients. How much of the astounding increase in hospital costs can be attributed to the purchase of computer-controlled devices? Does every hospital need the most expensive, but specialized, equipment? Would today's young doctors be willing to work in hospitals that do not have the latest technology?

Should computers be allowed to interact directly with patients during the diagnosis process? If programs can be developed, should they be allowed to converse with, for example, psychiatric patients? Would this improve patient care and reduce costs? Weizenbaum has argued that there are things that computers should not be allowed to do even if they have the capability.

Consider the interactive program MYCIN written by E. H. Shortliffe to assist doctors in diagnosing and prescribing treatment for infectious diseases. A doctor can ask for an explanation of the program's conclusions at any time during the conversation, and he can reject the advice if he wishes. In nonclinical tests MYCIN gave the same advice as experts in 75% of cases. When an incorrect answer is obtained, a doctor having expert knowledge can add that knowledge to the program. Thereafter, MYCIN will give the correct answer for that case. Should programs such as MYCIN be used in real medical situations?

Home Information Systems

Low-cost computers for home use open exciting possibilities for game playing, personal data recording, financial computations, household energy monitoring and control, home security systems, menu planning, and appointment recording. When the home computer is used as a terminal to other systems, it may be possible to bank at home, order groceries and other household items, obtain access to library materials, receive news and special reports, and participate in educational activities. At the national level, voting and participating in instant national referenda have been proposed. Useful applications seem to be almost unlimited.

The effect of home-based information systems is difficult to predict. Since for the foreseeable future the equipment and services will be relatively expensive, will economic class differences be increased? What will be the effect on privacy? How can security be maintained when so many individuals are using the system? Will our travel habits change as a result of being able to do so many things directly from the home?

Who could have predicted in 1895 the effect the automobile would have on American society?

Law Enforcement

The Law Enforcement Assistance Administration of the Department of Justice makes grants to local and state police agencies. Some grant funds have been used to purchase computers. At the national level, the FBI's National Crime Information Center (NCIC) is a nationwide, computerized police information system. Local police can use terminals to access data in the NCIC.

The NCIC is a valuable tool in combating crime. Although police are generally restricted to a small geographic area, criminal histories can be made available nationwide to help offset the mobility advantage of criminals. Further, the ready availability of information can make police work safer. The cost of law enforcement may, perhaps, be decreased.

Despite the advantages of computerized police information systems, the general public is reluctant to give more power to the police. Critics claim that a police state would be produced if the system were extended to include surveillance data. Even if safeguards could be developed to prevent this, serious threats to personal privacy would exist: an individual might be denied access to his records, arrests might be recorded but disposition of the case might not be entered, discriminatory or political arrest data may be recorded without qualifying information, and the existence of a file about an individual may result in a presumption of guilt in police dealings with the individual. How are legitimate needs for better law enforcement to be balanced against dangers to the rights of individuals?

Liability for Program Errors

Suppose that a programmer working for a bank makes an error in a program, and as a result many bank customers suffer serious financial losses. Who should be liable for the losses—the bank, the programmer, the government, or no one? A reasonable argument can be presented for each of these choices. A related question is whether or not programmers should be required to obtain professional certification and a license to practice.

The enumeration of social issues related to computing can be expanded almost indefinitely. In most cases the issues are quite complex and involve serious conflicts in value positions. Your attention to the consequences of using computers can affect the role that computers will play in the future of our society.

INDEX